# TRUE REFORM

## JESS MONEY

Finchville Publishing

# ACKNOWLEDGMENTS

**Christiana Miller**
For her advice in general,
and her editing prowess in particular.

**Janet Laughridge McCarter**
For her encouragement and especially,
her insight regarding the last two chapters.

**Jo Hrzina**
For pointing me in the right direction
regarding the legal intricacies of a non-fiction work.

**The late, great Nance Mitchell**
Without whom I would never have had a writing career,
much less the chance to write this book.

**Mark Iwasykiw**
Friends come no better than this man.

**Lori**
The extraordinary woman who passed through my life
for only a moment, but changed me forever.

And finally,
All those who graciously allowed me to cite their work
on the many subjects covered by this book.

# DEDICATION

**To James Money**
A man of courage, integrity,
determination, and style.

*This is for you, Dad.*

# CONTENTS

*Some men look at constitutions with sanctimonious reverence, and deem them like the Ark of the Covenant, too sacred to be touched ... In questions of power ... let no more be heard of confidence in man, but bind him down from mischief by the chains of the Constitution.*

-- Thomas Jefferson

# FOREWORD

This is only my second book and to say that I struggled with it is an understatement. In my novel *Public Enemies*, I took great pains to make it as authentic and technologically correct as possible. However, the bottom line in fiction is that things only have to sound plausible, whereas a book like *True Reform* is required to present facts, data, quotes, and citations to support its contentions and conclusions. The difficulty in finding the right balance between style and substance, between making the book readable and making it authoritative, proved daunting and substantial.

Rather than a lengthy academic tome crammed with footnotes, I wanted something relatively short. *So much for that idea.* The issues and solutions addressed here unavoidably required a certain amount of explanation and justification. In fact, most of these topics could fill up a book all by themselves, which is why I had to *force myself to stop writing.* New revelations of wrong-doing, which reinforce the need for one or more of these amendments, appear daily. They will have to wait for life on the True Reform website. In the end I had to settle for just making this book as conversational as possible. (Note: My conversations tend to be blunt, and my language sometimes colorful, so if you offend easily...)

Fortunately, in today's world, authors have the option to place supporting data, footnote material, and so forth on a website. This not only makes the book cleaner, it allows for more supporting or collateral information to be presented.

In e-book editions, links to the supporting material are included in the Sources Section at the back of the book. Readers of traditional print editions can visit the TrueReform.org website and search sources to their heart's content.

A note about sources: Some people will be quick to criticize a few of the sources cited here that are aligned with either the conservative right wing, or the liberal/progressive left, of American politics. I understand both sides. I also subscribe to the theory that even a stopped clock is right twice a day. Those on the right have agendas (both social and economic) with which I disagree vehemently, but the only important question about their statistics and examples is: *Are they wrong*? If the numbers are correct, if the examples are true and valid, that does not mean that we are obligated to adopt right-wing solutions. But when conservatives accurately point out real problems, it does us no good to hide behind left-wing or "centrist" propaganda designed to camouflage reality. You can only hide so much, for so long, before inconvenient truths become both public and incontrovertible. Likewise, just because someone along the "progressive" spectrum of American politics points out a problem, doesn't mean their proposed solution has merit. This book is about proposing fair, concrete, democratic solutions to real problems, which is why nobody on the left or the right is going to like all of the amendments proposed here, or the justifications for those amendments.

People may also criticize the use of Wikipedia as a source. However, I'm using Wikipedia simply to provide basic information, definitions, historical context, etc. Second, there are over 400 sources cited here. There would be more, but a number of publications and institutions denied permission to have their material quoted, either at all or without a fee that I was unwilling to pay. So, if the best you can do is criticize some sources, you need to up your game. Don't challenge something on the basis of who said or wrote it; **challenge it on the basis of whether or not it's correct**. (Which, by the way, does not mean that you should just counter with other stats that portray a different aspect of the problem, but which do not actually contest the accuracy of what has been presented here. If something written here is wrong, *prove it*.)

A few of the strategies and solutions presented here are my own creation, but most are variations on suggestions and proposals made by politicians, scholars, journalists, and regular people who comment on blogs, write letters to the editor, or post on social media. But be forewarned: Some of these proposed amendments may seem either so strict as to be impractical, or too idealistic to ever be enacted. When tempted by such emotions, please keep in mind that our Founding Fathers were aiming for the best possible structure of government based on their knowledge, and the conditions, of the times. So, why shouldn't we seek to reform our government in the best possible way? Why shouldn't our goal be a government that operates and performs as well as it can, and as well as it should, given our knowledge and the world we live in today?

If nineteen amendments seem like too many, in 2008, Larry Sabato, founder of the Center for Politics at the University of Virginia (where he has taught since 1978), and a Rhodes scholar who received his doctorate in politics from Oxford, wrote a book proposing twenty-*three* amendments. Included were some real head-scratchers, like increasing the size of the House of Representatives to 1,000 members (which would give more power to the larger states) *and* giving the larger states extra senators. Considering that amendments must be ratified by 3/4 of the states, those ideas would seem to be complete non-starters, evidence of the classic academic ivory-tower disconnect from the real world. Nevertheless, Sabato's book reinforces the premise that our constitution is in serious need of some major updating.

Because amendments must be ratified by 3/4 of the states, you will not find one here to eliminate the Electoral College. It is simply not going to happen. The less populous states that make up the geographical core of the country already feel ignored and disrespected by the coastal elites. And rightfully so. They are not going to willingly cede even more power and influence to population centers with whom they feel very little kinship, and from which they sense significant antipathy. Likewise, there is nothing here about repealing the Second Amendment, because it is also just not going to happen.

Many readers may embrace most of the reforms suggested here, but will find a few with which they disagree. Good. It is the nature of the beast. It is a natural human tendency to want what makes our life better, but to dislike that which imposes more obligations or responsibilities. In the end, the basic concepts of democracy on which the United States was founded demand fairness, justice, and balance. If government exists to provide various benefits and protections for its citizens, all sectors of society must contribute equally. This is the essence of concepts like the *common good* and the *general welfare*. It is also why the reforms contained in these Restoration Amendments interlock with each other to form a circle. Removing some amendments would result in loopholes through which today's favored few would escape responsibilities, avoid making a fair contribution, or dodge punishment for their corruption of government and abuse of society in general.

One group that will likely hate this book is the legal community. Lawyers tend to view the law as their exclusive domain. They bristle when non-lawyers attempt to suggest improvements in the law. To lawyers, laypersons simply don't understand the nuances of the law (*nuances* being a polite word for *loopholes*). Thus, many lawyers will not be enthused at the prospect of amendments, which don't just close loopholes, but cement over the doorway where the loophole used to be.

Since I am not a lawyer, elected official, or noted academic, some will ask, "What qualifies you to propose these amendments? What credentials do you have?" My answer is, many people in politics and economics today with sterling credentials are precisely the ones who have led us into our current mess. Their ideas and policy prescriptions have proven ineffective, defective, or downright disastrous, not to mention sometimes clearly criminal. That's because they belong to the ruling class. They grew up with the right parents and went to the right colleges. They are products of the system, and they are not going to bite the hand that feeds them. Devoid of morals, bereft of original thinking, and often harboring downright hostility to the lower and middle classes, they refuse to consider policies and solutions which do not reinforce the current system from which they benefit. Yet, because of the incestuous nature of our current system, they keep re-circulating, going from failed government position to some think tank, academic sinecure, consulting gig, or lobbyist job, only to re-emerge later, back in government after their previous failures have faded from memory. Therefore, I urge you to ignore the author and focus on the ideas. The only pertinent real question is: Are they a viable solution?

Furthermore, I submit that even our Founding Fathers could not salvage our republic as it is currently structured. They would have to do precisely what I'm suggesting here: amend the constitution. While their solutions might differ somewhat from those in this book, they would see the same core problems, and their suggestions would cover much of the same ground: public campaign financing, effective prohibitions against gerrymandering, a constitutional right to good government, firm government control of our currency, provisions for equal justice, and so forth. I therefore ask readers to evaluate each of the proposals here based on the logic and reasoning put forward to justify it.

Many readers will probably be surprised to see provisions that call for white-collar offenders to be incarcerated in maximum security prisons. Other than with regard to treason, impeachment, or prohibition of the death penalty, it is unusual to find sentencing standards addressed directly in a constitution. At first blush, the idea of sending people convicted of white-collar crimes to maximum security prison seems extreme. That's because we have been conditioned to believe that maximum security should be populated exclusively by the most physically violent offenders, who just happen to be mostly minorities and poor or blue-collar whites. And who conditioned us to this belief, who fostered these images in our mind? Politicians, business leaders, and journalists. The real truth: The biggest criminals wear ties, not tattoos. As Alexander Hamilton wrote in Federalist No. 15:

> It is essential to the idea of a law, that it be attended with a sanction; or, in other words, a penalty or punishment for disobedience. If there be no penalty annexed to disobedience, the resolutions or commands which pretend to be laws will, in fact, amount to nothing more than advice or recommendation.

Exactly. Without a sufficient penalty there is no deterrence, and no meaningful price for failure to obey. Therefore, we must be reminded in our revised Constitution of two essential principles of incarceration: First, that the punishment should match the severity of the crime. In this sense, incarceration is judicially-imposed societal revenge. Many white-collar crimes, especially those committed by those who wield great economic power or officials who betray their office, are far more damaging to society than offenses perpetrated by common criminals, even murderers. Which is worse: killing one person during a robbery, or killing thousands by lying the country into a war, as happened in Iraq and

Vietnam? Which is worse, robbing the local fast food place of a few hundred dollars, or robbing employees and investors of a lifetime of retirement savings, as happened with Enron and WorldCom? Stealing a car, or stealing the right to vote?

The second key principle of incarceration is that the punishment should be enough to deter other people from committing similar crimes. I recently saw a GIF that read, "Punishable by a fine means legal for rich people." The threat of going to some minimum-security Club Fed facility where inmates work on their tennis game, or do landscaping, has proven to have insufficient deterrent value for white-collar offenders. Instead, we must erect a *felony firewall,* reinforced by the prospect of living among cons who belong to prison gangs and are doing long sentences. This might make politicians, public officials, or corporate officers think long and hard before they break the law.

Sadly, there may be a temptation for many to look at these amendments and think that they are too ambitious. Too complicated. Too specific. Wildly unrealistic. Could never be enacted. That they don't allow for enough "flexibility" in government. I offer two responses:

First, *check the title.*

It's *True* Reform.

Not partial reform.

Not pseudo reform.

Not incremental reform.

Not cosmetic reform.

*True* Reform.

Second, simply because enacting these amendments is a daunting task, doesn't mean that it can't become a reality. As famed anthropologist Margaret Mead said, "Never doubt that a small group of thoughtful, committed citizens can change the world;

indeed, it's the only thing that ever has." A strategic plan to make these amendments a reality is spelled out in the last two chapters. It will not be easy, it will not happen overnight, and there will be great cost. But I am firm in my belief that it can be done.

If enough of us want it to happen.

One final note: While these amendments are very close to finished, I'm not above making revisions should readers point out loopholes that need fixing, doors accidentally left open for evasion, etc.

# PART I

---

## SITUATION REPORT

# Chapter 1

# THE STATE OF THE UNION

A national Situation Report is like the annual State of the Union message, which the president is constitutionally required to deliver to Congress at the beginning of every year. Despite some subtle language tweaks, the basic message is always the same: "The state of the union is strong."

No, it's not.

The initials D.C. now stand for District of Corruption. Our nation's capital isn't a swamp, it's a cesspool. Depending on politicians to clean it up is like expecting Bernie Madoff to reform Wall Street. The same holds at the state and local level. Even those rare, high-minded candidates who manage to get elected inevitably find themselves confronting an entrenched culture of corruption and crippled bureaucracies riddled with nefarious obstacles meant to block any meaningful reform. The system is rigged, and the people who rigged it like it that way.

The Founding Fathers, who wrote the Declaration of Independence and our Constitution, were not perfect. Some were slave-owners. Others believed that voting rights should only extend to men who owned property. These shortcomings notwithstanding, they were also undeniably men of great courage, considerable brilliance, and revolutionary vision; men who dared to imagine the kind of society under which men governed themselves. To heighten the contrast between those men and today's so-called leaders, and to further illuminate the pitiful depth to which we have sunk, I like to challenge people to name elected officials currently serving, or having recently served, in government who would have been allowed in the door at our 1787 Constitutional Convention. What leaders of either party have the intellect, vision, and devotion to democratic principles to engage in debate with our Founding Fathers? Ninety-nine percent of the people in politics today wouldn't have been allowed to deliver lunch to the Constitutional Convention for fear they'd screw up the food order.

Intent on creating a government that could endure for all time, our Founding Fathers built into the Constitution a system of checks-and-balances, and a separation of powers, to prevent any one branch of government from becoming too powerful. After demands from several states, they also incorporated a Bill of Rights to protect individual liberties. Yet even with these protections, some of them foresaw problems. When asked what kind of government the Constitutional Convention had created, Franklin said, "A republic, if you can keep it." Thomas Jefferson went even further: "Experience hath shewn [*sic*], that even under the best forms of government those entrusted with power have, in time, and by slow operations, perverted it into tyranny."

Even with all their intelligence and visionary thinking, Jefferson and his fellow patriots could not have imagined the world in which we now find ourselves. The power of money has polluted the entire political process. Presidents have become virtual kings, with Congress a weak sister, populated by professional politicians interested only in re-election, or in securing a lavishly paid position in the private sector after they leave office. Enabling it all has been the corruption of the federal judiciary, most notably the

Supreme Court. The slow perversion of democracy and descent into tyranny that Jefferson feared, has happened. Today, the Constitution is a quaint historical artifact having no real bearing on who governs or how the country is run. It took us over two hundred years, but here we are, facing the tyranny Jefferson warned us about. We've arrived, if not at the bottom of the governance barrel, at least within sight of it.

The solution to our problems will not be found in electing better politicians. Personalities are never a suitable substitute for principles, or for the ability to wield actual political power. We must put power back into the hands of the people through overarching constitutional reform designed to improve how our democratic republic functions. Thanks to the process to amend the Constitution provided for in Article V, we have the means to do so. Think of the Restoration Amendments not just as improvements to the architecture of our government, but as a fence, to both contain government *and* to keep out the influence of corporations and the wealthy. To address the flaws in our body of law as it currently exists, the Restoration Amendments:

- Clearly define what government must do.

- Clearly define what government cannot do.

- Provide specific and unavoidable punishment for government officials who do what they should not, or who fail to do what is required of them.

- To the maximum degree practicable, prevent lawyers and courts from evading the letter, intent, or spirit of the Constitution through creative semantics and the nefarious lawyerly parsing of language.

- Provide a mechanism by which individual citizens, representing the public at large, can compel adherence to the entire Constitution.

John Adams wrote in 1814 that:

> **Democracy never lasts long. It soon wastes exhausts and murders itself. There never was a democracy yet, that did not commit suicide**.

Is that our destiny? More importantly, is that what we are willing to accept? If not, then *we the people* must change how our government functions. We must become a nation where everyone in government, and in the private sector, is held accountable. The best part? Even though our so-called leaders are a dreadful pack of hypocritical idiots and corrupt scoundrels, there is a vast army of smart, principled everyday people all across the country, men and women who have the capacity and the will to fix what is wrong. All they need is the opportunity, and the right tools.

A modified version of the Manifesto from my novel *Public Enemies* follows. However, where the main character in that story used violence to achieve his ends, we will disavow violence. Instead, Part Four outlines a non-violent strategy to enact these Restoration Amendments and restore government of the people.

# MANIFESTO

*from the novel "Public Enemies"*

*"In a time of universal deceit, telling the truth is a revolutionary act."*

--George Orwell

America has become its corporations, not its citizens.

## America's Longest War is America's Institutional War on Us!

For the past thirty years, our institutions -- Congress, the Courts, State and Local Governments, Stockbrokers, Bankers, Lobbyists, Lawyers, Multi-National Global Corporations, and Presidents -- have waged war on America's poor and middle class:

*With promises that turned out to be lies.*

*With pensions and health care benefits that vanished.*

*With trade agreements and treaties that took away our jobs.*

*With security that took away our privacy.*

*With secret laws and Presidential decrees that took away our rights.*

*With no prosecution of the rich, and harsh prosecution of all others.*

## The American Dream has been replaced by the American Delusion.

Never before have the American people been so victimized, and never has the American public witnessed such disdain for the rule of law. The actions of recent presidents prove that it's not just they, and those who serve them, who are above the law. A class of corrupt financial fraudsters burned the economy to the ground, all without fear of prosecution. This shamelessly discredits the sacrifice of Americans who fought and died for the cause of liberty, democracy, freedom, and justice *for all*. It can not, and must not, continue.

The great nation that once was America is no more.
That America vanished because accountability vanished.

Without accountability, we have become
a hated Empire overseas and a Fascist Oligarchy at home.

Without accountability:

***Corporations*** make the decisions

***Special Interests*** get the representation.

***We*** pay the price in taxes, blood, and loss of freedom.

Without accountability, there is no justice.
And when there is no justice, there is no freedom.

**Democracy = Accountability and
Equal Justice for All**

**It's not too late. America can be saved.**

***It's time for the Second American Revolution,***

***a Crusade for Reform and Accountability.***

We, the people, are responsible for the actions of our government.

We, the people, are responsible for
how it operates, and what it has become.

We, the people, must replace the
Government of the Corrupt, by the Corrupt, for the Corrupt

With Government of the People, by the People, for the People.

***Bring Democracy Back to America.***
***Restore the Rule of Law.***

# Chapter 2

# LARGER ISSUES

We must fix our government, not just to salvage and improve our way of life, but so that we can deal with at least seven massive, over-riding issues facing our nation and the world.

## Global Climate Change

Most reputable scientists have concluded that global climate change, and an overall increase in the Earth's temperature, are a result of human activity, by-products of industrialization and our reliance on carbon-based fossil fuels such as oil, coal, and natural gas. A few scientists dispute man's influence on global warming, but a number of them have been shown to be beneficiaries of funding, directly or indirectly, from fossil fuel companies. However, for the sake of argument, let's assume that they are right, that recent increases in Earth's temperature and the resulting changes in climate are a natural occurrence, not affected by the actions of man. Stop and think about that for a moment:

> *If man's economic activity does not contribute to global climate change, presumably changes in how we live and use energy will have no effect on the climate going forward.*

In other words, Mother Nature will do what she wants to do, and we're along for the ride.

If this theory is correct, Mother Nature could turn around tomorrow and start cooling the Earth. Problem solved. But what if she doesn't? Geological studies have shown that when it comes to changes in climate, the swings are very long and slow. In climate terms, a hundred years is nothing. A thousand years is a blink of an eye. Recently, California went through its worst drought in 1,200 years. What was the world like 1,200 years ago?

- The Vikings were colonizing Britain.

- Pope Leo III crowned Charlemagne Emperor of Rome.

- It would still be six hundred years before Columbus landed in the Americas.

So, even if we accept the position of the climate-change deniers -- that we humans aren't causing it and therefore can't do anything about it -- this doesn't mean we won't have to deal with its effects. According to sea level models posted by National Geographic on its website, if all the glacier and polar ice melts, Pine Bluff, Arkansas -- where the operative geological feature is the *bluff* -- becomes the next New Orleans. What's left of Puerto Rico will become our new 49th state as both Florida and Louisiana **completely cease to exist**. The current New Orleans, as well as Houston, Boston, New York, Philadelphia, Washington, D.C., Norfolk, and Charlotte will become destinations for tourists in glass-bottom boats.

The Pacific Coast states will also get hit hard. Los Angeles as far inland as 30 or 40 miles will disappear. Coastal areas of San Diego and the Bay Area, the same. The big island of Hawaii will survive mostly intact, but Honolulu will vanish, and the other islands will shrink down to just a few ragged mountain tops dotting the sea.

Forget, for a moment, all the disruption along the rest of our three coasts and concentrate only on the effect on Florida. How do we redistribute twenty million people who will all need housing, utility services, schools, police and fire protection, medical facilities, jobs, and recreational opportunities? Where will these refugees get the money to pay for such items? An influx of new residents will produce some additional jobs in the new communities where they settle. But there is no guarantee that there will be enough new jobs. What about retirees whose present home or condo becomes an aquarium? All the insurance companies in America combined don't have the loss reserves to compensate this many families and businesses. Even if the federal government steps in, as it will surely have to do, how will fair compensation be calculated? What is the replacement value of property that was once worth hundreds of thousands, or even millions, but is now worthless except for scuba diving?

A mass migration of this sort doesn't just mean moving to new areas, it means environmental mitigation of the land left behind. The fuel storage tanks from every service station, and any contaminated soil, will have to be removed. The same goes for the equipment, buildings, and land of every industrial site. Toxic and non-biodegradable materials, from asbestos to fiberglass insulation to asphalt roof shingles, will have to be removed from every building. Old sewage systems and waste treatment plants will have to be dismantled. Asphalt roads and driveways will have to be scraped up and carted hundreds of miles away. The costs and logistics will be staggering.

It's not just the residential population along the coasts that is a problem. Much of the world's commerce depends on shipping. How will rising sea levels and higher storm surges affect the ports of Los Angeles, Long Beach, San Francisco, and Seattle? What happens to shipping in the Gulf of Mexico when Galveston, Baton Rouge, and Mobile are all under water? How do port cities and highway/rail hubs along the East Coast cope with rising sea levels and the loss of ports such as New York, New London, Baltimore, and Philadelphia? When people are forced inland, there will be inevitable clashes, quite possibly violent, between the refugees and those who already occupy higher ground.

As the world heats up, water will become a scarce, expensive, rationed commodity. One prediction has British Columbia losing 95% of its annual snowpack by the end of this century. If that sounds like it's a long way off, consider this: Know anyone who is 82 years old? A person born the year this book is published will be 82 by the end of the century.

The British Columbia prediction may be way too optimistic. In 2018, after just three years of drought, Cape Town, South Africa came dangerously close to running out of water. FastCompany.com reported that residents were limited to using only 13 gallons of water per day, per person. Washing cars and maintaining swimming pools were outlawed.

Cape Town isn't alone. The FastCompany.com story also highlighted pending water shortages in Morocco, Spain, Iraq, and India, where water levels fell so far that not only was drinking water threatened, but there wasn't enough water flow to operate electrical generators at major dams. In India alone, lack of water for irrigation has sent many farms into bankruptcy, prompting almost 60,000 suicides. Drought in Syria forced a million farmers into cities, where they became one of the forces sparking the Syrian civil war. (Not that the U.S. desire to control a trans-Syrian oil pipeline didn't influence our attempt to topple the Assad regime.)

Quick on the heels of the Cape Town crisis, *Macrobusiness.com* ran a story by Leith van Onselen headlined:

**Melbourne's water supply on verge of "disaster" as population balloons**

Melbourne's water supply depends on the retention of rainwater runoff from surrounding forests. However, extensive logging of old growth trees has necessitated the planting of new trees which absorb vastly larger amounts of water than mature, old-growth timber. Thus, the runoff captured for public use is drastically reduced. Compounding the problem is the fact that Melbourne's current population of 4.9 million is expected to balloon to 8 million by mid-century. The story concluded with this quote from prominent Australian research scientist Dr. Jonathan Sobels, given in an Australian Broadcasting Company interview:

> ...we are coming up towards physical limitations within our physical, built and natural environments that will lead to compromises in the quality of our life...

> Not only are the dams not filling, but the ground water supplies are not filling. The only option you have open to you is water efficiency use and whacking up desal plants. But if your population keeps increasing at the rates we have seen in recent times, you won't be able to afford putting up billion dollar desal plants, which also have their environmental impacts.

Dr. Sobel was referring to Australia, but his analysis applies worldwide.

If Cape Town, Melbourne, and India sound like far away problems, *grist.org* ran an article in May 2018 with the headline:

### The Water War that will decide the fate of 1 in 8 Americans

The conflict involves allocations from the Colorado River for California, Arizona, New Mexico, Nevada, and Utah. These states are not only a major food source, they are home to over 40 million residents. Then there's the report in the Denver University Law Review, published in June 2018, showing dangerous depletion in the Ogallala Aquifer under the Great Plains states. According to this report, this aquifer, which lies under eight states, is home to a staggering one-sixth of the world's grain production. Excess water extraction, far in excess of annual replenishment, is contributing to a cascade of follow-on environmental issues, including the extinction of some fish species.

Also close to home is the purchase of large farms in Arizona by both Saudi Arabia and the United Arab Emirates on which to grow alfalfa (hay) which, if supplied with enough water, flourishes in hot climes due to the long growing season. Saudi Arabia and UAE need this hay to feed their dairy cows *because their own aquifers, including an enormous one under the Saudi sands, have been sucked nearly bone dry.*

The negative impact of water shortages and rising temperatures on worldwide food production is a recipe for starvation and civil unrest on a scale never previously imagined. Developed countries will battle ferociously to hold on to what they have and not be swamped by refugees from the poorest and most low-lying countries. How much of the world's population will die? A third? Half? Two-thirds or even three-quarters? How about **everybody**?

In April 2018, The Guardian ran a story about eminent British professor Dr. Mayer Hillman, that led with the headline, "We're doomed." Dr. Hillman contends that we've already passed the point of no return, that fossil fuel use has already condemned us to complete melting of the polar and glacial ice caps resulting in catastrophic climate change. He argues that attempting to get to zero-emissions would require changes that societies around the world are simply unwilling to accept, including elimination of almost all air travel, automobiles, going to a strict vegan diet, etc. His prediction is that the northernmost areas of the U.S. and Europe will survive the longest, but even they will eventually succumb. In the meantime, billions will be turned away and die as the haves pull up the drawbridge over the moat.

Dr. Hillman is not alone. In October 2018, the U.N. released a climate change report stating that the world has only a dozen years -- until 2030 -- to act on reducing the greenhouse emissions that fuel temperature increases. Otherwise, the world will have passed the tipping point and there will be no way to prevent catastrophic climate change. In response to this report, Umair Haque wrote an essay in which he pointed out that:

> Catastrophic climate change is not a problem for fascists -- it is a solution. History's most perfect, lethal, and efficient means of genocide, ever, period.

He's right. The ruling class thinks that they, along with a hand-picked group of people deemed necessary to serve them, will survive.

Nobody knows how close Dr. Hillman is to the truth, but he could be off by quite a bit and the result would still be the catastrophic outcome predicted by Haque. In any event, the impending crisis is severe enough that the Pentagon and the CIA have already game-planned for the eventualities. But those institutions do not have the best interests of average citizens at heart. They serve themselves, and their masters in the oligarchy under which we now live. It is our challenge to change the entire equation. We will probably not be able to save those unfortunate people from other countries, but we can damn well ensure that all Americans, regardless of race, creed, or class, have an equal chance to survive in whatever the new world looks like.

This is certain: Our current economic/political system is a gargantuan runaway train, barreling toward Cassandra's Crossing, and we cannot hope to stop it unless we un-tether the politicians, who can apply the brakes, from those who benefit by keeping the momentum going right up to the moment of oblivion.

## Fukushima

Dr. Helen Caldicott gave her book about Fukushima an apt title: *Crisis Without End*. Nuclear reactors are cooled with water. After Fukushima's containment vessels collapsed, the only way to prevent a massive nuclear chain reaction was to pour water directly on the superheated radioactive rods. But that water has to go someplace. So, every day since shortly after the tsunami, the Japanese government and Tokyo Electric Power Company have dumped 300,000 gallons of radioactive water back into the Pacific. Three hundred thousand gallons. ***Every. Damn. Day.***

The result? In 2013, Stanford and the State College of New York at Stony Brook sampled 25 different commercial tuna catches between British Columbia and Baja California. Every single sample contained traces of radioactive Cesium 134 and Cesium 137. ***Every. Single. Sample***. More recently, visible evidence has started to show up of sharks, crustaceans, and fish with cancerous growths and genetic deformities. All the world's oceans have been in danger from over-fishing for decades. Factor in the damage from endless radiation and what you have is starvation on a global scale.

It's not just the marine food supply that's in danger. Carried east by the jet stream, fallout from Fukushima continues to fall on the U.S. and Canada. The heaviest concentrations -- up over 500% from pre-tsunami levels -- have been in the western third of the continent. But as long as Fuki continues to emit radioactive particles on a daily basis, the drift eastward will be continuous and inexorable. The first impact will be an increase in cancer caused by direct contact with these microscopic particles on the skin or absorption into the lungs. The second will be infection of the food supply, causing not only an increase in cancer and birth defects among humans, but also mutations and possible extinction among various plants and animals up and down the food chain.

Aside from the prospect of diminished or compromised food supplies on the domestic front, what kind of economic damage will result if foreign countries no longer permit foodstuffs to be imported from the U.S.? Don't think it can't happen. A number of countries already ban food imports from Japan over fears about high radiation levels. (This is sort of ironic, in that some foods from the U.S. are banned by over thirty other countries due to concerns about GMO crops and our reliance on highly suspect toxic insecticides, artificially-enhanced fertilizers, and so forth, a subject which is addressed in Chapter 16.)

There are three ways that governments, institutions, and corporations can respond to a crisis or a disaster. The first is to move aggressively to actually resolve the situation. The second is to rationalize away the situation by changing the criteria by which the crisis or disaster is defined. The third, which Japan has chosen, is to limit information. In 2013, the Japanese legislature passed a law making anything related to Fukushima a state secret, with publication subject to government pre-approval. Violations can land the offender in prison for ten years. Meanwhile, TEPCO (Tokyo Electric Power Company), and the Japanese government proposed, and later abandoned, various innovative but unproven solutions such as building an ice wall in the ground around the plant to contain the radioactive runoff in an artificial underground lake. In 2015, four years after the tsunami, the Japanese government finally approved an official clean-up plan. But, as FireDogLake.com (now Shadowproof.com) reported, it has a time span of 30-40 years, delays the removal of the remaining radioactive fuel rods, makes no mention of how highly dangerous corium elements will be disposed of, and depends on proposed technology that, "simply does not yet exist for a number of timelined [sic] operations."

Meanwhile, radiation levels continue to climb, both in Japan and North America. In fact, as of April 2018, radiation released by

Fukushima exceeded that from Chernobyl, making it officially the worst nuclear disaster in history. *And it ain't over yet.* Far from it.

How has the U.S. responded? By raising the levels of what is considered to be safe dosages of radiation, and then stopping all reporting of increased radiation at sites around the country which have been in place since the grimmest days of Cold War nuclear bomb tests. Why would the U.S. take such actions? First, to prevent public panic. Second, to protect our own, very powerful, nuclear energy companies (such as G.E., which was responsible for the deficient design and construction of the Fukushima plant). Whenever there is a nuclear accident anywhere in the world, the first two questions are: a) How safe are our plants? The answer: Not Very; and b) Why don't we close our nuclear plants, which in many cases are now beyond their planned life expectancy? The answer involves Money, Money, Money.

With no proven current solutions to the problems at Fukushima, massive technological assistance from other countries may be necessary. However, this kind of outside interference will run head on into Japan's deeply ingrained culture of hiding failure to avoid losing face. (Not to mention, resistance to the potentially bankrupting economic hit likely to impact the Japanese power industry.) Nevertheless, if Japan is unable or unwilling to solve the problem on its own, the time will come when the U.S. will have to actively intervene to stop a disaster, which originated over there but is producing dangerous results here. Otherwise the title of Dr. Caldicott's book, *Crisis Without End*, will became a stark and deadly reality.

## The War on Drugs

It only took the U.S. thirteen years to realize that Prohibition had failed. The War on Drugs, begun in 1971 with President Nixon's declaration that drugs were, "America's public enemy number one," has been going on for over four decades, but we still haven't wised up. Maybe that's because the war on drugs is really a war on the poor and minorities, a way to justify an outsized, over-paid, militarized, abusive police presence in the poor areas of every city and town.

Television has been justifiably criticized for dumbing-down the masses, but if you look at the right shows with a critical eye, you can learn much. Take the long-running *COPS*, for instance. Desperate gun-battles with hardcore thieves and murderers? Very few. Thrilling chases to capture escaping bank robbers, muggers, or car-jackers? Occasionally. But a huge number of episodes involve stopping a motorist for a broken tail light, failing to signal for a turn, and so forth. These types of discretionary stops are rarely seen in more affluent communities. That's because they're not really about traffic safety. They're a pretext to question drivers and conduct a warrantless search, justified on the grounds that it is necessary for the officers' safety.

Do they find weapons? Occasionally. But what they often find is dope of one kind or another. Weed, crack, meth, oxy, whatever. Then the occupants of the car get carted off to jail. But for what purpose? Drive or operate machinery under the influence? Lock 'em up. A person on drugs hallucinates, runs down the street naked, or attacks someone? Lock 'em up for even longer. But otherwise, why should we as individuals, or collectively as a society, care what people ingest to make themselves feel more comfortable?

Naturally, law enforcement is against legalizing or decriminalizing drugs. One reason is the natural tendency of the authoritarian mindset to want to dictate what other people can and can't do. What do you think the chances are that, if you went to a cop BBQ, they'd have plenty of beer to go with their burgers, hot dogs, and potato salad? Alcohol is okay. But weed and other drugs, BAD! So what's the big distinction? Comedian Chris Rock nailed it in one of his spot-on routines, when he noted that alcohol and tobacco production are "all right, 'cause it's all white."

Remember the scene in *The Godfather*, where the Mafia bosses get together to make peace? The other big decision they arrive at is to approve the drug business, as long as it is confined to the "colored" neighborhoods. That was fiction, but based on fact. It's no accident that drug use, from marijuana to heroin, first became entrenched in Harlem, Watts, and minority areas in every other major city. Weed use became widespread in the Hippie 60s, but it took the introduction of powdered cocaine in the 70s, before white America became a center of profits and addiction.

But ... but ... but ... we can't legalize or decriminalize drugs because ... drugs lead to crime!

Yes, but mostly because we make sale, and even mere possession, a crime. Because their product is illegal, drug pushers charge big money. (The MBA-types call this a *risk premium*.) So, addicts, and sometimes even recreational users short on funds, resort to crime to finance their urge to get high. If a dime bag actually cost ten cents -- or even a dollar -- and was available at the local CVS, Duane Reede, or Rite-Aid, drug-related crime would plummet. Membership in drug gangs would also fall off exponentially. How do we know? Because recreational use of marijuana is now legal in an increasing number of states. In others, medical use of marijuana has been legalized. Have crime rates skyrocketed in those states? No, *they've gone down*. And not just because there are no longer minor weed busts to inflate the statistics. Actual crimes like assault and burglary are also down. Colorado is a prime example. Since legalizing marijuana in 2014, crime is down, and the sales tax revenues have been put to good use helping pay for schools. In fact, by 2018, there was enough marijuana sales tax revenue coming in that some of it could be deferred to things like homeless shelters.

When Prohibition was repealed, the mobsters switched their emphasis to other rackets such as prostitution, numbers running, protection, and union corruption. So, too, would today's drug gangs. While not minimizing the threat that protection rackets pose to individuals and businesses, or the costs associated with labor corruption, this is small potatoes compared to the market in illegal drugs. Now that you can buy a lottery ticket at just about every convenience store in America, the numbers racket has long since faded into history. Which leaves prostitution. And guess what: many hookers are also addicts, working the street to pay for their expensive habit, which would no longer be nearly so expensive if drugs were legal.

Fighting the never-ending, never-successful War on Drugs has spawned a huge, multi-billion-dollar industry. Lots of people, from those who train drug-sniffing dogs to companies that produce SWAT team gear and aerial surveillance technology, make a financial killing year after year. It's a war we can't win, but it sure is great for sales. There is also another big payoff: The War on Drugs has proven to be a terrific Trojan Horse to facilitate the gradual erosion of civil liberties. Over the past half-century, we have accepted intrusions on our privacy and civil liberties -- in the name of fighting the War on Drugs -- that we would have never otherwise accepted. The *War on Drugs* and the *War on Terror* are really wars on constitutionally protected civil liberties.

However, the most compelling reason to end the War on Drugs is because ***it was never intended to be about drugs***. Here's John Ehrlichman, of Watergate infamy, explaining:

> The Nixon campaign in 1968, and the Nixon White House after that, had two enemies: the antiwar left and black people. You understand what I'm saying? We knew we couldn't make it illegal to be either against the war or black, but by getting the public to associate the hippies with marijuana and blacks with heroin, and then criminalizing both heavily, we could

disrupt those communities. We could arrest their leaders, raid their homes, break up their meetings, and vilify them night after night on the evening news. Did we know we were lying about the drugs? Of course we did.

Ending the war on drugs would allow states and communities to cut the size of their police forces and still have more officers available to solve or prevent real crimes. Without the money wasted on the war on drugs, states could afford to run DNA tests on the thousands of backlogged rape kits, and put genuine threats to public safety behind bars. An added benefit of fewer police is lower government costs across the board. Less money for current salaries and benefits, fewer expenditures downstream for pensions and retiree health care. Look at the budget for any city: the biggest cost is personnel, and the biggest chunk of that goes to law enforcement.

## The War on Education

The American educational system, public and private, is a mess from top to bottom. Kids in low-income and even some moderate-income areas either don't get adequate pre-school and kindergarten instruction, or get none at all. This puts them behind when they get to public elementary school. Inadequate resources and inferior teachers compound the problem, and the scenario repeats itself in high school. At the university level, student debt skyrockets while learning takes a back seat to marketing campaigns that encourage school administrators to think of students as *customers*. Those who earn a degree start life with huge debt and increasingly poor job prospects.

Education at all levels has been marked by an explosion in the number of administrators and their compensation, to the detriment of both teachers and students. According to a study by Benjamin Scafidi of The Friedman Foundation:

Between fiscal year (FY) 1950 and FY 2009, the number of K-12 public school students in the United States increased by 96 percent, while the number of full-time equivalent (FTE) school employees grew 386 percent. Public schools grew staffing at a rate four times faster than the increase in students over that time period. Of those personnel, teachers' numbers increased 252 percent, while administrators and other non-teaching staff experienced growth of 702 percent, more than seven times the increase in students.

Sure, teaching has changed quite a bit since 1950, so maybe the increase in administrators is warranted by new demands, such as IT departments and greater staff to handle all the reporting now required by the states and federal government? Not really. More from Scafidi:

Between FY 1992 and FY 2009, the number of K-12 public school students nationwide grew 17 percent, while the number of FTE [Full Time Equivalent] school employees increased 39 percent ... teachers' staffing numbers rose 32 percent, while administrators and other non-teaching staff experienced growth of 46 percent, 2.3 times greater than the increase in students over that 18-year period.

Scafidi goes on to list the annual amount -- *per teacher* -- that some states could have saved if the increase in administrators had simply matched the increase in students:

| | |
|---|---|
| Virginia | $29,007 |
| Maine | $25,505 |
| D.C. | $20,472 |

Scafidi also points out that Texas could:

[save] almost $6.4 bil [annually] if they had not increased the employment of administrators and other non-teaching staff more so than their increase in students. Texas public schools hired 159,228 additional non-teaching personnel, above and beyond

its growth in student enrollment during FY 1992 to FY 2009.

With a genius for understatement, Scafidi notes, "Those funds could have been spent on salary increases for teachers or some other worthy purpose." The problem is not that many public schools are underfunded, but rather that a big chunk of the money is going to the wrong people. And the problem is just as bad at the college and university level.

This hasn't happened by accident. While the *War on Drugs* has been waged with much fanfare, the *War on Education* has been a stealth campaign, hidden behind slogans like choice, charter schools, and "No Child Left Behind." The *War on Drugs* and the *War on Education* operate in tandem, producing a school-to-prison pipeline for the poor and minorities, and debt serfdom for anyone who doesn't come from a privileged family able to foot the obscene costs of college. Think this perspective is a little too extreme? In 2018, a federal judge dismissed a Michigan lawsuit claiming that the right to a decent education is covered by the Equal Protection clause of the 14th Amendment. The judge agreed with state education officials who argued that, "no fundamental right to literacy exists." No wonder people of color and the poor can't get ahead.

Everyone agrees that a productive modern economy requires a well-educated society. So why has college become so expensive? Because certain elements of the elite have a hidden agenda: Their claim -- that an improved education will help workers displaced by outsourcing qualify for new jobs -- is just a smokescreen to facilitate the dismantling of America's industrial capacity. Money allocated by Congress for these job-training programs is a handout to well-connected donors and special interests who run these generally useless programs. And, while it will come as a surprise to many white-collar elites, *not everyone wants to work in a cubicle.* Some quite talented people prefer to work with their hands, or outdoors, or both. Some derive enjoyment, even satisfaction, from making things other than deals.

Second, by raising the cost of education, especially a good education, the well-to-do ensure that their offspring have every head start in the race of life. This is why affluent schools and school districts not only have official funding, but are wildly successful raising supplemental funding through Educational Foundations. Take, for example, the Ed Foundation for California's Manhattan Beach School District, where the median home price hovers around $3 mil. For the 2017-2018 school year it raised $6 million. *Six. Million. Dollars*. By the foundation's own calculations, that's equivalent to 9% of the district's annual budget, enough to pay 73 teachers. Compare that with the Lawndale Elementary School District, which is just east of Manhattan Beach but in terms of affluence might as well be on another planet. (Median home price: $450K.) In 2014 (the last year for which figures are available), the Lawndale Ed Foundation distributed a mere $52,000. Remember, when parents talk about giving their children every advantage -- a perfectly natural and rational parental instinct -- what that really means is putting all other kids at a *dis*advantage.

By making the cost of college and technical schools so expensive, the elite ensure that most graduates leave with their diploma in one hand and a pile of debt in the other. Their dilemma is compounded by a dismal job market. According to former Secretary of Labor Robert Reich, "Since 2000, the real average hourly wages of young college graduates have declined 7 percent, adjusted for inflation. Yet according to yesterday's Times, the pay of America's 200 top CEOs has been rising 12 percent a year, to an average of $21 million." Meanwhile, from 2009 to 2012, Apple -- now the world's first trillion-dollar company -- dodged $74 billion in taxes, enough to provide tuition-free college to every student in America. (Could this be one reason Apple reached that trillion-dollar plateau? You be the judge.)

An indebted populace is important to the elite because people living paycheck-to-paycheck generally have neither the time nor the courage to engage with the political system, especially when that means demonstrations and protests and attempts at union organizing. People in deep debt tend to be scared, compliant people. The term of art for this is *debt peonage*. Others prefer the metaphor of Medieval serfdom.

Third, the elite want to control what is taught. Technically-proficient graduates who are ready to step into plug-and-play technical, managerial, or scientific jobs? You bet. More captains of financial exploitation? All good. Graduates with a well-rounded education that addresses things like morality, ethics, the true history of the labor movement, and the functions of democracy? *Not. A. Chance.* The *War on Education* is not as publicized as the *War on Drugs*, but it has caused just as much damage.

## The New Economy and Limits on Growth

While economics is sometimes referred to as the dismal science, it is in fact, not really a science at all. Economics is the analysis of economic events that happened in the past, and *theories* about what will happen in the future under various conditions and government policies. Certain facts from the past can be plugged into models: the market got to this level, trade imbalances reached this point, and then so forth happened. But why the people involved made the decisions they did is largely subjective or suppositional. It's historical psychiatry.

True science, on the other hand, is governed by laws. Physics has the *Law of Gravity*, or *The Law of Inertia*. Same with chemistry; combine copper and tin in the correct proportions and you'll get bronze. *Every time*. With economic theories, there is no such thing as surety of outcome. Some theories have been shown to work in the past, but fail now. Others *are failing*, but remain in use because those policies favor the banks and other ruling elite.

A lot of economics research is funded by grants and endowments from wealthy individuals and corporations that have a deep, vested interest in seeing that certain economic philosophies are presented *as if* they were true, indisputable, scientific laws, or at least, as highly credentialed opinions for which There Is No Alternative, known derisively in some circles by the acronym TINA. (There is an alternative: RITA. Reform Is The Alternative, and it is this book's goal to chart a path for that reform.)

Many economic theories fail because they are built on faulty assumptions. Some contend that everyone involved will be a rational actor. Others assume the existence of a perfect free market, devoid of corporate manipulation, regulatory bias, or government intervention. Some economic models attempt to separate the so-called free market from government influence entirely. This unwillingness to consider and weigh human factors is why so much of what passes for high level economics thinking is simply quackery, sold with a lot more skill -- but no more ethics -- than snake oil from carnival barkers. That's why it's important to understand the concept of *agency*: institutions, organizations, and government agencies don't do things. The *people* who command those entities do things. Shit doesn't just happen, *someone makes it happen*, even if merely through flawed decisions that set the stage for whatever climactic (and often eminently predictable) catastrophic event eventually transpires. Fifteen-hundred people didn't die on the Titanic because the ship hit an iceberg; fifteen-hundred people died because the owner, designer, and builder decided to put too few lifeboats on board.

The most dangerous and pernicious of these phony economic theories is neoliberalism, which unfortunately has held America, and much of the world, in a death grip for several decades. Wikipedia and Britannica provide handy summaries: First, Wikipedia: [Bold is original.]

**Neoliberalism** or **neo-liberalism** refers primarily to the 20th-century resurgence of 19th-century ideas associated with *laissez-faire* economic liberalism· Those ideas include economic liberalization policies such as privatization, austerity, deregulation, free trade, and reductions in government spending in order to increase the role of the private sector in the economy and society. These market-based ideas and the policies they inspired constitute a paradigm shift away from the post-war Keynesian consensus which lasted from 1945 to 1980.

### *The postwar Keynesian consensus which lasted from 1945 to 1980.*

Remember anything else about that period from 1945 to 1980, when average people made good wages, bought homes, worked a forty-hour week, and took regular vacations? The heyday of mom choosing to work, but not *having* to work? Although it was a period of upheaval in terms of civil rights, overall it was also a good, or at least improving, economic time for a number of people, including blacks and Hispanics.

Neoliberalism fell out of favor in the 1930s, but re-emerged in the 1980s, spurred at least in part by developments in Chile after the CIA engineered a bloody right-wing coup that killed thousands, including Chile's democratically-elected president, Salvador Allende. But, as Wikipedia notes, when neo-liberalism reappeared as a subject of economic and political discussion:

> ...it also had shifted in meaning from a moderate form of liberalism to a more radical and *laissez-faire* capitalist set of ideas. Scholars now tended to associate it with the theories of economists Friedrich Hayek, Milton Friedman and James M. Buchanan, along with politicians and policy-makers such as Margaret Thatcher, Ronald Reagan and Alan Greenspan.

Ah, yes, Alan Greenspan, ardent supporter of the idea that banksters would police themselves because of concern for the continued existence and well-being of the banks they ran. Turns out, as he finally admitted, that wasn't the case. Personal greed won out. Who could have predicted?!

Britannica.com adds this:

> ...neoliberalism is often characterized in terms of its belief in sustained economic growth as the means to achieve human progress, its confidence in free markets as the most-efficient allocation of resources, its emphasis on minimal state intervention in economic and social affairs, and its commitment to the freedom of trade and capital.

> Although the terms are similar, neoliberalism is distinct from modern liberalism. Both have their ideological roots in the classical liberalism of the 19th century, which championed economic laissez-faire and the freedom (or liberty) of individuals against the excessive power of government ... Modern liberalism developed from the social-liberal tradition, which focused on impediments to individual freedom -- including poverty and inequality, disease, discrimination, and ignorance -- that had been created or exacerbated by unfettered capitalism and could be ameliorated only through direct state intervention. Such measures began in the late 19th century with workers' compensation schemes, the public funding of schools and hospitals, and regulations on working hours and conditions and eventually, by the mid-20th century, encompassed the broad range of social services and benefits characteristic of the so-called welfare state.

> By the 1970s, however, economic stagnation and increasing public debt prompted some economists to advocate a return to classical liberalism, which in its revived form came to be known as neoliberalism.

Don't let *economic stagnation* and *increasing public debt* fool you. These are the direct result of policies imposed to create economic conditions conducive to the rollback of FDR's New Deal. They didn't have to happen. We did not have to have the savaged economy and society we confront today. There could have been a different present, and there can be a different future.

If neoliberalism is how we got here, what does the future hold? An example of how the elite see the rest of us fitting into their economic world occurred in October 2005, when Citigroup issued an Equity Strategy report to its investors titled, *Plutonomy: Buying Luxury, Explaining Global Imbalances*. After a slew of sites reported on the story, Citibank's lawyers started playing internet whack-a-mole, trying to get every site to delete the text on grounds that it was proprietary material. But once on the web, things are out there forever. You can still find it if you look hard enough. And there are plenty of sites which summarize and analyze the contents, which boil down to:

- The world is composed of two groups: the ruling plutonomy, controlled by the wealthy, and everybody else.

- The U.S., Canada, and UK lead the plutonomy.

- Countries like Japan and parts of Europe constitute sort of an aristocratic sublevel.

- Investors and companies should focus on people in the top income levels of the plutonomy countries because nobody else has enough money, or other value, to be worth pursuing.

The Plutonomy is supported on the twin pillars of globalization and eternal growth. The first is a disaster, the second is absurdly irrational. The Earth is a finite object, with limited resources, and an equally limited ability to sustain ecosystems in the face of unrestrained and misdirected resource exploitation. As economist Kenneth Boulding said, "Anyone who believes exponential growth can go on forever in a finite world is either a madman or an economist." So who was Boulding, and why should we pay attention to what he said? Both an economist and a sociologist, Boulding, a professor at Colgate and author of 36 books, was a pioneer in the field of system dynamics and what we now call interdisciplinary studies. His studies of the sociological effects of economic changes got him nominated for both the Nobel Peace Prize *and* the Nobel Prize in Economics. Given that he died in 1993, his conclusions about continuous growth were ahead of his time. In fact, among some reality-based economists, the term growth is now disparaged as "groaf." (Another favored parody buzzword: "jawbs.")

Much blame for our dismal state goes to the Mainstream Media, commonly abbreviated MSM. They only color within the lines, carefully avoiding any explanations, context, or truth that might upset advertisers and others among *The Powers That Be* (TPTB). If you get your news from CBS, NBC, ABC, Fox, or CNN, at best you're only getting part of the story. At worst, you're being flat-out lied to. One commenter at NakedCapitalism.com called it, "The New York Times/Washington Post Axis of Smug Insularity." Got that right.

America was built on the idea that it is the Land of Opportunity where, with initiative and hard work, anyone who is deserving can be successful and live a decent life. For some, that meant entrepreneurship, building their own business which, in the early days, was often a farm. For others it meant a decent job, earning enough for a house with a picket fence, appliances, perhaps a camper or a boat. This dream, which became a reality for many, included sending their children to college without bankrupting the family, or mortgaging their kids' future under a mountain of debt. That dream included the parents living out their Golden Years with a roof over their heads, food on the table, and decent health care.

The other side of this work ethic has been disdain for those "lazy, shiftless, no account" folks who don't apply themselves diligently. Many people who are well-off view poverty as a choice, rather than a fate, an attitude that conveniently neglects to consider barriers to advancement, ranging from inferior education to racial, ethnic, or religious discrimination. It was no accident that a huge split occurred in the ranks of the Democratic Party when the civil rights movement resulted in blacks pushing into the formerly all-white ranks of many unions. White union members -- who had come to think of a job at the mill or the plant, or in the construction trades, as an inheritance to be passed down to their kids -- split off from the party's white-collar social liberals whose jobs in academia, finance, or the arts weren't threatened by this new competition.

Over the past thirty-five years there has been a shift in the employment paradigm. Millions of jobs have been lost to technological advances, especially computer-controlled robotics. The men who used to weld car bodies have given way to robots that do the job faster, without ever making an error. Where once machining a part required a machinist, now that same part can be trimmed, bored, threaded, slotted, and whatever else needs to be done, many times faster, by a computer-controlled machine that feeds itself a new piece of raw stock after it has chucked the finished one into a bin or onto a passing conveyor belt. Even more devastatingly, millions of jobs that still require human labor have been out-sourced to foreign countries. (Don't you love *out-sourced* to describe the workers whose jobs are lost? Try this little exercise: every time you hear out-sourced, substitute rat-fucked. It might not make you feel any better, but it will be a lot closer to the truth.)

The situation was exacerbated in the Great Recession, which started in 2007-2008 but which, for many people, has never ended. That's because all the money to rescue the economy went to

Wall Street instead of Main Street. The result was the explosion of an economic underclass of people, many in their 50s, who were not able to get another job of any kind and thus stopped looking for work. Many others, who had good jobs with benefits prior to the Great Recession, have had to settle for minimum wage employment flipping burgers, standing behind retail counters, and so forth. The technical term for these people, including college grads who are waiting tables because they can't get a job in their professional field, is *under-employed*.

Every month the Department of Labor Statistics releases the latest unemployment figures. The one you see on the news, the official unemployment rate, is category U3, *Total Unemployed as a Percentage of the Civilian Labor Force*. The thing is, U3 does not include the long-term unemployed who have given up looking for work. Nor does it include folks working part-time because that's all they can get. The true unemployment number is category U6, defined as:

> Total unemployed, plus all marginally attached workers, plus total employed part time for economic reasons, as a percent of the civilian labor force plus all persons marginally attached to the labor force.

***Marginally attached***. More marvelous bureaucratic obfuscation. *Marginally attached* means that even if you only work one hour a week, you're not considered unemployed for U3. That's why U6 numbers are regularly double the U3 number. If U3 is 6.1%, the U6 count will be more like 12%. Some economists and academics contend that even U6 understates the problem by several percentage points. In 2018, when U3 fell to 3.9%, the Real News Network interviewed Robert Pollin of the Political Economy Research Institute at University of Massachusetts Amherst. Pollin explained that because the Labor Participation Rate has fallen so far since the Great Recession, that U3 number of 3.9% and its companion U6 number of 7.8% lag far behind the institute's projection of 12%. But that's nothing. In June 2018, economist

John Williams, who operates the Shadow Government Statistics website, posited that if those who are left out of U6 stats because they've left the workforce -- a number that is now estimated at 102 million people -- were included the true unemployment rate would be 21.5%

**One-hundred-and-two million people. Twenty-one-and-a-half fucking percent.**

Chew on those numbers for a moment.

The unemployment rate during the Great Depression of the 1930s, considered to be the greatest economic crash in history, topped out at 25%. Not only is Williams' 21.5% estimate way too close for comfort, even if we accept Pollin's estimate of 12%, that's still half what it was during the Great Depression. **This** is why people are homeless, suicidal, and homicidal. It's why those who have jobs can't get raises, or still can't make ends meet even working two jobs. It's why wages haven't risen in terms of actual buying power since 1972, even though, according to Pollin, worker productivity has *doubled*.

One goal of the 43rd Amendment, Economic Security, is to return out-sourced jobs to the U.S. This will be hard, but not impossible. Global multinationals will scream bloody murder, and relations with countries who lose those jobs will suffer. (Tough shit; those countries are looking out for what's best for their people, there's no reason we shouldn't do the same.) Such a re-shoring of jobs would open up opportunities for people now working part time to find full time employment. In addition, as Naomi Klein argues convincingly in *This Changes Everything*, the transition from fossil fuels to sustainable energy and a greener economy would create millions of new jobs representing a net increase over jobs lost as older, polluting, and unsustainable industries are phased out.

But what happens if all the out-sourced jobs return, and all the promised new green technology jobs appear as predicted, and there still aren't enough jobs for everyone? This will require not only a paradigm shift, but a massive adjustment in attitudes. The solution is in Chapter 19.

## Immigration

We also face problems of immigration and birth rate. Obviously, if our society cannot produce enough jobs for the current population, allowing anyone else into the country is pure insanity. Naomi Klein argues that since First World resource extraction and economic exploitation is responsible for much of the devastation visited on third world countries, major Northern Hemisphere nation-states have an obligation to rescue displaced people from poorer nations by climate change and degradation of their domestic economies. On a moral and humanistic basis, she's right. But as a practical matter, that idea is likely dead on arrival. First, there is no guarantee that the first world can rescue a significant percentage, much less all, of those people from countries that will be devastated by climate change and resource exhaustion. If the planet has exceeded its carrying capacity, simply distributing the same population over new geography is no solution. The massive rescue idea also hinges on being able to spread the same number of people over a much smaller area and get sufficient food production *from that same area*. As my father used to say, "Sometimes you can't get there from here."

Second, even if such a massive rescue was possible, as Dr. Hillman contends, it is unlikely that the populations of the prosperous countries will accept a tidal wave of new immigrants. It will be difficult enough to get Americans to accept a lower-consumption lifestyle just to accommodate folks already here, much less get them to accept a diminished lifestyle to facilitate continued large-scale immigration. In this respect, I think fears of a dystopian future, such as portrayed in the TV series *The Walking Dead,* are tied to a simmering realization among Americans that the future will feature a constant battle over vastly depleted resources between the citizen *haves* and the non-citizen *have-nots.* To sharpen the analogy, simply substitute "refugees" or "illegal immigrants" for "zombies."

The subject of population stabilization begs the next natural question: "How do we reduce our future population to bring it more in line with the number of jobs that actually need to be performed for society to function and flourish?" Historically, first- and second-generation immigrant families in the lower economic ranks tend to have higher birthrates. But once the third generation begins to establish itself on a more comfortable and secure economic level, the birthrate drops. In fact, if not for immigration and the higher birthrate of new immigrant families, the U.S. would have shown a net decline in population over the latter part of the last century.

In previous times, a declining birthrate was seen as a problem, first because it portended a future shortage in the labor pool and second, because it meant too few current earners to cover the cost of retirement benefits, like Social Security, that had been promised to former workers. However, in a world where technology and a reduction in conspicuous consumption driven by declining resources will require fewer jobs and a much smaller workforce, a declining population may be just the ticket. If it happens naturally, so much the better. But what if it doesn't? China has been criticized for its policy of only allowing families to have one child. (Most of this criticism has come from countries that don't have to worry about feeding a billion people.) But the day may come when the U.S. has to consider something similar. How to make that equitable, and enforce it, will be the subject of bitter public debate, especially given the emotional and religious aspects of hot-button issues like mandatory birth control or tax penalties for having more children.

## New Military Doctrine and Posture

In general, the men and women who serve in our Armed Forces are dedicated, courageous, and well trained. However, that does not mean that we should refrain from serious analysis of when, where, and why they are sent into harm's way. The reason we don't do a better job of this is because the history we learn in schools is truncated, incomplete, and often deliberately distorted. At best, true motives are often soft-pedaled. At worst, the truth is ignored and lies are substituted. Cynics have often said, "History is propaganda written by the victors." That's not always true, but it applies in too many instances of American history, both in the distant past and more recent times.

The size, composition, capabilities, and mission orientation of the United States military has evolved greatly since the nation's inception. Having watched the British Army impose the oppressive policies of King George, our Founding Fathers were justifiably wary of the potential menace posed by large standing armies. Thus, for the early decades of its existence, the U.S. was a minor military power with a Navy and Marine Corps just large enough to protect American merchant vessels from pirates, and an Army barely sufficient to protect the western border from marauding Indians. Later, as the country's push westward provoked increased resistance from tribes being shoved off their land, the army grew in size and professionalism. But, aside from the Civil War period, it was still small by comparison to those of the major European nations.

Things stayed that way until the Spanish American War of 1898, where the U.S. acquired the former Spanish colonies of Cuba, Puerto Rico, Guam, and the Philippines. After a short period of occupation, Cuba was granted its independence. However, the U.S. retained possession of the naval base at Guantanamo Bay. As Wikipedia points out:

The U.S. Navy now had a major forward presence across the Pacific [Guam and the Philippines] and ... a major base in the Caribbean guarding the approaches to the Gulf Coast and [after its completion in 1914] the Panama Canal.

What Wikipedia fails to mention is that this also marked America's transition into being a colonial power. America, a country founded by colonists throwing off the economic and military yoke of the mother country, now imposed itself as the ruler of other people, all (conveniently enough) non-white. This led to the Philippine Insurrection of 1889-1902, which the U.S. put down with the aid of a young officer who would later achieve victory in the Pacific, Douglas MacArthur.

Once the U.S. became a colonial power with global political, military, and economic agendas, the mission of the U.S. military changed radically. No longer intended simply to defend our sovereign soil, now our military became an instrument of economic dominance and exploitation. As Wikipedia notes, starting in 1898:

> ...the United States conducted military interventions in Panama, Honduras, Nicaragua, Mexico, Haiti, and the Dominican Republic. The series of conflicts only ended with the withdrawal of troops from Haiti in 1934 under President Franklin D. Roosevelt. ... Reasons for these conflicts were varied but largely economic in nature. The conflicts were called "Banana Wars", a term that arose from the connections between these interventions and the preservation of US commercial interests in the region.

> Most prominently, the United Fruit Company had significant financial stakes in the production of bananas, tobacco, sugar cane and various other products throughout the Caribbean, Central America, and Northern South America. The US was also advancing its political interests, maintaining a sphere of influence and controlling the Panama Canal

(opened 1914) which it had recently built and was important for global trade and projecting naval power."

Note the phrasing: *preservation of US commercial interests in the region* and *projecting naval power*. Not a word about democracy, or the right of local peoples to self-determination in either their form of government or their domestic economic interests and policies. And why was it necessary to project naval power? Because the U.S. was establishing its global colonial reach in order to get other countries to act in our best interests, not theirs. This remains the overarching reason for today's bloated U.S. military.

When FDR pulled the last of our occupation forces from Haiti, he did so under what he called the Good Neighbor Policy. As his Secretary of State, Cordell Hull, told a conference of Latin American countries, "No country has the right to intervene in the internal or external affairs of another." Roosevelt himself later confirmed that, "the policy of the United States from now on is one opposed to armed intervention."

There's no telling how things might have gone had WWII not happened. America, traditionally isolationist, was again drawn into massive conflict abroad. Successfully prosecuting the war meant taking the fight to the enemy, which required hundreds of bases far from our shores. Just because the war ended didn't mean these bases could all go away. There was the necessity of occupying Japan, Germany, and Italy as a means of ensuring that their new governments did not replicate the worst elements of previous regimes. With the U.S.S.R. exercising control of Eastern Europe from the Baltic states to the Greek border, in order to prevent the spread of communism (and potential Pearl Harbor-type surprise attacks), the U.S. and its Allies were forced to maintain military installations throughout Europe and the Pacific. As the battle against communism grew, U.S. troops and military support spread to countries throughout Asia, Africa, and Latin

America. The most obvious examples, intended to send a message to communist Russia and China, were Korea and Vietnam.

Although the battle against Russian and Chinese influence was branded as a battle between communism and democracy, in reality, it was a battle between communism and capitalism, which has all too often proven to be the exact opposite of democracy. All any corrupt dictator had to do to ensure full U.S. military and financial backing was declare his government anti-communist, even if that really meant anti-democratic and anti-human rights. Billions of dollars poured into these countries. Not content to merely support pro-capitalist regimes that came into power on their own, the US deployed the CIA to engineer, equip, and support violent regime change in countries with leftist or socialist regimes, even those that had been freely elected and were widely supported by the local populace.

Two of the most heinous and flagrant examples of this practice occurred in Iraq in 1953, and in Chile twenty years later. In Iraq, the motivation was ensuring Western access to oil, preferably at favorable prices. In Chile, the interests of ITT, which owned the nation's phone system, played a huge role, as did the desire of Henry Kissinger and Milton Friedman to create a real-world test case for Friedman's Chicago School of Economics theories about the privatization of traditional government functions.

Iraq and Chile were not isolated incidents. Wikipedia provides a summary of countries where the U.S. financed, promoted, and armed coup forces and their successor dictatorships. Among them:

> Syria 1949 (where we're currently at it again)
> Guatemala 1954
> Indonesia 1958
> Cuba 1959
> Iraq (again) 1960-63
> The Congo (1960-65)

Dominican Republic 1961
Vietnam 1963
Brazil 1964
Turkey 1980
Nicaragua 1981-90
Venezuela 2002

In all of these cases, the ostensible public relations goal was the institution or preservation of freedom and democracy. (Just ignore the fact that virtually all of the new governments that we helped install were harsh, authoritarian right-wing dictatorships.) The true overarching goal, however, was to ensure that economic alternatives to American-style unbridled capitalism did not take root and flourish. These policies and covert actions were designed to make sure that U.S. corporations and their free-world economic brethren had cheap, secure, unfettered access to that country's markets and/or resources.

Note that the Wikipedia summary omits the post-9-11 invasion of Iraq, the third time in fifty years that the U.S. was involved in the removal of an Iraqi government we did not like. (Iraq also marked the first time where America asserted it had the authority to wage "preemptive" war. Not surprisingly, this authority is one we reserve for only the U.S.A., because, we're like, you know, exceptional.)

Wikipedia also omits the 2009 coup in Honduras where democratically-elected reformist President Manuel Zelaya was rousted out of bed and sent packing in his pajamas on a flight *from a U.S. military base*. While the U.S. may not have engineered this coup, we certainly supported it, both before and after it happened. Unlike the European Union and other Latin American countries, we did not withdraw our ambassador in protest. Nor did we officially use the word *coup* because, under U.S. law, that would have required us to suspend military aid. (As if having a democratically elected President thrown out of the country by 200 armed men in the middle of the night could be anything else except a coup. But we can't call a coup a coup if doing so gets in the way of weapons-export profits, or the location of strategic bases that support our military's ability to intimidate nearby countries.)

It is interesting that this coup took place on Hillary Clinton's watch as Secretary of State. And who did the new Honduran government hire to run its public relations and lobbying campaign on Capitol Hill? Why longtime Clinton crony, attorney Lanny Davis, one of the most despicable people currently drawing air on the planet. Part of Bill Clinton's defense team during the Monica Lewinsky scandal, he's remained a member of Team Clinton ever since. And who hired Davis? The Honduran Chapter of the Business Council of Latin America. In other words, the anti-democratic elitist oligarchs whose control of the country was threatened when President Zelaya raised the minimum wage.

Many Americans have long turned a blind eye to our interference in the internal affairs of other countries. But the time is rapidly approaching when we will not be able to afford the luxury of willful ignorance. The day will soon come when we will have to determine whether or not we are going to be a full-fledged, traditional, territory-occupying colonial power.

The Pentagon has game-planned all sorts of scenarios that will arise when global climate catastrophes meld with massive poverty and inequality. Among these scenarios are resource wars, which come in two kinds. The first is when we militarily subdue or intimidate a country into providing us with its natural resources, usually at a bargain rate, with the money going to that country's oligarchs and government officials. The second is when we battle a country, like China or Russia, over the resources of a third country. Naturally, the people of that country will not be consulted.

If we decide to continue operating the American Empire, we will have to accept the animosity, terrorism, and perils of traveling abroad that come with that policy. If we decide to become a good neighbor to the rest of the world, we will have to accept some decline in our consumptive life-style. As Naomi Klein points out in *This Changes Everything*, our average middle-class lifestyle of the 70s was still a whole lot better than how most of the world lives today, and we will have to be content to go back to that level of relative luxury if we are to have any hope of effectively battling global climate change.

One reason we will have to face this choice is that while excessive war and military spending is profitable for the Military Industrial Complex, it ultimately bankrupts the nation. A second reason is that if we engage in military action in the conquest of resources, the elite and what's left of our middle class will enjoy a vastly disproportionate share of the benefits. It's only fair that we ensure that the well-off and their children share in the grief, bloodshed, and shattered lives that war always produces. (More on these issues in Chapter 17.)

## Summary

None of the over-riding issues that confront us can be resolved by Constitutional amendment. The subjects themselves, and the components of any solution, are too complex. Each will require carefully crafted laws, regulations, policies, and incentives that can only come out of the political process. However, any fair and viable solution to these problems can only result if that political process is untainted by the secrecy, conflict of interest, and influence peddling which describes our current system. The merits of the Restoration Amendments reside in their ability to sweep aside the existing barriers to good government.

# PART II

---

# ACCOUNTABLE
# GOVERNMENT

## *NOTE*

Since there are already 27 amendments to the U.S. Constitution, the Restoration Amendments start with number 28.

# Chapter 3

# THE RIGHT TO GOOD GOVERNMENT

In 1983 Walter Mitchell, Jr., a city councilman from Redondo Beach, California, was sentenced to prison for fraud after accepting $108,000 in bribes from developer Robert Ferrante. The court ruled that Mitchell had, "deprived the citizens of the honest and loyal services of a public official."

Six years later Mitchell's conviction was overturned by the Ninth Circuit Court of Appeals on the grounds that Mitchell had not defrauded the city. If he'd taken a bribe to push through a contract for city services, then he would have been guilty, because taxpayer funds were involved. But since he took money only from Ferrante and not the city, the federal fraud statute didn't apply. The Appeals court decision derived from a 1987 ruling by the Supreme Court, in *McNally v. United States,* that mail fraud convictions could not be based on an intangible, "right of good government" not specifically enumerated in the Constitution.

Yes, you read that right. Even though the Supreme Court inferred a right of privacy in the Constitution to underpin *Roe v. Wade,* and even though, as I'll discuss later, the courts have invented, out of thin air, other concepts such as "qualified immunity" for law enforcement, would SCOTUS dare to infer a public right to good government from officials and public employees?

### Not. A. Chance.

The following year Congress reacted to the Supreme Court's decision by passing the Honest Services Fraud Act. But, as Lyle Denniston reported on Scotusblog.com:

> Almost from the day Congress enacted the law specifying that fraud can be committed by denying someone the 'intangible right" to one's "honest services," lower courts have struggled to define just what kind of wrongdoing would fit within that concept.

Not surprisingly, over the next twenty-five years the Supreme Court used that vagueness to whittle away at the scope of what can be prosecuted as a theft of honest services. Thanks to Supreme Court rulings in cases involving Ken Lay (the notorious Enron fraud), publishing mogul Conrad Black, and others, the law can now only be used to prosecute cases of outright bribery or kickbacks. Ironically, under this definition, Walter Mitchell, Jr.'s conviction would have been upheld.

After this Supreme Court evisceration of the law, self-dealing and conflict-of-interest can no longer be prosecuted; indeed, they are not even crimes under the statute. So, if a company bribes a politician to obtain a government contract, that's a prosecutable offense. But if that same politician steers a government contract to a company he owns or has stock in, that's all fine and dandy under federal law. Same if he influences the awarding of a government contract to a company in which his wife, children, or other relatives have an interest. The get-out-of-jail-free card also applies in cases where a politician uses their power or influence to benefit their campaign donors. Which raises the question:

***What good is a Constitution that isn't based on a right of good government, and which has no mechanism to ensure delivery of the benefits it pretends to confer?***

The answer: Not much.

Often, when the courts wish to duck a contentious case, especially one involving civil liberties or the National Security State, a favorite and most despicable tactic is to dismiss the suit based on the pretext that the plaintiff cannot prove that they have been personally affected by the law in question, and therefore does not have standing to sue. This denies the concept that everyone has a vested interest in, and ultimately benefits from, the law being applied in a fair, legal and uniform manner. This has led to absurd, *Alice-In-Wonderland* decisions where lawsuits from persons and organizations attempting to discover if they were subjected to illegal surveillance and wiretapping have been dismissed because the plaintiff could not prove that they had been secretly monitored. Literally:

**You can't search for the evidence you need, because you don't already have the evidence you need.**

Another recent case that undermined democracy was the Supreme Court's decision in 2013 that the backers of California's anti-gay marriage Prop 8 lacked standing to appeal a lower court ruling invalidating the measure. To avoid having to rule on the issue of gay marriage itself, the justices decided to overturn a century of precedent that backers of initiatives, referendums, and recalls have legal standing to sue if the state or local jurisdiction refuses to enforce the measure after it had been passed. Regardless of personal feelings about gay marriage, consider the broader implications: the purpose of initiatives, referendums, and recalls is to let the people act when government will not, or to reverse government actions with which the governed disagree. Rather than address a controversial issue, the court threw out the right of the people to ensure that measures they pass at the ballot box are enforced. The highest court in the land literally gave state and local governments the power to ignore the will of the people. Here is how Justice Anthony Kennedy described this legal travesty is his dissent: [Emphasis added.]

> Under California law, a [ballot initiative] proponent has the authority to appear in court and assert the State's interest in defending an enacted initiative when the public officials charged with that duty refuse to do so. The State deems such an appearance essential to the integrity of its initiative process. ... The State Supreme Court's definition of proponents' powers is binding on this Court.

> The Court concludes that proponents lack sufficient ties to the state government. It notes that they "are not elected," "answer to no one," and lack "'a fiduciary obligation'" to the State. But what the Court deems deficiencies in the proponents' connection to the State government, the State Supreme Court saw as essential qualifications to defend the initiative system. ***The very object of the initiative system is to establish a lawmaking process that does not depend upon state officials***. In California, the popular initiative is necessary to implement 'the theory that all power of government ultimately resides in the people.'

> A prime purpose of justiciability [granting standing to argue a case] is to ensure vigorous advocacy, yet the Court insists upon litigation conducted by state officials whose preference is to lose the case. ... And rather than honor the principle that justiciability exists to allow disputes of public policy to be resolved by the political process rather than the courts, here the Court refuses to allow a State's authorized representatives to defend the outcome of a democratic election.

> In the end, what the court fails to grasp or accept is the basic premise of the initiative process, and it is this. ***The essence of democracy is that the right to make law rests in the people and flows to the government, not the other way around. Freedom resides first in the people without***

*need of a grant from government.* The California initiative process embodies these principles and has done so for over a century. In California and the 26 other states that permit initiatives and popular referendums, the people have exercised their own inherent sovereign right to govern themselves. The court today frustrates that choice by nullifying ... a state Supreme Court decision holding that state law authorizes an enacted initiative's proponents to defend the law if and when the state's usual legal advocates decline to do so.

A few years later the Supreme Court recognized the legality of gay marriage. But the original ruling, denying initiative and referendum backers legal standing at the federal level to defend their own ballot measures, remains in place.

The first step in reform is establishing in clear language that good government is a fundamental right assured to every citizen. Thus:

## The 28th Amendment --
## The Right to Good Government

**Section 1: The right of the people to fair and honest government, which neither favors nor discriminates, is hereby established, and any citizen shall have standing at law to enforce and preserve such right, and when they prevail to be fully compensated, including the full costs of litigation plus treble damages, which shall be calculated on the cost of litigation, or the total amount of fines and settlement awards, whichever are greater. All prior laws and decisions to the contrary are hereby null and void.**

There are already U.S. laws which allow private citizens to bring suit as private individuals on behalf of (or in lieu of) the government (thus benefitting the people at large). The first is Qui Tam, the legal abbreviation for a longer Latin phrase which translates as, "he who sues in this matter for the king as well as himself." It has its roots in medieval English common law and is embodied in U.S. law as part of the False Claims Act, which permits an individual with knowledge of fraud against the government to bring suit on behalf of the government. It is sometimes the only effective tool of whistleblowers. Typically, it involves employees or vendors who discover that their employers or clients are cheating the government on anything from inflated Medicare claims and watered-down medications to faulty military equipment or over-priced office furniture. Plaintiffs who are successful receive between fifteen and twenty-five percent of any fines and funds recovered by the government. Likewise, the attorneys for the plaintiff are awarded their fees and costs.

Sadly, despite various legal protections theoretically afforded whistleblowers, many of them, even if they merely expose wrongdoing but do not attempt to file a *qui tam* suit, end up being fired and find themselves effectively blackballed from future employment, not only in their current field but in other lines of work as well. Thus, the award that a successful plaintiff receives (fifteen to twenty-five percent of the penalty or settlement), is insufficient to fully compensate for the damage to their income, lifestyle, and often even their physical and mental health. A treble damage award provision makes it worthwhile for people with knowledge of fraud and wrongdoing to take the risk of blowing that whistle. Just as breaking the law must be painful for the criminal, enforcing the law for the benefit of the public when officials have failed to do so, must be made worth the effort and risks to the individual.

Another example of the law allowing civilians to file suit against criminal activity is the Civil Rico portion of the 1970 federal Racketeer Influenced and Corrupt Organizations Act. Attorney John Tollefson has posted an excellent summary of Civil Rico on Tollefsonlaw.com. Here are some key excerpts:

The Racketeer Influenced and Corrupt Organizations Act of 1970 ("RICO", 18 U.S.C.A. §§ 1961 et seq.) created a civil law cause of action (§ 1964) for violations of its provisions. Exclusive venue is in federal District Courts which are empowered to award triple monetary awards, attorney fees, and to issue equitable orders preventing and restraining violations, including divestiture of an interest in any enterprise, restrictions on future activities or investments of any person, and the dissolution or reorganization of the enterprise.

...In order to obtain relief, the plaintiff must prove two "predicate offenses" (violations of § 1962) which prohibits persons who derive income from a pattern of racketeering activity or through the collection of an unlawful debt to invest the income in any enterprise which engages in interstate commerce. The statute does not mention "organized crime" or limit its application to criminal endeavors and can be applied to legitimate businesses.

Note that the Civil Rico statute also empowers courts to award treble damages and attorney's fees. There is an added bonus in that when an individual, company, or organization brings a Civil Rico suit, if the federal government then steps in and piggy-backs on that suit by bringing a successful criminal prosecution, the civil penalties also apply, and the original civil plaintiff is entitled to their reward. There are however, two drawbacks to the government intervening by bringing a criminal case. One is that, due to the higher standard for conviction in a criminal case, if the government loses, the acquittal might adversely affect the prospects for success in the civil case. The second drawback is that the civil case is held in abeyance while the criminal case is pursued, which means that, in theory anyway, a Civil Rico defendant -- most likely a government contractor or big campaign donor with sufficient influence -- might get the government to file and then repeatedly delay prosecuting its own case, leaving the civil case in suspended animation for years, if not decades. Worse, the government could tank the criminal case, leaving on record an acquittal which would make it virtually impossible for the original plaintiff to prevail in the civil case.

A problem private individuals and small groups encounter when using the courts to enforce the law is encapsulated in the old saying, "You're only entitled to as much justice as you can afford." Having contributed to a number of lawsuits against my own corrupt local city government, I can tell you from first-hand experience that the process can eat up six-figures in a heartbeat. And even when legal fees are awarded, much of that money goes to the attorneys and is not reimbursed to those who originally went out on a financial limb to fund the suit. That's because judges will often not reimburse the full amount that the victorious attorneys requested, leaving the plaintiffs on the hook for the difference between what the court awarded and what the attorneys actually spent.

In cases where funds are put forward by charitable organizations which join in a suit because the central issue (perhaps dealing with civil rights or the environment) is related to their primary mission, those funds cannot be refunded due to laws governing charitable donations. So, those who fund the suit end up proving that the government was wrong, but are still out their litigation costs. *Their reward for being right is to lose money.* This does not even include the irritating irony that the government used your tax dollars to fight your lawsuit, and then used more of your tax dollars to reward your lawyers, while all you can do is stand back and applaud your victory with an empty wallet.

Notice, too, that while the justices will labor to infer powers (or imagine some restriction) in the specific articles and amendments of the Constitution, they never cite the duties implied by a reading of the purposes for which the Constitution was drafted, as enumerated in the Preamble:

> *We the People* of the United States, in Order to form a more perfect Union, establish Justice, insure domestic Tranquility, provide for the common defence [*sic*], promote the general Welfare, and secure the Blessings of Liberty to ourselves and our Posterity, do ordain and establish this Constitution for the United States of America.

How many bad laws and bad decisions could be reversed if the criteria were establishing justice, promoting the general welfare, or securing the blessings of liberty? But that is not the case. It is high time that the legal system reflects the fact that the sections of the Constitution *only exist to implement the principles and goals embodied in its Preamble*. The Preamble states the goal, and the rest of the Constitution is simply a map for how to get there. Therefore:

**Section 2: In interpreting the applicability of laws the Supreme Court shall consider the degree to which said laws conform to and support the principles enunciated in the Preamble to the Constitution.**

Another example of how entrenched elites avoid accountability for law-breaking involves pardons, commutations, and suspended sentences. Scooter Libby was convicted of perjury and obstruction of justice after publicly revealing that Valerie Plame was a covert CIA agent. This ended her career and endangered many people abroad with whom she had had contact over the years. Libby was sentenced to thirty months in prison and a $250,000 fine. But George W. Bush commuted Libby's sentence, and, to rub salt in the wounds, four years later Libby appealed and got his license to practice law reinstated. And if that wasn't enough, in 2018, President Trump pardoned Libby in a move which some saw as a signal to Trump's associates that he would pardon them if Special Prosecutor William Mueller started to close in on possible wrongdoing by Trump, either while in office or in his business dealings.

Prior to Libby's conviction there was considerable speculation that he had been ordered to reveal Plame's status by Vice-President Cheney, and that presidential advisor Karl Rove also had a hand in the matter. With the threat of a prison term hanging over his head, Libby may have implicated one or both men. With his sentence commuted, Libby was free of such pressure, and now the public will never know for sure if Cheney or Rove had any involvement.

George W. Bush learned well from his father. Remember Iran-Contra, where the Reagan administration agreed to illegally sell arms to Iran, and use the money to bypass the refusal of Congress to fund the Nicaraguan Contras? Reagan's VP, George H. W. Bush, was implicated in the plot. If proven, this would have resulted in his impeachment, possible conviction on criminal charges, and spelled an end to his presidential aspirations. So, good old H.W. pardoned six people, including former Secretary of Defense Caspar Weinberger, who reportedly had meeting notes proving Bush's participation in the scheme. (Which, we later learned, also involved the CIA helping drug traffickers import cocaine destined for our cities.) With typical corrupt timing, Bush announced the pardons on Christmas Eve and then lammed out of town to Camp David. Here's the New York Times headline:

### Bush Pardons 6 in Iran Affair, Aborting a Weinberger Trial; Prosecutor Assails 'Cover-Up'

Reporter David Johnson characterized the pardons as "decapitating" the investigation led by the independent prosecutor, Lawrence E. Walsh. Furious, Walsh said the pardons were:

> "evidence of a conspiracy among the highest ranking Reagan Administration officials to lie to Congress and the American public."

The cases of Libby, Weinberger, and five other Iran-Contra conspirators also pardoned (three of whom had already been convicted or entered guilty pleas), demonstrate that it will do no good to enact mandatory sentences if they can vanish with the swipe of an official pen, whether wielded by the president, governor, judge, or even a parole panel. Thus:

> **Section 3: Inescapable accountability being a cornerstone of good government, all powers of the President, governors, judges, and official bodies to pardon, parole, commute, suspend, or otherwise reduce mandatory minimum sentences for crimes involving corruption, misuse of office, or violation of election statutes is hereby abolished.**

It is also not enough to ensure that political criminals face incarceration. We must also not allow government to escape from itself. One common complaint about Congress and lesser legislative entities is that they impose laws on the public, but exempt themselves from the same mandates, restrictions, and penalties. A classic example was Obamacare. Once the bill went into effect, Congress and the White House suddenly realized that it would prevent members of Congress, and congressional staffers, from retaining their existing, federally-subsidized, gold-plated health plans. Presto! Suddenly, that provision of the new law was magically waived by the Office of Personnel Management. (No need to, you know, revise the law. And perish the thought that similar waivers be granted to, you know, regular people.)

What does it say about the lack of principles and courage of Congress, or a lesser legislative body, that exempts itself from laws and regulations governing everyone else? Where is the *justice for all* in that? There is none. This classic, "Do as I say, not as I do," attitude breeds contempt for the law. Aside from the rank hypocrisy, it also defies reason. If something is harmful enough to be outlawed, then no one should be allowed to do it. Conversely, if some act is desirable enough to be required by force of law, then that law should apply to everybody. And if complying with the law costs money, then everyone should pay. Therefore:

> **Section 4: Neither Congress nor any lesser legislative or regulatory body shall exempt itself from compliance with any statute, rule, or regulation of its own enactment. Nor shall Congress or any legislative body confer on itself by virtue of office any benefit, other than those related to compensation, which is not available to all citizens.**

One problem our system of government has had, ever since its inception, is effectively defining corruption. Fordham law professor Zephyr Teachout wrote the compelling book, *Corruption In America,* which traces the long struggle to construct both definitions and commensurate penalties. Not surprisingly, much of the problem stems from a political class unwilling to subject itself to a harsh, confining definition. Teachout, a devout reformer, has no such problem. The following is a slightly tweaked version of the definition she arrived at:

> **Section 5: Corruption is hereby defined as the self-serving use of public office for private gain, including, without limitation: bribery; public decisions to serve private financial gain made because of economic, professional, or familial relationships; public decisions to serve executive power made because of economic, professional, or familial relationships; use of public positions to become wealthy, whether by the officeholder, public official, or others seeking privately to influence same; and any failure to recuse by an officeholder, official, or public employee which thus creates the appearance of possible corruption or conflict of interest.**

Now here is my proposed solution to the issue of satisfactory punishment for corruption:

**Section 6: All offenses involving corruption or fraud upon the public, or against the cause of good government, shall be felonies punishable as prescribed in Section 10.**

Few things are more galling than government officials being convicted of corruption or other abuse of office and then, after serving whatever sentence is imposed, retiring with a fat public pension. Despite being convicted of taking $700,000 through kickbacks from ghost employees, and by embezzling from the House Post Office, Illinois Congressman Dan Rostenkowski kept his congressional pension, which reached $125,000 a year by the time he died in 2010. But "Rosty" was no exception. As the *Deseret News* noted, even though Congress has the power to revoke pensions for abuse of office: "Since the turn of the century, **two senators and 32 House members** have been jailed for felonies. None was denied a congressional pension." [Emphasis added.]

*Thirty-four convictions in a single century. One every three years.*

Clearly, corrupt and felonious activity by members of Congress is not a rare or isolated event.

By some measures, Rostenkowski was a piker. Pennsylvania State Senator Robert Mellow got a sixteen-month prison sentence for mail fraud but still kept his $245,000 a year pension. You can find similar examples in almost every state. Some state pension laws actually prohibit public pensions from being forfeited due to criminal convictions. If the crooked politicians are determined to protect their own, we simply have to take that power out of their hands. Which is why pension forfeiture is included along with criminal penalties in Section 10.

As long as we're establishing that laws involving corruption should have strong criminal penalties attached, how about we address the process in which laws are made? One critical step for achieving good government is limiting bills to singular subjects which are clearly identified in the bill's title. It is equally critical to ensure that responsibility for every element of legislation is clearly and permanently made public so that voters can know who among their elected representatives is serving whom, and why. No more sneaking special tax breaks into legislation funding the Defense Department or the Department of Agriculture. Bills that can't pass on their own merit don't deserve to pass. And once the reforms dealing with gerrymandering outlined later in Chapter 10 are enacted, bills that do deserve to pass, will.

> **Section 7: No legislation at any level of government shall contain any provision not explicitly germane to the central purpose and title of said legislation. Every element or provision of every bill shall include the name and title of the person who introduced or drafted said provision. Any element or provision that is not germane, or not identified as to author, shall be null and void, and shall impose on the bill's primary authors a prison term as prescribed in Section 10.**

It's not enough just to identify which officials are behind each provision of proposed legislation. The entire process of drafting bills needs to be open to public examination. Shouldn't the running of *our* government, which is the ultimate business of the public, be conducted in a way that the public can observe? Why should discussion of laws and the drafting of regulations take place behind closed doors, at cocktail parties, or on golf courses, yachts, and private jets? Most people don't even realize that many laws are drafted, not by legislators and their staffs, but by lobbyists or outside private organizations. Some of these lobby shops produce model legislation, plug-and-play bills that legislators can introduce to assist the elite in avoiding more regulations, evading more taxes, or extracting more money by privatizing more government services. Therefore:

**Section 8: Except for true matters of national security, subject to judicial review if necessary, all actions and discussions by public officials or employees of government bearing on the creation, drafting, enactment, revision, repeal, or implementation of legislation, or regulations deriving from legislation or from an order of the Executive or Judicial branch, shall be conducted only in open public proceedings, contemporaneously disseminated by mass media and subsequently archived for convenient public examination.**

Opponents of open government will argue that if not guaranteed confidentiality, experts will not give honest advice to everyone from the President on down. Think about that for a moment:

- What assurance do we have that what these experts and advisors say in their private discussions is the truth? We cannot judge because we do not know.

- If what these experts and advisors say in private is not the same as what they are willing to say in public, why should the framework of our government provide them a platform for lying?

Those who benefit from the current veil of secrecy that surrounds the drafting of laws and regulations will argue that confidentiality is necessary to keep from hurting people's feelings and creating animosity between individuals or organizations on the opposite side of any particular issue. (It's ironic that many people who make this argument can often be seen grandstanding, in front of the television cameras, saying awful things about their opponents.)

Anyone who can't stand having their feelings hurt shouldn't go into politics or advocate on behalf of businesses, organizations, and social causes. They need to leave the hard work of running the greatest nation in history to those adults who are tough enough for the conflict that entails.

There are also those who will say that these discussions often involve trade secrets. Bullshit. If the purpose of a proposed law or regulation is not to favor one company against another, why would a trade secret even enter the conversation? Legislators and regulators don't need to know secret formulas or the particulars of various patents. They don't need to know marketing plans or sales projections. All they need to know is why a law or regulation is necessary **to serve the public**, and how best to draft it to accomplish that purpose. The public is best served by the truth, and anyone who is unwilling to make an argument in public should not be allowed to make it in private. Experience has shown that private discussions involving laws and regulations most often disserve the public. What we don't know can't hurt *them*, but it sure as hell can, and does, hurt *us*.

The final argument against Section 7 is that the cost of recording all discussions of legislators, staffers, and regulators, archiving them, and making them available over the Internet or other future means of mass distribution would be prohibitive. This from a government that collects and archives over 1.5 **billion** public phone calls and emails ***a day***? A government where the former head of the National Security Agency stated that the agency's goal was to collect ***all electronic communications by anyone in the world***? Better we put that money and technological capability to work ensuring that the business of democracy is conducted in the harsh light of day. In short:

***Allowing private discussion of public business merely enables lying.***

Either somebody lies in private, or they lie to the public. People who are not lying should not mind having their discussion of public business viewed by the public.

One more step remains, however, in cleaning up the process of law-making. No bill can become law unless, and until, it is voted on by the appropriate legislative body. Ever since the Supreme Court's 1964 *Reynolds v. Sims* decision, both Congress and state legislatures have been elected on the basis of "one man, one vote." (Prior to *Sims*, in many states gerrymandered districts gave greater proportional representation to rural voters.) Unfortunately, once legislators are in office, the rule often becomes, "one man, NO vote." That's because the leaders of each chamber, and many committee chairs, can bottle up legislation or block confirmation of official appointments by simply refusing to bring the matter to the floor for a vote. The supreme offender here is the U.S. Senate. Wikipedia explains:

> ...a **hold** is a parliamentary procedure permitted by the Standing Rules of the United States Senate which allows one or more Senators to prevent a motion from reaching a vote on the Senate floor.
>
> If the Senator provides notice privately to his or her party leadership of their intent (and the party leadership agreed), then the hold is known as a **secret** or **anonymous hold**. If the Senator objects on the Senate floor or the hold is publicly revealed, then the hold is more generally known as a **Senatorial hold**.

Although it has become harder to hide the identity of a senator placing a hold, the practice itself remains indefensibly resistant to reform. The problem isn't just that it gives a single person veto control over legislation, but that it is often used as a form of hostage-taking. If a senator wants something from the White House, all he or she has to do is put a hold on the nomination of a judge or cabinet official. Want to prevent a sitting president from appointing a particular person to the Supreme Court? Simply refuse to bring the nomination forward for hearings.

Politicians and political scientists like to point out that, technically, we're a republic and not a democracy, as was, say, ancient Athens. But on the other hand, those same people are fond of using the phrase "democratically elected." Well, if democracy is good enough to get them elected, it's good enough for them to practice once in office. Both parties play this disgusting hold game. If Congress won't end this crime against democratic government, we'll have to do it.

> **Section 9: No member of any legislative body shall have the power, granted by rule or courtesy, to prevent in any way the advancement of any matter before said body or committee thereof. Any matter may be advanced by a vote of twenty-five percent of the members of the relevant committee or twenty percent of the legislative body as a whole. Refusal to grant such a vote, or refusal to abide by the results of such a vote, shall result in the immediate disqualification and removal from office of the committee or chamber chair by the Chief Justice of the State Supreme Court, or in the case of Congress, by the Chief Justice of the U.S. Supreme Court.**

In keeping with Hamilton's admonition that any law without a specific penalty is merely a recommendation:

> **Section 10: Violation of Section 6 shall be a felony punishable by mandatory incarceration for a period of not less than ten years. Violations of Sections 7 and 8 shall be felonies punishable by mandatory incarceration for a period of not less than five years. All sentences prescribed herein shall be served in maximum**

security and not subject to pardon, parole, commutation, suspension, or other reduction of sentence. Conviction or plea of guilty shall result in the forfeiture of all pension benefits accrued while in public office or employment.

# Chapter 4

# THE PUBLIC'S RIGHT TO KNOW

Just as the Constitution currently contains no right to good government, there is also no explicit right to know what government is doing for the people, *to* the people, or in their name. The First Amendment protects the right of the press to report on the actions of government, but the press can only report what they know, and government has become very good at preventing the press from knowing a great many things, especially those which, while not endangering our security, are nonetheless embarrassing to those in power. And yes, we have Freedom of Information laws at the federal and state level, but these vary wildly in strength and application. As legislative acts they are subject to revision and even repeal, and usually there is no criminal penalty for evading or even defying these laws.

For example, the citizens of the Phoenix suburb of Tempe voted overwhelmingly (*by 90%!*) to amend their city charter to require that any group spending over $1,000 in a city election disclose the identity of their donors. It took less than a month for the Arizona state legislature to outlaw such ordinances. Apparently, the legislature is a little sensitive about the fact that, as Newsweek reported, anonymous donations, "accounted for just $35,000 in 2006 elections. By 2014, that figure rose to more than $10 million."

While a constitutional Right to Information amendment would still be subject to judicial interpretation, it would put plaintiffs and reformers on much firmer legal ground than currently exists, and thus make it much harder for government at all levels to avoid disclosure. The bottom line, which many in government will find disturbing, is that citizens should have a constitutional right to know what their government is up to in all matters that don't genuinely involve national security. Thus:

**The 29th Amendment --
The Public's Right to Information**

**Section 1: An informed electorate being critical to the health and survival of a democratic government, no person disseminating information to the public at large shall be compelled to reveal any source of information or documentation alleging a violation of law or regulation, abuse of power or position, or act against the public good, nor shall any such person supplying or disseminating such information as described herein suffer prosecution under any statute or definition of espionage.**

**Section 2: No person deemed a possible source of information or documentation obtained by the press, or otherwise disseminated to the public at large, alleging a violation of law or regulation, abuse of power or position, or act against the public good shall be asked, compelled, or coerced to waive confidentiality, and any attempt to do so shall be a felony punishable by incarceration in a maximum security facility for a period, not subject to pardon, parole, commutation, suspension, or other reduction of sentence, of at least ten years.**

**Section 3: Acts of retaliation taken against any person invoking these rights, or against their employer or supporters, shall be a felony punishable by incarceration in a maximum security facility for a period, not subject to pardon, parole, commutation, suspension, or other reduction of sentence, of at least ten years.**

The 29th Amendment is necessary to protect the right of the public to know when government officials violate the law, improperly use government funds, or abuse the powers of their position. The prohibition against charging whistleblowers, or those engaged in journalism, with espionage is necessary because of the Obama administration's insistence on using the Espionage Act of 1917, which was clearly intended to punish true acts of espionage, as a cudgel to attack those who revealed illegal and unconstitutional government actions. In the first six years of his administration, President Obama's Justice Department filed Espionage Act charges against six whistleblowers, more than double the number of times that all prior administrations had invoked the act during the ninety years since it was enacted. We can only assume that Trump and other ensuing presidents will avail themselves of the same weapon when it suits the purpose of keeping the citizenry in the dark.

Another repulsive procedure we must eliminate is the use of Non-Disclosure Agreements to muzzle former government officials and employees after they leave public service. Trump's use of NDA's for members of his administration has called attention to this issue which, as reported by Katherine Barrett and Richard Greene at *governing.com*, Washington Post reporter Ruth Marcus described as, "not just oppressive, but constitutionally repugnant." But the matter goes much deeper, not just to the state level, but to local communities. I've seen it in my own city, where NDA's were undoubtedly used to cover up the misuse of funds, sweetheart contract deals, and all manner of other crimes against residents.

Aside from matters of true national security, which are already covered by laws and security clearance agreements signed at the time a person is hired or promoted, there is no justifiable reason that former officials and employees should not be able to benefit the public by revealing what they know. If what they reveal is just embarrassing, people in government might, over time, do and say fewer embarrassing things. If what former officials or employees reveal involves criminal activity, then the guilty parties should rightfully be prosecuted and jailed. Therefore:

> **Section 4: Except as pertains to true issues of national security, subject to federal judicial review and confirmation, no official or employee of government at any level, nor any vendor or consultant thereto, shall be required to sign, as a condition for hiring, transfer, or promotion, or as a condition of benefits upon retirement, a Non-Disclosure Agreement that prohibits or penalizes disclosure of fraud, waste, abuse of position, or violations of law or civil liberties. This provision shall not apply to legal staff bound by attorney-client privilege, or to those involved in the negotiation of contracts during the negotiating period.**

Public exposure to information about government failures, whether those failures stem from deliberate bad conduct, good ideas gone wrong, or just plain bad luck, has been the catalyst for many reforms, and has ended many careers which needed ending. The bottom line is always:

*The government can only get away with what the public does not know. If the facts get out, sooner or later the public rebels, and forces a correction.*

This is why, despite the separation of powers that we learned about in sixth-grade civics class, often multiple branches of government collude and cooperate in hiding embarrassing truths from the public. One particularly pernicious example of this collaboration involving the judicial community and the intelligence community (aka the National Security State) is the concept of state secrets, which rests on a court case, *United States v. Reynolds*, where it was later shown that the government lied about the need for secrecy.

On October 6, 1948 one engine of a B-29 bomber overheated and caught fire, causing the plane, on a mission to test some secret electronic gear, to explode in mid-air. Only three of the eight crewmembers, and one of the five civilian technical advisors on board, managed to parachute to safety. The widows of three of the civilian advisors eventually filed a claim against the government for negligence under the Federal Tort Claims Act of 1946, which authorizes lawsuits for injuries or damage, "caused by the negligent or wrongful act or omission of any employee of the Government while acting within the scope of his office or employment." During the discovery phase, lawyers for the widows questioned government witnesses, including Air Force officers, under oath about whether the plane had a history of maintenance problems, and if the government had prescribed modifications to reduce fire danger due to overheating. After the witnesses answered, "No" to both questions, the plaintiff's counsel requested a copy of the official Accident Report. The government refused, claiming that to do so would result in public disclosure of confidential information about the equipment on board and the secret nature of the mission. It also refused to provide a copy of the report to the judge in the case, William H. Kirkpatrick. During questioning by Kirkpatrick, Assistant U.S. Attorney Thomas Curtin asserted that, once the head of a government department -- in this case, Secretary of the Air Force Thomas Finletter -- asserted the state secrets privilege, *the decision was final and unreviewable by anyone in the judiciary*. [Emphasis added.]

Faced with the government's refusal to let him examine the report, Judge Kirkpatrick entered a verdict for the plaintiffs, which was upheld by the Third Circuit Court of Appeals. The government appealed to the Supreme Court, where once again, government lawyers lied about the contents of the report. The court took their word for it, did not examine the report, and using the kind of tortured reasoning for which the judiciary has become infamous, overturned the verdict.

Fifty years later the Accident Report was routinely declassified. Judith Loether, the daughter of one of the civilian advisors killed in the crash, stumbled across it on a website devoted to military accidents. In an examination of the Reynolds case for Political Science Quarterly, Louis Fisher noted that:

> The report revealed clear negligence on the part of the Air Force, which had not installed [the recommended] heat shields [on the engines] and had failed to brief the civilian engineers before the flight on the use of parachutes and emergency aircraft evacuation. Had Kirkpatrick looked at the report, it would have been clear that the government had lied ... [when] asked whether any modifications had been prescribed for the B-29 engines to prevent overheating and reduce the risk of fire hazard.

Once Loether discovered that there was no classified information in the report, she contacted the survivors of the other civilian victims and, in 2003, filed a new lawsuit seeking to have the original Supreme Court verdict overturned because the government had committed a fraud upon the Court. In September 2004, District Judge Legrome Davis granted a government motion to dismiss the suit, arguing that, "In all likelihood, fifty years ago the government had a more accurate understanding on the prospect of danger to [national security] from the disclosure of secret and sensitive information than lay persons could appreciate or that hindsight now allows." As Fisher explains, "That is not only pure assumption on Davis's part but improperly implies that 'disclosure' to Judge Kirkpatrick would have been disclosure to the public."

The families appealed and, in 2005, the Third Circuit upheld Judge Davis' decision. The court's stated reason is truly mind-boggling:

> Actions for fraud upon the court are so rare that this Court has not previously had the occasion to articulate legal definition of the concept. The concept of fraud upon the court challenges the very principle upon which our judicial system is based: the finality of a judgment.

So, if the government wins a case by lying to the court, it's better for the government to prevail rather than reversing an unjust decision? As Fisher noted:

> What counted most for the Third Circuit was not having to revisit and redo an earlier decision, even if the government had misled the judiciary.

So much for that part in the Constitution's Preamble about establishing justice.

Further defying belief, the Appeals Court concluded that the state secrets the government had an interest in shielding were: "[that] the project was being carried out by the 315th Electronics Squadron ... that the mission required an aircraft capable of dropping bombs ... and that the mission required an airplane capable of operating at altitudes of 20,000 feet and above." Guess what? The name of the squadron, the type of plane, the altitude at which the plane was flying when the accident occurred, and the fact that the plane carried confidential equipment, *had all been reported in the local newspaper the following day*. Fisher asks:

> Why not simply concede mistakes and pay the widows the sums that Judge Kirkpatrick had awarded: $80,000 each to Phyllis Brauner and Elizabeth Palya,

and $65,000 to Patricia Herring? The answer to the three families in 2003 was the desire of the government to "fabricat[e] a test case for a favorable judicial ruling on claims of an executive or state secrets ... privilege -- a case built on the fraudulent premise that the documents in question contained secret military or national security information."

Nobody in their right mind would suggest that there are not situations where the government has a legitimate reason to conceal sources, methods, or capabilities with genuine national security implications. However, without the judiciary playing its intended role as arbiter of government claims, justice is not merely blind, it is castrated. Arbitrary prevention of judicial review invites use of the state secrets privilege to conceal government fraud, abuse, waste, and violation of civil liberties. Failure of the courts to compel revelation of such conditions prevents the legislative oversight necessary for an effective system of checks-and-balances. As Professors William G. Weaver and Robert M. Pallitto stated in another article for Political Science Quarterly:

> [T]he incentive on the part of administrators is to use the privilege to avoid embarrassment, handicap political enemies, and to prevent criminal investigation of administrative action.
>
> In several prominent cases, the evidence that the government successfully excluded was later revealed to contain no state secrets: *United States v. Reynolds, Sterling v. Tenet, Edmonds v. Department of Justice,* and the *Pentagon Papers.*

As Fisher concluded, in the Reynolds case:

> The Court surrendered to the executive branch quintessential judicial duties over questions of privileges and evidence. The Court served not justice but the executive branch. It signaled that in this type of national security case, the courtroom tilts away

from the private litigant and becomes a safe house for executive power.

*A safe house for executive power*. You betcha.

Not satisfied with having the judicial blessing to exclude certain evidence from trials purely on its own say-so, after 9-11 the Bush administration successfully argued that assertion of the state secrets privilege was enough to get entire lawsuits dismissed without the judge -- any judge, including those on the Supreme Court -- being allowed to review the underlying material to ascertain if this is, in fact, the true situation. Wikipedia explains:

> Under its original formulation, the state secrets privilege was meant only to exclude a very narrow class of evidence whose revelation would harm national security. However, in a large percentage of recent cases, courts have gone a step further, dismissing entire cases in which the government asserts the privilege, in essence converting an evidentiary rule into a justiciability rule. The government response has been that in certain cases, the subject of the case is itself privileged. In these cases, the government argues, there is no plausible way to respond to a complaint without revealing state secrets.

As we have seen from the Edward Snowden revelations, in at least some instances, trying the case would result in disclosure of government programs that are illegal and unconstitutional.

Another way to understand why the administrations of both George W. Bush and Barack Obama pushed this expansion of the state secrets privilege is found in the Unitary Executive Theory, which argues that in his capacity as Commander-in-Chief in the War on Terror, the President **cannot be bound by Congress or any law, national or international**. If this sounds like our Presidents are claiming the powers of a king, it's because they are. And invoking the state secrets privilege is a handy way to avoid trials (and therefore, judicial review) of this expansionary new power claim. Which explains the need for:

> **Section 5: No claim of secrecy invoked by government in furtherance of national security shall prevent the inspection, by a court of competent jurisdiction, of all materials the government wishes to deny plaintiffs or defendants, for the purposes of determining the validity of the government's assertion. No claim of state secrets alone shall be sufficient to prevent an action for remedy at law.**

Another area which screams out for the cleansing effect of public observation involves what actually happens in courtrooms. Judges want the public to believe that televising court proceedings would compromise the dignity of the court, that attorneys and witnesses would pander to the camera. Bullshit. Too many judges like to rule their courtrooms like medieval fiefdoms. Too many lawyers and judges don't want the public at large to witness what actually goes on in court. More importantly, going back to the years of Court TV, there is now plenty of evidence that justice is not thwarted by television coverage. Countless defendants have been tried under the eye of the television camera, and either convicted or acquitted, without the world coming to a stop. Moreover, portions of many trials are already taped and later appear on true crime shows. If the public can watch police in action on shows like *Cops* or *Live PD* or *Jail!*, and overdose to its heart's content on documentaries like *Lockup* which take place in prisons, why shouldn't that same public get to watch what happens in court? Answer: They should. Therefore:

> **Section 6: Except as may apply to proceedings involving juveniles, neither Congress nor the States shall pass any law, and no court shall issue any order, preventing the live audio and visual dissemination of any proceeding, or**

**permanent preservation by private parties of records of said proceedings. Any attempt to do so shall constitute a felony punishable by incarceration in a maximum security facility for a period, not subject to pardon, parole, commutation, suspension, or other reduction of sentence, of at least five years.**

We also need to address the issue, not just of what is known, but what is publicized and disseminated. In a democratic republic, such as ours claims to be, the media is supposed to fulfill one over-riding function: investigating and exposing corruption, abuse of power, and other excesses of government or business interests in order to set the stage for public pressure which can lead to changes and reforms. Presenting diverse viewpoints, independent from centralized corporate control, is essential if the media is to fulfill this role as a check on the powers of both government and corporate interests. Unfortunately, the United States has devolved into a place where a handful of corporations own all the major media outlets, national and local.

These media monoliths don't just stop with determining what is presented as news; they own or exercise programming and content control of sports stations, movie studios, television networks and the companies who supply them with product. TV and feature films are handy vehicles to disguise propaganda as fiction. *Zero Dark Thirty* was an entertaining and award-winning film, and while it may be accurate in how the raid unfolded on the ground, if anyone believes the part about how the U.S. discovered Bin Laden's location, Pulitzer Prize-winning author Sy Hersh has a surprise for you. In a 2015 article in the London Review of Books titled, *The Killing of Osama Bin Laden,* Hersh contends that the tale of tracking Bin Laden's couriers is simply a cover story and that a Pakistani intelligence officer ratted out OBL for a big chunk of the $25 mil bounty the U.S. put on his head after 9-11.

The concentration of ownership power in radio is equally distressing. In 2016, the top five radio networks owned 1,982 stations, which means that these networks control the overwhelming majority of stations in virtually all markets, large, medium, and small. Given this kind of market penetration, it's not surprising that the top ten station groups earned 47% of all radio ad revenue. The top two radio networks alone accounted for 27% of ad revenues. And it could get worse. As one market analysis report noted, "After many years of acquiring stations and merging larger radio companies, the radio industry is characterized by a greater degree of national consolidation."

*A greater degree of national consolidation*. Really? No shit? You don't say.

Although radio may be seen by some as a weak sister to television and the internet, remember that many of the most influential media personalities achieved, and in part maintain, their prominence from radio. Rare is the popular radio show that is not also simulcast on the internet or available as a podcast. We must end the stranglehold on viewpoints imposed by the concentration of media ownership and control.

> **Section 7: Concentration of media in the hands of an elite few being contrary to the public good, no person or entity shall own or control more than one entity engaged in the dissemination of news by electronic, digital, print, or other means, in any geographical area comprising a market as determined by Act of Congress. Nor shall any person or entity own, or control the news or informational programming, of more than ten such entities on a national basis.**

The efforts by corporate entities who pulled the puppet strings at the FCC to kill net neutrality means that the same forces, who also control the traditional media, are intent on doing the same to internet sources of news and opinion. They dare not let the public have widespread access to facts and opinions which run counter to the official narrative, whether it concerns government policies and activities or the rape and pillaging of the economy by our overlords in the private sector. This stranglehold on the power to shape both opinions and actions must be broken. Thus:

> **Section 8: The free exchange of ideas and information being critical to the effective functioning of the republic, the internet, and such future technologies as may supplement or replace it, shall be delivered, at the lowest possible cost to the user, either as a service of municipal government or as a public utility, without discrimination in any way as to speed of service, cost of service, or ease of access to content.**

If the idea of a municipality providing internet service strikes you as odd, that's because you don't live in Chattanooga, Tennessee, which has GIG, a fiber optic network operated by the city-owned Electric Control Board. GIG offers the fastest internet service available anywhere in America, up to 1,000 times faster than the minimum service provided by rival AT&T in surrounding areas. *One. Thousand. Times.* The gigabit service is $69.99 per month, and GIG's minimum plan delivers 100 Mbps for $57.99. Businesses, or individuals who so desire, can pay $299.99 a month for 10 Gbps. *Ten Gigabytes Per* **Second.**

As a result of providing its own ultra-high-speed internet, Chattanooga has become a burgeoning tech center, with its own innovation incubators, a number of start-ups, and even a Tomorrow Building, run by a venture capital incubator, which combines living and working spaces for young entrepreneurs. Unlike many smaller communities, which are slowly dying from an exodus of young people, Chattanooga has become a destination city. Tech types, tired of the intensity and high costs of Silicon Valley, the New York tech scene, and even Austin, have flocked to Chattanooga's more relaxed, family-friendly, and much less pricey lifestyle.

Chattanooga is not alone. Other municipalities also offer broadband internet service, but the big ISPs like Comcast, AT&T, and Charter want no part of that, and they've shown no reluctance to deploy the corporate capitalists two favorite weapons: litigation and lobbying. They sued Chattanooga four different times, but lost all four battles. Realizing that their best hope was in having states usurp local community options, they spread around enough money to induce politicians in twenty-three states to outlaw municipal broadband service. As Craig Settles, who consults with cities considering building their own networks, told Jason Koebler at Motherboard:

> "The general rhetoric behind these laws, from the incumbents, is that cities are too incompetent to run their own networks, so it's a risk to taxpayers. But then, the other side of it is that cities are so competent that they represent unfair competition."

Koebler goes on to briefly summarize the three general categories of laws that the big telcos and cable companies use to thwart the wider rollout of municipal broadband:

> There are "If-Then" laws, which have some requirements for municipal networks such as a voter referendum or a requirement to give telecom companies the option to build the network themselves, rather than restrictions (some are easier to meet than others). Then there are "Minefield" laws, which are written confusingly so as to invite lawsuits from incumbent ISPs, financial burden on a city starting a network, or other various restrictions. Finally, you've got the outright bans. Some of these are simple, others are worded in a way that make it seem like it'd be

possible to jump through the hoops necessary to start
a network, but in practice, it's essentially impossible.

For traditional ISPs, there is huge money in providing internet service. In 2015, Bruce Kushnick, Executive Director of the New Networks Institute, wrote an article for The Huffington Post, complete with charts -- using Time Warner Cable's own financial statements -- showing that TW made a profit of 97% providing internet service. ***Ninety-seven percent***. Perhaps that's why, after Time Warner spun off its cable systems and the enterprise was renamed Spectrum, some have taken to calling it *Rectum* Cable. Sadly, in many areas, Rectum is an improvement on the fiber optic offering of notoriously awful Frontier. And for these outrageous prices, customers get painfully slow operating speeds, far slower than those offered in other industrialized countries.

Given that the current for-profit ISPs own the existing system build-out, how do we wrestle away ownership and control? First, we kneecap the power of the lobbying community through public financing of campaigns, which is covered in Chapter 8. This opens the door to repealing these anti-consumer and anti-competition laws. This will rip away the underpinnings of corporate litigation power. Then we can get our state governments to regulate internet service as a public utility, with rates set by Public Utility Commissions, which are likely to see a 7% profit as a lot more equitable than 97%. Public Utility Commissions would also be able to mandate system upgrades with higher operating speeds and more reliable service. That way all of us might enjoy the same service offered by one little city on the Tennessee River.

# Chapter 5

# LIMITS ON THE
# POWER OF THE EXECUTIVE

One of the touchstone concepts of our country that we learn in school is the mantra *liberty and justice for all*. It is not enough to eliminate the ability of presidents, governors, judges, and parole panels to cancel or reduce the sentences of those who commit crimes against the cause of good government. There can be no rule of law if certain officials are seen as above the law. That is why we must preclude all possibilities, and close any loopholes, that might allow officials to dodge accountability for actions that violate our newly-expanded constitutional rights.

Justice requires not only that the innocent go free, but that the guilty are punished. This is why Gerald Ford committed the gravest crime ever against our republic when he pardoned Richard Nixon. Many believe that the promise of a pardon was either explicit or implicit in Nixon's decision to nominate Ford as vice-president after Spiro Agnew resigned in disgrace. The instant he pardoned Nixon, Ford enshrined the concept that the president is above the law. Indeed, what Nixon once proclaimed, "If the president does it, it's not illegal," Ford's pardon confirmed as the de facto law of the land. From that moment on, any president was, for all practical purposes, above the law.

Note: I do not put much stock in the great liberal dream that a prosecution of President Trump would change things. First off, we do not yet know how presidential pardons might impact the outcome of any investigation. Second, even if Trump is indicted, courts -- and even the Justice Department itself -- have previously held that presidents, while in office, are protected from active prosecution because a trial would conflict with the time required to discharge presidential duties. Some have speculated that one reason Trump nominated Brett Kavanaugh to SCOTUS was due to his willingness to protect presidents from indictment and trial. So, the most likely path would involve Trump first being impeached and convicted. (Impeachment is a fairly easy bar to hurdle with a partisan House, but conviction requires a 2/3 vote in the Senate. Considering that the GOP actually increased its Senate majority in the 2018 mid-term elections, this is a rather remote possibility. And even if it did happen, the new incoming president, at this point Vice-President Pence, would have to not pardon Trump. But even if all those obstacles were surmounted, what would likely result is not the establishment of the principle that presidents can be prosecuted, but rather that *some* presidents -- those who incur the wrath of the state security apparatus, the Pentagon, or select elements of Congress -- are not above the law. In other words, presidential immunity from the law would be subjectively applied, but not eliminated.

Once Ford established that the presidents were exempt from punishment, it was only a matter of time until the exempt class expanded. The relevant question became, "How far down the line, and how wide through the rest of society, does this immunity extend?" Unfortunately, as we have now seen, the answers are: very far and very wide.

We can speculate how history might have been different if Ford had not sold out. If Nixon had been tried, convicted, and sentenced to prison, would Ronald Reagan, and his lackeys like Oliver North, have been so quick to engage in the Iran-Contra weapons deal? Probably not. What if North, instead of a three-year suspended sentence, had received a long term in a high-security federal penitentiary? Might Reagan have been inclined, or forced, to pardon him in order to protect other people and/or secrets of his administration? But there is a solution:

### The 30th Amendment --
### Limits on Presidential Power

**Section 1: No President may pardon, parole, commute, suspend, or grant other reprieve from sentence to any person serving, or who has served, as President or Vice President, or who has advised or served in an official or unofficial capacity any administration or campaign of the President or the Vice President.**

One argument put forth for not prosecuting presidents and their key aides is that we, "shouldn't criminalize policy differences." News flash:

*Any action that violates the law isn't a policy, it's a crime.*

Policies that are illegal are illegitimate, and have no place in a democratic society governed by laws and a constitution. Government is supposed to make and enforce laws, not ignore those already on the books.

Another argument is that prosecuting former presidents would turn the U.S. into some kind of Third World banana republic. (This presumes that we haven't already descended to that dubious status.) And while politically and economically unstable countries are more prone to imprison or execute former leaders for offenses ranging from corruption to crimes against humanity, other nations that definitely fit the definition of working First World democracies have imprisoned former leaders. South Korea sent to prison both of its presidents who served from 1980 to 1993. Park Guen-hye, who served as president from 2013-2017, was also impeached, convicted, and recently sentenced to twenty-four years in prison. None of this has prevented South Korea from continuing to function, from continuing to send us plenty of Kia Sorrentos and electronics equipment. Similarly, Israel imprisoned former Prime Minister Ehud Olmert for bribery, fraud, falsifying documents, and tax evasion. Current Israeli Prime Minister Benjamin Netanyahu is presently under investigation for corruption and may eventually be indicted. But Israel hasn't fallen into the sea. Its parliament still meets and exercises its duties, business gets conducted, the lights work, as do the plumbing and the transportation systems. In short, jailing the highest officials in South Korea and Israel hasn't led to the ruination of either country.

Meanwhile, we live in an absurd and twisted reality, where whistleblowers who reveal fraud and misconduct are ruthlessly prosecuted, but officials who violate the law are shielded from punishment. Companies that conspire with the government to violate Constitutional civil liberties are given retroactive immunity. People and institutions with influence skate free, while those who commit far less serious crimes spend long terms behind bars.

Despite the role that wide-spread fraud played in the financial crisis of 2007-2008, banks not only became Too Big To Fail, their CEOs and other key executives became Too Big To Jail. Not one leading executive of the financial institutions that perpetrated the biggest fraud in history was indicted, much less convicted. We have the appalling spectacle of our alleged chief law enforcement officer, Attorney General Eric Holder, admitting before Congress that the chief officers of key financial institutions were not prosecuted because doing so might have endangered the economy and the world financial system. The implication was clear: these executives are thought of as being the companies they head, which plainly they are not. It all makes for a convenient excuse not to antagonize the people who hand out big campaign contributions, and who determine who gets lucrative jobs once public service is over. Indeed, Holder came from Covington & Burling, a law firm frequently counted on by many financial institutions when they need legal representation and lobbying muscle. And wouldn't you know it, as soon as he resigned from the administration, Holder went right back to Covington & Burling, taking up residency in his old corner office -- which the company had kept vacant *and undisturbed* during all those years that he was ostensibly serving the public as attorney general.

President Nixon's disregard for the law and constitutional rights only became apparent after he was elected, but it had been there all along. Sadly, ever since Nixon's pardon, many candidates for the presidency and vice-presidency have run for office with the express notion that they can break laws. With the exception of Bernie Sanders, modern presidential candidates only follow any specific policy to the extent that such a policy enhances their power, repays their big-money donors, or provides for a lucrative retirement. Justice, integrity, loyalty to campaign promises -- not to mention the concept of right and wrong -- have nothing to do with the presidential decision-making process. Depending on the situation, laws are either vehicles to achieve presidential goals, or impediments to imposing presidential power. Being able to count on immunity from prosecution for breaking the law is both a powerful allure of the office, and a dangerous tool for imposing anti-democratic policies.

But surely, a president's opposition party must be interested in holding him to account, right? Not at all. Despite the illusion of two parties, and the rhetoric coming out of alleged progressives, when it comes to issues of economic policy or the national security state, the actions of President Obama clearly demonstrated that there are no substantive differences between Democrats and Republicans. This is why many have come to dub our current ruling class the *Uni-party*, the *Demopublicans*, or the *Republicrats*. The Uni-party is always in control of Congress, and with the corrupt version of government we currently live under, it is always subservient to the moneyed class. It is in the best interests of those in Congress to invalidate our system of checks-and-balances by allowing the president to break the law. This saves Congress from having to exercise leadership and accountability, which might offend their donors.

One of the favorite ways for presidents to violate the law is by issuing signing statements claiming that, in the opinion of the administration, certain provisions or sections of a new law are either unconstitutional, in conflict with other existing laws, or an impermissible intrusion on the powers of the Executive Branch. This is made to seem as if the president is simply trying to faithfully carry out the duties of his office. But in reality, it's a president defying a law and ordering the entire executive branch to ignore it. Signing statements are the rule of *President as King*, the *Imperial Presidency,* ruling by proclamation. Don't take my word for it. Here's Wikipedia:

> In July 2006, a task force of the American Bar Association stated that the use of signing statements to modify the meaning of duly enacted laws serves to "undermine the rule of law and our constitutional system of separation of powers".

> [The committee opposed] "as contrary to the rule of law and our constitutional system of separation of powers, a President's issuance of signing statements to claim the authority or state the intention to disregard or decline to enforce all or part of a law he has signed, or to interpret such a law in a manner inconsistent with the clear intent of Congress;"

Prior to the Reagan administration, signing statements were rare, mostly limited to rhetoric extolling the virtues of the new law or warning about unintended consequences. However, Reagan's then-Assistant Attorney General (now Supreme Court Justice) Samuel Alito, issued a 1986 memo arguing for interpretive signing statements which, according to Wikipedia, Alito saw as, "a tool to 'increase the power of the Executive to shape the law." He suggested adding them to certain bills as a pilot project but warned that, "Congress is likely to resent the fact that the president will get in the last word on questions of interpretation."

Once no Congressional challenge occurred, the use of signing statements escalated, and it is by no means limited to Republican administrations. Wikipedia again provides valuable context:

> A Congressional Research Service report issued on September 17, 2007, uses as a metric the percentage of signing statements that contain "objections" to provisions of the bill being signed into law:
>
> President Reagan issued 250 signing statements, 86 of which (34%) contained provisions objecting to one or more of the statutory provisions signed into law. President George H. W. Bush continued this practice, issuing 228 signing statements, 107 of which (47%) raised objections. President Clinton's conception of presidential power proved to be largely consonant with that of the preceding two administrations. In turn, President Clinton made aggressive use of the signing statement, issuing 381 statements, 70 of which (18%) raised constitutional or legal objections. President George W. Bush has continued this practice, issuing 152 signing statements, 118 of which (78%) contain some type of challenge or objection.

As further proof of bipartisan support for signing statements, Walter Dellinger, who, according to the New York Times, "helped develop the legal framework for signing statements as a Clinton administration official," co-authored several essays and legal commentaries suggesting that the problem isn't signing statements *per se*, but the manner and purpose in which George W. Bush used them.

While Clinton was certainly aggressive in using signing statements, the floodgates really broke open under President George W. Bush. The New York Times reported in 2009 that in his eight years in office, the Bush 43 administration used signing statements, "to challenge about 1,200 sections of bills ... about twice the number challenged by all previous presidents combined."

That's right, President George W. Bush issued more than *twice as many signing statements as all previous presidents combined*. And despite his explicit campaign promise not to use signing statements to invalidate sections of laws, President Obama immediately did so. As Wikipedia notes:

> During his presidential campaign, Obama rejected the use of signing statements. He was asked at one rally: "when congress offers you a bill, do you promise not to use presidential signing statements to get your way?" Obama gave a one-word reply: "Yes." He added that "we aren't going to use signing statements as a way to do an end run around Congress." On March 11, 2009, Obama issued his first signing statement, attached to the omnibus spending bill for the second half of the 2009 fiscal year.

Yessiree, it only took six weeks for Obama to issue his first signing statement, expanding his own power and further castrating Congress. (Not that Congress hasn't shown great ability to self-castrate.) Dellinger's defense of signing statements can be summed up as, "If your guy does it, it's bad; if my guy does it, that's okay."

There has only been one legislative effort to abolish signing statements. The late Senator Arlen Specter introduced the Presidential Signing Statements Act of 2006, which not only would have instructed courts to ignore signing statements, but also proposed giving each house of Congress the power to file suit directly with the Supreme Court to determine the constitutional validity of signing statements. The bill died in the Senate Judiciary Committee and was reintroduced the following year, but again failed to advance out of committee. Why would Congress not pass a bill that forced the executive branch to enforce all laws faithfully, as required by the presidential Oath of Office? Because the career politicians now occupying Congressional office love to appear as if they are exerting power and authority, but in truth they are loathe to put themselves on the line and take responsibility for actions which could offend their donor base, or open themselves to attack by opposing candidates. Thus, they pass laws that technically apply to big corporations or the national surveillance security state, but rely on the president not to enforce those provisions. Congress-critters then get to brag in glossy campaign materials about how they voted for this or that, without fearing retribution from powerful elites.

Presidents have at their disposal an easy alternative, the *non*-signing statement. The Constitution allows bills to become law if the president does not sign or veto them within ten days, as long as Congress is in session during that period. Therefore, all the President has to do is issue a non-signing statement explaining his reservations about certain portions of the bill, then allow it to become law without his signature. Non-signing statements serve three valuable functions:

- They guide the relevant government agencies in the implementation of the bill. Officials in the legal departments of those agencies press forward more slowly on provisions that are likely to result in a legal challenge that may prove, as attorneys like to say, "dispositive."

- They guide the Justice Department in enforcing the applicable civil or criminal penalties attached to violation of the law. Again, the agency may be careful in bringing cases or may even intervene on the side of a private civil suit challenging a particular provision of the new law.

- They provide guidance and ammunition to private parties wanting to bring suit against specific provisions of the bill. ("Hey, look, even the President thinks this is a problem.")

Presidents do not like *non*-signing statements because a non-signing statement still allows the law to go into full effect. Only a signing statement enables presidents to pretend that they have the power to ignore the law and do as they damn well please. This is the same reason presidents and their administrations don't race over to the Supreme Court to get a definitive ruling. Why hasten the process of judicial review when a test case can take years, even a decade or more, to wind its way through the federal court system? Even when the problem of standing to challenge laws is resolved by enacting the 28th Amendment, the Right to Good Government, there will still be ways in which the Supreme Court can try to avoid addressing the issues raised in a suit contesting a signing statement. (Not to mention the costs incurred by the plaintiff, which under the 28th Amendment, could only be recovered after a favorable verdict.) Eliminating signing statements and mandating immediate Supreme Court review immediately strips away much of the power of the Imperial Presidency and returns the office to the status of elected official rather than temporary dictator. Therefore:

> **Section 2: No President, Vice President, or official of any branch of government shall be exempt from full and complete compliance with any law.**

> **Section 3: Should the President disagree with Congress over the constitutionality or enforcement of any provision of any law, or a regulation derived there from, the Supreme**

**Court shall hear arguments and issue a binding ruling forthwith. Any order or directive asserting the power of the President or the Executive branch not to comply with any provision of any law, regulation, or resolution passed by Congress shall result in the immediate automatic impeachment and trial of the President. All such statements or assertions previously made by any President, and any rulings, regulations, procedures, or precedents derived as a result thereof are null and void.**

The lust for unbridled power by the executive branch and the national security state, combined with the unwillingness of a captured and impotent Congress to act, means that the only mechanism left to restore our system of checks and balances, indeed to restore the rule of law and democracy itself, is for *we the people* to force enactment of the 30th Amendment.

# Chapter 6

# OFFICE OF SPECIAL PROSECUTOR

What if a President doesn't bother with a signing statement and simply issues an Executive Order, or even verbal instructions, for agency or executive branch personnel to ignore certain laws? What if members of Congress, state legislatures, and their staffs commit crimes, especially involving bribery and corruption? And how about officials and staff at government agencies who fail to vigorously enforce the law because they have become captured by the very industries they are supposed to regulate?

Unfortunately, since the attorney general is a partisan political appointee who may share a party affiliation with the offender, the A.G. can have great motivation not to prosecute. It happened during the Obama administration when Eric Holder declined to pursue criminal investigations against bank executives, even though evidence of fraudulent mortgage loans was documented in investigations carried out by government agencies, congressional committees, and through private lawsuits. The fact that Holder came from one of Wall Street's favorite law firms, and returned to the same firm after leaving the DOJ, is purely coincidental.

It happened again when Holder's replacement, Loretta Lynch, decided not to prosecute Hillary Clinton for violating federal law by failing to secure classified documents through the use of a private email server. Once again, Lynch's meeting with Bill Clinton shortly before the decision not to prosecute was purely coincidental. (There are so many coincidences in modern politics and government that someone should form a new national Coincidence Party.)

Holder and Lynch are just recent examples. They are by no means exhaustive, and don't even begin to scratch the surface of the problem, which has plagued every administration of both parties since Nixon, if not before. Even after we succeed in establishing the good government right of individuals and private entities to ensure the enforcement of laws, there is still one problem: sometimes the biggest crimes require insider knowledge. They require a whistleblower to come forward, or someone in an enforcement capacity to spot something suspicious and then bring considerable resources to bear. The vast scope of our corruption problem is such that there has to be a permanent, fully funded office, independent of both Congress and the president, charged solely with ensuring that the laws of the land are faithfully executed and enforced against everyone, regardless of position. There has to be an office specifically charged with seeing that we really have justice for all, which, in actuality, means *prosecution of all offenders.*

We already have an initial framework in place for this task. The General Accounting Office was established in 1921 to, as Wikipedia notes:

> ..."investigate, at the seat of government or elsewhere, all matters relating to the receipt, disbursement, and application of public funds, and shall make to the President ... and to Congress ... reports [and] recommendations looking to greater economy or efficiency in public expenditures". According to the GAO's current mission statement, the agency exists to support the Congress in meeting its constitutional responsibilities and to help improve the performance

and ensure the accountability of the federal government for the benefit of the American people.

The name was changed in 2004 to Government Accountability Office by the GAO Human Capital Reform Act to better reflect the mission of the office.

[snip]

the GAO has been referred to as "The Congressional Watchdog" and "The Taxpayers' Best Friend" for its frequent audits and investigative reports that have uncovered waste and inefficiency in government. News media often draw attention to the GAO's work by publishing stories on the findings, conclusions and recommendations of its reports. Members of Congress also frequently cite the GAO's work in statements to the press, congressional hearings, and floor debates on proposed legislation. In 2007 the Partnership for Public Service ranked the GAO second on its list of the best places to work in the federal government

[snip]

the GAO is headed by the comptroller general of the U.S. a professional and non-partisan position in the U.S. government. The comptroller general is appointed by the president by and with the advice and consent of the Senate, for a 15-year, non-renewable term. The president selects a nominee from a list of at least three individuals recommended by an eight-member bipartisan, bicameral commission of congressional leaders.

Despite its efficiency and well-deserved reputation for integrity, the General Accountability Office suffers from one fatal flaw: *it can't actually hold anyone accountable*. All the GAO can do is produce reports and refer findings to the Department of Justice for *possible* criminal prosecution (or even weaker civil action). The same holds true for the many agencies at both the federal and state level who have an Inspector General. The solution is to make the General Accountability Office a separate branch of government and give it the power to bring prosecutions through the creation, within the GAO, of an Office of the Special Prosecutor.

**The 31st Amendment --
Accountable Government**

**Section 1: The Government Accountability Office is hereby established as an independent branch of government. Within sixty days after ratification of this Amendment, a GAO Office of Special Prosecutor shall be established. The Special Prosecutor shall be appointed according to the same procedures as currently used to appoint the Comptroller General, and shall serve a single, non-renewable term of fifteen years.**

**Section 2: Should the President at any time abrogate his responsibility to appoint a Special Prosecutor, the Senate shall appoint one, subject to confirmation by two-thirds vote of the House of Representatives.**

**Section 3: The Comptroller General shall retain all existing current investigative and audit powers and duties, and shall continue to issue reports as necessary, or as Congress or the President may request.**

**Section 4: The Special Prosecutor shall have the authority and duty to prosecute any and all crimes involving officials in federal, state, or lesser government office, and in furtherance thereof, without limitation or restriction, to compel the production of records for examination; compel testimony under penalty**

**of perjury, contempt, or imprisonment; and issue grants of immunity.**

A full-time permanent Special Prosecutor eliminates the political infighting and partisan grandstanding that accompanies the appointment of temporary Special Prosecutors charged with looking into specific issues. Those who are considering illegal acts will perhaps think twice knowing that there is someone in a powerful office who is getting paid handsomely to pounce at the first hint of impropriety. The ability of the Special Prosecutor to look into wrongdoing by any entity at any level of government reduces the ability of institutions to protect their own by attempting to cover-up misdeeds. Many of what are now internal investigations in various departments and agencies will likely be referred to the Special Prosecutor's office.

A constitutional mandate for a Special Prosecutor isn't enough. A favorite trick of legislative bodies at all levels is to under-fund offices and programs which some legislators find objectionable or bothersome. In the horse-trading for votes that goes on to get bills passed, it is possible for a motivated minority to negatively impact funding for individual programs, and even entire agencies. In past instances when a temporary Special Prosecutor has been appointed to investigate a specific matter, the longer the investigation went on, the more wailing was heard about the costs Congress was asked to approve. (This wailing almost always comes exclusively from the party whose official is being investigated. Shocking, I know.)

We must provide a mechanism to ensure that Congress does not hamstring the Special Prosecutor's office by denying proper funding. Therefore:

**Section 5: Congress shall appropriate all funds necessary for the Government Accountability Office and the Office of Special Prosecutor to faithfully and completely discharge their**

**duties and obligations. Should Congress, in the judgment of the courts, fail to properly fund the Office of the Special Prosecutor, Congressional immunity from arrest during session shall be void and all members of the House Appropriations Committee shall be immediately confined without bail until such time as Congress appropriates sufficient funding.**

It may sound unfair to slap members of the Appropriations Committee in jail while letting the rest of Congress off the hook. However, it is unlikely that other members of Congress are going to let their powerful and influential colleagues languish in jail for any appreciable time, lest those committee members exact revenge when finally released. Persisting in an action that keeps committee bigwigs behind bars is not the way to get support for bills you wish to see move forward. Nor is it a good way to get future appropriations for projects in your state or district.

Allowing everyone in the office of Special Prosecutor to share in the proceeds from successful prosecutions would incentivize pursuit of tough cases, force lawbreakers to foot some of the bill for their own prosecution, provide additional resources for future investigations, boost morale among all agency employees, and act as a powerful tool to recruit high-caliber talent. Returning some of the fines or settlement amounts to the agency of government that was exploited would also be beneficial. Therefore:

**Section 6: One-third of all fines and proceeds resulting from successful prosecutions shall be retained as supplemental funding for department operations; one-third shall be distributed as bonuses to all GAO employees, pro-rata according to position; and one-third shall be remitted back to the government agency exploited by the actions of the individuals or entities convicted.**

Having a Special Prosecutor with power to investigate and prosecute corruption at the federal level is not enough. There are thousands of departments, districts, commissions, legislative bodies, and law enforcement agencies spread across state and local jurisdictions. Many states are part of multi-state entities handling issues like water allocations, resource extraction, flood control, and electric power generation. Given the number of these entities, and the proclivity for corruption at the state and local level, it is crucial that the GAO and the Special Prosecutor's office be able to investigate and prosecute criminal activity when state or local bodies lack the resources, prosecutorial power, or political will to do so. Giving the GAO and Department of the Special Prosecutor mandatory access to all state and local Inspector General reports will provide leads on wrongdoing. The same goes for reports from citizen's oversight committees, which are often created as supposed watchdogs over programs like bond expenditures but more often than not are toothless tigers with no power to compel the production of the documents necessary to actually perform oversight.

Putting the muscle of the Special Prosecutor's office behind state inspector generals, and local citizen oversight boards, is likely to result in a lot less criminal behavior at the state and local level. At the same time, when private citizens and citizen groups are forced into action under the 28th Amendment, The Right to Good Government, the office of the Special Prosecutor should be available to lend assistance. Therefore:

> **Section 7: The Inspectors General or equivalent officials of all federal and state agencies, and all public or civilian oversight boards, shall provide the Government Accountability Office and the Special Prosecutor with the results of their audits, investigations, and oversight functions, together with all supporting material as may be requested.**

**Section 8: The Special Prosecutor may assist citizens filing suit to enforce laws under the 28th Amendment Right to Good Government.**

We don't need attorneys in the office of Special Prosecutor, we need hunters, people who, at their gut level, hate corruption and the misuse of public funds or public power. At the same time, we must recognize that these people need to live in one of the most expensive areas of the country. We also have to provide a salary commensurate with their skill level and commitment to clean government. They and their families should not suffer a quality of life that is significantly less than what they could earn in the private sector, especially since anyone appointed to the office of Special Prosecutor will usually have already spent considerable time, and demonstrated their worth, at lower levels of government, where compensation is usually not lavish. (At least not by the standards of equivalent private sector employment.)

The only way we can reduce the possibility that financial factors may influence them not to pursue the tough cases is to provide them with a substantial salary and pension. Since the Comptroller General will work hand-in-hand with the office of the Special Prosecutor, we need to compensate the Comptroller General in the same way. Therefore:

**Section 9: The annual salaries of the Special Prosecutor and the Comptroller General shall be One Million Dollars each, adjusted every five years using the cost-of-living formula set for retiree benefits by the Social Security Administration. Upon completion of their term in office, the Special Prosecutor and the Comptroller General shall continue to receive the same salary and benefits of office for life.**

One million dollars is not an exorbitant amount given the responsibilities of these positions. A salary and pension at that level would be a powerful inducement for the brightest and most dedicated to accept nomination to the office, while at the same time greatly reducing any financial issues that might compromise them in the pursuit of their duties.

We must also ensure that once they leave office, at the end of their term, they are not faced with the temptation to take their skills, talents, and knowledge to private law firms, where they would be uniquely qualified to defend the most disreputable against future Special Prosecutor actions.

For example, former Comptroller General David Walker resigned before his term was over and took a far more lucrative position with the late, but not lamented, billionaire Pete Peterson's Peterson Foundation. Walker then traveled the country, shilling for Peterson's pet crusade to cut Social Security and Medicare. His previous position as Comptroller General gave his efforts far greater credibility and media attention than they deserved. In addition, Walker explored running for office several times, an endeavor in which Peterson's financial backing and that of his billionaire buddies would have been most helpful.

Rising to become Special Prosecutor or the Comptroller General must be seen as the culmination of a career. After they leave office, they can still write books, make speeches, and lecture, but the money must go to some charitable cause such as scholarships or endowments. To prevent a recurrence of the regrettable actions of David Walker it is necessary to combine a lucrative lifetime pension with a prohibition against lecturing, consulting, or practicing law (except on a pro bono basis). Therefore:

> **Section 10: During their term of office and upon retirement the Special Prosecutor and the Comptroller General shall not receive any other compensation except as might derive from properties and investments held prior to appointment, nor shall they accept any gifts or**

**benefits from any organization, person, foreign government, or business entity. Retired Special Prosecutors and Inspector Generals shall not obtain other employment, publish or speak for profit, or represent litigants except on a pro bono basis.**

Finally, since some officials at all levels succumb to either temptation or their inherently venal character, we must ensure severe punishment for any Special Prosecutor or inspector general who betrays the office.

**Section 11: Willful or negligent failure by the Special Prosecutor or the Inspector General to perform the duties of office shall be a felony punishable by incarceration in a maximum security facility for a period, not subject to pardon, parole, commutation, suspension, or other reduction of sentence, of not less than ten years.**

Prosecution for negligent failure to perform their duties ensures that a compromised Special Prosecutor can't skate simply by pretending to be inattentive or inefficient. That strategy is just too easy to employ. So once again, we must remember Jefferson's advice to place no confidence in any man.

# Chapter 7

# ROTATION FROM POWER

*"Politicians and diapers must be changed often, and for the same reason."*

--Mark Twain

**The 32nd Amendment -- Rotation from Power**

**Section 1: Senators elected subsequent to ratification of this Amendment shall serve no more than twelve years. Senators appointed to serve out unfinished terms shall serve no more than fourteen years. Senators in office upon the ratification of this Amendment shall serve no more than one additional term.**

**Section 2: Members of the House of Representatives elected subsequent to ratification of this Amendment shall serve no more than twelve years. Members of the House of Representatives in office upon ratification of this Amendment who have served less than twelve years may serve additional terms until reaching twelve years.**

Term limits are not a new idea. As Wikipedia explains, back when the former colonies were debating ratification of the Constitution:

Several leading statesmen regarded the lack of
mandatory limits to tenure as a dangerous defect,
especially, they thought, as regards the Presidency and
the Senate. Richard Henry Lee viewed the absence of
legal limits to tenure, together with certain other
features of the Constitution, as "most highly and
dangerously oligarchic". Both Jefferson and George
Mason advised limits on reelection to the Senate and
to the Presidency, because said Mason, "nothing is so
essential to the preservation of a Republican
government as a periodic rotation".

Wikipedia also quotes historian Mercy Otis Warren:

"There is no provision for a rotation, nor anything to
prevent the perpetuity of office in the same hands for
life; which by a little well-timed bribery, will probably
be done."

***Well-timed bribery***. Sound familiar?

By the 1830s, things had further devolved. Rotation from office
became a system whereby Congressional and state legislative
terms were rotated among various party faithful as rewards. With
gerrymandering elevated to a science, by the 1950s, the ability of
officials to homestead a lifelong career in the Congress or state
legislatures became epidemic. In response, by the early 1990s,
virtually every state where citizens had the power of the initiative
passed term limits for its legislators. Twenty-three states also
enacted limits on the number of terms Congressmen from their
state could serve. Some of these Congressional term limit bills
passed by a margin of two-to-one. Unfortunately, the U.S.
Supreme Court overturned congressional term limits in 1995 on
the grounds that, "state governments cannot limit the terms of
members of the national government." Of course, what the
Supreme Court was really saying was that the ***people*** of a state
cannot limit the terms of their representatives in Congress.

After the Supreme Court overturned voter-imposed Congressional term limits, there were several attempts by members of the House to put forth term-limit constitutional amendments. Only one, which would have limited terms in both the House and Senate to twelve years, managed to garner a majority of votes. Unfortunately -- and conveniently -- constitutional amendments require a two-thirds vote of each house of Congress before they can be sent to the states for ratification. (This allowed certain members of Congress to vote for term limits, and use that in their re-election campaigns, while knowing all the time that the bill would never actually pass.)

Thirty-six states impose some limit on the terms of governors. In eight states, absolute limits prohibit the governor from serving more than two terms. The other twenty-eight states impose rotational or cyclical limits, in which a candidate must sit out at least one election cycle and is usually limited to a total aggregate number of years in office. Legislative term limits are not so widespread. Only fifteen states currently limit the number of terms legislators may serve. State Supreme Courts in Washington, Oregon, Wyoming, and Massachusetts overturned previously enacted term limits. In 2002 and 2003, the Idaho and Utah legislatures repealed the term limits on the books there. Why is it so easy to limit the terms of governors but not legislators? Simple: a lot of legislators want a shot at the governorship some day. Or, if they currently serve in the state's lower house, they want a shot at the upper house when a member of that body runs for governor, lieutenant governor, U.S. senator, state attorney general, etc.

At the city and county level, term limits are common. But even when limits are imposed by voters, unscrupulous politicians attempt an end run. The most notorious example was former New York City Mayor Michael Bloomberg. Limited to two terms by a voter-approved 1993 referendum, in 2008, Bloomberg got the City Council to amend the law to allow him to run for and win a third term. Two years later, outraged voters passed another referendum reinstating the two-term limit.

One argument put forward against term limits is that it arbitrarily disqualifies candidates with whom voters are pleased and would otherwise re-elect. Given the ever-declining performance ratings of Congress, and negative opinions from voters about their own representatives, this argument, as judges like to say, "fails to persuade." In truth, the fundraising advantage of incumbents, paired with gerrymandered districts, has created a Congress composed almost entirely of the inept, the corrupt, and the captured. Logic suggests that a regular influx of new members could not possibly result in a worse overall outcome, and is more likely to help, rather than hinder, Congress in the performance of its duties to the *voters* (instead of its cronies and donors).

Another common defense of unlimited terms is that it takes newly-elected legislators years to "learn how the institution functions," and "effectively get things done." Translation: It takes time to learn how to manipulate the system, and engage in the backroom deals necessary to enrich legislators, donors, lobbyists, and their respective cronies. Opponents of term limits argue that a lack of experience by newly-elected officials shifts the "institutional memory," and thus undue power and influence, to professional staffers. Seriously? Any official re-elected to a second term should already know the ropes, inside-out. If they don't, the voters in a fairly drawn district will quickly find someone with a greater ability to absorb on-the-job training.

The amendment proposed here uses a twelve-year limit for House members but extends Senate service to a maximum of fourteen years. This would enable Senators to still run for two full terms after having been appointed to serve less than two years of the unexpired term of a senator who left office prematurely, which sometimes happens when a senator dies, becomes too ill to serve, or leaves early to become a cabinet official.

Under this formula, a candidate could conceivably serve a total of twenty-four, or in rare cases, twenty-six years, in Congress. However, to do so they would have to win election six times at the district level and twice statewide. Assuming passage of the fair districting procedures and public financing proposals outlined in coming chapters, any candidate re-elected this many times would have a strong following and generally reflect the political sentiments of their constituents.

The SCOTUS decision overturning Congressional term limits is not surprising when you consider that the Supremes have also ruled that Congressmen and Senators do not have to be residents of a state in order to be eligible to represent that state or district. Supposedly, a residency requirement prevents voters from selecting the candidate of their choice. What makes this particularly offensive is that the Constitution requires that candidates for president and vice-president on the same ticket cannot be residents of the same state. Thus, when George W. Bush picked Dick Cheney as his VP, Cheney had to fly up from Dallas and re-register using his Montana vacation home as his residence. Characteristic of the morass that the American political system has become, no one bothered to challenge this charade in the courts. It probably wouldn't have mattered anyway.

Illinois requires that candidates for state and local office be residents of that particular district or jurisdiction for at least the year preceding election. When Rahm Emanuel resigned as Obama's Chief of Staff to run for Mayor of Chicago, his eligibility was challenged in court. Despite the fact that Emanuel had moved his entire family to D.C., enrolled his kids in local Washington schools, rented his house in Chicago, and even re-registered his cars in D.C., the court ruled that he still met the Illinois residency requirement. This proved, once again, that judges must be trained at the best law schools in the country, not just to distort the common meaning of words, but to keep a straight face when doing so. Only the brilliant wordsmiths in the federal judiciary can define a *representative* of a state or district as someone who does not live there.

Henry Waxman was the poster child of an arrogant Congressman for whom their district is nothing more than an afterthought. For the last twenty of his forty-two years in Congress, Waxman lived year-round in Washington, and didn't even own or rent a residence anywhere in California, much less in his district. Waxman's case is a stark example of how gerrymandering, combined with the absence of term limits, ensconces Congress members in seats that are perpetually safe and non-competitive. Waxman's free ride went off the tracks when California voters approved a 2010 ballot measure to have districts drawn by a non-partisan volunteer commission. Placed in a much more balanced district, in 2012, Waxman faced his first serious primary challenge in decades, then had a bruising general election battle against a first-time GOP candidate.

Insulted by the notion that he would have to seriously campaign and be responsive to his new constituents, Waxman decided not to run for a twenty-second term in 2014. If the concept that representatives should be elected from states, or districts within states, in order to accurately represent their constituencies is to mean anything, then candidates and office holders must be required to live in that state or district for some period, both before and after election. Therefore:

> **Section 3: Except for persons returning from active government service abroad, candidates for congressional, state, or local office shall have maintained a residence in that jurisdiction for at least one year prior to election, and shall have been present in said jurisdiction for at least 120 days during that year. Officeholders shall maintain a residence in their district, or for Senators, in that state, throughout their term of office, and shall be**

**physically present thereat for at least 60 days
of every year. Violation hereof will result in
immediate removal from office by order of the
Chief Justice of that state's Supreme Court.**

Unfortunately, simply ensuring that members of Congress actually
reside in their state or district, and rotating them out of office
through term limits, is not enough. To break up the increasingly
incestuous and dynastic Permanent Political Class, we must end
the revolving door that allows officials to move from positions of
power in government to lucrative jobs in the industries over which
they formerly exercised authority. This malignant merry-go-round
is social and economic murder-for-hire. Campaign contributions
are a down payment on the hit. An obscene salary for post-
government employment in the private sector is the payoff after
the hopes, futures, and in some cases, the actual lives of the
citizens have been killed off in service of fascist oligarchy.

Make no mistake about it: government policies that favor the elite
often result in real death. Coal miners dying in unsafe mines
because there is no meaningful enforcement of safety regulations
isn't an accident, it's murder. The same applies to sending troops
into action with defective body armor. Both are murder-by-
spreadsheet, a cost-benefit analysis tilted toward profits over lives.
The same for obscene hikes in the price of life-saving medications,
or the deliberate refusal to address pollution of our air, water, and
food.

For those inclined to believe that this characterization is a little
over the top consider, once again, the case of Eric Holder. After
serving in the DOJ under Bill Clinton, Holder went to work for
Covington & Burling, the firm that helped create the Mortgage
Electronic Registration Service (MERS), a way for financial firms
to avoid the labor and fees involved in filing the *legally
required* change-of-title documents with state or local officials.

When the subprime mortgage meltdown hit, MERS was revealed as a complete scam. Foreclosure firms were unable to produce accurate title and loan documents, so they forged replacement docs. Some sharp judges and a few diligent attorneys caught the errors, but tens of thousands of other homeowners were foreclosed upon by banks and mortgage servicing companies even though those companies could not prove legitimate title to those properties. Anybody who thinks that some victims of these fraudulent foreclosures weren't driven to suicide is simply in denial.

Did Holder's Justice Department prosecute anyone from MERS? Or the CEOs of the financial institutions that wrecked the global economy? *Of course not*. Instead, Holder offered the lame excuse that prosecuting banks would imperil the global financial system. The problem is, people weren't asking him to prosecute banks, just evil bankers, a distinction conveniently beyond his ability to grasp. Holder's Assistant Attorney General in charge of the criminal division, Lanny Breuer, echoed this argument in an infamous *60 Minutes* interview. A week later, Breuer resigned from the DOJ and returned to -- did you say, Covington & Burling? -- at a salary of approximately $4 million a year. ***Four. Million. Dollars. A. Year***. Blood money.

Then there's Tim Geithner, who went from President of the New York Federal Reserve Bank to Secretary of the Treasury, where he helped shield his banker cronies from both financial collapse and criminal prosecution by funneling them trillions of dollars in government subsidies. And where did little Timmy land after leaving Treasury? As president of the giant private equity firm Warburg Pincus. His compensation was not revealed, but it is known that he, like the firm's other partners, benefit from the carried interest provision of the tax code which allows those in private equity to have their compensation taxed at the much-lower capital gains rate rather than as regular income.

Another example of the revolving door screwing of Americans is former Louisiana Congressman Billy Tauzin. While chair of the House committee that oversees the drug industry, Tauzin helped push through the Medicare Prescription Drug Act, commonly known as Medicare Part D. A highly controversial element of this bill specifically prohibits Medicare from negotiating lower prices from drug manufacturers, and prohibits re-importing cheaper versions of drugs from countries such as Canada. After the bill passed, Tauzin resigned from Congress and became President of the Pharmaceutical Research and Manufacturers of America (PhRMA). His annual House salary? Less than $200K. His PhRMA compensation started at $2 million a year and in 2010, hit $11.6 million, making him the highest paid lobbyist in the health care field. Of course, much of that money came out of the pockets of elderly Americans on Medicare who paid higher prices for covered drugs, and exorbitant prices if they fell into the coverage gap known as the donut hole.

Or how about Eric Cantor? Here's Jon Walker at FireDogLake.com describing Cantor's transition from defeated Congressman -- at $193,000 a year as Majority Leader -- to Wall Street lobbyist:

> Eric Cantor's new job sends a clear message to all incumbents: toe the Wall Street line and you'll be rewarded later.
>
> Bribing people with big bags of money or expensive gifts is so 20th century. Not only is it gauche to carry around suitcases full of hundred dollar bills, it is also stupid ... The perfectly legal way to influence policy makers is to simply let it be known that if they hold favorable voting positions, they will very likely be rewarded with lucrative jobs. There is no need for a quid pro quo or even explicit promise as long as a clear and consistent norm is established. This is what happened to Rep. Eric Cantor (R-VA). From Market Watch:

"Talk about victory in defeat: Former House Majority Leader Eric Cantor will be pulling in about $3.5 million thanks to his new job with Wall Street investment bank Moelis & Co."

Chris Dodd left the Senate, where his base salary was $174,000, to become head of the Motion Pictures Association of America, where his compensation totals $3.3 million. Needless to say, his position on subjects related to the entertainment industry, such as copyright protections, net neutrality, and so forth, have magically morphed from pro-consumer to pro-corporation. Gen. Keith Alexander, former head of the NSA, founded a consulting firm that charges its corporate clients from $600,000 to $1 million a month. (This is why former high-level national security officials were so up in arms when Trump revoked ex-CIA chief John Brennan's security clearance; losing access to classified intelligence makes these ex-officials far less valuable as corporate consultants.)

These stories are not unusual. We cannot tolerate situations where someone can get elected to office, get termed out or defeated, and is then lavishly rewarded by the very companies and industries that he or she was previously supposed to regulate and restrain. We cannot continue to foster an environment where those we elect, those who advise them, and those who execute the daily grunt work of governing, remain cloistered in a bubble, totally out of touch with people in other walks of life.

**Section 4: Perpetuation of a permanent political class being detrimental to the health of the republic, for a period of five years after having left elected office, appointed Cabinet or sub-cabinet position, or employment of any type in a government agency, no person shall be employed or retained in any capacity by any person or entity having previous or current business under the authority of any office, committee, or department position previously**

**held by former official or employee. No family member shall succeed another family member in the same office until six years has elapsed.**

**Section 5: Except for true matters of national security, subject to judicial review if necessary, after leaving elected office, appointed Cabinet or sub-cabinet position, or employment of any type in a government agency, no person shall attempt in any way to influence policies or legislation, or to provide advice pertaining thereto, except through public testimony or written communication subject to unrestricted public review.**

Section 5 merely extends to former government officials and employees the same restrictions imposed by Section 8 of the 28th Amendment, the Right to Honest Government, on those currently serving in the public sector.

In August 2018, Senator Elizabeth Warren introduced the *Anti-Corruption and Public Integrity Act* which proposed, among other things, to:

- Erect a lifetime ban on lobbying by former Presidents and members of Congress.

- Require members of Congress and Cabinet Secretaries to either divest their stock portfolios or place them in special "conflict-free" accounts managed by the Federal Retirement Thrift Investment Board, a small agency established during the Reagan administration.

- Prohibit all government officials from owning stocks with enough value to possibly influence their decisions while in office.

- Prohibit American citizens from lobbying on behalf of foreign governments and businesses.

Interestingly enough, Warren's proposal contains a six-year restriction on former government officials trying to influence pending legislation which is similar in some respects to the five-year ban that I propose in Section 5 of the 32nd Amendment.

There was immediate criticism of Warren's bill on two fronts. First, that it would be an unconstitutional interference with these people's First Amendment right to petition government. It would be interesting to see this contention adjudicated. If Warren's prohibition on "lobbying" did not prevent former members of Congress and ex-Cabinet Secretaries from giving public testimony, then the contention that it violates the First Amendment right to petition government would seem to not apply. By its very nature, the First Amendment can only apply to public speech. It has never applied to private speech between two or more people in a private setting.

The second criticism is that the bill is window dressing which has no chance to pass the current Republican-controlled Congress. This assertion is ludicrous, but only because it implies that somehow the ravenously corrupt Democrats would pass it, if only they came to power. ***Not. A. Chance.***

Just because it is window dressing, and a campaign prop for a possible presidential candidacy by Warren, doesn't mean that elements of it might not have merit as part of a revised 32nd Amendment. For that reason, when it comes time to move forward to get the Restoration Amendments enacted, such revisions could be, and perhaps even should be, considered.

Regardless of the final form of this amendment, to enforce its provisions we must erect a felony firewall:

**Section 6: Any violation or attempted violation of the provisions of this Amendment shall be a felony punishable by incarceration in a maximum security facility for a period, not subject to pardon, parole, commutation, suspension, or other reduction of sentence, of not less than ten years.**

An obvious argument against the restrictions proposed by this amendment is that it will force motivated, experienced, and highly qualified people out of government service. That argument ignores the fact that these motivated and highly qualified people are only forced to leave politics *for a limited period of time* and *after they have already served*. Moreover, the idea that we have a shortage of capable replacement candidates is absurd. At the time of the American Revolution the colonies had a total population of about one million. Today that number is over three hundred times larger. Discounting children, the elderly, felons, and aliens ineligible to hold office, out of the more than two hundred million or so remaining people, we can't find capable officials? Bullshit.

# Chapter 8

# PUBLIC ELECTION FINANCING

**The 33rd Amendment -- Campaign Financing**

**Section 1:** All elections shall be funded exclusively by grant of sufficient public funds, distributed equitably without favor or discrimination as to candidate, party, or measure. No candidate shall contribute to their own campaign any amount in excess of a reasonable filing fee for said office. Except as provided for in Section 5 below relating to the support of political parties, no business, domestic or foreign government entity, foundation, organization, association, or person shall contribute any funds to any candidate, party, campaign-related activity or event, or to either side in a measure before the voters.

**Section 2:** Unions, associations, charitable or non-profit organizations, and entities created for the purpose of engaging in business or advocating on behalf thereof, shall be artificial persons not accorded or entitled to the same political rights and free speech protections as

**natural persons, and therefore prohibited
from participating in any way in any election.**

Numerous polls and studies consistently demonstrate that
Americans loathe most of their elected representatives. Voters also
have equal contempt for how those representatives get elected.
Elections have become auctions, with the office generally going to
the candidate who can raise the most money. Even in
gerrymandered districts that favor candidates of one party, there
can still be hard-fought primary campaigns. The common
denominator in all of these races is that candidates who are
significantly underfunded rarely triumph. During presidential
campaigns in key battleground states, besieged voters can barely
escape the avalanche of campaign ads long enough to check the
weather report.

Not surprisingly, an overwhelming majority of Democratic,
Republican, and independent voters believe that there is way too
much money in politics. According to a May, 2012 Ipsos Public
Affairs poll:

> Seventy-five percent of Americans feel there is too
> much money in politics, and only 25 percent feel there
> is an intrinsic right to unfettered election spending, an
> argument commonly used by opponents of controls on
> campaign finance.

> [snip]

> The poll found 79 percent of Democrats believe there
> is too much money in politics, compared with 68
> percent of Republicans. Independents largely agreed
> with Democrats on the issue, with 77 percent saying
> there is too much money in politics and campaigns.

> [snip]

> Many past controls on campaign spending have been
> lifted thanks to the U.S. Supreme Court's 2010

*Citizens United v. Federal Election Commission* decision, which ruled that corporate and labor union spending in elections is protected free speech.

[snip]

Two-thirds of respondents -- 67 percent -- also believed public officials change their positions to appeal to campaign donors, compared with 33 percent who think campaign donations mostly go to officials who already agree with donors' positions.

There was little disagreement between members of the different parties on that issue, with 69 percent of Democrats, 64 percent of Republicans and 68 percent of independents agreeing that officials change their stances.

A few months later a poll cited by TheHill.com showed that 76% of the people questioned supported laws that would require corporate campaign spending to be publicly disclosed, including prohibitions on back-door spending channeled through trade organizations and other trade fronts. About 81 percent of people surveyed said the current campaign spending rules are "bad for democracy."

The following year, MSNBC reported the results of a poll commissioned by Represent.us:

A huge majority of Americans favor aggressive measures to stem the influence of money in politics ... 90% of respondents said they'd support a law that imposes tough new campaign finance laws. When "campaign finance" was changed to "corruption," that figure rose to 97%...

A year later, things hadn't changed. According to a May 2014 CBS News poll:

- 75% of voters believe that the wealthy have a better chance of influencing elections;

- 71% thought individual contributions should be limited;

- 76% felt that political ad spending by outside groups not directly tied to the candidates campaign should also be limited.

Even voters who don't follow elections closely know that campaign costs have skyrocketed. A look at the numbers reveals the escalation to be staggering. Here are some numbers compiled by the Campaign Finance Institute using Federal Election Commission data:

Cost of winning House race in 1986,
adjusted for inflation to 2012 dollars: $753,274
Actual 2012 cost: $1,596,953

Cost of winning Senate seat in 1986,
adjusted for inflation to 2012 dollars: $6,426,200
Actual 2012 cost: $10,351,556

But these are averages. In 2000, John Corzine spent a staggering $69,209,506 to win his New Jersey Senate seat. Across the river in New York, Hillary Clinton spent just under $30 million in her Senate race. 2018 blew the top off the chart once again. As of September 2018, here are the numbers compiled by OpenSecrets.org:

| House races: | Democrats | $ 850,195,336 |
| | Republicans | $ 576,457,936 |
| | Total | $1,431,223,399 |
| | | |
| Senate races: | Democrats | $ 489,647,047 |
| | Republicans | $ 353,194,087 |
| | Total | $ 870,702,044 |
| | | |
| Combined total: | | $2,301,925,443 |

By election night in November that number was up to $4.7 billion, with the final projected total, after all required financial reports are filed, estimated at $5.2 billion.

*Five billion, two hundred million dollars.*

It's not just the candidates who raise and spend money, it's also parties and their subordinate committees. In 1994, the Democratic Party National Committee plus its separate House and Senate campaign committees raised $132.4 million. By 2012, that figure had ballooned more than 400% to $631.1 million. In the same period, the equivalent three committees on the Republican side of the aisle went from $233.1 million to $697.7 million, just under a 300% increase. And these are only expenditures by official committees. In 1978, non-party independent campaign expenditures, for and against candidates from both parties in House and Senate races, totaled $303,000. By 2012 that figure was an astounding $457,215,466. From $300,000 to $457 **million**.

Presidential election costs have risen even more dramatically. Total expenditures for the 1976 Presidential race between Jimmy Carter and Gerald Ford were only $171 million. By 2008, that figure zoomed to $1.749 **billion**. Adjusting for inflation, that's still an increase of 400%. Or put another way: adjusted for inflation, the $730 million Barack Obama spent on his 2008 election campaign is more than double the total amount spent by **both** candidates combined in 1976. Here are some of the 9 Incredible Campaign Money Stats compiled by Andy Koll in 2012 for Mother Jones: [Bold is original.]

- Estimated amount of disclosed spending in 2012 election: **$6 billion**.

- Amount of dark money (with no donor disclosure) spent in the 2008 election: **$70 million**

- Minimum amount of dark money spent on the 2012 election: **$213 million**

- Amount super-PACs, dark money groups, and other outside groups spent <u>in October</u>: **$526 million**

- Percentage of outside spending coming from disclosed donors in 2004: **96.5 percent**

- Percentage of outside spending coming from disclosed donors in 2012: **40.5 percent**

All these previous campaigns were pikers compared to the 2016 Clinton campaign that set fire to $1.2 ***billion*** -- and lost.

The solution most often suggested, and put forward by this amendment, is public funding of political campaigns. But what, exactly, does public funding mean? How far down the hierarchy of office should it extend? To the local town council? School board races? Should any form of private funding be permissible? Should wealthy candidates be able to self-fund their campaigns? (With public campaign funding, limiting a candidate's self-funding to an amount equal to the public funds allotted to rivals is self-defeating, because no wealthy candidate would use their own money unless it gave them an advantage, which in this case it would not. They would simply apply for and use the public money.)

One huge adjustment to the political process that public financing of campaigns would have is the elimination of private advocacy group spending on election campaigns. Under current law, private PACS can run ads for or against candidates. They just lack that familiar endorsement, "I'm so-and-so and I approved this ad." Some organizations governed by IRS regulations are limited, in theory anyway, to running ads for or against specific issues, such as environmental protection, educational reforms, reproductive rights, and so forth. However, through close but unofficial coordination with a candidate's campaign (and/or the candidate's state and national party organizations), it's easy to transform an issue ad into a stealth ad for a candidate or against their opponent. Thus the line between permissible and impermissible political activities by non-profit organizations has become meaningless. A July 2014, Huffington Post article by Ashley Alman headlined:

### IRS Surrenders, Won't Check Whether Political Non-Profits Are Breaking The Law

...the Internal Revenue Service has decided to award most nonprofit groups tax exemption status without being screened

According to articles in Time, The Huffington Post, and others, the IRS will now be granting charitable 501(c)3 status to organizations without a background check, and without monitoring to see that they are not illegally using the money to fund political advertising. Previously, political expenditures were limited to 501(c)4 organizations. Unlike their 501(c)3 counterparts, money given to 501(c)4 organizations is not tax deductible. Now donors will be able to remain anonymous, give unlimited amounts, and write it off on their taxes. Reportedly, there may be as many as 50,000 new organizations a year who will get to skate by because the IRS has waved the white flag.

Is America great, or what?

A true ban on private campaign spending would eliminate all political ads from any group other than the candidate's formal, publicly-funded campaign. This means that while the Chamber of Commerce and organizations funded by the Koch brothers could no longer run ads, neither could the Sierra Club, MoveOn.org, Blue America and so forth. This sets a lot of progressives (both real and faux) on edge. Overall, the mere suggestion of limiting paid private ads provokes an emotional reaction in many Americans: "I ought to be able to speak my mind and tell anyone what I think about a candidate or an issue." This is true. But unlike personal conversation, a letter to the editor of the local paper, or even a blog comment, regardless of which side you're on, communicating your views over mass media, other than via a viral Internet meme, requires money. Lots of it.

***The benefits of free speech should not be limited to those who have the power of free spending.***

As a woman who comments under the name Carla wrote on NakedCapitalism.com in 2018:

> Since "democracy" is a public project, and voting is a public act, and the whole infrastructure of elections is publicly funded, and those elected to serve in the public sector are called public servants, why would we not need to have public financing of political campaigns?

If private money is to be eliminated, we must also address the issue of volunteer campaign manpower, which is support in lieu of money. Many activists freely volunteer their time to campaigns, or staff local party offices, which is fine, should be encouraged, and need not change just because campaigns are publicly financed. However, we must guard against various strategies to circumvent the ban on private funding of campaign activities.

For example, unions have traditionally provided massive manpower for Democratic candidates. This comes in the form of operating phone banks, walking precincts talking to voters one-on-one, distributing campaign handouts, putting up signs, and sometimes manning voter registration drives aimed at increasing the number of registered voters within a target area that has a demographic profile traditionally favorable to Democratic candidates. If unions were allowed to continue providing this in-lieu-of-cash support, what would prevent companies from hiring temporary employees for their public relations division and then assigning them to work for GOP candidates? The short answer is: nothing. Nor should there be.

What's fair for one side must be fair for the other. However, allowing this to happen would open the door for an end-run around the goal of public campaign financing. The solution: prohibit unions from organizing or formally aiding political activities by their members, while also making it a crime for both the management and the employees of a company to lend the services of those employees to a campaign. (The employee could still volunteer on their own time, but could not work for the campaign on company time with company compensation.) Given the communication capabilities of today's political and social networks, there is no reason that parties and campaigns cannot easily recruit volunteers for their candidates and issues.

When voters hear the word *election*, many tend to equate it with candidates running for office. However, the corrupt financial web underpinning our electoral system is a beast of infinitely greater proportions. Take, for instance, the party presidential nominating conventions. In addition to appropriating about $18 million to both the Democratic and Republican parties for the cost of hosting these orgies of insider glad-handing, the government also supplies each party with $50 million in security services. That sounds like a lot of money for people to gather for four days, but it's not nearly enough for the party pigs. That's why they also set out to raise enormous amounts from corporate sponsors.

One way the parties camouflage these contributions is to not take them at the national party level, but instead funnel them through a Host City committee. PublicIntegrity.org noted that for the 2012 Charlotte convention, the Democratic National Committee pledged not to accept money from lobbyists, corporations, or PACS, and made a big show of soliciting small donations. "This convention is relying on a grassroots network made up of people like you to give small amounts to help make this convention a success," Obama wrote in one fundraising appeal. In keeping with the true spirit of small donors the party graciously capped donations from individuals at a mere $100,000, which is understandable since, according to Bloomberg, the Host Committee's goal was $36 million.

Finding it unthinkable to hold a convention on a measly $36 mil (plus $68 million in federal funding), the Dems also set up a second committee, *New American City*, ostensibly to showcase Charlotte. This committee happily solicited millions from lobbyists, corporations, and PACs. But only to help defray administrative costs, you understand. Of course, this second committee had *nothing whatsoever to do* with trying to appear not to take special interest money while actually doing so. Such is the corrupt nature of American electoral politics.

According to the Center for Public Integrity, in 2008 the Democrats' Denver host committee brought in $63 million, with $9 million of that coming from unions. Except for the part about unions, the 2008 GOP convention in Minneapolis was no different, where the Minneapolis Post ran an article headlining 51 corporate sponsors. A partial list:

Target
General Mills
Best Buy
Wells Fargo
3M
Ameriprise Financial
US Bank
United Health Group
Anheuser-Busch
Astra Zeneca Pharmaceuticals
Cisco
Comcast
Fed Ex
Google
Hewlett-Packard
Koch Industries

Microsoft
Coca-Cola
UPS
Verizon
AT&T

2012 was the same, only larger. Here's a partial list of sponsors for the Democratic convention in Charlotte, NC:

Bank of America
Duke Energy
Time Warner Cable
Coca-Cola
Wells Fargo
UnitedHealth Group
Piedmont Natural Gas
US Airways
AT&T

Speaking of AT&T, one article quoted a spokesman describing the company's participation as "being a good corporate citizen."

*A good corporate citizen.* How about we eliminate corporate citizens? Sounds good to me.

Of course, all those AT&T donations had nothing at all to do with the bill Congress passed, just prior to the 2008 conventions, granting the telecom companies retroactive immunity from civil suits and criminal prosecution for the massive warrantless electronic surveillance of the Bush administration, right? *Of course not.* And it is mere coincidence that, as soon as he had the nomination secured, Obama, who had campaigned on filibustering that bill, turned around and supported it. No surprise that once in office he eagerly expanded the scope of the national security state's relentless, unconstitutional, and unwarranted invasion of citizen privacy.

Despite the fact that the 2012 Democratic convention was held in the virulently anti-union, right-to-work state of North Carolina, union leaders showed how few principles they have by again spending big. The first five all gave from $1 million to $1.5 million:

Service Employees International Union

International Brotherhood of Electrical Workers

American Federation of Teachers

Laborers' International Union

National Education Association

United Food and Commercial Workers

American Federation of State, County
and Municipal Employees

International Union of Bricklayers
and Allied Craftworkers

National Air Traffic Controllers Association

United Automobile Workers of America.

Once again, except for the absence of unions, the 2012 GOP convention in Tampa, FL was more of the same. Duke Energy and Coca Cola led a list of the usual suspects. Bloomberg reported that Chevron gave $250,000 directly and that oil industry trade groups like Teco, Inc., and the American Petroleum Institute were also major donors. These sponsorships are all about ensuring access and maintaining the relationship between the buyer and those anxious to be bought. But rest easy. Supposedly, these events have no official connection with the convention. It's just *so* fortunate that delegates can go all week and never have to pay for a meal.

If we ban corporate contributions, how in heaven's name will parties afford their conventions? The same way normal people afford seminars, conferences, and things like the Boy Scout Jamboree: Have the delegates pay their own way, which already happens a lot, especially to those who support anti-establishment candidates. A number of GoFundMe efforts were required to get some Bernie Sanders' supporters to the 2016 Democratic convention. The conventions can also dispense with all the fancy parties. It is, after all, supposed to be a working environment, key (if not critical) to the proper functioning of our political system.

Corporations and the wealthy don't stop with contributions to candidates, party committees, and conventions. Once their guy wins the world's top job they are eager to help him celebrate in an orgy of excess known as the Presidential Inauguration, with its attendant gala balls. Once again, it doesn't matter which party's candidate wins. The usual suspects will still be lining up to buy access, influence, and goodwill. Who can blame them? If the new president is a good boy or girl, the corporation will get lots of preferential treatment, and when their term is over, the former president will get obscene book deals, speaking fees, consulting gigs, board memberships, and contributions to their library or whatever high-sounding foundation they establish.

As Wikipedia notes, for George W. Bush's second inaugural:

> Some $40 million was raised by private sponsors such as ExxonMobil, Chevron, Cinergy, Occidental Petroleum and the Nuclear Energy Institute. ... Donors received special tickets and seating at the events.

Bill Clinton's second inauguration in 1997 raised $42.7 million from private donors. Despite all his phony rhetoric about "Hope and Change," Barack Obama continued the practice but added another cynical layer of deception. Trumpeting his commitment to "take on" the entrenched power of federal lobbyists, Obama banned them from donating to his inaugural. However, he placed no such prohibitions on contributions to the inaugural *from corporations that employ those lobbyists*. So instead of a lobbying firm making the contribution and then billing their client, the company's public relations or governmental liaison office paid the money directly.

The Center for Public Integrity reported that corporations and unions who contributed to the 2013 inauguration had previously spent $160 million on lobbying during Obama's first term. In addition to the usual suspects, other big contributors included Genentech, a major biomedical firm, Southern Co., an energy giant, and four unions: The American Federation of Government Employees, International Brotherhood of Electrical Workers, Laborers International Union of North America, and the American Postal Workers Union, which was undoubtedly trying to offset the stealth campaign of private delivery companies like Fed Ex to slowly strangle, and then ultimately privatize, the Post Office.

How much do these companies and organizations fork over for the privilege of partying with elected officials and party apparatchiks? Inauguration committees are not required to report the amounts, but the World Socialists Website reported that the 2013 Obama Inauguration Committee established four sponsorship levels: Washington at $1 mil, Adams at $500,000, Jefferson at $250,000 and lowly Madison at a mere $100,000. The same article described these invitation-only events as, "a pageantry of wealth and power that serve as the American ruling elite's answer to a British coronation."

Sandwiched between the party conventions and the presidential coronation comes the nationally televised debates between the Democratic and Republican candidates. For a brief period between 1976 and 1984, these debates were sponsored by the League of Women Voters with the goal of informing the voting public. But soon Democrats and Republicans alike realized that they could not allow anything as sacred as election debates to be handled by a third party. Especially when the LWV insisted on such things as the dreaded "follow up question" (which makes ducking the intent of the original question much harder). In 1988, the Dukakis and

Bush campaigns met secretly and drafted their own debate rules and formats. Relegated to figurehead status, the League of Women Voters promptly denounced the new agreement as, "a fraud upon the American voter," and quit hosting the debates, a task quickly taken up by the Committee on Presidential Debates (CPD), a wholly-owned, and nominally non-profit, creation of the legacy parties.

The CPD has controlled every debate since. Every detail is negotiated between the two parties: who will moderate the debate, who the panelists will be, what kind of questions can be asked, and even the height of the podiums. Naturally, the audiences are handpicked, by invitation only. To give a false impression of fairness, CPD rules require that a third-party candidate appear on a sufficient number of state ballots to win the 278 electoral votes needed to become president. But because Ralph Nader and Jill Stein (both running as candidates of the Green Party) proved able to meet this threshold, the CPD also instituted another qualification: the candidate must have the support of at least 15% of the voters according to public opinion polls.

The 15% public provision was added because the CPD, under immense public pressure in 1992 from Ross Perot's high-visibility Reform Party campaign, had made the mistake of allowing Perot into the debates despite his having only 7% support in the polls. Perot performed brilliantly and captured 19% of the vote on Election Day. His 12-point jump from pre-debate poll support to actual vote tally was, and still is, the greatest by any candidate in the televised debate era. The CPD learned its lesson and excluded Perot from the 1996 Dole-Clinton debates. From that time forward, the CPD has excluded all independent candidates. In 2000, when Ralph Nader obtained a ticket, the CPD had him forcibly removed from the live debate audience. In 2012, Jill Stein was arrested for merely trying to enter one of the debates.

The brazen CPD makes no effort to hide the identity of its real bosses, proudly listing major donors going back to the first CPD debate in 1988. Among them:

Anheuser-Busch
Southwest Airlines
American Airlines
Continental Airlines
JetBlue Airways
US Airways
Sprint
Ford Motor Company
Phillip Morris
Lucent Technologies
And, of course, AT&T

The donor roll also includes those not well known by the public but nonetheless charter members of the insider elite. Law firms like Crowell & Morning, LLP; Sheldon S. Cohen, Esq; and Morgan, Lewis & Brockius, LLP. Foundations such as The Knight Foundation, the Howard G. Buffett Foundation, The Marjorie Kovler Fund, and The Ford Foundation provide a glossy veneer conveying that this is all somehow in the public interest. After all, the CPD website Mission Statement proudly claims that it was established to, "ensure that debates, as a permanent part of every general election, provide the best possible information to viewers and listeners." Just as long as none of that information comes from third-party candidates, or is accidentally blurted out by a candidate responding to a follow-up question.

Of course, even though the CPD website acknowledges its corporate masters, the debates themselves, which one journalist described as corporate carnivals, are off-limits to the public. Here's Washington Post reporter Dana Milbank describing one of the 2000 presidential debates:

...inside the debate area ... there is beer flowing, snacks, Budweiser girls in red sweaters, the baseball playoffs on television, ping-pong and fusbol.

The sight of all those massive sponsor tents might result in adverse optics. Being corrupt is okay, but let's not allow the public to see first-hand how captured our political process is.

Not surprisingly, the co-chairs of the CPD are two of Washington's most prominent and powerful lobbyists, Frank Fahrenkopf, a lobbyist for the gaming industry, and Mike McCurry, who represents the telecommunications industry.

Another issue that must be addressed regarding public campaign financing involves referendums, initiatives, and recall campaigns. Referendums are employed to challenge or repeal a law or government action. Initiatives are used to put a new law on the books when the legislative body, for whatever reason, is either unable to act or has seen fit not to do so.

Some states allow the legislature or the Governor to place either advisory or legally-binding measures on the ballot. Over two dozen other states permit voter-sponsored initiatives and referendums. In Chapter 11, the 36th Amendment, Participatory Democracy, proposes to expand the right of initiative, referendum, and recall to all states.

Once a measure reaches the ballot, public financing will ensure a level playing field for both sides. The problem occurs in the process by which a measure makes it to the ballot in the first place. The fact is, no matter how many volunteers a petition drive has, it still needs baseline funding. The petition application has to follow each state's prescribed format, meaning that those promoting the measure must hire a lawyer to see that each element conforms exactly, even down to the size and type of font used.

The entire text of the law being challenged must be included with every referendum petition so that a prospective signer can examine exactly what they're being asked to support. Likewise, initiative petition books must contain the entire text of the proposed measure. It's not unusual for a petition book to run 50 pages. Even in a small city, just printing the petition books for a local referendum or initiative can run several thousand dollars. For statewide initiatives in states with large populations and significant geographic area like California, the cost can run six figures. Paper is heavy, so in addition to the printing cost, in a statewide campaign there can be significant shipping costs just to get the books from the printer to the circulators in the field. (Proponents of a measure dare not have petitions printed in more than one location for fear that an accidental or deliberate printing error -- such as a paragraph or even a sentence left out -- would invalidate sufficient books to prevent the measure from qualifying.)

In almost all cases, for every side pushing a ballot measure there is a group opposing it, and that group will often mount an intense counter-offensive in an effort to dissuade voters from signing the petition. (After all, the easiest way to defeat a ballot measure is to make sure it fails to get on the ballot in the first place.) So, long before anyone even knows if the petition drive will succeed, both sides incur costs for mailings, handouts, phone bank voter outreach, and even running TV commercials arguing their side of the issue. Where the measure involves zoning, development, or business issues, often the battle pits an under-financed group of local activists against big money commercial interests. Voter-led efforts to reform public employee pension excesses naturally incur organized resistance from public worker unions. Even in small communities, a successful petition drive requires an informative website that is updated regularly. That may not cost much, but it still costs.

One argument against voter-instigated ballot measures is that, while their original purpose was laudable, special interest groups have succeeded in co-opting the process, using it as a way to circumvent the legislature and/or hoodwink voters into approving measures that secretly or artfully benefit the measure's backers. This complaint has some validity, but that is no reason to throw the baby out with the bath water. States that permit private citizens to circulate ballot measures have found them to be a valuable tool in keeping government honest, and in protecting the rights of citizens against special interests who pull the strings in the state or local legislative body. Issues such as term limits, controls on runaway property taxes, requiring voter approval for new taxes, zoning controls on over-building, the acquisition or preservation of recreational and open space, or changing public employee pension formulas have all been put on the books through ballot measure drives led by motivated citizens.

The solution to the cost-of-activism issue is a system whereby the proponents of a ballot measure are reimbursed for their substantiated out-of-pocket costs if the measure qualifies for the ballot. Ballot measures are democracy's safeguard because they ensure the voting public a way to either address or correct matters when the formal institutions of government -- *which are already funded by the taxpayers* -- have fallen short. It stands to reason that those who go through the effort and expense to circulate a petition should not have to pay for good government twice. And reimbursing people for their out-of-pocket hard costs does nothing to repay the tax on their time. In an ideal world -- something akin to the fairy tale we were told in sixth grade civics about "how a bill becomes law" -- citizens would not have to resort to referendums, initiatives, and recalls. Just making their opinions known to lawmakers through public or written testimony, telephone calls, and email should be enough. But of course, it's not. Therefore:

> **Section 3: Proponents of initiatives, referendums, and recalls may raise and spend the funds necessary for the petition drive, but upon the measure qualifying for the ballot shall be reimbursed on a timely basis, by the legislative body or office or jurisdiction subject to the petition measure, for the true, documented, and, if necessary, court-approved expenses involved in securing the required number of signatures.**

Reimbursing proponents of a measure only if it qualifies for the ballot erects a reasonable barrier to frivolous measures not based on issues of sufficient concern to voters. There is also ample legal precedent for doing so. In many cases, the law provides that if a person or organization successfully sues a government entity, the plaintiff's legal expenses (as documented and approved by the judge in the case) are reimbursed by the losing government body. Again, the justification is based on the premise that citizens should not have to pay twice to get government to do its job correctly. Opponents will argue that under this proposal, tax money paid by people opposed to a measure would go to the measure's proponents. But this can be considered a cost of democratic government, a price everyone must pay to ensure that elected and appointed officials act as their constituents wish.

> **Section 4: For 120 days prior to any election, all electronic media falling under the jurisdiction of, or licensed to operate, by any branch of government shall grant, at no cost, without favor or discrimination as to candidate, party, or issue, adequate periods of time across all hours and days of the week for campaign advertising.**

The best way to reduce the cost of campaigns is to reduce the cost of TV advertising. Currently television and radio stations -- as well as the cable and fiber-optic systems which retransmit their signals

-- are required, in certain designated periods of time prior to each election, to provide campaign ads in all time periods at the lowest commercial rate offered in any time period. In municipal elections, the cost of a 30-second ad between two a.m. and five a.m. on a local cable system, such as the one serving my community, can be as low as $20. (No, that's not a typo.) But during the designated election period, a candidate, or groups contesting a ballot measure, can run the same ad, at all hours of the day and night, at that same $20 price on CNN, ESPN, or during an episode of primetime programming such as *NCIS*, *Dancing With The Stars*, or *Survivor*. While this helps reduce campaign costs, given the total costs of the campaign examples cited at the beginning of this chapter, it is certainly not enough. Especially when the airwaves, the cable systems, and the internet are all either directly, or indirectly, subsidized. For example, over-the-air television stations pay the government a license fee to use certain specific spectrum frequencies that are designated by law as *public property*. The same is true for traditional over-the-air radio.

Thus there is a vested public interest and often, a public subsidy as well. The poles and utility tunnels are either on, or under, public roads or sidewalks. Without those roads, and the regular, taxpayer-funded maintenance they require, there would be no homes for the company's subscribers. Without the franchises granted by state public utilities commissions to power companies, there would be no electrical power for TVs. That's why almost all states regulate cable and phone companies as some form of public utility. Even wireless devices exist and function only as a by-product of government permission and assistance. When a phone company needs to put a relay tower in a particular community, often the local municipality is required to allow it, even if the property owner or neighbors object. Eminent domain law can be used to forcibly wrest the property in question from its owner. The satellites that relay wireless transmissions for data, voice, and images are all regulated by various federal government agencies to ensure that they use only specific frequencies, follow approved orbits, and meet certain launch standards so that a malfunctioning rocket doesn't drop the satellite on a mall or an elementary school.

Internet Service Providers are also regulated by the Federal Communications Commission, and the Internet itself was originally developed using taxpayer dollars by funding from DARPA, the Defense Advanced Research Project Agency. (The transfer of governance of the internet to private companies, for comparatively miniscule amounts of money, may have been the biggest heist of public assets in world history.)

The companies that make or import and sell the TVs, computers, routers, modems, smart phones and other instruments of modern technology benefit from taxpayer-funded government services. The company's products travel along public roads on trucks inspected for safety by the Interstate Commerce Commission and state law enforcement agencies. Both imports and exports are inspected by Customs Agents, and the shipping containers are stored on public harbor lands until picked up or loaded aboard ship. The cargo ships themselves are inspected by customs agents and/or Coast Guard personnel, then guided to a safe berth by harbor pilots. Company stores and warehouses rely on power generated by utility companies which have their rates regulated by state governments. Those same stores and warehouses are protected from theft, vandalism, and fire by local police and fire departments. Last, but not least, to spur innovation, or accelerate the growth of new industries, Congress often grants companies preferential tax treatment. Just as with the creation of the internet, many of the most popular advances in today's consumer devices resulted from funding quietly supplied by the CIA or the Defense Department.

Anyone who claims that they or their company is completely self-made, without any assistance or support from government, is delusional. It is for that reason that the communications entities, on which we depend, must be compelled to offer free and equal time to all candidates in publicly funded elections.

> **Section 5: Commencing one year after ratification of this Amendment, all operation and administration of national political party offices and entities shall be funded solely and exclusively by membership dues not to exceed $50 per year. Membership dues for the operation and administration of each state or territorial party office shall not exceed $50 each per year. After ten years, and each ten years thereafter, the dues limits imposed herein shall be adjusted for compound inflation according to the same formula used to calculate Social Security increases.**

A frequent complaint about political parties is that they are not responsive to their members except in the run-up to each new election. That's because at the institutional and administrative level, the two major parties have become completely captured by, and beholden to, the same wealthy donors and major corporate sponsors. The solution: make the operation of party offices at every level dependent on dues, from a single class of members, all paying a modest and equal amount. With publicly funded elections there would be no more need for continuous fundraising by the myriad House, Senate, and state legislative campaign committees. Each party's central office could be underwritten by the dues of rank-and-file party members, not by PACs and corporations.

Need $10 million to operate the national party office for a year? Fine. Instead of getting one donor to write one check, or ten donors to write ten checks, get 20,000 party members to each send in $50. In addition to reducing each party's bloated staff and forcing more people out of the Political Industrial Complex into the normal workforce, over time this might transform the District of Corruption back into the District of Columbia. Before this can happen, there are more areas from which private and corporate funding must be eliminated. Sadly, in June of 2014, Congress voted to go in exactly the opposite direction. As Shane Goldmacher, reporting in the National Journal, proclaimed: [Bold in title is original. Emphasis in final paragraph added.]

## Congress Quietly Deletes a Key Disclosure of Free Trips Lawmakers Take

House Ethics reverses decades of precedent as lobbyist-sponsored lawmaker travel expands.

It's going to be a little more difficult to ferret out which members of Congress are lavished with all-expenses-paid trips around the world after the House has quietly stripped away the requirement that such privately sponsored travel be included on lawmakers' annual financial-disclosure forms.

The move, made behind closed doors and without a public announcement by the House Ethics Committee, reverses more than three decades of precedent. Gifts of free travel to lawmakers have appeared on the yearly financial form dating back to its creation in the late 1970s, after the Watergate scandal. *National Journal* uncovered the deleted disclosure requirement when analyzing the most recent batch of yearly filings.

[snip]

The change occurs as free travel, which critics have criticized as thinly veiled junkets, has come back into vogue. Last year, members of Congress and their aides took more free trips than in any year since the influence-peddling scandal that sent lobbyist Jack Abramoff to prison. There were nearly 1,900 trips at a cost of more than $6 million last year...

Now none of those trips must be included on the annual disclosures of lawmakers or their aides.

The tabs for these international excursions can run into the tens of thousands of dollars. One trip to Australia earlier this year cost nearly $50,000. Lawmakers are often invited to bring along their husbands or wives, fly in business class, and stay in plush four-star hotels. In the wake of the Abramoff scandal, lobbyists were banned from organizing or paying for these travels. But some of the nonprofits underwriting them today **have extremely close ties to lobbying groups, including sharing staff, money, and offices.**

Another curse of modern presidential elections is the early reporting of results from eastern and Midwest states while polls are still hours from closing in western states. If we really want to drive voter turnout, simply outlaw the reporting of results or exit polls from any state until the last polls in Alaska and Hawaii have closed. No more cases where people in western states don't go to the polls because their presidential candidate has already been projected to lose. Or win. Every time this occurs, candidates and measures farther down the ballot suffer.

The news media, and the professional political consulting class, will be aghast at this idea. So what? We have no responsibility to tailor election night for the benefit of Wolf Blitzer or Rachel Maddow. They -- and we -- will survive not knowing who our next president is going to be until after all the polls close. Therefore:

**Section 6: No person or entity shall disseminate, attempt to disseminate, or otherwise facilitate the dissemination of the presidential voting results from any state, or any predicted outcome of a presidential election, prior to the closing of the last polling place in the last state. Violation hereof shall be a felony punishable by incarceration in a maximum security facility for a period, not subject to pardon, parole, commutation, suspension, or other reduction of sentence, of**

not less than five years. This applies to the press in all forms, and revises the First Amendment accordingly.

# Chapter 9

# ELECTION INTEGRITY

The process by which America currently nominates its candidates for president is both absurd and irrational. The only people in favor of the current system are residents of Iowa, which conducts the first caucus, and New Hampshire, which holds the first primary. That these two tiny states go first isn't merely tradition, it's mandated by state law. New Hampshire requires the Secretary of State to schedule the New Hampshire primary at least one week prior to any other state. In 2012, attempts by other states to dislodge New Hampshire's privileged position led to the threat that the 2012 New Hampshire primary would actually be held in December of 2011. As it was, the primary barely made it past the dawn of the new year, occurring on January 10th. Iowa also has a provision to ensure that it holds the first state presidential caucus.

Iowa has a mere six electoral votes and New Hampshire even fewer, four. With just under 3,100,000 residents, Iowa ranks 30th in the nation in population. The City of Los Angeles (not the metro area, just the city itself) has a population of 3,792,000, making it twenty-three percent more populous than the entire state of Iowa. New Hampshire, with 1,323,000 residents, has only about 15,000 more people than the *City* of San Diego (1,307,000), and approximately 100,000 *fewer* than the New York borough of the Bronx. The largest city in Iowa, Des Moines, has 203,400 residents, about 9,000 fewer than the southern California suburb of Irvine. With 109,500 people, Manchester, the largest city in New Hampshire, has virtually the same population as Costa Mesa, CA (109,960), Odessa, TX (110,720), and Arvada, CO (111,700).

Neither Iowa nor New Hampshire represents an accurate cross-section of the nation at large. New Hampshire is 92% non-Hispanic white. Its $49,467 median household income places it seventh in the nation, and it consistently has the country's lowest poverty rate. New Hampshire has no state sales tax and no state personal income tax except on interest and dividends. Iowa is over 88% non-Hispanic white, and in an age of unprecedented mobility, 72% of Iowa residents were born there. Thanks to a diversified economy with manufacturing, biotech, and insurance services on top of its traditional agricultural base, Iowa has weathered the economic impact of the Great Financial Crisis of the last decade relatively unscathed. At a time when the official national unemployment rate hovered around 6%, Iowa's was only 4.4%.

Would anybody suggest that the City of Los Angeles hold the first presidential caucus? Or that the Bronx conduct the first primary? Of course not. The idea would be ridiculed as completely unrepresentative of the country as a whole. But we continue to do the same thing by giving Iowa and New Hampshire perpetual priority privileges.

Residents, politicians, and business leaders in both of these states argue that their small size, combined with certain local campaign traditions and customs, makes them ideal early sorting grounds for candidates. They talk about the need for candidates to do retail campaigning, get out and meet the voters, answer tough questions at supermarkets and backyard barbecues. But what these supporters are really trying to retain is the prestige of being first, of having the national spotlight on their state for as much as a year, not to mention the considerable economic benefits that come from these marathon campaigns. According to a study by George Washington University:

> It is no exaggeration to say that the long courtship of New Hampshire voters provides a comparable and probably greater boost to the state than a major party nominating convention provides to a host city. That figure is more than $100 million. For New Hampshire the visits are spread out over a year-plus. The candidates, their aides, reporters, camera crews, representatives of a number of interest groups seeking to get their messages out, and various hangers-on all flock to the state and spend money on rental cars, hotel rooms, taxis, food, event costs and advertising campaigns.

$100 million every four years is a nice chunk of change. And although the numbers are smaller, the effect is the same in Iowa. In 2008, when there was an open seat and a large field of candidates from both parties, the caucuses brought Des Moines alone about $25 million. According to the Washington Post, in the final week of the campaign one group spent $3.3 million just attacking Newt Gingrich's campaign. After the Supreme Court's 2010 *Citizens United* ruling outlawed caps on campaign spending, the money that poured into Iowa and New Hampshire was bound to increase. Some 2012 Iowa caucus spending figures:

- Amount spent directly by candidate campaigns: $15.55 million

- Amount spent in Des Moines alone for lodging, meals, transportation, etc. by campaign staff and press: $17.00 million

- Number of hotel room nights used by press alone: 10,500

But 2012 came a cropper compared to 2016. According to IowaCaucus.biz, the Democrats spent a little over $20.5 million, while the Republicans spent a whopping $57,761,134 for a combined total of $72.4 million. TV ads accounted for $65 million of that.

There is a reason for all this spending: winning, or at least finishing high in the Iowa caucuses and New Hampshire primary, determines whether or not a candidate is taken seriously and can raise additional funds for the ensuing primaries. It's gotten so bad that in 2011, Connecticut Senator Chris Dodd uprooted his entire family and moved to Iowa for the final months leading up to the caucus. (Wonder how his constituents back in Connecticut appreciated that move?) Sadly for Dodd, he finished sixth and immediately dropped out of the race.

So how could we allocate primaries and caucuses to ensure a fairer and more representative system?

### The 34th Amendment -- Election Integrity

**Section 1: On the first Wednesday of October of the year preceding each Presidential election, Congress shall conduct a random drawing to determine the order and dates on which states may conduct a Presidential primary or caucus.**

**Section 2: States having twenty or more electoral votes, and those having four or fewer, shall be excluded from the first drawing. From the remaining states and jurisdictions the Parliamentarian shall draw five to conduct their primaries or caucuses on the third Tuesday of February.**

**Section 3: All remaining states and jurisdictions not yet assigned dates shall then be drawn in groups of five. The first group drawn shall conduct primaries or caucuses on the first Tuesday of March; the next on the third Tuesday of March. All subsequent groups**

**shall, in the order of their selection, conduct their respective primaries or caucuses at their discretion on the first, second or the third Tuesdays of April, May, and June as necessary.**

Currently six states have twenty or more electoral votes:

| | |
|---|---|
| California | 55 |
| New York | 29 |
| Texas | 38 |
| Florida | 29 |
| Illinois | 20 |
| Pennsylvania | 20 |

Taking these states out of the first round ensures that no candidate would be able to grab an overwhelming early lead simply by capturing two or three large states. It would also guard against an over-representation of coastal states. Twelve states have four or fewer electoral votes:

| | |
|---|---|
| Alaska | 3 |
| Delaware | 3 |
| Hawaii | 3 |
| Idaho | 4 |
| Maine | 3 |
| Montana | 3 |
| New Hampshire | 4 |
| North Dakota | 3 |
| Rhode Island | 4 |
| South Dakota | 3 |
| Vermont | 3 |
| Wyoming | 3 |

Eliminating these twelve guards against the problem we have now, of early leaders emerging based on an unrepresentative sample of the national electorate. Any five of the remaining thirty-two states would certainly represent a more accurate economic, cultural, and political cross-section of America with which to start the presidential selection process. And, although it is theoretically possible for a random drawing to come out lopsided, with too many states clustered in one region, odds are that the distribution would be reasonably widespread. Winning South Carolina and Oklahoma would give a candidate the same sixteen electoral votes as a rival candidate winning Michigan. Winning Tennessee and Oklahoma would count the same as winning Ohio.

Is this proposed new system foolproof? No. But its random nature would change the dynamics of the primary process. Not knowing which states would go first until the October prior to the election year would prevent candidates from camping out and campaigning for years in advance as they now do in Iowa and New Hampshire.

Simply changing the timing and geography of presidential elections will not be sufficient to fix the problem of how elections, especially partisan primaries, are run. Over the years, courts have concurred with the contention -- absurd as it is -- that primaries are a party function not subject to judicial interference. This is simply another case of the judiciary screwing the voters under the guise of impartiality.

How can a primary election be purely a party function when state and local officials -- collecting public office salaries -- administer the voter rolls, produce and distribute the ballots and official campaign statements, hire and train polling place staff, supply the actual voting machines, and then secure, tabulate, and certify the election results?

This *Alice In Wonderland* judicial reasoning is why, during the 2016 Democratic primary in Brooklyn, 120,000 registered voters simply vanished from the rolls on election day. Of course, the fact that Brooklyn was a hotbed of enthusiasm for Bernie Sanders -- *and* his birthplace -- had absolutely nothing to do with it. *Riiiight.*

Similar machinations took place in California where millions of people who changed their 2016 registration from Independent or Decline-to-State/No Party Preference to Democratic found out that the voter registration rolls had not been updated, and they had to cast provisional ballots. *2.4 million* provisional ballots, which took so long to count that the Secretary of State had already certified Hillary Clinton as the winner before the actual vote counting concluded.

In the 2016 Arizona Democratic primary, election officials in Maricopa County, the most populous in the state, closed 70% of the normal polling places. (Down from 200 to just 60.) If you're a career party hack, worried that a high voter turnout might help Bernie Sanders, just drop the number of polling locations and make people -- many of whom are taking time off work or are elderly -- stand in line for hours in the hot sun.

In case you think that Maricopa County officials might eventually get their act together, in 2018 they pulled off this little gem, reported by Kira Lerner for ThinkProgress.org:

### 140,000 Arizona residents weren't sent voter ID cards, official calls it a 'little hiccup'

Maricopa County officials have not sent all voters the cards they can use to cast a ballot under Arizona's voter ID law because of an issue with the company used to print the materials. The paper reports that just 60,000 ID cards have been mailed to people who recently registered or changed their registration, while about 140,000 have not been sent.

Adrian Fontes, the county recorder who oversees elections in Maricopa County, told ThinkProgress on Monday that he's not concerned with what he sees as a "little hiccup in printing."

[snip]

According to the secretary of states' office, "a county recorder must issue a voter ID card to any new registrant or an existing registrant who updates his or her name, address or political party preference."

But because of an error by the company used to print the ID cards, they have not been mailed out since December.

*Not mailed out since December.*

*For an election in late April.*

*Because of a little hiccup in printing?*

You can't make this shit up.

And it gets better.

On election day, voters were turned away from numerous polling places due to technical problems with the electronic voting machines after about 1/3 of the staffers from the voting machine vendor failed to show up to ensure that the machines were properly set up and working. At some poll locations the problems also included *failure to receive election materials*.

Not wanting to let Maricopa get all the attention, election officials in Nevada, Los Angeles, and New York City also decided to screw the voters' pooch. For Nevada's June 2018 primary, there were over 300 reported machine malfunctions, including candidates who were left off the ballot and instances where voters were confronted with the wrong slate of candidates for a particular office. Things were so bad in Clark County (home of Las Vegas, and the state's most populous county) that the state had to call another, special election to correct the problems.

In Los Angeles, county election officials managed to lose 118,000 names from the voter rolls for its June 2018 primary. Naturally, this caused an outcry from officials demanding an explanation, which so far has been that it was another "printing error," this time involving the roster of voters sent to about 35% of the precincts. In some areas, entire city blocks were omitted from the rolls.

Across the country in New York City, voters showed up to their 2018 primary election polling places only to find that they either were not listed on the voter rolls at all, or were shown with the wrong party affiliation. A few months later, in the November general election, Brooklyn firefighters had to break open the doors at one polling place when both voters and election staff showed up bright and early, only to find it locked up tight. At other sites across New York City, machines failed to work and voters had to use backup paper ballots.

Speaking of backup paper ballots, in May 2018, a Florida court ruled that the Broward County Supervisor in charge of elections, Brenda Snipes, had illegally destroyed all of the 2016 paper ballots in a case where challenger Tim Canova was contesting his loss to the reprehensible incumbent Rep. Debbie Wasserman Schultz (infamous for rigging 2016 Democratic primaries against Bernie Sanders). As Canova told the press:

> The governor has the power to dismiss Snipes from office for malfeasance and misfeasance. The judge also pointed to the supervisor's bad faith for continuing to litigate for months after admitting she destroyed the ballots, which will certainly run up the cost to taxpayers.

Reportedly, Canova's legal fees for more than a year of litigation amounted to over $200,000. But instead of firing Snipes, Florida Gov. Rick Scott simply announced that he would appoint someone to oversee future county elections. Of course, Governor Scott didn't seem concerned that, according to a story by the Times Herald Tallahassee bureau, mail-in ballots in Florida **are ten times more likely NOT to be counted than votes cast at polling places**.

In a case of irony of cosmic proportions, Scott later had to sue Snipes over her failure/refusal to turn over ballots and election records after his 2018 bid to unseat Senator Bill Nelson produced a margin so thin that a recount was ordered by the Secretary of State. To top it off, a fleet of trucks were suddenly parked at the Broward County Election Center in what appeared to be a deliberate attempt to block views into the building where vote tabulating was still apparently in progress.

Another common tactic is to make voting quick and easy in affluent areas, while poverty and minority areas are short-staffed and provided with only a few booths, which turns voting into an arduous, sometimes nearly day-long process. In places where paper ballots or provisional paper ballots are used, sometimes minority polling places get shorted on those, too.

For the November 2018 general election, officials in heavily Hispanic Dodge City went so far as to locate the city's **only** polling place **outside the city limits,** and a considerable distance from the nearest public transportation. Gives a whole new meaning to *Get Outta Dodge.*

Georgia went even farther. Locked in a tight general election battle for governor with black Democratic candidate Stacey Abrams, former Minority Leader in the Georgia House of Representatives, Secretary of State Brian Kemp -- the state's chief election officer -- tried to pressure the Randolph County elections board into "consolidating" polling stations by closing 7 of the 9 normally in use -- including one at a school where 97% of the local voters are black. That's right; Kemp wanted to leave an entire county with **two** polling places.

Public outcry and bad press forced the board to reject the proposal, but polls in other heavily black areas of the state were "consolidated." This comes after Kemp used a particularly biased "exact match" state law governing voting I.D. to purge 1.4 million voters -- over 70% minorities -- from Georgia's rolls since 2012. Almost 690,000 voters were purged from the rolls just in 2017. (Exact Match disqualifies a voter registration if anything at all varies from the voter's approved I.D. This includes things as minor as *Street* being abbreviated as *St.* It also includes instances where someone **in the Registrar of Voters office** incorrectly spells a person's name when entering it on the voter rolls!)

Kemp also prevented 53,000 people -- again, 70% of whom are minorities -- from registering or re-registering. But that wasn't enough. Early voters began to report that voting machines (which do not produce a paper ballot) were flipping votes for governor from Democrat Abrams to Kemp. And to top it off, on election night some polling places in heavily minority precincts were sent voting machines **without the special power cords required to plug them in**. (Special plug configurations help prevent tampering with machines between elections. If you can't power it up, you can't reprogram it.)

In Fulton County, Elections Director Rick Barron blamed a staff error for the fact that only three voting machines were sent to a heavily black voting location. That excuse sounded hollow from the get-go. It became absolutely ludicrous three days later when Georgia Public Broadcasting reported that 700 brand-new voting machines, still in the factory shrink-wrap, were discovered hidden in a Fulton County warehouse.

And to top things off, Georgia's electronic touch-screen voting machines do not produce a paper backup, a defect which almost caused a federal judge to make the state use paper ballots in that upcoming November election. That the judge failed to require paper ballots is both astounding and appalling, considering that only months earlier, in the May 2018 primary election, somehow the 276 registered voters in Habersham County's Mud Creek precinct managed to cast 670 ballots -- **all of which were completely unverifiable**.

On election night, Kemp appeared to win by about 66,000 votes. However, the day after the election Abrams refused to concede. Georgia law provides for a mandatory run-off election if either candidate fails to get more than 50% of the vote. Abrams indicated initially that she was banking on provisional ballots and mail-in ballots that arrived at the last minute being enough to trigger a run-off. Lacking that, in view of the blatant voter suppression that occurred, she could also challenge the results of the election in federal court. In fact, two weeks prior to the election the NAACP had already filed suit challenging the election on the basis of the machines which had been seen flipping votes. However, given the heavily conservative makeup of the federal judiciary, all the way up to and including the current Supreme Court, the chances of her or the NAACP prevailing appear to be slim. After all, why pack the judiciary if you can't count on it to steal elections?

Georgia isn't the only place where voter rolls have been purged and the reduced number of voters has been used as an excuse to "consolidate" polling places. Here's where almost 1,100 polling stations have been closed since 2012:

| | |
|---|---|
| Arizona | 212 |
| Texas | 403 |
| Louisiana | 103 |
| Mississippi | 44 |
| Alabama | 66 |
| Georgia | 214 |
| S. Carolina | 12 |
| N. Carolina | 27 |

Notice anything here? First, all of these states have substantial minority populations. Second, all except North Carolina were formerly covered by provisions of the 1965 Voting Rights Act, which required them to get prior federal approval for changes in election procedures. But thanks to the Supreme Court under John Roberts, those restrictions were abolished in 2013.

All of these examples of election manipulation or election management incompetence share one thing in common: no one ever goes to jail, gets fined, or fired for rigging an election. Apparently, all anybody involved in election theft has to do is say they're sorry and promise not to do it again. Next time your kid stays out past curfew and drives home drunk, instead of grounding them or taking away the car, just make them apologize and promise not to do it again. Fortunately, to correct election procedures and prevent future attempts to steal or manipulate election results we can always try a time-honored solution and make such activities a crime:

> **Section 4: All elections, including partisan primaries, shall be conducted completely under the control of each jurisdiction's primary election officer. Any failure to ensure a fair and impartial election, with equal access to materials, equipment, and staffing across all polling sites, or any failure to properly maintain voter rolls that results in the disenfranchisement of eligible voters, shall be a felony punishable by incarceration in a maximum security facility for a period, not subject to pardon, parole, commutation, suspension, or other reduction of sentence, of not less than ten years.**

Some will argue that while outright election manipulation should be a crime, mere incompetence should not. This is understandable, but wrong. There are many occupations where incompetence -- the failure to do your job as required -- makes the offender subject to incarceration. Ship captains are one example. Bus and truck drivers are another. So are heavy lift equipment operators. Doctors are often targets of civil malpractice suits, but they are also subject to criminal prosecution when they blatantly fail to properly discharge their obligations to patient care.

Unfortunately, even if we criminalize incompetence or discrimination by people involved in conducting elections, that won't necessarily make us safe from those who want to steal elections by other means, which in this age involves electronic manipulation. Let me be blunt:

***Electronic voting machines exist to enable election theft and vote manipulation. That the manufacture, sale, and maintenance of these machines is a profitable endeavor is merely an ancillary benefit.***

In many cases, the state or jurisdiction using a particular voting machine, or vote-tabulating scanner, is not allowed to inspect the software which operates the machine because that's a trade secret of a private, for-profit company. That's right: *public elections are conducted using private equipment which no government agency has the right to inspect to ensure that it is working properly*. In too many cases, these machines do not use any form of paper ballot and are not required to produce a paper trail as each vote is cast. ***Thus they cannot be audited for accuracy***.

Dismayed by this, voter-rights groups, computer security conferences, and university computer departments have performed demonstrations where they successfully hacked voting machines. One of these took place at the 2017 DEF CON Cybersecurity Conference in Las Vegas as Joe Uchill reported for TheHill.com: [Emphasis added.]

> ...for the first time, the conference is hosting a "Voting Machine Village," where attendees can try to hack a number of systems and help catch vulnerabilities.

> The conference acquired 30 machines for hackers to toy with. ***Every*** voting machine in the village was hacked.

The fallibility and easy manipulation of electronic voting machines is so flagrant that there have been cases where people casting votes actually saw the machine switch their vote to another candidate, right in front of their eyes. One problem with the ExpressVote machine made by Election Systems and Software involves a voter's ability to confirm their electronic vote against the paper version. If the voter hits the *Check* Your Vote button, the machine spits out the paper copy of the ballot. After confirming that the ballot is correct, the voter then hits, *Cast* Your Vote and deposits the paper ballot in the bin under the machine. Thus the electronically-recorded vote and the paper ballot match.

However, if the voter bypasses *Check* Your Vote and goes straight to *Cast* Your Vote, the paper ballot is automatically deposited in the bin *without the voter ever having a chance to look at it*. In both cases, the electronic vote and the paper ballot will match, but in the second scenario the voter has no way to know if what the machine recorded, and what the matching paper ballot show, reflect how he or she intended to vote. A single vote could be changed, or the entire ballot might have been altered. In fact, more than one line on the ballot can be altered to make the overall results look more consistent. Let's say that there is a measure on the ballot to legalize marijuana in that state. Democrats are more likely to vote "Yes" on such an issue. So, if the machine's programming is altered, either by hackers or election officials, it could change Democratic votes for the marijuana initiative to votes against it, and also alter that voter's choice for president, governor, senator, etc., from Democratic candidates to Republicans to make it seem like the same people who rejected marijuana legalization also favored Republican candidates.

Not content with merely producing corruptible voting machines, ESS has now gone a step farther and decided to remove what used to be the one most reliable safeguards for election management systems, namely that they are not connected to the internet. Unfortunately, ESS recently admitted that for six years it had installed modems, and a remote access software called *PCAnywhere,* on some of the election management systems it sold. These are not the machines at polling stations; *they're worse*: These machines are in county election officials' headquarters, and are used to either program the polling place machines and/or tabulate the votes after they are cast! But because of these modems and the imbedded *PCAnywhere* software, ESS technicians -- or hackers -- can gain remote access to all the voter data and the complete network system. In fact, the code to *PCAnywhere* was stolen by hackers in 2006, but never detected, and only made public by a hacker in 2012. It is strongly suspected by various computer experts that other voting machine manufacturers also installed some form of remote access software on their management systems, but efforts to prove so have been stonewalled.

What was it that I said before? Oh, yeah: ***You can't make this shit up.***

Perhaps the most insidious trick -- and one that is facilitated by any kind of remote access -- is fractionalized tabulation, in which a voting machine is programmed so that it takes a small percentage off each vote and gives it to a rival candidate. Take one-twentieth off twenty votes for Candidate A and you've added one more vote to Candidate B. But you've also taken one vote away from Candidate A. That changes a 50-50 contest into 51-49, but does so in a way that the total number of votes tabulated will match the number of voters who signed in at the polls. But the result is fraudulent, and ***an election has been stolen.***

When it comes to the subject of voting machine vulnerabilities and manipulation, Bev Harris at BlackBoxVoting.org is probably the reigning expert. Here she explains why fractional tabulation is so dangerous:

> A fractional voting framework is treacherous because it can be scaled to run across multiple jurisdictions very quickly. False results precisely mimic known patterns to appear plausible. In the demonstration we

performed, Smith's one-size-fits-all utility showed that a person without any programming skills at all could seize control of election results in several counties at a time, even though each county had different precincts, races, and candidates. Vendors and well-placed middlemen can alter results in multiple states.

Ms. Harris and her associates have done fantastic work ferreting out irregularities and outright election fraud all across the country, including how machines can be hacked both through the use of external devices such as USB drives, and remotely from locations far from the polling place or tabulating location.

Fortunately, there is a simple cure for virtually all types of election fraud:

**Section 5: All elections shall be conducted using hand-marked paper ballots which shall be deposited in transparent ballot boxes which are under constant public observation and constant recorded electronic surveillance. All ballots shall be hand-counted in public at the location where cast, and the results shall be announced to the public and disseminated via live media before said ballots are moved to any other location. All ballots shall be maintained under security by the chief election official of that state or jurisdiction for a period of five years. Any violation hereof shall be a felony punishable by incarceration in a maximum security facility for a period, not subject to pardon, parole, commutation, suspension, or other reduction of sentence, of not less than ten years.**

If we want fair and credible elections, this is how to do it. Paper ballots, tabulated where they are cast, in full public view and reported to the media, before those ballots get a chance to magically disappear out of the back of a police cruiser on their way to the County Clerk's office. And keep them long enough that any appeal of the results, or any prosecution for violation of election laws, can be safely completed.

Mail-in ballots present their own set of problems. In Florida, the 2018 general election for both the U.S. Senate and for the governor's office produced razor-thin margins, and yet another Florida recount battle looms. (Can you say, *Bush v. Gore 2.0*?) Vote counting in Broward County appears particularly suspect, and at least one news outlet has published a photo of bins of mail-in ballots still sitting in a Post Office processing center three days after the election. Initially, it has not been determined if these ballots were received after the deadline, and the question is further muddled by the fact that this particular facility was temporarily closed after a number of pipe bombs passed through it on their way to CNN and various Democratic officials.

There is also the problem of excessive disqualifications, such as the situation in Florida where things have gotten so bad that Patrick Murphy, who represented Palm Beach county's 18th Congressional district for four years, had his 2018 mail-in ballot disqualified over a "signature mismatch."

If mail-in ballots must be permitted, then they must be handled, by specially-trained and bonded USPS personnel, as they come in, and then deposited in transparent ballot boxes in public view, under constant video monitoring throughout the process. Why do these employees have to be specially trained? And why can't the post office's machines do the sorting? Because those machines, and regular post office personnel, simply can't be counted on to do the job accurately. Three days after the 2018 general election, the American Reformers website published a photograph they had received from a voter of their mail-in ballot -- which had been returned as undeliverable by the Post Office -- even though it was in the ***official pre-printed return envelope provided by*** *the state*. And what state would that be? Did you say, Georgia? *Give that man a cigar.*

Not only must mail-in ballots be handled with special care, the total number of ballots received each day must be published daily, along with the names of the voters who sent them in. Then, on election night, those ballots need to be counted right there, in public, under the watchful eye of the camera and recording devices.

Hand-marked paper ballots, counted by hand at each polling place, were used in Britain for the historic referendum on whether or not to leave the European Union. Over 33 million votes were cast, counted, and reported by the end of the night. If the British can do it, so can we.

Having elections which produce valid and verifiable results is beneficial only if we ensure that only eligible voters -- meaning *citizens* -- are allowed to vote. Sadly, this is not always the case. Since the Constitution leaves determination of voter eligibility up to the states, some have begun to permit non-citizens (legal resident aliens, non-citizen property owners, etc.) to participate in local elections. San Francisco and ten cities in Maryland are in this group. The latest example of this lunacy comes courtesy of Boston. In July 2018, The Hill headlined a story:

### *Officials in Boston are considering allowing non-citizens to vote in local elections*

Even worse is California legislature's Motor Voter legislation, which automatically registers those 18 years of age to vote when they get their license. The defenders of this program argue that the DMV verifies citizenship and voter eligibility before registering license recipients. Except, as it turns out, *that's not true*. This should not come as a surprise, given that in California the DMV is a subject of scorn, a model of bureaucratic inefficiency. The California DMV has been forced to add Saturday hours in an effort to cut down wait times which often reach *seven* hours in line. Maybe these delays are caused by things like people sleeping on the job; one employee slept at her desk for at least three hours a day *for four fucking years*, racking up 2,000 hours of accumulated nap time at a salary cost of $40,000.

Seven hours in line, employees napping on the clock, overtime up over 200% from previous years, but state officials are still *absolutely sure* that citizenship is being rigorously verified? In August 2018, a study by the Public Interest Legal Foundation (PILF) documented 3,120 instances of non-citizens being registered to vote in 13 "sanctuary" cities around California. Proving that this is not a recent phenomenon, one of the illegal voters originally registered in 1998, and voted in ten elections. A month later, it was revealed that the DMV had mistakenly registered at least 23,000 people *under the wrong political party affiliation*.

A month after that the DMV, California's vigilant defender of our sacred right to vote, revealed that it had somehow improperly registered 1,500 "non-citizens" to vote. Of course, the DMV spokesman assured us that none of those affected were illegal immigrants. Really? We're supposed to take their word for it? The L.A. Times doesn't think that's good enough. On October 11, 2018, it ran an editorial calling for the California Motor Voter program to immediately be suspended until its accuracy could be ascertained, and any needed modifications put in place. Because, after all:

*What aspect of citizenship is more sacred than the right to vote?*

I find it a massive example of cognitive dissonance that those who advocate for expanding the rights of non-citizens are often the very same people who decry global rule by corporate elites which is, by its very nature, supra-national and respects neither borders nor citizenship. The right to vote is what ultimately separates citizens from non-citizens, and thus must be sacred. You can bet that allowing non-citizen legal residents to vote in local elections is the camel's nose under the tent. Supporters of illegal immigration (a topic addressed in Chapter 15: Sovereign Security), have begun to push even further, clamoring for the most precious right of citizenship -- the right to vote -- to be extended to **illegal aliens**. This cannot be allowed to happen:

> **Section 6: No person not a citizen of these United States, or its territories or possessions, shall be eligible or allowed to vote in any election. Any legislation, regulation, practice, custom, or court ruling which is, or may be, contrary to this principle, including those attendant to the process of voter registration, is hereby null and void. Any non-citizen who votes shall be guilty of a felony punishable by incarceration in a maximum security facility for a period, not subject to pardon, parole, commutation, suspension, or other reduction of sentence, of not less than five years, followed by deportation.**

> **Section 7: Any person charged with responsibility for the enforcement of election laws who fails to act diligently to prevent voting by non-citizens, or who in any way facilitates such illegal voting, shall be guilty of a felony punishable by incarceration in a maximum security facility for a period, not subject to pardon, parole, commutation, suspension, or other reduction of sentence, of not less than five years.**

In discussing voting security it is important to distinguish between *election* fraud, which is the stealing of elections by means such as electronic tampering or voter suppression, and *voter* fraud, which is voting by those not eligible to do so. (Illegals, disenfranchised felons, and of course, the good old Chicago favorite, dead people. The dirty ward politics of Chicago long ago gave birth to the saying, "Vote early. And vote often.")

The Republicans are masters at election fraud, in all its various forms. One tactic, called caging, is to purge voter rolls by sending out first-class postcards to voters in heavily Democratic precincts. If any postcard is returned as undeliverable, or if a person fails to return the tear-off portion to confirm that they still reside at that address, then that person is assumed to have moved or died, and their name can be stricken from the rolls. This tactic assumes that no one ever misses their postcard, never has it accidentally caught up in the folds of all the junk advertising pieces that contaminate the average mailbox on a daily basis. It also ignores studies that show that certain categories of people -- the elderly, minorities, students -- tend to respond less often to things that are mailed to them.

Most importantly, caging assumes that the Post Office never screws up. As someone with nearly three decades of direct mail experience, who has sent out millions of pieces, I can tell you for a fact that the post office does screw up. (Surprise, I know.) In fact, on one occasion I had a brochure -- part of a mass mailing for a client -- addressed to my home (as a way to track Post Office delivery time on the mailing) come back to my office return address with a notation that I was *No longer at this address*. Certainly came as a surprise to me, my neighbors, my dog, etc.

Another tactic is to use a particularly evil invention of former Kansas Secretary of State Kris Kobach, perhaps the most malignant and unrepentant advocate of voter suppression currently drawing air on the planet. This is a software program officially titled the Interstate Voter Registration Crosscheck Program, or more commonly, Crosscheck. This program purports to compare voter registration data from multiple states and process out duplicates so that people who have moved cannot vote twice, or vote in jurisdictions where they no longer live. The idea sounds reasonable, but the devil, as always, is in the details. The program is deliberately designed to use the most primitive and inaccurate matching criteria. For instance, it does not differentiate according to middle names or initials. Thus, like in *Saving Private Ryan*, James Francis Ryan of Iowa, is not the same as James Albert Ryan of Pennsylvania, but both can end up purged from the rolls in their respective states. Same problem with generation identifiers like Sr., Jr., or III, all of which are ignored by the program.

Of course, it's not the Ryans of the world that are most likely to be targeted and victimized. That distinction belongs to minorities. Care to take a wild guess at what the racial breakdown is of people with the last name Washington? Any idea how many Garcia's there are in America? Try 858,000. Not surprisingly, this led to absurdities such as in 2014, when a whopping 342,556 people were allegedly registered to vote both in Virginia and some other state. Use of this deliberately flawed and anti-democratic software program has undoubtedly caused millions of voters in over a dozen states to be illegally and unfairly tossed off the rolls. Most were minorities. How do we know? Because racial information on individual voters by address can be obtained from census records, Crosscheck conveniently ***includes the race of the voter***, right there on the spreadsheet. In fact, anyone with a mind to do so can sort all of the *allegedly* duplicate names by race, and then only delete those who are non-white. Like I said, *convenient.*

Unlike the unfortunate Stacey Adams in Georgia, the Gods of Karma intervened against Kobach in the 2018 Kansas general election. Despite all the voter caging and other dirty tricks, he lost his bid to become governor to Democrat Laura Kelly.

The Democrats, on the other hand, love to decry election fraud -- and rightfully so, because they are usually on the receiving end --

but claim that voter fraud, previous examples notwithstanding (and generally not acknowledged) -- doesn't happen. Of course, as Steve Salvi, founder of the Ohio Jobs and Justice PAC noted, "If you don't look for it, you're not gonna find it." Fortunately, some people do look for it. The Heritage Foundation, perhaps the most prominent conservative think tank, has a voter fraud database of over 1,000 convictions for individual voter fraud. These cases include everything from buying votes to illegally submitting stolen vote-by-mail ballots. Just a few days before the 2018 mid-term elections, KCBS-TV in Los Angeles ran a story showing that 265 people were still on the rolls and had somehow managed to cast ballots even after they had been dead for up to 26 years. One person died in 1988, voted in 2014. And what made this possible? Mail-in voting. Seems that officials in multiple counties aren't very diligent about checking the signature on the mail-in envelope against the voter registration form on file. ***Who could have guessed?!***

Conservatives love to use the specter of voter fraud as a reason to pass laws which require proof of citizenship or identity in order to vote. Behind the ostensible goal of preventing fraud lurks the real intent of these laws: to disadvantage the elderly, minorities, and students. The elderly and minorities often have difficulty acquiring the necessary birth certificate in order to prove citizenship. College students, who tend to be generally more liberal in their attitudes toward social issues that can drive voter turnout, often have a different residence address every year. In many states they are also permitted to keep their home state driver's license. So, if you live in a dorm or a frat house, and/or your mail comes to a campus mailbox, plus you only have an out-of-state driver's license, you can have trouble either registering or actually casting a vote. Some states have even gone to the extreme of closing DMV offices in minority areas, or near colleges, just to make it harder to obtain vote-valid I.D.

If people have to present a photo I.D. for everything from buying cigarettes or alcohol to opening a bank account or boarding a plane, it is pretty hard to construct a rational argument against requiring the same kind of identification to vote. (Progressive author and media personality Thom Hartman has noted that one seldom-discussed reason many conservatives oppose universal single-payer healthcare is that in Canada, the most recommended and accepted vote-valid I.D. is a person's national healthcare card.) So, if conservatives are really concerned about protecting the right to vote they will have no problem embracing:

**Section 8: All states and lesser jurisdictions thereof shall ensure that every person eligible to vote has free and convenient access to any documentation necessary to prove citizenship. Any person responsible for implementation of voter identification documentation who fails to discharge those duties with the greatest possible diligence shall be guilty of a felony punishable by incarceration in a maximum security facility for a period, not subject to pardon, parole, commutation, suspension, or other reduction of sentence, of not less than five years.**

Section 8 is necessary to ensure that voter I.D. requirements are not used as a strategy to exclude the poor, elderly, minorities, and students from obtaining the documents necessary to exercise their voting rights. American elections are already often way too close. If anyone doubts how close, consider these numbers: 537, 8, and 0.

- 537 is the number of votes that gave Florida, and presidency, to Bush in the 2000 election.

- 8 is the number of votes by which a local ballot measure in my community passed.

- 0 is the number of votes which separated state legislative candidates in Virginia (1971 and 2017), Rhode Island (1978), Massachusetts (1988, 1990 and 2010), Wyoming (1994), South Dakota (1996), and Alaska (2006). In these cases, methods employed to break the tie ranged from calling special elections to conducting a random drawing. (I kid you not, a random drawing determined control of the 2017 Virginia House of Delegates.)

We can also go one step further and make presidential election days a national holiday.

**Section 9: All presidential general elections shall be a national holiday. Government agencies (other than those engaged in public safety or election management) and private companies who cannot suspend operations for the entire day shall give all employees a minimum of four hours paid leave in which to vote. Public safety employees shall be given a minimum of two hours paid leave, and shall have priority at their appropriate polling place.**

# Chapter 10

# FAIR APPORTIONMENT

It's no secret that Congress is now held in contempt by most Americans. A December 2012 CBS/New York Times poll put Congress' approval rating at 9%. A year later, in November 2013, it was still either 9% (according to Gallup) or had fallen to 6% (a poll by The Economist and the online opinion research firm YouGov.com). Even after a modest uptick to 13% in early 2014, dissatisfaction was still spread evenly across the board: only 17% of Republicans, 11% of independents, and 14% of Democratic voters approved of the job Congress was doing. In 2018, things have not improved. According to a January NPR/PBS News Hour poll conducted by Marist, only 9% of Americans have a great deal of confidence in Congress. Congress, as a whole, ranked lower than both major political parties. (But not by a lot, since both parties were in the bottom four institutions surveyed.)

Low approval ratings for Congress are nothing new. It was only 22% back in 1994. And since then, even when one party has controlled both houses of Congress, *only a minority of that party's members* have approved of the job Congress was doing.

There was, up until recently, a disconnect between Congress' overall approval rating and the rating most voters gave their individual representative or Senator. While increasing numbers of voters expressed dissatisfaction with Congress (and by inference the performance of government in general) they approved of the job their individual Congress-critter was doing. That is no longer always the case. According to a 2014 Rasmussen Reports poll, only 25% of voters thought that *their own representative* in the House deserved re-election. Even fewer, just 20%, thought their current rep was the best person for the job. The lack of respect for Congress and politicians in many states is now so low that it would be laughable, if the situation the country finds itself in wasn't so dire.

The fact that members of Congress who are not well liked in their own districts can still get re-elected is easily explained. Every ten years, after the most recent census, Congressional districts are re-aligned according to changes in state populations. Some states gain a seat or two, while others lose one or two. With few exceptions, the redrawing of Congressional districts is done by state legislatures and involves redrawing state legislative districts as well. Obviously, these legislators have a deep, vested interest in protecting their own reelection prospects, and ensuring that their party holds as many seats as possible. Aside from the federal goodies that their party brethren may channel down from D.C., many of today's state legislators often have their eye on being the next Congressperson when the reigning incumbent from their area leaves office.

This has led to gerrymandering, drawing district lines to tilt the number of voters in any one district toward one party or the other. Depending on differing historical accounts, the term was coined in either 1811 or 1812, when the Massachusetts legislature, which the Democrats controlled, drew grotesquely misshapen new districts in order to improve their prospects against the Federalist party in the next Congressional election. The *gerry* part refers to then-Governor Elbridge Gerry, and *mander* derives from the perceived resemblance of one district to a salamander. The effort was a resounding success. As the website flaglerlive.com notes:

> The Democratic party carried everything before them
> at the following election, and filled every office in the
> State, although it appeared by the votes returned that
> nearly two-thirds of the voters were Federalists.

Although it didn't have a formal name until then, the practice may pre-date even our first Congress. Some historians believe (and many Founding Fathers claimed at the time), that prior to the first Congressional election of 1789, when the newly independent former colonies were still operating under the Articles of Confederation, Patrick Henry conspired to place James Madison in an oddly-shaped Virginia district to ensure that Madison lost to Henry's political ally, James Monroe. (The history of this rivalry involves differences between Thomas Jefferson and his supporters versus the ascendant Federalists led by Monroe, Henry, and Alexander Hamilton.) In fairness to Henry, other scholars argue that the district was not improperly drawn, with all counties within the same natural geographic cluster. At any rate, it did not seem to matter, as Madison ran a superior campaign and defeated Monroe in the only congressional election in American history where future presidents ran against each other. Regardless of the outcome of that election, the idea of deliberately drawing biased and distorted districts was clearly present in the minds of politicians, and it only took two decades for the tactic to have an official title.

Jon Walker, writing for the now defunct (but still beloved by many former readers) website FireDogLake.com, summed up gerrymandering as, "Instead of voters choosing their elected officials, our democracy is often decided by elected officials choosing who their voters will be." That process comes in various forms known as packing, cracking, and mutual benefit, or incumbent protection. In packing, voters with a history of backing one party are herded into a single district, making surrounding districts easier pickings for the rival party. In cracking, densely concentrated voters from one party are split into minority enclaves spread over adjoining districts. Under the mutual benefit method, a party without a large enough majority to completely control the redistricting process simply makes a deal with their rival party to protect incumbent districts, regardless of the officeholder's party affiliation.

This happened in California after the 2000 census gave the state one new seat, which was created by combining some of Congressman Gary Condit's existing district with portions of surrounding districts. Condit was extremely unpopular at the time due to his involvement in an extra-marital affair with Chandra Levy, a government intern who disappeared and was later found murdered. Sure enough, Condit (later cleared of involvement in Levy's murder) lost his reelection bid. However, in 2004, with 120 seats in the state legislature and 53 Congressional district seats at stake, ***in not one case*** did the party affiliation of the winning candidate change.

Gerrymandering distorts the political will of voters across the state, and wastes votes. Republican voters in a district where they are over-represented waste their votes because victory by their candidate is virtually pre-ordained. The same for Democrats in districts where their party constitutes a disproportional percentage of voters. As Wikipedia notes: [Emphasis added.]

> Because gerrymandering can be designed to increase the number of wasted votes among the electorate, the relative representation of particular groups can be drastically altered from their actual share of the voting population. This effect can significantly prevent a gerrymandered system from achieving proportional and descriptive representation as the winners of elections are increasingly determined by who is drawing the districts rather than the preferences of the voters.
>
> Gerrymandering may be advocated to improve representation within the legislature among otherwise underrepresented minority groups by packing them into a single district. This can be controversial, as it

may lead to those groups' remaining marginalised [sic] in the government as they become confined to a single district. Candidates outside that district no longer need to represent them to win elections.

As an example, much of the redistricting conducted in the United States in the early 1990s involved the intentional creation of additional "majority-minority" districts where racial minorities such as African Americans were packed into the majority. This "maximization policy" drew support by both the Republican Party (who had limited support among African Americans and could concentrate their power elsewhere) and by minority representatives elected as Democrats from these constituencies, who then had safe seats.

The 2012 election provides a number of examples as to how partisan gerrymandering can adversely affect the descriptive function of states' congressional delegations. In Pennsylvania, for example, Democratic candidates for the House of Representatives received 83,000 more votes than Republican candidates, yet the Republican-controlled redistricting process in 2010 resulted in Democrats losing to their Republican counterparts in 13 out of Pennsylvania's 18 districts.

In the seven states where Republicans had complete control over the redistricting process, Republican House candidates received 16.7 million votes and Democratic House candidates received 16.4 million votes. The redistricting resulted in Republican victories in 73 out of the 107 affected seats; in those 7 states, Republicans received 50.4% of the votes but won in over 68% of the congressional districts. While it is but one example of how gerrymandering can have a significant impact on election outcomes, *this kind of disproportional representation of the public will seems to be problematic for the legitimacy of democratic systems*, regardless of one's political affiliation.

***Problematic for the legitimacy of democratic systems.***
Really? You think?

In some cases, major sections of grotesquely-shaped districts are connected only by narrow strips of land that may not even have a single resident. A freeway or railroad right-of-way is a favorite, as are industrial areas where the only "resident" might be a security guard or night watchman. The Illinois 4th District is a notorious example.

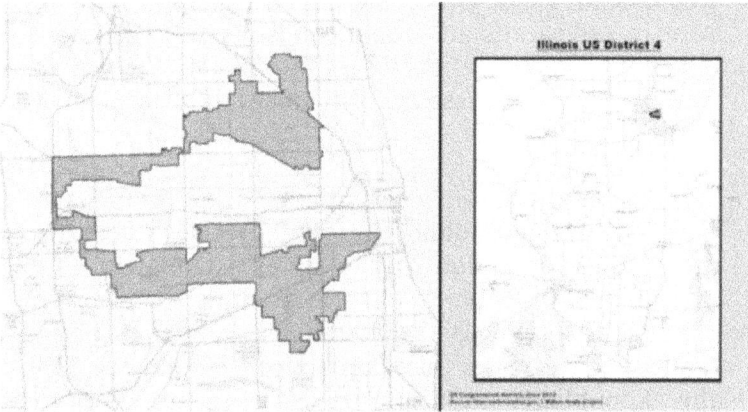

Illinois CD-1 is also a doozy:

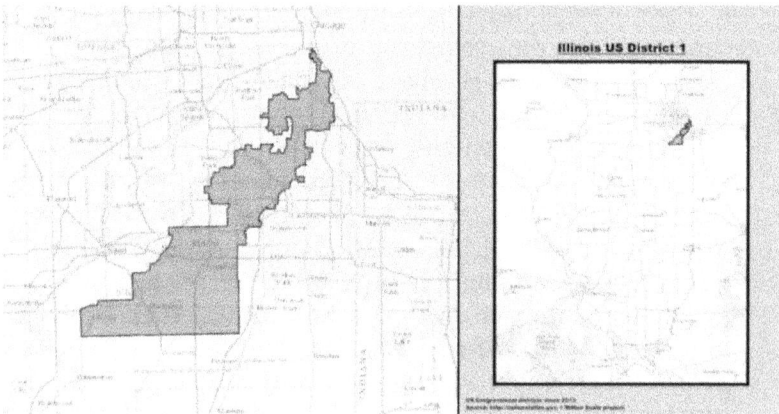

And here's the current South Carolina CD-1:

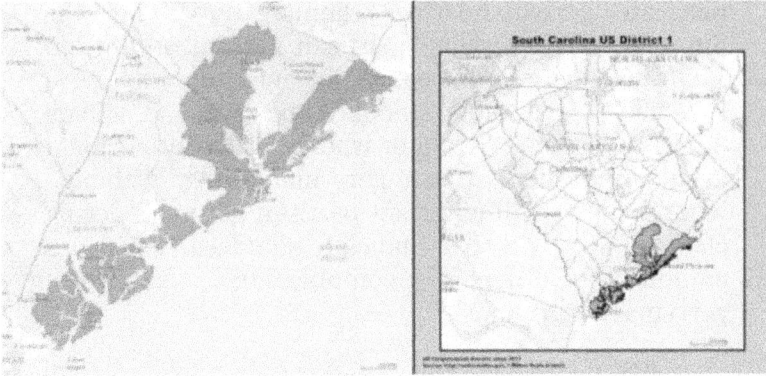

*Images courtesy of Wikipedia*

Look closely and you can see that SC-1 includes areas that are not contiguous with each other. This is only one example of the absurdities involved in gerrymandering. In some cases, prison inmates are counted in order to make the number of residents in each district appear equal enough to avoid a court challenge. This is a complete sham because, aside from the fact that they don't really reside in the district, they are *ineligible to vote*, which further distorts the votes of those who can legally cast a ballot.

As Whitney Eaton noted in 2006 in the University of Richmond Law Journal *Where Do We Draw The Line? Partisan Gerrymandering and the State of Texas* (40 U. Rich. L. Rev. 1193):

> During most of the two-hundred-year history of gerrymandering, federal courts steadfastly refused to police partisan gerrymandering because drawing electoral districts was considered the province of the legislative branch under the United States Constitution and, therefore, beyond the reach of the federal courts. Finally, in 1986, the Supreme Court of the United States entered the arena in *Davis v. Bandemer*, holding that political gerrymandering claims are justiciable. Since that decision, the Supreme

Court and the federal courts have grappled with finding a judicially manageable standard to adjudicate partisan gerrymandering claims. In 2004, the Supreme Court revisited partisan gerrymandering in *Vieth v. Jubelirer* but could not agree on whether a judicially manageable standard exists to adjudicate partisan gerrymandering or whether the courts should even adjudicate partisan gerrymandering. Although federal courts still entertain partisan gerrymandering claims, no workable judicial standard exists to adjudicate them, complicating successful gerrymandering suits.

What successful gerrymandering suits? Even after the Supreme Court's 1986 ruling that suits challenging gerrymandered districts could be heard, the tests which courts have imposed for evaluating the merits of gerrymander suits are stiff, not to mention confusing, contradictory, or at odds with essential American concepts of fairness. For instance, "severe" gerrymandering is illegal, but lesser forms that still confer significant partisan advantage are not. Dissenting from this view, Justices Lewis Powell and John Paul Stevens wrote:

> ...district lines should be determined in accordance with neutral and legitimate criteria. When deciding where those lines will fall, the State should treat its voters as standing in the same position, regardless of their political beliefs or party affiliation.

But despite their reasoning, the court held:

> The Equal Protection Clause does not supply judicially manageable standards for resolving purely political gerrymandering claims, and no group right to an equal share of political power was ever intended by the Framers of the Fourteenth Amendment.

Only judges from the best law schools, sitting on the highest court in the land, could argue with a straight face that the Equal Protection Clause -- which, under the legal doctrine of rational basis, "prohibits government use of power solely to augment the influence of those with a favored political agenda at the expense of those who disagree with them" -- does not mean that everyone should have equal protection, or that groups of voters (which is what parties are) should not have political power equal to other groups of the same size. As Justice Breyer noted in his dissent from the 2004 *Vieth* case:

> The use of purely political considerations in drawing district boundaries is not a "necessary evil" that, for lack of judicially manageable standards, the Constitution inevitably must tolerate ... Sometimes purely political 'gerrymandering' will fail to advance any plausible democratic objective while simultaneously threatening serious democratic harm.

As recently as June 2018, SCOTUS demonstrated once again how its members will go to absurd lengths to avoid ruling on gerrymander suits. In this instance, it remanded a Wisconsin case because the Democratic party plaintiffs had brought suit alleging that all districts statewide had been gerrymandered. SCOTUS ruled that they should have filed suit separately for each district being challenged. A nice technical way to dodge the substantive issues, and force plaintiffs into many more years of effort and expense as they start again from ground zero. Then, just a few weeks after punting on the Wisconsin suit, SCOTUS overturned lower court rulings and *reinstated* blatantly gerrymandered districts in Texas. Let's hear it one more time for the law schools of Harvard and Yale. Because of the unwillingness of the Supreme Court to establish clear principles and definitions of what constitutes illegal gerrymandering, successful gerrymander suits have been few and far between.

Voters in Michigan, frustrated by adverse court rulings, took matters into their own hands. Over 425,000 of them signed an initiative petition to outlaw gerrymandering on the November 2018 ballot. The state chamber of commerce -- a "dark money" group that does not have to disclose its donors -- tried to block the measure from appearing on the ballot. Supporters of the measure, Represent.us, responded with a brilliant and intense lobbying campaign, which included outing eleven donors to the lawsuit, among them the head of the committee, Chamber Chair Mark Davidoff, a Managing Director at the Deloitte accounting firm. Not surprisingly, Deloitte has $400 million in contracts with the state. The public pressure paid off, as the Michigan Supreme Court rejected the suit and then the voters approved the measure resoundingly. Similar anti-gerrymandering ballot measures passed in Colorado, Missouri, and Utah, joining one passed by Ohio voters in the June 2018 primary election. All were backed or supported by Represent.us

On the other end of the spectrum, there's North Carolina, where a successful lawsuit against gerrymandered districts turned out to be a Pyrrhic victory. By the time the suit wound its way through the state court appeals process, there wasn't enough time to implement the court-ordered changes before the November 2018 election. Now that Brett Kavanaugh is on the U.S. Supreme Court, an appeal of the suit at the federal level is virtually certain to be heard, and then overturned. Meanwhile, using the old district boundaries, Democrats in North Carolina racked up 1,771,061 votes but won only 3 Congressional seats. The GOP garnered only 74,980 more votes but captured 9 seats.

We can no longer allow this kind of disenfranchisement of voters, this disparity in how much votes are worth in varying states and districts. Nor can we depend on the success of ballot measures to solve the problem. We must have national constitutional reform to abolish the practice in all states, not just those which currently enjoy the benefits of citizen-led initiatives.

With so many gerrymandered districts having an artificially higher number of voters who identify with one party, naturally a majority of the residents of those districts were likely to approve the job their rep performed. However, now even this has changed. Results of a poll by Rasmussen released in June 2014, headlined:

### New Low: Only 25% Think Their Member of Congress Deserves Reelection

That same report notes:

> Sixty-nine percent (69%) think most members of Congress don't care what their constituents think ... Fifty-three percent (53%) say their [own] representative doesn't care what they think...

Why do so many voters believe that *their* representative (much less Congress as a whole) doesn't care what they think? *Because it's true*. Congress members only care what their major donors and party leaders want. Donors provide the majority of funds needed to win re-election, and are the gateway to cushy jobs in the private sector once a member leaves Congress. Party leaders wield enormous power not only because they determine crucial committee assignments, but because they also decide on which races to focus the party's financial and manpower resources.

Although the influence of money, both directly and filtered through the party bureaucracy, has long been known, two political science graduate students, Joshua Kalla of Yale and David Brockman at the University of California Berkeley, set out during the Congressional summer recess of 2013 to prove the theory with a novel experiment. They organized a group of volunteers to send emails to almost 200 members of Congress, asking for a meeting to discuss a particular bill banning certain dangerous chemicals which was pending in the House. One email simply asked for a meeting; the other identified the person as an "active political donor." As Aaron Sankin reported in TheDailyDot.com:

> Unsurprisingly, saying that the meetings were with donors made a huge difference.

When congressional schedulers were told that meetings were with constituents, CREDO members were able to meet with members of Congress or their chiefs of staff a mere 2.4 percent of the time. When they were identified as past donors, those meetings occurred 12.5 percent of the time.

That is a 429 percent increase in someone's ability to get face time with a lawmaker's top staffers if they approached in the context of having given money in the past. Put another way, members of Congress themselves were three times more likely to meet with people identified as donors than regular constituents. Similarly, people who want to meet with their representative in Congress have a 231% greater chance if they've donated.

As the Washington Post noted, because the office staff didn't know if the donor had previously donated to that particular congressperson, "the study may actually underestimate the access of political donors."

In short, Congress members and key staff don't even need to know a person's previous history as a donor, only that they have shown a willingness to open their checkbook. Elected officials at the federal and state level are like teenage boys, who will tell girls anything to get them into bed. At election time, when these politicians proclaim how much they love and respect you, what they really want is to get you to mark the box next to their name. The next morning, and from then until the next election cycle, they see no reason to take your call.

The combination of gerrymandered districts and private campaign financing allows this distortion of democracy to flourish. The claim that, "no workable judicial standard exists to adjudicate," partisan gerrymandered redistricting plans is absurd. *We the people* can break the stranglehold the parties have over those who hold elected office, which the parties control through the redistricting process. We can, and must, take the drawing of districts out of the hands of judges and politicians from both parties by entrusting it to properly designed computer programs. Computers are already used to draw districts, the only difference being that party affiliation and previous voting patterns are currently the priority parameter inputs.

### The 35th Amendment -- Fair Apportionment

**Upon completion of the first census after ratification of this Amendment, and continuing with each census or other redistricting thereafter, all federal, state, and local election districts shall be drawn by a computer, or other automated program, that utilizes, to the maximum degree possible with the technology available at the time, features of terrain and geography, whether natural or man-made, and the existing boundaries of parks, educational institutions, penal or military facilities, and subordinate political jurisdictions to minimize odd-shaped districts. Technologies employed to create election districts shall not consider the race, ethnic origin, or political party affiliation of any voter, and shall draw the most compact districts possible.**

One method of using computers to draw compact fair district boundaries, known as the Shortest Splitline Algorithm (SSA), has been proposed by the Center for Range Voting. As Wikipedia explains: "The algorithm uses only the shape of the state, the number N of districts wanted, and the population distribution as inputs." It includes tie-breaking criteria when the initial result is impractical, such as when a district boundary bisects a residence. Arguments against the SSA include the fact that, because it does not take into account existing political boundaries, cultural clusters, or geographic features, the method can arbitrarily separate communities with common interests, and thus can be even less fair and representative than districts drawn by (allegedly) unbiased humans. In addition, if political or racial/ethnic minorities are not concentrated in clusters, the SSA will fail to create "majority-minority" districts, which have come into favor over the past several decades as a mechanism to correct previous under-representation by those groups.

This, of course, begs the question as to whether or not we still need such specially designed districts. While the U.S. Senate remains a bastion of white power and privilege, minorities are increasingly well-represented in other offices that are not elected by district, including big city mayors and governorships. And it is inherently racist to argue that quality minority candidates in fairly drawn districts can't win election. After all, Barack Obama won the world's most important elective office in a race where the country amounted to one gigantic district.

Another method for creating computer-generated district boundaries is the Minimum District to Convex Polygon Ratio (MDCP Ratio), which has been described as wrapping a rubber band around the smallest possible area sufficient to create the proposed district. A big advantage of this method is that it permits easier use of existing irregular borders, such as county or municipal boundaries, housing developments, and even voting precincts. In addition, because it includes geographic features in its design criteria, it can be argued that the MDCP Ratio method does a better job of drawing districts along bodies of water. However, because MDCP Ratio districts can be adjusted by human input, it merely reduces, but does not eliminate, the temptation to gerrymander.

An interesting byproduct of using computers to design unbiased district configurations is the Public Mapping Project created by Professors Micah Altman of Harvard and Michael McDonald of George Mason, together with Norm Ornstein of the American Enterprise Institute. As the website socialcapital.com explains, a handful of states and the city of Philadelphia have used software developed by the Public Mapping Project to hold competitions, where citizens and groups can create their own redistricting maps for comparison with those from official bodies, whether the state legislature or some form of nominally non-partisan state commission.

Rather than let humans interfere with the MDCP Ratio method, why not create a computer program that ignores party affiliation, previous voting history, and other forms of data mining, but also takes into consideration, to the maximum extent practical, major natural and manmade geographic features to determine district boundaries? Highways, freeways, major streets, park or school boundaries, as well as the borders of cities, counties, military bases, and even golf courses or country clubs, can all easily be used in conjunction with rivers, lakes, and coastlines to draw fair districts that do not favor or discriminate against voters from any party.

One way to test the validity of such a program is to create four different versions, one starting at each of the farthest north, south, east, and west compass point of the state, then compare the differences in the makeup of the districts. It should certainly be possible to design a program so that none of the four versions varied by more than a set percentage, say 5%. A further way to ensure fairness would be to allow each state to write into its constitution a provision wherein, after every census, the new redistricting map is drawn starting at a different corner of the state. For example, the first time it's the northeastern-most compass point. Ten years later it switches to the southwestern-most. Then to the southeastern most, and finally the northwestern.

A fairly drawn district should elect officials who accurately reflect the will and wishes of its residents. This benefits both the local voters and the nation at large. When candidates must appeal to a wider diversity of political opinion (not to mention differences in economic conditions within a district), they need to be less dogmatic and less highly partisan. Much of the gridlock that now strangles Washington is that too many members of Congress need only retain the support of the most radically hyper-partisan party faithful who dominate primary turnout. In fact, many districts are so gerrymandered that the opposition party simply fails to field a candidate, and the winner of the primary goes straight to, *or back to*, Congress. The only people who should fear fair redistricting are the politicians who benefit, at the expense of the public, from the current corrupt system.

# Chapter 11

# PARTICIPATORY DEMOCRACY

It's always convenient when Wikipedia provides the perfect introduction to a subject, in this case direct democracy and the first Progressive movement:

> Fired by the efforts of millions of farmers, exposes written by investigative journalists (the famous muckrakers), and correlations between special interests' abuses of farmers and special interests' abuses of urban workers, Progressives formed nationally connected citizen organizations to extend this democracy movement. From 1898 to 1918, the Progressives, supported by tens of millions of citizens, forced direct democracy petition components into the constitutions of twenty-six states.

> The constitutional placement of direct democracy petition components was seen by those citizen majorities as necessary. Given the obvious corruption in state governments, the lack of sovereign public control over the output of state legislatures was seen as "the fundamental defect" in the nation's legislative machinery. Advocates insisted that the only way to make the founding fathers' vision work was to take the "misrepresentation" out of representative government with the sovereign people's direct legislation.

[snip]

Initiative and referendum (I&R) citizen lawmaking spread across the United States because state legislatures were unresponsive in creating laws that the people needed to protect themselves from lobby groups, laissez-faire economics, and the era's robber barons. Additionally, while legislatures were quick to pass laws benefitting special interests, both legislatures and the courts were inflexible in their refusals to amend, repeal or adjudicate those laws in ways that would eliminate special interest advantages and end abuses of the majority.

Hmm, let's see:

Lobbyists corrupting government at every level.

Laws and courts that favor corporations and laissez-faire economics over people.

Robber barons.

Sound familiar? It's exactly the situation we face today, and part of the solution is the same now as it was then: expanding the right of the initiative, referendum, and recall to every state and subdivision thereof.

Initiatives and referenda have been responsible for many major advancements in democracy. In 1914, Colorado Senator John Shafroth proposed a constitutional amendment to give the people in every state the right to use the initiative process to put a women's suffrage measure on the ballot. Although his proposal did not pass, it helped highlight the cause of women's suffrage, achieved five years later with passage of the 19th Amendment.

Another efficient early use of the initiative process occurred in 1934, when the citizens of Nebraska replaced their 133-member bicameral legislature with a unicameral one having only 43 members. As Wikipedia notes:

It reduced cost, waste, secrecy and time (no conference committee required), while at the same time making the legislature more efficient and more cooperative with the press and civil society. The success of combining direct democracy governance components with a unicameral legislature has stood the test of time.

At the federal level, a Congress with two houses is necessary to protect small states from being bulldozed by larger ones. This might also be true for states that have large cities combined with vast, sparsely populated areas. But for many states, a unicameral legislature would be a vast improvement on their current legislative mess. Imagine the money saved by eliminating an entire house of elected officials and their staffs. Imagine how many fewer people would have a career in the Professional Political Class. Think about all the times when members of one house cast phony symbolic votes for measures they don't really support, but they know will never pass the other house. With a unicameral legislature, all that public relations spin goes out the window. Armed with the power of the initiative process, the people in many states could enact such a change.

One of the most historic examples of a people's initiative is California's Prop 13, passed in 1978. In the inflationary aftermath of two oil embargoes earlier in the decade, home values in many areas spiraled out of control. Politicians made token cuts in the tax rate, but those were more than offset by assessments that doubled every two or three years. As young, two-income professionals snatched up homes at high prices, many blue-collar survivors of the Depression faced the prospect of being taxed out of the modest homes they had purchased during the post-WWII boom. Prop 13 returned all property tax assessments to their 1975 levels and froze the base tax rate at one percent of assessed value, with annual increases limited to two percent until the property was resold, at which time the sales price becomes the new base assessed value.

Prop 13, which passed with over 62% of the vote, established what is, in effect, a means test for property taxes. If you can afford the house, presumably you can afford the property taxes. This is a far cry from the previous system in which, just because your neighbor could afford his house and taxes, presumably you could too, even if you had bought your house decades earlier at a fraction of the price your neighbor paid. This kind of protection against skyrocketing property taxes is particularly important during periodic bubbles in house prices. Absent Prop 13, during the fraud-driven speculative housing bubble that preceded the Great Financial Crisis (GFC, also known as the Great Recession) of 2007-2008, millions of lower-income and middle-income California homeowners would have paid out billions in unnecessary and unfair taxes based on values inflated by speculators and flippers. Prop 13 also made property taxes predictable. Going in, buyers know what their tax obligations will be in coming years. And in one of the great ironies of recent political history, Prop 13 proved to be a stabilizing influence on state and local government income. Even a former L.A. County Tax Assessor admitted that, because of its two percent annual inflation index, Prop 13 established a floor on property tax revenues and thus modulated what would otherwise be huge swings in revenues as the value (and assessment) of all properties, not just those recently sold, tumbled.

Of course, Prop 13 has its detractors, primarily those politicians and their supporters who depend on government largesse for their power and position. Public employee unions generally hate it, because they see limitations on revenue as limitations on their salaries and pensions (a subject addressed in Chapter 20). Almost yearly, there is some attempt by the legislature to circumvent either the letter or the spirit of Prop 13, or seduce voters into amending it, but (with one exception) those attempts have either died in the legislature or failed at the ballot box. (In 2000, voters approved Prop 39, which lowered the threshold for approving school bonds from two-thirds to 55%. From then until the GFC of

2007-2008 hit, school bonds passed right and left.) Overall, California voters still approve highly of Prop 13.

Spurred by the passage of Prop 13, in 1980, proponents of citizen government in Massachusetts got Proposition 2-1/2 passed. It not only established a Prop 13-type formula for property tax assessments, but also applied a similar restriction to the state's auto excise tax. That same year, sixty percent of voters in Nevada used a ballot referendum to enshrine existing state abortion law into the state constitution. A great advantage of initiatives is that they can only be repealed by another vote of the people, so the legislature cannot snatch them away.

The initiative and referendum process allows state and local governments to let the public decide critical or contentious issues. From 2000-2007, state legislatures placed 600 measures before the voters, nearly twice the 311 voter-initiated measures that qualified for the ballot. In California, ballot measures have been used to approve tax increases for road improvements and mass transit projects, as well as hundreds of millions of dollars in bonds to acquire or protect parklands, wetlands, and other open space. Initiatives and referenda have also allowed local communities to hash out zoning questions, limit over-development, preserve civic charm and character, and regulate the shipment of hazardous materials through their neighborhoods.

An area where citizen initiatives have been put to extremely good use is in the establishment of term limits for state and local officials. As Wikipedia notes: [Emphasis added.]

> The elections of 1990-94 saw the adoption of term limits for state legislatures in **almost every state where citizens had the power of the initiative**.

Subsequently, term limits were overturned in six states. The Idaho legislature repealed term limits because they had been approved in a vote which was only advisory and not binding. In 2003, the Utah legislature repealed the term limits they had enacted in 1995 when faced with the likelihood that a citizen initiative would qualify and pass. In Massachusetts, Washington, and Wyoming, state supreme courts invalidated term limits because they had been enacted as statutes when they should have been amendments to the state constitution. In 2002, the Oregon Supreme Court tossed out term limits enacted ten years earlier because the initiative containing them violated a state requirement that initiatives deal with a single subject. (Funny how courts rarely consider "reform" a single subject. And how it took ten years for the decision to be rendered, which conveniently happened just as a number of lawmakers were about to be termed out.)

Seventeen states currently have legislative term limits of one sort or another. Fifteen of those are the result of either initiatives or referendums. As Wikipedia again notes:

> Where rotation in the legislative branch has withstood court challenges, term limits continue to garner popular support. As of 2002, the advocacy group "U.S. Term Limits" found that in the 17 states where state legislators served in rotation, public support for term limits ranged from 60 to 78 percent.

Thanks largely to initiatives, or the threat of same, thirty-six states impose some form of term limits on governors. Similar limits usually apply to other statewide offices such as lieutenant governor, attorney general, secretary of state, etc. In addition, the citizen's power of the initiative is also responsible for term limits in countless cities, counties, school boards, special districts, and even some judicial offices. Unfortunately, in some cases where these limits were enacted as the result of a referendum placed on the ballot by the legislative body, they can also be overturned by that body. This happened in 2008 when, as previously noted, New York Mayor Michael Bloomberg coerced the City Council into extending the two-term limit to three. He got his third term, but another referendum reinstated the two-term limit in 2010. Sadly, that limit will likely last only until some other power-mad politician wants to extend their reign as mayor of the Big Apple.

Direct democracy has its detractors, chief among them the political establishment, which feels that the business of governing is best left to professionals like themselves. That's right: the corrupt spineless riff-raff who are most responsible for our sad current state of affairs think the public would just mess things up. A good response to this elitist claptrap is: ***How much worse could it get?***

Another criticism is that the initiative process has been co-opted by business interests, with the money to fund expensive signature-gathering campaigns. This is a throw-the-baby-out-with-the-bathwater argument. In fact, despite the best efforts of special interests, voters often see through these attempts. In her book, *The Populist Paradox*, University of Michigan professor Elisabeth Gerber studied the impact of money and special interest groups on the initiative process and concluded:

> Economic interest groups are severely limited in their ability to pass new laws by initiative. Simply put, money is necessary but not sufficient for success at the ballot box. By contrast, research found that citizen groups with broad-based support could much more effectively use direct legislation to pass new laws. When they are able to mobilize sufficient financial resources to get out their message, citizen groups are much more successful at the ballot box, even when economic interest groups greatly outspend them.

The Los Angeles suburb of Inglewood is a prime example. After listening to residents who didn't want their local merchants put out of business, the City Council refused to make zoning changes necessary to accommodate the building of a Walmart. The company countered by placing a zoning change measure on the ballot, but it was rejected by voters. The smaller city of Redondo Beach is another example. In recent years it has rejected two corporate-backed measures which attempted to gain voter approval for massive building projects, one a mammoth residential and retail development, the other a brain-dead proposal to convert valuable harbor property into a mall (at a time when malls are closing at a record pace). Between the two measures, the corporate sponsors spent nearly $2 million in a city of 66,000 residents. The citizen opposition spent $36,000. The citizens prevailed, and by wide margins. (Two-to-one, in one case.)

A study conducted by Dennis Polhill and published by the Initiative & Referendum Institute at the University of Southern California described other failures of initiatives pushed by well-heeled special interests:

> George Soros, Gene Sperling and Peter Lewis spent millions of dollars in 2000 to try and [sic] get a drug policy reform initiative passed in Massachusetts only to be defeated. Dick DeVos (the founder of Amway), along with several other wealthy individuals spent almost $30 million dollars in the 2000 election cycle to try and [sic] get school choice initiatives adopted -- they too were left empty handed on election night. In yet another example, millionaire Ron Unz, the successful architect of the California and Arizona initiatives to require that schools teach in English only (with some exceptions), saw his campaign finance reform initiative handily defeated in California in 2000 -- after spending a substantial amount of his own money.

This doesn't mean that business interests won't win some of these battles, or that they will quit trying. Currently, special interests not only have an advantage in being able to qualify a ballot measure, but also have a huge edge in spending on the ensuing election. But if the public financing provisions of the 33rd Amendment are implemented, and both sides of a ballot initiative are limited to equal spending, the chance that special interests will prevail becomes more remote.

The right of citizens to counter-balance elected officials through the use of ballot measures was one of the great triumphs of the original Progressive movement but, unfortunately, it was not adopted by every state. It's up to us to finish the job:

## The 36th Amendment -- Participatory Democracy

**Section 1: The right of voters in all states and lesser jurisdictions thereof to participate by legally binding initiative, referendum, and recall is hereby established. Any initiative or referendum petition containing valid signatures, of voters residing within the jurisdiction subject to said measure, equaling ten percent of the votes cast in that jurisdiction during the last general election, shall be put before the voters within a period of not less than 90 nor more than 150 days after certification of qualification.**

**Section 2: For measures to recall elected officials, the percentage of registered voter signatures necessary to qualify for the ballot shall be no more than fifteen percent of the votes cast in that jurisdiction during the last general election, and said recall election shall take place no less than 60 nor more than 90 days after certification of qualification.**

**Section 3: Proponents of initiative or recall measures shall have 180 days to collect and present the necessary signatures. Proponents of referendums shall have 70 days after official approval of the resolution, law, or other action of government being contested.**

**Section 4: Certification of petition signature validity shall be performed in a timely manner**

by the official who is normally responsible for the conduct of elections in that jurisdiction. In the event that a petition is deemed short the required signatures, proponents shall have a reasonable right of appeal, including to court of law, to protest disqualified signatures.

Section 5: Once approved by voters, an initiative shall not be repealed or amended except by another vote of the people. If any portion of a measure is later overturned by a court of law, all other provisions shall remain in full force and effect.

# Chapter 12

# EQUAL JUSTICE

Currently, federal judges serve lifetime appointments unless they resign, die, or are impeached for failing to maintain what the Constitution calls "good behavior." The only justice of the Supreme Court ever impeached was Samuel Chase in 1805. A signer of the Declaration of Independence, Chase was caught up in the battle between President Thomas Jefferson and the Federalist party of Alexander Hamilton. Charged with allegedly abusing his office, Chase was acquitted in his Senate trial on all counts.

In 1969, it was discovered that Associate Justice Abe Fortas had made a secret lifetime retainer agreement for $20,000 a year with a Wall Street financier facing serious legal troubles. Had Fortas not immediately resigned he would certainly have been impeached and convicted. Thirteen District Court judges have been impeached. Seven were convicted, three resigned rather than face trial, and the remaining three were acquitted. A single Appeals Court Judge, Robert Archbald, appointed to the Middle District Court of Appeals for Pennsylvania by President McKinley, was convicted for accepting bribes from litigants in cases before the court. Clearly, judicial impropriety rarely rises to a level where it can clear the high threshold of impeachment, but this doesn't mean that there aren't several problems with lifetime appointments to the bench, especially when it comes to the

Supreme Court, which lately has become the lynchpin of our descent into a fascist oligarchy.

It is a misconception that justices only recently began serving very long terms. True, the length of service for justices of the Supreme Court started out modestly enough. The original nine justices served an average of nine years. However, starting with Chief Justice John Marshall, that figure more than doubled. Marshall and the next nine justices averaged 22 years on the court. Forty-three justices have served at least twenty years, and fourteen exceeded thirty years. At the time of his death, Justice Antonin Scalia was closing in on the thirty-year mark. Four others -- Thomas, Ginsberg, Breyer, and the recently retired Kennedy -- have all served for at least twenty years.

The pivotal point in the court's history coincided with the term of Earl Warren as Chief Justice, which lasted from 1953 to 1969. The so-called Warren Court was at the forefront of many momentous decisions that changed the way Americans lived. The Court's unanimous 1954 *Brown v. Board of Education* decision outlawing racial segregation in schools transformed a nascent struggle for equal rights into a national movement. The Civil Rights Act of 1964 and the Voting Rights Act of 1965 paved the way for subsequent rulings that struck down other discriminatory state laws. The emphasis by the Warren Court on equal rights for all members of society represented a huge change from the court's traditional focus on property rights and issues involving commerce. The court's new direction spawned a push for equality for women, the disabled, the LGBT community, and seniors. The impact eventually spread to everything from marriage, adoption, and abortion to affirmative action, hiring practices, and freedom from sexual harassment in the workplace.

The Warren Court's one man/one vote ruling ended practices that gave over-representation to conservative rural areas at the expense of generally more liberal and more densely populated cities and suburbs. During the same period, the Warren court ruled that indigent defendants must be provided with legal counsel. Later, it instituted the Miranda ruling requiring that persons being interrogated be advised of their right to remain silent, and to have an attorney present during questioning. On the First Amendment front, the Warren Court outlawed mandatory prayer in public schools, and announced that everyone had a constitutionally-protected right to privacy, which provided the basis of the *Roe v. Wade* decision granting women the right to have an abortion. (Note that this right of privacy was *inferred*. It's only on matters like good government where the right has to be explicitly stated.)

The Warren Court ended business as usual, not just for many businesses, but also for state party political machines as well as the entire educational infrastructure, from local school districts to university admission policies. Any time traditional institutions of government and business are forced to radically change the way they operate, those whose ox is getting gored by the new rules are inspired to fight back. Just such a movement began in the 1970s, largely inspired by the infamous "Powell Memo." Written by Lewis Powell just a few months before his appointment to the Supreme Court, and directed to the National Chamber of Commerce, the memo contended that America's free enterprise system was under attack. Wikipedia describes the memo as, "a road map to defend and further the Chamber of Commerce's concept of free-enterprise capitalism against perceived and/or real socialist, communist, and fascist cultural trends." As Wikipedia notes:

> Powell argued, "The most disquieting voices joining the chorus of criticism came from perfectly respectable elements of society: from the college campus, the pulpit, the media, the intellectual and literary journals, the arts and sciences, and from politicians." In the memorandum, Powell advocated "constant surveillance" of textbook and television content, as well as a purge of left-wing elements.

The idea that Powell's memo was intended to head off fascist trends is laughable. The free enterprise system he purported to be protecting has become a model of Benito Mussolini's classic definition of fascism: the perfect combination of business and state. Suggestions contained in the Powell Memo are credited with inspiring the formation of influential right-wing think tanks and lobbying firms, including The Heritage Foundation, Cato Institute, Manhattan Institute, and the particularly pernicious spawn of the Koch brothers, the American Legislative Exchange Council (ALEC), which specializes in secretly drafting model pro-business, anti-labor, anti-environment, and anti-consumer legislation which legislators can introduce in their home states. Powell's characterization of academics, religious leaders, intellectuals, artists, and scientists as the enemy is a classic fascist approach straight out of Senator Joe McCarthy's blacklist playbook. The notion that textbooks and television content should be under constant scrutiny, with an eye toward purging progressive influences, is totalitarian.

In 2011, journalist Bill Moyers wrote in The Nation magazine:

> The rise of the money power in our time goes back 40 years. We can pinpoint the date. On Aug. 23, 1971, a corporate lawyer named Lewis Powell -- a board member of the death-dealing tobacco giant Philip Morris and a future justice of the Supreme Court -- released a confidential memorandum for his friends at the U.S. Chamber of Commerce. We look back on it now as a call to arms for class war waged from the top down.

***Class war waged from the top down***. It's taken more than four decades, but the strategy inspired by the Powell Memo has now burrowed into nearly every valued institution and critical aspect of American life.

None of this should come as a surprise, given that Powell spent a quarter-century at a white-shoe law firm representing big corporations and trade groups. Prior to his law career, Powell served in Army Intelligence during WWII, and strongly believed in the need for government to keep secrets. In *United States v. Nixon*, Powell tried unsuccessfully to convince his fellow justices to let President Nixon keep his secret Oval Office tapes out of the hands of Leon Jaworski, the Special Prosecutor investigating Watergate. Powell also wasn't above lying in order to silence critics of government wrongdoing. Frank Snepp was a former CIA agent that Wikipedia describes as, "one of the first whistle-blowers who revealed the inner workings, secrets and failures of the national security services in the 1970s." In *Snepp v. U.S.*, Powell "misstated" the factual record in the case in order to convince his fellow justices to issue an order requiring Snepp to pre-clear all of his writings with the CIA for the rest of his life.

The problem of justices serving long terms isn't simply a function of how long they are on the bench, but also of how the political process has corrupted the way in which prospective justices are identified, nominated, and confirmed. Part of the campaign that grew out of the Powell Memo was a long-term effort to yank the Supreme Court back from the liberal direction it was being led in by Earl Warren, Thurgood Marshall, William Douglas, and John Paul Stevens. It took a long time, but as these lions of civil liberties died or retired, Republicans in Congress obstructed the nomination of anyone who did not meet certain conservative, pro-business criteria. Every decision, every speech, every law school lecture ever given by anyone who might be considered a potential nominee, is now subjected to scrutiny. Thus it has become standard practice for judges who aspire to the high court to avoid writing or lecturing about controversial legal issues. (This is also why the Trump administration went to unprecedented lengths to prevent disclosure of most writings of Brett Kavanaugh, whose career created a massive paper trail covering everything from his part in the Whitewater Investigation and drafting of the Patriot Act to decisions made while on the D.C. Circuit Court of Appeals.)

Normally, Senate confirmation hearings for Supreme Court nominees produce a form of kabuki. Every attempt to elicit a nominee's true feelings on critical issues is now met by either a solemn promise (later broken), to be guided by the concept of *stare decisis* (relying on the precedent of previous rulings) or the catch-all evasion, "It wouldn't be appropriate for me to comment on cases and issues that might come before the court." That strategy worked for the appointments of Roberts, Alito, Sotomayor, Kagan, and Gorsuch. For Kavanaugh, the old rules went out the window. His confirmation hearing was undoubtedly the most controversial and heated since the rejection of Robert Bork in 1987.

Most notable about the Kavanaugh hearings was the fact that the Democrats chose to focus on his use of alcohol, and his history of alleged sexual misbehavior (including rape) as a high school student. The Democrats on the Judiciary Committee did little to address his known positions on the law, some of which many people consider extreme. He is a known defender of torture, advocate of mass surveillance and metadata collection, and supporter of presidential immunity from prosecution. (Or even investigation, for that matter.) The great undertone of Kavanaugh's nomination was, of course, the 1973 *Roe v. Wade* decision which legalized abortion. Religious conservatives have been on a forty-year crusade to pack the Supreme Court with enough judges to overturn *Roe*. They have finally succeeded. As conservative pundit and zealous abortion opponent Pat Buchanan noted, the Supreme Court was the last fortress. Those in the pro-life movement either accepted the argument that these charges of sexual impropriety were not true, or simply didn't care. Getting enough justices to overturn Roe was worth virtually any price.

As a result of Kavanaugh's appointment, the court is now stacked with conservative ideologues determined to finish rolling back the gains of both the Warren Court and decades of progressive legislation. By appealing to a religious issue, the GOP has succeeded in creating a court that will give anti-abortion forces the victory they seek. Unfortunately, these same justices are firmly committed to interpreting the law in a manner which solidifies the power of the oligarchy and the national security state. That all of these conservative judges are relatively young, and may serve for thirty years or more, brings us to the subject of whether or not federal judges, including those on the Supreme Court, should enjoy lifetime appointments.

Prime examples of justices who (in the opinion of some, myself included), served too long are William Rehnquist (1972-2005) and William O. Douglas (1939-1975). Rehnquist's thirty-three years on the court spanned the presidencies of Nixon, Ford, Carter, Reagan, George H.W. Bush, Clinton, and George W. Bush. During that time, the country went from Vietnam and Watergate through 9-11 and the wars in Iraq and Afghanistan. When the conservative Rehnquist joined the high court, the home VCR was just being introduced. By the time he died, cell phone use spanned the globe, and the internet was in daily use by billions of people worldwide.

Justice Douglas is the same story on the other end of the political spectrum. Appointed two years *before* Pearl Harbor, Douglas' tenure also spanned seven presidents: FDR, Truman, Eisenhower, Kennedy, Johnson, Nixon, and Ford. This is simply too long, especially considering the accelerating pace of social and economic change. Indeed, one of the problems the current Court faces is ruling on matters of privacy and business practices raised by new technologies that many of the court members either don't use, or don't fully understand.

The idea of term limits for Supreme Court justices is not new or novel. In his book, *A More Perfect Constitution*, law professor Larry Sabato, chair of the University of Virginia Center for Politics, suggested a single fifteen-year term. In May 2014, a Democracy Corp poll found that 74% of voters favored a single eighteen-year term. The support was uniform across Democrats (80%),

Republicans (72%) and Independents (73%). Because justices are nominated by presidents who have been elected by the people, limiting Supreme Court appointments to fixed terms ensures that new presidents, who may reflect changing views, priorities, and realities of our society, will be able to nominate justices better equipped to deal with those issues. It also reduces the chance that one party enjoying a temporary hold on Senate power can put in place justices who will continue that party's judicial ideology long after control of Congress, the will of the people, and the direction of the country has changed. Therefore:

### The 37th Amendment -- Equal Justice

**Section 1: Supreme Court justices appointed subsequent to ratification of this Amendment shall serve for a single term of 15 years, or to age seventy-five, whichever shall occur first.**

It is not enough to simply limit how long justices can serve. We must also insulate them from the temptations of outside compensation. There are two ways to accomplish this. The first is by raising the salaries of the justices. Currently justices of the Supreme Court make $253,300. The Chief Justice makes slightly more, $267,000. This is ridiculous. There is great prestige involved in being on the Supreme Court but really, less than $300K for ruling on the most important legal issues facing the entire country? This is not only absurd, it is indicative of obsolete concepts and an ignorance of economic realities. Many lawyers who argue before the Court make millions a year. We shouldn't necessarily try to match that, but we need to put a much higher monetary value on the job we ask Supreme Court justices to do. We also have to be realistic about the costs of living in one of the most expensive areas of the country. Therefore:

**Section 2: Immediately upon ratification of this Amendment the annual salary for justices of the Supreme Court shall be One Million**

**Dollars, adjusted every five years using the cost-of-living formula set by the Social Security Administration for retiree benefits. Upon retirement, not resulting from impeachment or threat thereof, justices shall continue to receive the same salary and benefits of their office for life.**

If paying each justice a million dollars a year sounds like it's a lot of money, consider this: if, at any time, there were nine justices currently serving and three more in retirement, that would only total $12 million a year. Our justice system is only as good as it is at the very top, and $12 mil a year is a pittance of a price, not worthy of argument or discussion.

Because they are currently so poorly paid, Supreme Court justices are naturally inclined to seek outside sources of income. According to recent financial disclosure forms, all but one, Justice Breyer, earned outside income from writing or lecturing at various law schools. This causes problems because, as it stands now, Supreme Court justices are not required to follow the *U.S. Judicial Code of Ethics* that forbids all other federal judges from being, "a speaker, a guest of honor, or featured on the program," of a fundraising event. Thus, a judge sitting on a federal District or Appeals court must abstain from participating in cases where they have a financial interest or other conflict-of-interest. But because the Supreme Court has exempted itself from compliance with the code, justices can, and do, make rulings that benefit themselves, family members, and former partners or clients. They are free to accept speaking fees, trips, and other gifts from the same parties who have business before the court. This loophole has allowed Justice Thomas to be a speaker and honored guest at fundraising events held by the conservative Federalist Society.

An even more notorious example was the attendance in 2010 by Justices Scalia and Thomas at a secret Koch brothers event in Palm Springs, where the two justices met with supporters of the

*Citizens United* suit then working its way up to the Supreme Court. In 2011, Scalia and Thomas sided with the majority by ruling in favor of the plaintiffs. The *Citizens United* ruling held that individuals and corporations cannot be limited in the amount of money they spend supporting candidates, or trying to influence legislation, something very beneficial to the deep-pocketed Koch brothers.

But it is not just the conservative justices who have ethical problems. Alleged liberal Justice Sonya Sotomayor received $3 million from Knopf Publishing for her memoir, *My Beloved World*. Aside from the dubious merits of a memoir by a relatively young justice, who had just joined the court, there is the fact that Knopf is owned by the enormous German multi-media firm Bertelsmann. If a matter affecting Knopf, or any other tentacle of the Bertelsmann empire, comes before the court, Sotomayor will be free to sit in judgment. Should, for instance, Bertelsmann seek permission to buy one of the American media companies that dominate the dissemination of news and information, Justice Sonya will have three million reasons to render a verdict in Bertelsmann's favor. Therefore:

> **Section 3: Justices of the Supreme Court shall be bound by the U.S. Judicial Code of Ethics, and shall recuse themselves accordingly. Under no circumstances shall a sitting justice participate in cases which involve, or might reasonably be seen to involve, any financial benefit to themselves or to those with whom they have a personal, professional, or familial relationship. Failure to adhere to this obligation shall be punishable by impeachment followed by felony criminal prosecution carrying a mandatory sentence of incarceration in a maximum security facility for a period, not subject to pardon, suspension, commutation, parole, or other**

**reduction of sentence, of not less than ten years. Conviction, or plea of guilty for violation hereof, shall result in the forfeiture of all pension benefits accrued while in public office or employment.**

Interestingly enough, one of the provisions of Senator Elizabeth Warren's *Anti-Corruption and Public Integrity Act* mentioned in Chapter 7 would also require justices of the Supreme Court to adhere to the *U.S. Judicial Code of Ethics* specified by Section 3 above.

Limiting the terms of justices will mean that we have to confront another problem: the revolving door, where former officials and key political staffers leave government and are immediately rewarded with lavish salaries as lobbyists or executives in industries they formerly regulated, or dealt with on a legislative basis. Supreme Court justices facing only a limited term of office will be sorely tempted to curry favor with future employers. As George Washington noted, "Few men have virtue to withstand the highest bidder." We must remove that temptation. By raising their salary to a million dollars a year for life (plus cost-of-living increases) we can ensure that retired justices continue to be more than adequately compensated after they leave the Court.

**Section 4: During their term in office, and upon retirement, Justices of the Supreme Court shall not receive any compensation except as might derive from properties and investments held prior to appointment, nor shall they accept any gifts or benefits from any organization, person, foreign government or business entity. Nor shall retired justices represent future litigants, or lecture at any institution, except pro bono.**

Under Section 4, if a retired justice wishes to write a memoir, or a law school text, they can donate the proceeds to law school scholarships, legal aid societies, or some other charity.

Serving on the Supreme Court is the pinnacle of achievement in the legal profession. If the prestige of being on the Supreme Court, plus a million-dollar annual lifetime salary/pension, lifetime health care, and other perks that go with the position is not enough, there is a simple solution: ***decline to be nominated***.

Removing the temptations of outside income, and preventing justices from following their legislative brethren through the revolving door, will be significant achievements. But we must also solve the problem of the absurdly narrow field from which SCOTUS candidates are drawn. ***All nine current Justices*** (as well as the four most recent Justices to leave the court), attended law school at either Harvard or Yale. (Ruth Bader Ginsburg attended Harvard Law, but actually graduated from Columbia, after she moved to New York because her husband got a job there.) Is this because Stanford, Duke, Notre Dame, Princeton, Cornell, Michigan, Texas, Virginia, U.C. Berkeley, and all the other law schools in the land, including those located in and around D.C., like Georgetown and George Washington, cannot produce lawyers qualified for the Supreme Court? Is it because the *professors* at these other law schools are unfit to serve on the Supreme Court? Of course not.

It's because Harvard and Yale have become America's Academic Axis of Evil, a vetting ground where the current ruling elite ensure that their offspring become the future ruling elite. Harvard and Yale aren't just elite schools, they are the schools *of* the elite. At the top of the student body pyramid sit the children of our rich and entitled reigning oligarchy. Some are from old money, others from the more recently rich. Many are "legacy admits," selected because their parents are influential alums. Next come the children of the rich and entitled ruling elite from other countries.

(Gotta develop those life-long international crony networking opportunities.)

Last comes a cross-section of bright, ambitious students from more humble backgrounds attending on scholarship. These students already know the real way of the world, who holds the levers of power and how that power is wielded. (This is why they, and their parents, strive so hard to get them into Harvard or Yale in the first place.) These students know that if they want that Harvard or Yale degree, and the school's vast, influential alumni network to pay off with a spot in the ranks of the plutocracy, they need to adhere to certain values and shun others. Social liberalism -- support for gay rights, abortion, racial equality, women's rights, etc. -- is tolerated. But true economic liberalism (or, if you prefer, socialism), the idea that the wealth of a nation should not be concentrated in the hands of a few dozen families, is verboten.

Occasionally, some of these talented and ambitious strivers from less-than-exalted backgrounds emerge from Yale or Harvard, get some real-world experience, and realize just how skewered and biased the system is. One such man is Steven Brill, a kid from working-class Queens, who got an undergrad scholarship to Yale, went on to graduate from Yale Law in 1975, then founded *The American Lawyer* magazine and Court TV. In his book, *Tailspin*, Brill wrote about the decline of America into what he calls "the protected few" and "the unprotected many." He referenced portions of a rather striking commencement address given to the Yale Law Class of 2015 by one of the school's esteemed professors, Daniel Markovits, who lectures on the relationship of law and behavioral economics. The gist of Brill's argument, and Markovits' address, is that a meritocracy, through which deserving students gain access to the best schools, and which was instituted to break up dominance by inherited wealth, has morphed to create a new dominant caste. As Markovits described it, "American meritocracy has thus become precisely what it was invented to combat, a mechanism for the dynastic transmission of wealth and privilege across generations. Meritocracy now constitutes a modern-day aristocracy."

It's not just the penetration into the halls of business, law, and finance of this meritocratic aristocracy that is pervasive, nor is it just the composition of the Supreme Court. Look at the extreme over-representation of these two institutions among the major party candidates for President starting in 1988:

| *Year* | *Democratic* | *School* |
|---|---|---|
| 1988 | Michael Dukakis | Harvard |
| 1992 | Bill Clinton | Yale |
| 1996 | Bill Clinton | Yale |
| 2000 | Al Gore | Harvard |
| 2004 | John Kerry | Yale |
| 2008 | Barack Obama | Harvard |
| 2012 | Barack Obama | Harvard |
| 2016 | Hillary Clinton | Yale |

| *Year* | *Republican* | *School* |
|---|---|---|
| 1988 | George H.W. Bush | Yale |
| 1992 | George H.W. Bush | Yale |
| 1996 | Bob Dole | Washburn |
| 2000 | George W. Bush | Yale |
| 2004 | George W. Bush | Yale |
| 2008 | John McCain | Annapolis |
| 2012 | Mitt Romney | Harvard |
| 2016 | Donald Trump | Penn |

Any critical examination of the anti-democratic, pro-corporate, anti-civil liberties policies that the administrations of these presidents followed demonstrates why some refer to the Ivy League as the Poison Ivy League. Nor is it hard to understand why the Supreme Court now interprets the Constitution, sometimes narrowly and other times widely, depending upon:

- Which interpretation will produce a decision most favorable to corporations, business entities, and the wealthy ruling elite?

- Which interpretation most favors or enhances the powers of the Imperial Presidency and the National Security State?

Even with public financing of campaigns, addressed in Chapter 8, we can do little to preclude alumni from Harvard or Yale dominating presidential options from the legacy parties. But we can damn sure reduce the influence of these two institutions on the Supreme Court. The notion that there is only a tiny pool of judges and attorneys smart enough, and skilled enough, to be on the Supreme Court is not only ludicrous and fallacious, it's insulting to the public and our purported national values. Every year attorneys trained at other law schools argue and win cases before the court. Every year, decisions crafted by federal district and appeals court judges who did not attend Harvard or Yale are upheld. This is self-evident proof that there is a sizable community of attorneys and judges qualified to sit on the high court.

There is nothing we can do about the present preposterous imbalance of law schools currently represented on the Supreme Court. Attempting to remove even a few current justices would not only provoke a political conflict of unimaginable proportions, the suggestion alone could well be a poison pill preventing the entire slate of Restoration Amendments from being palatable to the public. But through Section 5 we can ensure a broader representation of schools in the makeup of future courts:

**Section 5: No person shall be nominated to the Supreme Court after attending the same university or school of law as two or more justices currently serving.**

Cleaning up the Supreme Court will not be enough to achieve the goal, which so far has eluded us, of equal justice for all. That will also require reform in the lower levels of the justice system, from the cop on the street to the attorneys charged with seeing that justice prevails.

Chapter 3 of this book opened with the story of Walter Mitchell, Jr., and the legal ruling that citizens have no constitutional right to good government. If you think that was jaw-dropping, try the case of *Pottawattamie County, IA v. McGhee.*

In 1978, two black teenagers, Curthis McGhee and Terry Harrington, were convicted of killing a retired white police captain. Twenty-five years into life-without-parole sentences, the convictions were overturned after it was shown that prosecutors used perjured testimony, and withheld exculpatory evidence which pointed to another suspect, a man who happened to be a) white, and b) the brother-in-law of the local fire chief. Harrington (who had been in line for a scholarship to Yale at the time of his arrest), and McGhee subsequently sued the two former prosecutors, Pottawattamie County, and the city of Council Bluffs for $60 million. The case eventually made its way to the U.S. Supreme Court. Here's how Nina Tottenberg of National Public Radio described the case: [Emphasis added.]

> Iowa prosecutors, **backed by the federal government and prosecutors across the country**, contend that there is, quote, "**no freestanding constitutional right not to be framed**." For most Americans, that's a breathtaking proposition.

Breathtaking? Really? No shit? You think that's bad, listen to the arguments about why the men should not be able to sue. Again, from Tottenberg: [Emphasis added.]

> Representing the Iowa prosecutors, lawyer Stephen Sanders says there are good reasons for prosecutorial

immunity. Otherwise, **"there would be a flood of lawsuits."**

Let's parse that. Those who support prosecutorial immunity argue that if it was significantly modified there would be a flood of lawsuits that would tie up prosecutors in civil court. This assertion rests on the notion that there are a lot of attorneys out there who are willing to file frivolous lawsuits when they lack evidence of actual wrongdoing. So how do these lawyers get paid? Well, one could argue that the jurisdiction being sued would simply settle out of court. But that begs the question: Won't judges grant motions for summary dismissal if the plaintiff's attorney cannot show sufficient cause? And won't judges sanction and fine attorneys who repeatedly bring such suits? The answer to both questions is likely to be *yes*.

This brings us to the fact that the only way there could be a flood of civil damage lawsuits for tainted convictions *is if there is a flood of prosecutors who are suborning perjury and withholding evidence*, thereby subverting the cause of justice and public belief in the fairness of our legal system. Think that matters to lawyers, judges, and government in general? Think again. More from Tottenberg:

> ...the lawyer for the prosecutors pointed to a long line of Supreme Court decisions saying that prosecutors are immune from civil lawsuits for their actions at trial. The question posed was whether prosecutors who work side by side with police at the investigative stage of a case are also immune even though the police are not. The prosecutor's lawyer, Mr. Sanders, told the justices that it's impossible to separate the investigative phase of a case from the trial because without a conviction, there's no deprivation of liberty for the defendant and he has no legal claim that his constitutional rights were violated.

Read that closely, again. The prosecutor's defense lawyer -- joined by friend-of-the-court briefs from other jurisdictions and agencies including the U.S. Department of Justice -- argued that despite the fact that the men were held without bail prior to the trial, there was, "no deprivation of liberty," and, "no legal claim that his (defendant's) constitutional rights were violated," in the pre-trial phase of the case. (Remember, the claim was that the prosecutors engaged in misconduct not just during the trial, but in the investigatory and trial prep stages, while the suspects were in custody. In fact, one of the violations committed by these prosecutors was scripting the perjured testimony of a key witness.)

It gets even worse. Before the Supreme Court could rule, Pottawattamie County settled for $12 million, Council Bluffs agreed to fork over another $6 million, and the suit was dropped. But without a Supreme Court ruling there is no clear civil liability for prosecutors **who frame innocent people**. And while a total of $18 mil might sound like a lot of money, the plaintiffs' attorneys undoubtedly took a sizeable chunk. Split two ways, the remaining money is scant recompense for spending a combined total of **fifty years** in prison, for a crime prosecutors knew that someone else committed! To top it off, the settlement includes this provision, reported by David Pitt in the Lincoln, Iowa Journal Star newspaper:

> The agreement specifies no admission of fault, liability or wrongdoing by any party and bars anyone from making public statements suggesting otherwise.

No admission of fault. No admission of wrongdoing. A perfect example of the concept of lack of agency. Nobody did anything, all this bad shit just happened.

It's time to face facts: A prosecutor's primary interest is not in seeing justice done, but in getting a conviction. Their second priority is preventing convictions from being overturned because this embarrasses them, their predecessors and colleagues, the entire judicial system itself, and can lead to more defendants being acquitted by virtue of reasonable doubt. They have taken the old adage, "Better that ten guilty men go free than one innocent man is convicted" and turned it on its head. For them it has become, "Better ten innocent men are convicted, than one criminal goes free for lack of sufficient evidence."

The ideal case for a prosecutor is one in which the jury believes every word and every exhibit the prosecution puts forth, believes nothing from the defense, and returns a guilty verdict without ever leaving the jury box. This is why district attorneys and attorney generals will go to almost any length not to admit error, and not let convicted defendants prove their innocence. But often these people *are* innocent. Way back in 2007, the Death Penalty Information Center reported that 200 prisoners had been exonerated using DNA. The New York-based Innocence Foundation has a list of 161 Death Row prisoners who have had their convictions overturned.

One of the most notorious recent examples of prosecutorial misconduct is the infamous Duke Rape case. In 2006, a stripper accused three white Duke Lacrosse players of raping her at a party. Following much outrage, the three men were arrested, the Lacrosse coach was forced to resign, and the team's remaining games were cancelled. Despite many holes in the woman's story (which changed no less than four times), District Attorney Mike Nifong, engaged in a tough re-election fight, went ahead with the trial.

Eventually it was proven that the charges were completely false, made up by the woman in an effort to explain why she had left her child unattended at home. In the aftermath, D.A. Nifong was convicted by the North Carolina State Bar Disciplinary Committee of **twenty-seven** ethics violations. There were also calls for his criminal prosecution. As Wikipedia notes, Nifong was also:

> ...charged with having violated at least a dozen laws, rules and court orders designed to protect defendants' rights by playing "a game of hide and seek" with

evidence that could have cleared the players. The players' motion also alleged that Nifong's misconduct "shocks the conscience and defies any notion of accident or negligence".

In the end, after inflicting untold harm on the lives and reputations of not only three innocent men, but an entire fraternity, sports team, and university, for all that "shocking of the conscience," Nifong spent exactly one night in the local jail. ***One night***. But that's not the end of the story. Again, Wikipedia:

> In July 2014 there was a call for all the cases Nifong had prosecuted to be reviewed on the basis of his having been shown to ignore due process in some cases including the murder trial against Darryl Howard, who had been convicted in 1995 of a 1991 murder of a woman and her daughter.

In 2014, Darryl Howard, who at that time had been imprisoned for murder for 20 years, was granted a new trial because Nifong had withheld evidence in the trial that led to his convictions. Two years later, following a hearing where the state was asked why the convictions should stand, the murder conviction was vacated, and Howard released from prison, noting that DNA evidence not presented to the jury would likely have exonerated him.

Mike Nifong again went unpunished, this time for depriving an innocent man of twenty years of his life. The Duke Lacrosse and Darryl Howard cases highlight the differences in how the justice system operates, not only on the basis of race, but even more so, money. The big difference between Howard and the white Duke players was that the Duke players were from affluent families who could assemble a top-drawer legal team. Like O.J. Simpson's criminal case, the access to a great legal team made a huge difference. It is telling that Howard's case was only investigated after Nifong's wrongdoing in the Duke case had been exposed.

No system administered by humans is ever going to function perfectly. Some convictions which have been overturned were the result of human error and not malice. Eyewitness testimony is often problematic. Criminals have been known to wrongfully implicate other people just to get a deal on their own charges. In many past cases, forensic capabilities were far less than they are today. Before DNA testing, blood could only be identified by type and a few markers for abnormalities or certain hereditary conditions. Other advancements, which no one even dreamed about in the past, now allow fingerprints to be raised from surfaces like human skin, and facial characteristics of suspects to be determined from DNA samples.

But far too many of these overturned convictions came about because police and prosecutors engaged in deliberate fraud against innocent defendants. Perhaps no case is more appalling and frightening than that of former Chicago Police Detective Reynaldo Guevara, who some defense attorneys claim may have framed more than 50 defendants on murder charges.

A particularly chilling aspect of these cases is the allegation that Guevara took bribes of $20,000 to drop charges against suspects he had arrested for crimes that they probably hadn't committed. The whole sordid mess is compounded by the numerous times that city, state, and federal officials failed to take action, even when appeals courts issued statements describing Guevara's actions as, "profoundly alarming acts of misconduct," which led to "palpable injustice."

When questioned during a civil suit brought by Armando Serrano, whose murder conviction was overturned, Detective Guevara invoked his Fifth Amendment right against self-incrimination over 200 times. Eventually, the Cook County State's Attorney dropped the cases against nine men who had appealed their convictions. A number of others had their convictions overturned, and were either freed outright by a judge or acquitted in retrials. In 2009,

Arturo Reyes, another defendant framed for murder by Guevara, won a $16.4 million civil suit against the city. In 2013 alone, the city of Chicago paid $84.6 million in judgments for police abuse and wrongful conviction civil cases. With many of Guevara's cases still pending, the taxpayers are potentially on the hook for many more millions.

If you think the idea of framing 50 people, many for murder, is so outlandish that it has to be an outlier, a one-off event, stop right there. New York City, not wanting to be outdone by Chicago, offers the sordid story of disgraced former detective Louis Scarcella. Here's Wikipedia: [Emphasis added.]

> District Attorney Charles J. Hynes reopened the cases of **56** people arrested by Detective Scarcella;

> ...as of May 2018, Scarcella's police misconduct has resulted in wrongful convictions for at least 13 individuals, with a combined 245 years in prison for crimes which they did not commit. Because of Scarcella's tainted evidence, misleading testimony, and forced confessions, the city and state have been forced to pay at least $53.3 million in legal settlements.

But this isn't the end of the NYPD scandals. Indeed, it's hardly the tip of the iceberg. In 2017, the City of New York paid a $75 million class-action settlement because officers wrote **900,000** bogus summonses (tickets and infraction-level offenses) to meet quotas. According to a New York Post report in September 2018, in the preceding five years New York City paid out $384 million to settle cases of police misconduct. (Pretty sure you're not going to see that in an episode of *Blue Bloods*.)

Then there's Jackson County, Florida, northwest of Tallahassee, where in September 2018, Assistant State Attorney Laura Parish had to drop charges in **119** cases where former Deputy Zachary Wester is accused of planting evidence. Down state in Biscayne

Park, near Miami, the former police chief pleaded guilty to ordering three officers to arrest innocent citizens in order to clear unsolved burglary cases.

While not quite in the big leagues with Chicago, New York, or Florida, Orange County, California is another putrid example of malignant prosecutorial abuse. Revelations about systemic corrupt use of professional jail house informants has resulted in three sheriff's deputies committing perjury, and eighteen convictions being overturned. Investigations by multiple agencies, including the federal Department of Justice, are not yet completed so the final total of overturned convictions -- and the civil judgments that will surely follow -- is still to be determined.

A year earlier and just up the freeway, former Los Angeles County Sheriff Lee Baca got three years in federal custody for obstruction of justice and lying to federal agents investigating systemic abuses in the L.A. County Jail, where a majority of the inmates are awaiting trial, and thus entitled to the presumption of innocence. The bottom line:

**Big city, little city, north, south, east, west, this kind of shit goes on all the time.**

Police officers are human and mistakes, however unfortunate, happen. But any time that a single officer is involved in multiple instances of questionable behavior, any sane and fair legal system should react swiftly to see that justice is done. There can be no justification for allowing flagrantly suspect behavior to result in innocent people going to prison, especially for murder, where sentences can include the death penalty or life without parole. To allow prosecutors, cops, and others in the criminal justice system to get away with such behavior, behind a cloak of civil immunity, is a travesty that cannot continue. When the administration of justice fails to produce actual justice, because the system was subverted, then those responsible must pay such a high price that others are forever discouraged from imitating that behavior. Thus:

**Section 6: Fair enforcement of the law being critical to the cause of justice, all persons charged with the administration of justice who perjure, falsify evidence, or withhold that which is exculpatory, shall forfeit all immunity from civil liability and shall be guilty of a felony punishable by incarceration in a maximum security facility for a period, not subject to pardon, parole, commutation, suspension, or other reduction of sentence, of not less than ten years. Conviction, or plea of guilty for violation hereof, shall result in the forfeiture of all pension benefits accrued while in public office or employment.**

Our current legal system is founded on the premise that the truth will be discovered and justice will prevail when two adversarial sides, those of the prosecution/plaintiff and the defendant, battle it out according to arcane rules of procedure. The theory is, because each side is trying its hardest to win, eventually all the facts will come out and a jury, or a judge, can thus render a just verdict. This is preposterous, a judicial fantasyland. Because the focus is not on justice, but on winning, each side has insurmountable incentives to lie, conceal, and distort. It's all a carefully choreographed exercise in legal kabuki.

A prime example of this is when a judge rules that a prospective piece of evidence cannot be introduced because, "its prejudicial potential outweighs its probative value." Note that this is different from ruling that something cannot be introduced because it has *no* probative value. In applying a balancing test between prejudicial and probative, there is explicit acknowledgement that the evidence or claim has at least *some* probative value. Witnesses are compelled to tell the whole truth, but juries are not allowed to see the whole evidence. Again, only lawyers trained at the best schools of legal malfeasance can concoct such ridiculous reasoning. The simple truth:

***We must reduce the ability of lawyers to lie for a living***.

Instead, we need to make the truth paramount. The best way to do that is not to leave it to weak bar association panels to enforce regulations, and impose penalties, designed by lawyers for the benefit of lawyers. A constitutional mandate is required:

> **Section 7: The objectives of our legal system being truth and justice, all attorneys and other officers of the court shall, at all times in matters before the court, be bound to tell the whole truth and nothing but the truth. Violation hereof shall be a felony punishable by maximum security incarceration for a period not subject to pardon, parole, commutation, suspension, or other reduction of sentence, of not less than ten years.**

Eliminating, or minimizing, the damage from perversion of justice after a case makes it to court will be a great step forward. But we must also address the most grievous sin against the concept of justice: the killing of suspects before they even make it to court.

Police in America annually kill 1,000 or more people. A disturbing number are not only unarmed, they are not guilty of any crime (much less a serious felony). Examples abound, but it is almost impossible to get prosecutors to file criminal charges against the officers involved, partly because prosecutors fear antagonizing the police, whose testimony they depend on to get convictions. But even when prosecutors, either driven by genuine outrage or simply bowing to public pressure, bring charges against officers, guilty verdicts are hard to come by. The reason lies in two Supreme

Court decisions. As Chase Madar explained in *Why It's Impossible to Indict a Cop* for The Nation magazine:

> The legal standard authorizing deadly force is something called "objective reasonableness."

> This standard originates in the 1985 case of *Tennessee v. Garner*, which appeared at first to tighten restrictions on the police use of deadly force. The case involved a Memphis cop, Elton Hymon, who shot dead one Edward Garner: 15 years old, black and unarmed. Garner had just burgled a house, grabbing a ring and ten bucks. The US Supreme Court ruled that a police officer, henceforth, could use deadly force only if he "has probable cause to believe that the suspect poses a significant threat of death or serious physical injury to the officer or others." The ruling required that the use of force be "objectively reasonable." How this reasonableness should be determined was established in a 1989 case, *Graham v. Connor*: severity of the crime, whether the suspect is resisting or trying to escape and above all, whether the suspect posed an immediate threat to the safety of officers or others. All this appeared to restrict police violence -- even if, in the end, Officer Hymon was never criminally charged for fatally shooting Edward Garner.

> "Objectively reasonable" -- what could be wrong with that? But in actual courtroom practice, "objective reasonableness" has become nearly impossible to tell apart from the subjective snap judgments of panic-fueled police officers. American courts universally defer to the law enforcement officer's own personal assessment of the threat at the time.

> The Graham analysis essentially prohibits any second-guessing of the officer's decision to use deadly force: no hindsight is permitted, and wide latitude is granted to the officer's account of the situation, even if scientific evidence proves it to be mistaken.

According to Erwin Chemerinsky, dean of the UC Irvine Law School, recent Supreme Court decisions are not a path towards justice but rather a series of obstacles to holding police accountable for civil rights violations.

[snip]

The first step to controlling the police is to get rid of the fantasy, once and for all, that the law is on our side. The law is firmly on the side of police who open fire on unarmed civilians.

If admitting that the law is not always on our side is the first step, then the second step is:

**Section 8: The right to life being the bedrock of innocent until proven guilty, deadly force by law enforcement officers shall be employed only after actual danger to their own lives, or that of others, is clearly established, and non-lethal measures are unable to be employed with sufficient speed and effectiveness. Any violation hereof resulting in death shall be a felony punishable by maximum security incarceration for a period not subject to pardon, parole, commutation, suspension, or other reduction of sentence, of not less than twenty years.**

Police love to have it both ways: they proclaim how, "they risk their lives to protect the public," but they also want the freedom to use deadly force, not when the public is in danger, and not when the police are actually in danger, but when they *think* they *might* be in danger. Their argument is, essentially, that they need the right to take the risk out of a risky profession, even if it means the death of innocent people. This is a situation that has been compounded by the recent push to militarize the police. Our military doctrine ever since Vietnam has been to minimize battlefield casualties, which seems like a no-brainer. The problem is, this has led to a mentality where protecting our soldiers comes at the expense of eliminating certainty about who is, and who is not, the enemy. Rather than send in troops to determine the identity of the enemy, or confirm that enemy forces are even present, we just unleash a drone strike on a village, a car, a funeral, or even a wedding because we **think** someone in that group **might** be a terrorist or enemy combatant. Or, we're right that there is a terrorist or two in the groups, and we're just willing to blow away a couple dozen other people as a cost of doing business. But somehow, we are too stupid to figure out that this just breeds more terrorist jihadis. Just as the indiscriminate killing of civilians breeds more distrust and hostility in minority communities.

The difference between a drone strike because a terrorist might be present, and a *peace* officer shooting a person, because the object in their hand **might** be a gun, is one only of scale, not substance. This is also why many departments now have armored vehicles, which belong on a foreign battlefield and not a city street. In fact, most of these vehicles are military surplus and were deployed against the enemy in Iraq, Kuwait, or Afghanistan. But who's the enemy here?

Let's also be honest about the tremendous racial disparity in how suspects and ordinary citizens are treated by police. Ohio provides a classic, yet tragic and needless example: John Crawford III.

Ohio is an "open carry" state, meaning that, as long as you are of legal age, and are not otherwise prohibited from possessing a firearm due to a felony conviction, restraining order, or adverse mental health ruling, you can openly carry a firearm on your person when in public. Crawford, who was black, was shot to death by police in a Walmart store in Beavercreek, Ohio, while holding **a BB gun** he intended to purchase. Does anyone in their right mind think that two white cops would have been so quick to open fire if a white parent was holding that BB gun? Of course not.

Anyone who needs more proof should go watch the YouTube video, *Open Carry Experiment Exposes Racist Cops*. It shows two separate incidents of men walking down the street in an open carry state, each with an AR-15 slung over their shoulder. In the first video, involving a white man, the white police officer calmly gets out of his car and approaches the individual to ask for I.D. and politely inquire why he is carrying the weapon. In the second video, when a black man is carrying the weapon, the first officer on the scene takes a position behind his car, gun drawn, and forces the black man to get face down on the street until two backup units arrive. Open carry state. Both weapons slung, not hand carried. Two completely different reactions. That, folks, is the kind of racial discrimination in law enforcement which requires passage of Section 8. And it's been going on for a century or more.

Way back in 1963, I was pulled over by the LAPD, with three high school friends, two of whom were black. The cops were astonished at this integrated group, and demanded to know what Pete and I were doing with "two niggers." The next morning, I told my parents that someday the black community was going to react to one of these racially-profiled traffic stops and rioting would break out. Two years later, prompted by the beating of a young black man during a traffic stop, the Watts Riot erupted only a mile from where I had been pulled over.

In 2018, the Supreme Court made it even harder to prosecute cops who use lethal force as their first tool out of the bag. Here's how the L.A. Times reported the case where an Arizona woman was shot by police in her own front yard while holding a kitchen knife:

> Rather than decide whether Kisela used excessive force, the court instead ruled he could not be sued because the victim could not cite a similar case involving a police shooting of a person holding a knife.

So, because there were no previous cases where a person holding a knife was shot by a cop and then sued, this case can't be examined? Are you kidding me? These are the best and brightest legal minds we can produce? Of course not; they're simply the ones who can be most reliably counted on to preserve a key tool -- *law enforcement* -- that the elite use to control society through fear. This is also a great example of the Supreme Court refusing to recognize what everyone else would consider common sense -- an implied constitutional right to good government -- but instead conveniently inventing a right, in this case, "qualified immunity," when it suits the establishment. Again, from the L.A. Times story: [Emphasis added.]

> University of Chicago law professor William Baude, a former clerk for Chief Justice John G. Roberts Jr., has argued the justices ***invented the doctrine of "qualified immunity"*** in the 1980s and have steadily expanded it to block suits in cases of excessive force.
>
> In her dissent, Sotomayor quoted a law review article by Judge Stephen Reinhardt from Los Angeles ... "Nearly all of the Supreme Court's qualified immunity cases come out the same way -- by finding immunity for the officials," Reinhardt wrote in 2015."

***Invented the doctrine.*** Beginning to see a pattern here?

The same day this L.A. Times story hit, officers in New York city shot and killed a bipolar black man holding what they thought was a gun. It turned out to be a length of plumbing pipe with a shower head attached. A shower head -- mistaken in broad daylight -- for a gun by four officers who had the suspect contained. Thanks to these ridiculous Supreme Court rulings, the police preach, "to serve and respect," but the reality is, "comply or die." Except lots of times the victim isn't even given time to comply. Counterpunch ran an article soon after the Kisela and New York shooting titled,

*Badge of Impunity*. The problem of trigger-happy cops can only be remedied with Section 8 of the 37th Amendment.

The end of this chapter seems about as good a place as any for a note about the Supreme Court: Enactment of the Restoration Amendments through peaceful political action (as outlined in chapters 23 and 24) will only be part of the battle. Subsequent enforcement by the court system, all the way up to SCOTUS, will determine whether or not true reform actually occurs. Over the past half-century, we have seen how adept the Court has become in perverting the intent of the constitution. Because the Restoration Amendments have been drafted with so much specificity and detail, it will be difficult for the Court to evade or dilute enforcement of them. If the Supreme Court should go to such extraordinary lengths to frustrate true reform, we will be left with only two choices: Surrender to authoritarian fascism, or take to the streets in revolt, which could easily turn violent. Hopefully, this is a bridge we will never have to cross.

# Chapter 13

# SANCTITY OF PRIVATE PROPERTY

The Fifth Amendment is known primarily for its right against self-incrimination, but it ends with, "nor shall private property be taken for public use, without just compensation," which has become known as the Takings Clause. For two centuries, public use was interpreted to mean that as long as they paid the current owners a fair price, governments could use the power of eminent domain to acquire lands for roads, schools, public buildings, flood control projects, parks, etc. However, in the latter part of the 20th century, the definition of public use was expanded to include blight abatement.

As residents and businesses fled older neighborhoods, local governments wanted a way to acquire properties that had been allowed to deteriorate. Unfortunately, blight soon became whatever the local government said it was. Abandoned buildings turned into drug dens? Rusting, derelict cars stripped of everything valuable? Fields overgrown with vegetation tall enough to hide LeBron James? None of that was required. An area could be economically blighted simply if it did not produce as much local sales and property tax revenue as another type of use might. Before long, real economic blight was no longer necessary; eminent domain could now be used if an area was merely, in the opinion of someone in government, economically depressed.

The concept of economic blight and economic depression became handmaidens to a process called redevelopment. The way redevelopment generally works is that an area is designated as blighted and its current tax base becomes the floor for what is known as tax increment financing (TIF), in which the local government gets to keep (rather than share with the state or county) all the additional tax revenue (over and above the floor) that results from the new development. Supposedly, these increased tax revenues help pay for costs associated with the new project, like improved roads, new water and sewer lines, street lighting, and even increased police presence.

Unfortunately, there is almost always a pernicious condition attached: to use tax increment financing, the local government entity must incur debt on the project. That's because TIF is an invention of our old friends on Wall Street, the municipal bond industry. No pay-as-you-go financing using current revenues or accumulated reserves. Instead, the local government must issue bonds which have upfront fees paid to the underwriters, and typically end up costing taxpayers at least double in interest over the life of the bond.

Not surprisingly, local governments soon found ways to abuse the process. One California community declared the entire city blighted. In another classic example, my city of Redondo Beach, California, tried to declare a major portion of its harbor economically blighted. If an economically blighted harbor conjures up images of rotting wharfs and vacant warehouses, it's time to re-visualize. Imagine three boat marinas, three upscale hotels, an eclectic mix of small shops, and a Fisherman's Wharf featuring an El Torito, a Kincaid's Steak House, and L.A.'s renowned seafood restaurant, Tony's On The Pier. (In truth, *none* of Redondo Beach is blighted. Homes of less than 2,000 square feet on tiny lots miles from the beach, with no view, go for over a million dollars.)

The practice, and the result, are the same all across the country. Take the landmark case of *Kelo v. City of New London*, where the evil triplets of eminent domain abuse, redevelopment, and corporate giveaways came to a head. In 2005, New London, Connecticut tried using eminent domain to seize a large section of the working-class Fort Trumbull neighborhood in order to make room for a redevelopment plan anchored by a new research facility for the pharmaceutical giant Pfizer. Susette Kelo and six others sued. The case went to the Supreme Court and in 2005, the four traditionally liberal justices serving at the time -- Stevens, Breyer, Souter, and Ginsburg -- were joined by Justice Kennedy in ruling that this use of eminent domain was legal. This was the first time where merely wanting to increase tax revenues from a more affluent class of residents and shoppers was the sole justification for use of eminent domain.

The dissent, led by Justice Sandra Day O'Connor, was blistering. She suggested that what would come to be known as "reverse Robin Hood" -- take from the poor, give to the rich -- would become commonplace rather than exceptional:

> Today, the Court abandons [the Fifth Amendment's] long-held, basic limitation on government power. Under the banner of economic development, all private property is now vulnerable to being taken and transferred to another private owner, so long as it might be upgraded, i.e. given to an owner who will use it in a way that the legislature deems more beneficial to the public...

> [snip]

> [the decision eliminates] any distinction between private and public use of property -- and thereby effectively deletes the words 'for public use' from the Takings Clause of the Fifth Amendment.

> [snip]

...the fallout ... will not be random. The beneficiaries are likely to be those citizens with disproportionate influence and power in the political process, including large corporations and development firms.

In a concurring dissent, Justice Thomas castigated the majority for replacing the public use terminology actually in the Constitution with a court-concocted public purpose:

This deferential shift in phraseology enables the Court to hold, against all common sense, that a costly urban-renewal project whose stated purpose is a vague promise of new jobs and increased tax revenue, but which is also suspiciously agreeable to the Pfizer Corporation, is for a 'public use.'

By *agreeable to Pfizer*, Thomas meant that in addition to the private developer getting 91 acres of prime waterfront property for $1 a year (no, that's not a typo), Pfizer was promised a property tax rebate of 80% a year for ten years. Thomas also noted:

Something has gone seriously awry with this Court's interpretation of the Constitution. Though citizens are safe from the government in their homes, the homes themselves are not.

[snip]

Allowing the government to take property solely for public purposes is bad enough, but extending the concept of public purpose to encompass any economically beneficial goal guarantees that these losses will fall disproportionately on poor communities. Those communities are not only systematically less likely to put their lands to the highest and best social use, but are also the least politically powerful.

Just to show what a great bunch of guys the New London City Council was, after the verdict they tried to collect back rent from each of the seven plaintiffs for the years while the case worked its way through the courts. Although justice was not served, in this case the Gods of Irony did prevail:

- Instead of having to pay back rent, the seven plaintiffs received additional compensation over and above the city's original offer for their properties.

- When Kelo moved, the city had to agree to move her house to the new location.

- Pfizer merged with Wyeth and instead of a new research center in New London, the company closed its New London operations -- costing the city 1,500 jobs -- and expanded its facility just across the river in Groton. (To no one's surprise, the move to Groton came just as Pfizer's previous sweetheart tax deal was set to expire and the company's property taxes were about to go up 400%.)

- Unable to secure financing, the private developer abandoned the project. To this day the property still stands vacant. The cost of acquiring the land and bulldozing the old buildings cost the city of New London $78 million, and it has not received a cent of revenue of any kind from the project site.

- A small monument, and commemorative plaque, stand on the site where Kelo's house once stood. Since 2011, the rest of the area has been a dumpsite for debris from Hurricane Irene.

- Spurred by public outrage over the *Kelo* verdict, forty states amended their laws to either ban, or greatly limit, the use of eminent domain to transfer property to private entities for strictly economic reasons. For example, after years of efforts by reformers, California finally repealed its redevelopment law in 2011, transferring over $10 billion back to the state treasury. (As a side benefit, the repeal of redevelopment gave the municipal bond industry a sad.)

However, state laws are not sufficient to protect sacred property rights as envisioned by the Founding Fathers, who put the Takings Clause into the Bill of Rights for very specific reasons having to do with the way their property rights had been trampled by the Crown.

## The 38th Amendment --
## Sanctity of Private Property

**Section 1: The sanctity of one's home and business being of utmost importance, no process of government, except as results from a criminal conviction, shall seize or transfer directly, or indirectly, real property belonging to any person or private entity to another person or private entity.**

Not content with whittling away at the Takings Clause and the Due Process portions of the 14th Amendment, government and courts at all levels have learned to abuse civil asset forfeiture laws, in a practice that has become known as *Policing for Profit*. Most Americans generally know asset forfeiture law in the context of the 1970 RICO Act, which justified seizing assets of suspected drug kingpins before they went to trial in order to limit their ability to finance legal dream teams. However, the practice has roots going back to biblical times. An article in the Regent University Law Review explains:

> In *Calero-Toledo v. Pearson Yacht Leasing Co.,"* the Supreme Court located the origin of forfeiture in biblical practices: "[i]f an ox gore a man or a woman, and they die, he shall be stoned and his flesh shall not be eaten." This concept was broadened and changed in

a unique way by early English law. Under the English medieval law of "deodand" ... any property causing the death of a person was subject to forfeiture.' While the object itself was not necessarily seized, its value was assessed and remitted to the king as a forfeiture." Whereas biblical law prevented anyone from benefiting from the guilty property ("his flesh shall not be eaten"), under English law the property was forfeited to the crown.

Although the U.S. never established deodand (which was outlawed in England in the mid-1800s) as a legal doctrine, "forfeited to the crown" has morphed into forfeited to your local, state, or federal government. That's because the U.S. did adopt a variation of deodand used by the British Admiralty to justify imposing English Maritime Law on foreign merchant ships. (One not-so-quaint aspect of British Maritime Law allowed its warships to stop foreign vessels on the high seas and kidnap anyone it wanted into serving in the British Royal Navy. America's victory in The War of 1812 put an end to the practice, at least as far as American flag vessels were concerned.)

The adoption of British Maritime Law led to the legal fiction of personification, in which a person's money and property substitute, or personify, the offenses for which they're charged. Over time, this concept was distorted to the point where now you don't even have to be charged.

Government agencies, from local police departments to the Department of Justice and DEA, can seize and keep your property ***without an indictment, much less trial and conviction***. Bottom line: even if you're innocent, your money and property aren't. As the ACLU noted way back in 2001:

> Thanks to civil asset forfeiture laws, possessions that took you a lifetime to acquire can be taken in the blink of an eye, or, more accurately, the flash of a badge.

[snip]

Allowing authorities to take away and sell a person's vehicle or home without proving that he or she has done something wrong flies in the face of basic American values. Forfeiting a person's property without a conviction undermines the bedrock principle of our legal system: that a person is innocent until proven guilty.

As the Regent Law Review article noted, in writing about the case *Burnham v. Superior Court*, Justice Scalia quoted from an earlier case, *Schaffer v. Heitner*:

[the] fiction that an assertion of jurisdiction over property is anything but an assertion of jurisdiction over the owner of the property supports an ancient form without substantial modern justification.

Not surprisingly, the fiction of personification has led to widespread civil forfeiture abuse, where police departments finance significant portions of their budget by seizing money, cars, and valuables *from people who are never charged with a crime*. A few examples:

Condensed from the Regent University Law Review article:

Albert Wright, a local Las Vegas businessman, hired Billy Munnerlyn, owner of a successful Las Vegas air charter service, to fly him to Ontario airport in San Bernardino County. When they landed, the DEA arrested both men, seizing not only $2.7 million in Wright's briefcase but also Mannerlyn's plane, his $8,500 charter fee, and eventually all of his business records. It was only then that Mannerlyn learned that Wright was a convicted drug dealer. However, charges were dropped against both men, and eventually Wright even **got his entire $2.7 million back**. Mannerlyn wasn't so lucky. He had to sell three other planes to finance a lengthy legal battle. After winning at trial in Los Angeles, Mannerlyn saw the verdict overturned by a Federal District judge. Billy

Mannerlyn ended up filing for bankruptcy and at last report was working as truck driver.

From watchdogwire.com/texas:

In October of 2007, Roderick Daniels was traveling through Tenaha, Texas on US Route 59. Just outside of the city, he was pulled over for allegedly traveling 37 miles-per-hour in a 35 miles-per-hour zone. The officer then asked Mr. Daniels if he was carrying any cash. The very aim of the trip being to purchase a car, he revealed to the officer that he was carrying a substantial amount of cash; about $8,500. Little did Mr. Daniels know he was about to be become a textbook case of civil asset forfeiture abuse in Texas.

The officer promptly placed Mr. Daniels under arrest and transported him to the jail. It was here that Daniels was given an ultimatum: sign pre-notarized documents agreeing to forfeit the money and jewelry found in his car, or be charged with money laundering. Scared and far from home, Mr. Daniels complied. Ron Henderson and Jennifer Boatright had a similar experience with the Tenaha Police on US Route 59. While traveling through the area with their two children, they were pulled over and questioned as to whether they were carrying cash. They, too, were looking to purchase a used car and were carrying over $6,000. The officers began searching the car, turning up no contraband. Neither officer issued a citation for the alleged offense -- driving in a left-hand turn lane -- and Ms. Boatright and Mr. Henderson were told that they could either sign the same documents relinquishing all ownership interest in the cash or face money laundering charges. In addition, they were told that challenging the charge would result in them being placed in custody with their two small children being placed in foster care. The couple signed over their property rather than face the dissolution of their family.

"Incidents such as these, while abhorrent, are not uncommon. In Tenaha alone, it is estimated that between 2006 and 2008 the police seized $3 million worth of property from motorists. Over 150 of these seizure cases are believed to be invalid. With only 923 residents and two sworn police officers, these enforcement actions represent a windfall to the Tenaha and Shelby County government and have the potential to underwrite a significant portion of their budget."

From *When Did "To Protect and Serve" Become "To Seize and Profit"?* at FireDogLake.com:

Consider the case of an African-American man driving from Virginia Beach to Wilmington, Delaware:

He was stopped by police on June 16, 1998, while driving from Virginia Beach to Wilmington, Delaware. The police officer who stopped him claimed that a taillight was out, which was untrue. Once stopped, the officer subjected him to a search by a drug dog, claiming that he "looked like a drug dealer." The officers asked him if he was carrying drugs, guns or money. He replied that he had $3,500 in cash. The officer seized the money, claiming that it must be the proceeds of drug dealing ... The gentleman was never charged with a crime.

The man never got his money back.

From Nick Sibilla at the Institute for Justice in a story picked up by forbes.com:

Last month, the Fort Worth Star Telegram reported that the District Attorney's Office in Tarrant County, Texas seized $3.5 million, plus almost 250 cars and 440 computers in fiscal year 2013, roughly equal to about 10 percent of its budget.

[snip]

Between 2001 and 2007, law enforcement agencies (in Texas) seized and kept over 35,000 cars, homes and electronics, forfeiting more than $280 million. District attorneys have used these forfeiture funds on ridiculous purchases, including visiting casinos, a vacation to Hawaii and a margarita machine.

Civil forfeiture abuse isn't confined to just a few states; it goes on from Michigan to Florida, Nevada to Virginia. Some states, like Minnesota, have tried to address this abuse of power by requiring conviction of the crime before assets can be sold. However, as Sibila explains in the Forbes piece, local law enforcement agencies are able to make an end run around that restriction, thanks to a federal program known as equitable sharing: [Emphasis added.]

> By partnering with a federal agency, local and state law enforcement can keep up to 80 percent of the proceeds from a forfeited property. Incredibly, police can collaborate **even if doing so would circumvent their own states' protections for property owners**.

The problem is so bad that the Institute for Justice has published, *Policing for Profit: The Abuse of Civil Asset Forfeiture*. When corrupt, power-mad law enforcement agencies that have lost all concept of justice stand to profit from asset forfeiture abuses, the only solution is:

> **Section 2: Assets of individuals, organizations, and business entities may not be forfeited except upon conviction of a crime or as the result of civil judgment. Victims of illegal asset seizure shall be awarded return of the seized property, reasonable attorney's fees, and punitive damages of three times attorney's fees or the value of the seized property, whichever is greater.**

Sadly, there is a third way that government takes people's hard-earned property unfairly: through duplicate taxation. Make no mistake: At the state and local level, where the government cannot simply print the money it needs, taxes are the price we pay for what we recognize as a civilized society. Want safe roads with working traffic lights? Firefighters to save your home, family, or business? Police to control crime? Zoning regulations that prevent a strip club from setting up next to a school? Trash picked up every week? All these things require revenues from taxes and fees.

However, it is inherently unjust to require Americans to pay taxes on taxes. Whatever you pay in state and local taxes, sales taxes, gas taxes, and so forth, should be deductible on your federal income tax filing. This is the way it was until Congress, first under Reagan and now Trump, went hunting for ways to replace the income taxes lost by giving the über-wealthy and huge corporations massive tax cuts. (There was no actual need to replace the tax cut money; the Reagan and Trump administrations simply needed an excuse, one good enough to fool the average voter, to justify cutting domestic programs.)

In October 2017, just as this traditional deduction was under fire in the battle to pass the Trump tax cuts, Joseph J. Thornberg at TaxHistory.org wrote a superb article for Tax Notes titled, *The SALT Deduction Has Always Been Hard to Defend -- And to Kill*, which summarized the history of the state and local tax deduction, commonly known by the acronym SALT:

> The provision has been a feature of federal income taxation since 1862, but its roots run even deeper in U.S. history. Since the early years of American nationhood, political leaders have been arguing about the need to protect state revenue sources from federal encroachment -- as well as the dangers of double taxation to individual taxpayers.

The article explains how the deductibility of state and local taxes was incorporated into the Revenue Act of 1862 where, for the first time, a tax on income was imposed in order to fund the Union cause in the Civil War. After the war, the income tax temporarily disappeared. But when it was finally enacted for good in 1913, the SALT deduction was also restored. As Thornberg explains:

> Over the decades, the deduction evolved to reflect its fiscal environment. When states began to rely on sales taxes, the deductibility of those levies in the federal system was made explicit. The introduction of the standard deduction in 1944 also reshaped the SALT deduction, reducing its scope dramatically (and shifting the distribution of its benefits up the income scale). Later revisions in the 1960s and 1970s modestly curbed the deduction, but it remained largely intact through the 1980s.
>
> [snip]
>
> By the late 1970s, however, the SALT deduction had a target on its back, and tax reformers began to call regularly for its elimination. Most notably, Treasury urged its repeal in its famous series of tax reform studies conducted in the late 1970s and early 1980s. The 1984 version of the indictment was especially clear:

> The current deduction for State and local taxes disproportionately benefits high-income taxpayers residing in high-tax States. The two-thirds of taxpayers who do not itemize deductions are not entitled to deduct State and local taxes, and even itemizing taxpayers receive relatively little benefit from the deduction unless they reside in high-tax States. Although the deduction for State and local taxes thus benefits a small minority of U.S. taxpayers, the cost of the deduction is borne by all taxpayers in the form of significantly higher marginal tax rates.

> [snip]

> Ultimately, the 1986 Tax Reform Act eliminated the deductibility of state sales taxes, but it preserved the deductibility of income and property taxes.

What is conveniently not mentioned by those who oppose the SALT deduction, because it favors high-tax states, is that those high-tax states also have both high living costs *and* they generally provide more government benefits and services to their residents. If your vision of government is one where only minimum services should be provided, naturally you don't want to help residents of other states fund services which you see as extraneous. The fact that some of the states most affected by eliminating the SALT deduction -- New York, New Jersey, California, Maryland -- traditionally back Democratic party candidates is mere coincidence and has no connection to the fact that the war on the SALT deduction has been led by Republicans. *Yeah, riiight.*

Economist Michael Hiltzik noted in the L.A. Times that the state of politics in this country has sunk to such a low level that, "the idea that Republicans in Congress would turn their gun sights on Democratic states is seen as sort of adorable." Interestingly enough, the Trump tax bill's elimination of the SALT deduction may not survive constitutional challenge. Hiltzik cited both prominent Democrats and Republicans who argue that the SALT deduction has both historical precedent (going all the back to the Civil War) and legal foundation, including a decision about Maryland taxes written by the Justice Samuel Alito. However, at this time there is no guarantee how, or even if, the Supreme Court will rule. Even if it overturns this provision of the Trump tax bill, it is unlikely that it will reach back to retroactively reinstate the deductibility of state sales taxes that was eliminated in the 1988 Reagan tax bill. Nor have state gas taxes, on the rise in many states, ever been deductible. The easiest and most surefire way to ensure that double taxation does not occur is to enshrine protection in the 38th Amendment:

**Section 3: The right not to be taxed twice on the same income being fundamental to economic justice, all taxes, fees, and assessments levied by federal, state, or local**

**governments shall be deductible from federal taxes levied on income. Home ownership being a cornerstone of a stable society, all residential mortgage interest shall also be deductible from state and federal taxes levied on income.**

By enshrining mortgage interest as tax deductible, Section 3 ensures that the average family has the best possible opportunity to acquire its single biggest asset, the family home. Homes are more than just residential structures. They are a community's signature feature, the thing that most defines that community's quality of life. Home ownership provides neighborhood stability. The ability of residents to own and adequately maintain a house and grounds is essential if poorer communities are to achieve or maintain any sense of dignity, not to mention a reasonable tax base. Ownership of a decent home is the most frequent and accurate measure of the American Dream. Tax policies that discourage or impede home ownership are inimical to the ideals that Americans hold dear, and a threat to the image and example America should project to the world. For that reason, it deserves constitutional protection.

The primary objection from those who wish to abolish or limit the mortgage interest deduction is that it favors wealthy people who itemize deductions. The corollary argument is that rich people will deduct vacation homes, even multiple properties. Yes. *And so what?*

The residential construction industry has always been a primary driver of the national economy, and is one lynchpin of employment that can't be off-shored. Better to let a few rich people get an extra deduction than to deny it to the vast majority. I'm no fan of Mitt Romney or the late John McCain, but so what if they each own a half-dozen expensive homes? They're still paying local property taxes, bonded indebtedness levies, and special district assessments. Their property taxes support schools which their children do not attend. Their utility taxes still benefit the local community.

In addition, once state and local taxes become deductible, a lot more people will find it worth their while to file itemized returns, especially since software programs make itemizing deductions relatively quick, simple, and cost-effective. Moreover, once national industrial policy (Chapter 19) creates sufficient well-paying domestic employment, more people will have enough income to make itemizing deductions worthwhile, even if they have to go beyond Intuit or TurboTax and hire a CPA or professional tax preparer.

Most importantly, the build-up of equity through home ownership has traditionally been a bedrock of class mobility. Being able to retire in a paid-off home, and eventually leave it to your children, has been a way in which families have traditionally climbed the economic ladder. Just as being the first person in a family to attend college is a marker of economic progress, so, too, is being the first to be able to buy a home, and more importantly, to finally own it free and clear. There is something quite reassuring in waking up on New Year's Day knowing that, if you can simply pay the property taxes and utilities, you'll have a roof over your head for the year.

Finally, the principle of home ownership, of people being able to afford a permanent place in their community, is crucial to the core strength of the republic. The rich and powerful would like nothing better than denying as many people as possible the security that comes with home ownership. People whose jobs are constantly in danger, and whose ability to keep a roof over their heads is constantly threatened, tend toward desperate compliance with whatever their overlords desire. ***Keep 'em scared, keep them economically imperiled, and they will remain submissive***, is the mantra of the elite. No less than former Federal Reserve Chairman Alan Greenspan, an economics spawn of the devil if there ever was one, described how there is very little pressure for wages to rise when workers are *traumatized*. That's the word he used to describe the fear that pushing for higher wages will simply result in the company moving your job overseas or to Mexico.

Letting people keep more of what they make by not paying taxes on taxes, and by not making a mortgage act as more of a strain on their finances than is absolutely necessary, are part of a multi-pronged strategy to make things better for the average person. Leaving the right to deduct mortgage interest and subordinate taxes in the hands of Congress runs counter to that goal.

Alas, there is still one more area where property must be protected from the rapacious malevolence of politicians who seek to appease one segment of voters at the expense of another: rent control. In no other sector of the economy is an artificial limitation imposed on the price and value of a commodity or service. (There is an exception for emergencies where state governors and the President can enforce temporary bans on price gouging. But otherwise, there is no artificially imposed limit on prices.) Take, for example, cars: Imagine you tell your city council that you want to drive a Bentley, but you can only afford a Kia Sorrento, so you want the council to force the Bentley dealer to sell you a $235,000 Bentley Bentayga for the $26,000 price of a Sorrento. Once they stopped laughing, the council would ask you to have a seat until the men in the white suits with the butterfly net arrive. Same if you demanded that the city council force the supermarket to sell you organic ribeye steak for the same price as mass-farmed ground chuck.

But when it comes to rental control, all fairness and logic goes right out the window. Let's be clear; rent control exists for one reason:

*To allow politicians to curry favor with renters by forcing landlords to suffer financial loss so that some voters can live where they otherwise could not afford.*

Want to live in a nice area but can't afford it? Here's a solution: Have government make it affordable by forcing the property owner to subsidize your preferred lifestyle.

Rent control is often justified on two grounds:

- That renters who have lived in a particular place for "x" number of years should not be forced to move by rents that increase beyond their ability to pay.

- That it is better for society as a whole if communities contain a mix of various socioeconomic groups. (Poor, minorities, etc.)

The first argument pretends to grant renters a partial right of ownership -- a right to continue to reside -- to the homes or apartments they occupy. What is even worse is when the particular form of rent control does not permit what is known as *vacancy de-control* where the rent can be raised to current market rates when the current tenant moves out. But regardless of the specific elements of any rent control regulations, at its core rent control is nothing less than a transfer of partial private property ownership rights to a government entity without compensation to the owner. Although courts have weaseled their way around it, in strict constitutional terms, it amounts to a "taking," justified on the basis of political convenience.

The second argument, about the benefits of living in a blended society, is not without merit. In fact, it is an argument that I use later in this book regarding universal military service. However, rent control is neither the best way, nor a fair way, to achieve that goal. The equitable solution is rent subsidization, such as federal Section 8 vouchers, in which the government assists people in paying market rate rents. However, you rarely see proposals for communities to enact local taxes to subsidize renters who cannot afford market rates. Why? Because it is anathema to most voters: *Tax me in order to facilitate other people living someplace they can't afford, and perhaps even I can't afford? Fuck you.* Instead, their attitude is, *let's have somebody else -- specifically landlords -- pay for this.*

This is also why, even though rent control is justified on the grounds that *housing* is too expensive, that you never see proposals to regulate how much the sale price of a home can increase in a given year. This would bite too many hands. State and local governments would lose too much revenue because valuations would not continue to escalate. But more importantly, homeowners would suffer drastic decreases in the equity buildup and the cash-out value of their homes. Many homeowners who are quick to support rent control simply want to feel good about themselves without having any of their own skin in the game. *Socialism for thee but not for me.* (There is nothing wrong, at least in my opinion, with a social democratic approach to government. But it is inherently unfair -- and hypocrisy at its finest -- to advocate for a governing premise but then not want it to apply to yourself.)

Rent control also appeals to the idea of punishing the caricature of the evil landlord. Sure, there are slumlords. And there are landlords, especially those with a large number of units, whose primary focus is always on profits, to the exclusion of all other considerations. But there are also a lot of mom-and-pop landlords, who live in one half of a duplex and rent out the other. Or who rent out the old family home after the parents pass away. This is why many rent control ordinances exempt small landlords. While well-intentioned, and beneficial to those exempted, this just reinforces the bottom line: a certain narrow slice of rental housing owners are expected to pay the bill for what others think is a societal good, just one which they themselves are not willing to financially support.

Many liberal homeowners are perfectly willing to vote for rent control because it makes them feel good. But rent control often causes more problems than it cures.

In 2018, California voters rejected Prop 10, a state-wide rent control ballot measure, in part because the non-partisan legislative analyst concluded in the official ballot materials that over the long term, passage would decrease the number of current rental units and reduce the number of new units that might be built. The loss of current units would occur when landlords sold single family homes to buyers who would occupy the units. The reduction in future units would be caused by investor worries about Return on Investment (ROI). The legislative analyst also concluded that state and local governments would both lose tax revenues (because landlords would be taxed on lower profits), and incur increased costs from having to establish rent control boards and fund enforcement efforts.

Rent control is often propagandized as a way for low-income people to afford decent housing. However, in practice, it is most often imposed in middle-class, and even prime residential areas, so that the 10% can continue to enjoy a subsidized lifestyle. One of the most prominent examples of this is Santa Monica, California. (Also derisively known as the People's Republic of Santa Monica.) At one time, back in the 1990s, the average income of a person living in a rent-controlled unit in Santa Monica was $85,000. I personally knew young professionals with good jobs who drove BMW and Mercedes Benz automobiles, and took vacations to places like the Bahamas, who lived in prime beach areas for $800 a month when the market rate would have been $2,000 or more.

Rent control favors employers, because it allows them to have a convenient local workforce without paying commensurate wages.

But the real reason behind rent control is the arrogant belief by some people that they are entitled to live where they like, not where they can afford. What is left out of this equation is the fact that, almost always without exception, these people are taking away housing opportunities from others who could pay -- and would pay -- market rate. This occurs because rent control is often imposed where there are a limited number of rental units available due to building constraints. Sometimes, all the land that can be used has been used. In other cases, people who live in the area are dead set against continuous, never-ending, over-development that ruins the existing quality of life. The bottom line is:

*If more housing cannot be built in a given area, and some people who could not otherwise afford it are allowed to live there because of capped rents, then other people who have the financial means to rent at market prices are unfairly and arbitrarily denied that opportunity.*

When you strip away all the excuses and emotional appeals, it really is that simple. (This also applies to rent subsidies; some tenants who could afford the rent would be excluded by those receiving a subsidy. It's a variation on a law of physics: two objects cannot occupy the same space at the same time.)

As I pointed out earlier, at some point we have to come to grips with three harsh realities:

- Continuous growth as we know it cannot continue.

- Not everyone is entitled to live where they want just because they want it.

- The concept of being first has to have some value.

Therefore:

**Section 4:** The imposition of price controls on rental property constitutes a taking of value from the property owner without just compensation and is thus illegal in all forms and in all circumstances.

# Chapter 14

# THE RIGHT TO PRIVACY

Ernest Hemingway famously said, "The only kind of writing is rewriting." As luck would have it, just when it came time to rewrite this chapter, news broke about Cambridge Analytica's use of Facebook data to create voter profiles and targeted ads for the Trump campaign. Several days later, it came out that Facebook *allowed* the Clinton campaign to access similar information. So many articles poured out in the next few weeks that at one time just listing them by title might be sufficient to justify a constitutional Right to Privacy. Eventually I settled on samples from a select few. First and foremost was this from Edward Snowden, ironically posted by Act.tv on its Facebook page:

> Businesses that make money by collecting and selling detailed records of private lives were once plainly described as "surveillance companies". Their rebranding as "social media" is the most successful deception since the Department of War became the Department of Defense.

Here's what Ben Shapiro wrote for The Hill.com on March 20, 2018:

**What's Genius for Obama Is Scandal When It Comes To Trump**

The former Obama director of integration and media analytics stated that, during the 2012 campaign, Facebook allowed the Obama team to "suck out the whole social graph"; Facebook "was surprised we were able to suck out the whole social graph, but they didn't stop us once they realized that was what we were doing." She added, "They came to [the] office in the days following election recruiting & were very candid that they allowed us to do things they wouldn't have allowed someone else to do because they were on our side."

***Because they were on our side***. If the thought of a company, with Facebook's data and clout, secretly picking sides to manipulate election results doesn't make you tremble, you should probably stop reading because it's unlikely that anything in this book will be of use to you.

Here's tech and civil liberties writer Robert X. Cringely on Cringely.com: (Emphasis original.)

### Facebook, Cambridge Analytica, and Our Personal Data

...the quizzes on Facebook about "Which Star Wars character are you?" are there just to get you to authorize them. Then they go harvest your data. *The authorization is built into the terms of service when you take the test.*

***So don't take any Facebook quizzes, surveys, or tests -- EVER.***

**The aspect of this story that ought to be of most concern to Facebook members is that once I have authorized someone to use my Facebook data, I have authorized them to use not only my data but also that of *all my Facebook friends*!**

Jason Koebler, who covers tech and civil liberties for Vice.com, on Mar 19, 2018:

### Cambridge Analytica's Ad Targeting Is the Reason Facebook Exists

Thousands of third-party apps were designed solely to obtain and sell your data. It's no surprise that the data ended up being used again on Facebook, one of the biggest advertising platforms on Earth.

Voter rights and civil liberties expert Greg Palast, on GregPalast.com, also on March 19, 2018, pointing out that there are other firms, perhaps even more sinister, than Cambridge Analytica:

### Cambridge Analytica Ain't Nuthin: Look Out for i360 and Data Trust

Jon Talon in The Seattle Times on March 17, 2018:

### Big Tech needs to face a Theodore Roosevelt-style trust busting

The giants of the technology sector are falling from public favor. Busting them up isn't an impossibility.

Writers at the Guardian and the Observer, which the Guardian publishes, argued that the entire method by which the internet is run needs to be revised, and that to permit things to continue as they are would allow the tech titans to imperil democracy.

One of the most frightening stories appeared in The Guardian, from Irish writer Dylan Curran, who took advantage of provisions that allow anyone to look at their personal data that Facebook and Google maintain. The article was full of screen grabs and photos of the files he obtained. Some of the items included highly sensitive material that he had *deliberately deleted,* like financial records and encryption keys. Also included: geo-location data, all his apps, photos, all emails sent and received, complete search history, plus nearly a half million documents, photos, and videos. Facebook and Google can also remotely access the camera and microphone on your electronic devices, which is why there is a photo floating around of Mark Zuckerberg, at a desk, with tape over the camera and the microphone on his laptop. Curran also noted that Windows 10 has 16 different privacy setting sub-menus, and all the options are enabled by default upon installation. To make matters worse, if you Google things like medical conditions, symptoms, or treatments, that goes into your file as well. (Do I need to mention that this is highly valuable information, not only for those pushing various drugs and treatments, but for insurance companies and even future employers? Nah, didn't think so.)

Facebook and Google aren't the only ones spying on you. FitBit, Siri, your Apple watch, your car's onboard computer, even your heart's pacemaker all transmit information, which is not only used to compile private dossiers, but can also be subpoenaed and used in court against you.

Alexa is a really special case, and not the good kind. It not only answers your questions and activates devices for you, it also records your voice and conversations, *even when you're not addressing it*. In at least one reported instance, Alexa recorded a conversation and *sent it to a random person on the Alexa owner's contacts list*. The danger doesn't stop there. Turns out, Alexa, Siri, and Echo can hear commands at frequencies that are undetectable to humans. So while you're listening to your favorite songs or an audio-book the device may be hearing commands to do something like purchase an item on your credit card and ship it to some far away location.

If all this isn't bad enough, in 2017, Stacy Liberatore of the U.K. Daily Mail shot a video of what happened when she asked, "Alexa, what is the CIA?"

*Alexa:* CIA is the American Central Intelligence Agency.

*Liberatore:* Alexa, would you ever lie to me?

*Alexa:* No, I am programmed never to lie. I may be wrong, but I would never lie.

*Liberatore:* Alexa, are you connected to the CIA?

Alexa paused and then shut down. And continued to do so every time the question was asked.

Just because Alexa models no longer respond this way does not diminish the fact that they may still be eavesdropping, or that, because it has a $600 million a year contract to provide cloud storage for the CIA, Amazon -- which makes Alexa -- has an uncomfortably close relationship with our premier spy agency.

Then there's the Internet of Things, those web-enabled TV's, refrigerators, ovens, pool heaters, children's toys, and so forth. (Or, as Techdirt.com writer Karl Bode likes to call it, The Internet of Broken Things.) Got a Roomba robot vacuum? It sends info about your furniture back to the company. Roomba is not an exception. Virtually all of these devices transmit information back to their parent company, and most of them have a very low level of security, which makes them the easy entry point for hackers to get at everything in your house. As an example of how skilled hackers can use low-security entry points to penetrate even higher-level systems and devices, here's an example presented at a security conference by Nicole Eagan, CEO of Darktrace, about a case her company worked on:

> "a casino was hacked via a thermometer in an aquarium in the lobby. The attackers used that to get a foothold in the network," she said. "They then found the high-roller database and then pulled that back across the network, out the thermostat, and up to the cloud."

Articles about the evils of Big Tech and Big Data have been around for at least a decade before the Cambridge Analytica story broke. Three experts covering the topic are Jason Koebler at Vice.com (quoted earlier in this chapter), Caitlin Johnstone (caitlinjohnstone.com), and Yasha Levine, a former reporter for tech publication Pando.com, who has written several books about the subject. His latest, and certainly the timeliest, is *Surveillance Valley: The Secret Military History of the Internet*, which traces the genesis of Google. Here's the book description posted on Amazon.com: [Emphasis is original.]

**The internet is the most effective weapon the Government has ever built.**

In this fascinating book, investigative reporter Yasha Levine uncovers the secret origins of the internet, tracing it back to a Pentagon counterinsurgency surveillance project.

A visionary intelligence officer, William Godel, realized that the key to winning the war in Vietnam was not outgunning the enemy, but using new information technology to understand their motives and anticipate their movements. This idea -- using computers to spy on people and groups perceived as a threat, both at home and abroad -- drove ARPA to develop the internet in the 1960s, and continues to be at the heart of the modern internet we all know and use today. As Levine shows, surveillance wasn't something that suddenly appeared on the internet; it was woven into the fabric of the technology.

But this isn't just a story about the NSA or other domestic programs run by the government. As the book spins forward in time, Levine examines the private surveillance business that powers tech-industry giants like Google, Facebook, and Amazon, revealing how these companies spy on their users for profit, all while doing double duty as military and intelligence contractors. Levine shows that the military and Silicon Valley are effectively inseparable: a military-digital complex that permeates everything connected to the internet, even coopting and weaponizing the antigovernment privacy movement that sprang up in the wake of Edward Snowden.

Just days before the Cambridge story broke, Caitlin Johnstone wrote this about Google, which owns YouTube and has begun removing videos, banning certain content providers, and de-monetizing others in what is blatant censorship:

### Tell Me More About How Google Isn't Part Of The Government And Can Therefore Censor Whoever It Wants?

When you tell an establishment Democrat that Google's hiding and removal of content is a dangerous form of censorship, they often magically transform into Ayn Rand right before your eyes.

"It's a private company and they can do what they like with their property," they will tell you. "It's insane to say that a private company regulating its own affairs is the same as government censorship!"

This is absurd on its surface, because Google is not separate from the government in any meaningful way. It has been financially intertwined with US intelligence agencies since its very inception when it received research grants from the CIA and NSA for mass surveillance, pours massive amounts of money into federal lobbying and DC think tanks, has a cozy relationship with NSA and multiple defense contracts.

Johnstone then quotes Yasha Levine:

"Some of Google's partnerships with the intelligence community are so close and cooperative, and have been going on for so long, that it's not easy to discern where Google Inc ends and government spook operations begin," wrote journalist Yasha Levine in a 2014 *Pando Daily* article titled "Oakland emails give another glimpse into the Google-Military-Surveillance Complex".

One particularly laughable article that came out in the wake of the Cambridge Analytica revelations appeared on dealbreaker.com with the headline:

**Silicon Valley Is Begging For Wall Street-Style Regulation**

*Wall Street-style Regulation.* The same kind of regulation that allowed Enron, Worldcom, and Bernie Madoff to defraud millions of people out of billions of dollars? The same kind of regulation that let banksters skate free with $26 **trillion** in bailout funds while millions of Americans lost their homes, jobs, futures, and even their lives? That kind of regulation?

*No.*

*Fucking.*

*Way*.

What America needs is a constitutional right to privacy that prevents private industry from spying, tracking, and compiling dossiers on people, and the government from doing so without a warrant. (It is interesting to note that while the Supreme Court invented an inferred right to privacy as the foundation for *Roe v. Wade*, the court has never seen fit to extend that right to wider areas, such as the right to be free of government or private sector snooping.)

As if to highlight the danger of private businesses imposing censorship on behalf of the government, shortly before the 2018 general election, Facebook, YouTube, Instagram, and Twitter deleted -- in what clearly was a coordinated action -- over 500 accounts of people and organizations that, *supposedly*, violated the Terms and Conditions of those sites. In virtually every case, no specific violation was cited. Among the sites blocked (with their number of followers) were:

- The Free Thought Project -- 3.1 million
- The Anti-Media -- 2.1 million
- Police the Police -- 1.9 million
- Filming Cops -- 1.5 million
- Cop Block -- 1.7 million
- Rachel Blevins (a Russia Today journalist) -- 69,000

The fact that three of these sites deal with monitoring incidents of police brutality and violations of civil liberties by law enforcement is even more proof that we must enact the Equal Justice Amendment as well as a privacy protection amendment. Medium.com summed up the situation with this succinct headline:

### *In a Corporatist System of Government, Corporate Censorship is Government Censorship*

As Edward Snowden explained when he released his game-changing information about the NSA's spying program, the reason behind these programs was never fighting terrorism or foreign enemies. It was always about being able to exert social control over the public. That's why:

### *The War on Privacy is a War on Civil Liberties, and a War on Democratic Government.*

Whether you call it oligarchy or plutocracy, control of mass numbers of people by a small elite depends on the elite being able to employ methods to prevent the disgruntled masses from making effective use of legal and democratic methods of reform. (Or, should that fail, taking to the streets in violent insurgencies and mob action, as has happened in other countries.) Here's Jon Evans in Techcrunch.com on the conflict between security and privacy: [Emphasis added.]

...Except this dichotomy between "personal privacy" and "public security," all too often promulgated by people who should know better, is completely false, a classic ... argument in bad faith. When we talk about "personal privacy" in the context of phone data, or license plate readers, or genetic data, or encrypted messaging, we're not talking about anything even remotely like our instinctive human understanding of "privacy," ... Instead we're talking about the collection and use of personal data at scale; governments and corporations accumulating massive amounts of highly personal information from billions of people.

This accumulation of data is, in and of itself, not a "personal privacy" issue, but a massive public security problem.

At least three problems, in fact. One is that the lack of privacy **has a chilling effect on dissidence and original thought**. Private spaces are the experimental petri dishes for societies. If you know your every move can be watched, and your every communication can be monitored, so private spaces effectively don't exist, you're much less likely to experiment with anything edgy or controversial; and in this era of cameras everywhere, facial recognition, gait recognition, license plate readers, Stingrays, etc., your every move can be watched.

A second problem is that privacy eradication for the masses, coupled with privacy for the rich, will, as always, help to perpetuate status-quo laws/standards/establishments, and encourage parasitism, corruption, and crony capitalism ... Imagine how much easier it gets if the establishment has access to everything any dissident has ever said and done, while maintaining their own privacy. How long before "anti-terrorism" privacy eradication becomes "selective enforcement of unjust laws" becomes "de facto 'oppo research' unleashed on anyone who challenges the status quo"?

A third problem is that technology keeps getting better and better at manipulating the public based on their private data.

[snip]

When accumulated private data can be used to manipulate public opinion on a massive scale, privacy is no longer a personal luxury. When the rich establishment can use asymmetric privacy to discredit dissidents while remaining opaque themselves, privacy is no longer a personal luxury. When constant surveillance, or the threat thereof, systematically chills and dissuades people from experimenting with new ideas and expressing contentious thoughts, privacy is no longer a personal luxury.

Our Founding Fathers feared many possible future scenarios, including control of government by those with wealth and influence. But perhaps nothing scared them more than a loss of personal privacy. It's no accident that the Bill of Rights lists those rights in a certain order. First came the freedom of speech, press, assembly, and religion. Next came the right to keep and bear arms, which many argue was designed to ensure that the public could rebel against any government that failed to live up to the first amendment. But the next two amendments, the third (the right to keep troops out of private homes), and fourth (the right to be free of unreasonable and unsupported searches and seizures) go directly to the heart of the concept of personal privacy. Unfortunately, thanks to the relentless march of technology, now both the government and private companies (not to mention individual hackers and other miscreants) don't have to enter a person's home or business to know virtually everything they need or want to know about that person's life.

No sane person would argue that law enforcement should not be able to use wiretaps and other forms of surveillance to fight crime, or that the CIA and NSA should not be able to keep tabs on possible terrorists or suspected spies. Likewise, some personal information should be collected, archived, and publicly available. Going into business or entering a relationship with someone and want to know if they have a criminal record? No one would deny this right. About to loan money for a house, car, or business venture? Knowing the potential borrower's financial situation and credit history is essential to making a fair and informed decision.

But this is not what is happening. Mammoth tech firms, joined at the hip to government agencies, are now able to compile dossiers and profile regular citizens without their permission, not just for economic exploitation but in ways that inhibit public expression of critical or dissenting views. Big tech is now able to profile people with sufficient accuracy to predict how they will vote in elections, and this has got to stop. Needless to say, it also has all the information necessary to blackmail millions of citizens, either directly or by providing that info to employers. Speaking of embarrassing info, it has been revealed that Facebook has a previously secret program that allows its executives to not only delete emails from their accounts but also go in, retrieve, and delete it from the *recipients'* email accounts as well. Can't let any of Facebook's embarrassing, perhaps even illegal, acts be archived for posterity (or trial).

Some people may argue that if an individual wants to voluntarily surrender information to a private party, they should be able to do so. Or that they should be able to allow access to the information, in lieu of paying to access a site or use a product. The first problem with these arguments is, as has been demonstrated in the articles cited above, giving over your social media information inevitably results in turning over information from friends, business associates, and generally whomever you interact with or follow on the web. Second, if companies are allowed to require a fee for those who refuse to give up access to their information, the companies will simply price their fees so high that only the well-to-do or corporations will be able to afford the privacy that should be everyone's right.

In fact, the same day that Facebook's secret email retrieval program was revealed, Facebook COO Sheryl Sandberg, stated that if network users want to opt out of targeted ads, they might have to pay to use the service. Does any sane person think that Facebook would not be profitable if it was just a social networking site, or that it wouldn't be able to generate enough advertising revenue to stay in business? Of course not. What are the odds that Facebook would be a lot cheaper to run, and still be quite profitable, if it didn't have such a huge staff devoted to data mining, selling the mined information, and coordinating with the national security state? But there's a good chance that then Mark Zuckerberg might no longer be one of the richest men in the world. Oh, *boo hoo.*

People in other parts of the world take privacy much more seriously than we do in America. Europe is most notable, perhaps because of its history, which includes the Gestapo, the Stasi, and the KGB. Experience with these types of privacy-invading repressive entities could also explain why so many Europeans are more engaged with politics and civil liberties than we are. Not long after the Cambridge Analytica story broke, the European Union came out with its new General Data Protection Regulation (GDPR), expanding internet privacy and limiting how social media can track or sell data about its users. Among the privacy benefits of this new regulation are the ability to learn what data a firm has collected, as well as the "right to be forgotten," meaning that the firm has to expunge any data upon request. The GDPR also prohibits collecting data without a specific reason, thereby eliminating data collection simply because a person signs up or logs on to a site.

So how did Facebook respond to the GDPR? Reuters.com supplies the answer in a headline:

**Exclusive: Facebook to put 1.5 billion users out of reach of new EU privacy law**

The story explains that people who use Facebook, but live outside the U.S. and Canada, are governed by a Terms of Service Agreement that Facebook set up in Ireland where, for tax purposes, it has located its nominal "international headquarters." Faced with the GDPR, Facebook moved all its not-EU users out from under the Ireland TOS agreement. How many people are affected? Facebook has approximately 600 million users in the U.S. and Canada, but over 1.5 billion in the rest of the world.

But even this strategy may not be enough for Facebook and Google to escape the wrath -- and power -- of the EU. On the very first day that the GDPR went into effect, Facebook and Google were hit with lawsuits asking for $8.8 billion in damages for violation of GDPR regulations.

Remember the good old days when Google was just a really good search engine? How about we go back to that? Google can still give priority placement in its search rankings to advertisers, it just doesn't have to track its users and sell their information for billions of dollars. In fact, there is a perfectly good search engine out there, which often produces superior results, and does not track your information: duckduckgo.com. Give it a try. And if Google or Facebook can't survive without selling our data? Richard Stallman, somewhat of a legend among Silicon Valley programmers, supplied the answer in this headline quote for an article by Noah Kulwin in New York Magazine:

### 'No Company Is So Important Its Existence Justifies Setting Up a Police State'

Stallman's proclamation takes on even greater relevance when one considers that social media platforms like Facebook, Google, Instagram, Expedia, etc., are public entities that we are drawn to more or less of our own volition. We know their names. But, behind the scenes, more sinister companies also track us and mine our data. One of the most frightening and dangerous from a civil liberties and privacy perspective is Palantir, the creation of Silicon Valley billionaire Peter Thiel.

The value of Palantir's software programs derives from their ability to pull together data from many different sources, indeed many different *types* of sources, arrange it in a coherent manner, and then present it in an easily accessible series of charts, diagrams, and other visuals. Palantir programs like Gotham, Kite, and particularly XKEYSCORE Helper, allow analysts to combine, in just minutes:

- Information from open sources. (Social media accounts and posts, newspaper stories, graduation/ wedding/promotion announcements, etc.)

- Internet searches, web browsing history, and phone records.

- Financial data. (Bank balances, direct-deposit payroll, ATM and credit card transactions, loan applications, tax returns, business licenses, etc.)

- Real time and historical geo-location data from your phone, laptop, car's electronic control module, and license plate readers.

- Historical and planned travel data from airlines, hotels, passports, etc.

- Affiliations with and/or contributions to political, social activism, and environmental organizations and unions.

- Criminal and civil case records.

- Medical records.

Palantir's software can then map relationships between you and virtually everyone you know, have come in contact with, or crossed paths with, even unknowingly. It can then map all the relationships that those people have, presenting everything in easy to follow, brightly colored charts and graphs. This makes the task of analyzing mountains of data from disparate sources much easier for those in the intelligence community. This is not surprising in that initial funding for the company came from the CIA's In-Q-Tel program.

Because Palantir's software programs can be focused on anyone, for any purpose, the capabilities which makes them so effective are precisely what makes them so dangerous. Turn all that power on terrorists planning an attack, great. Turn it on political or environmental groups agitating for greater economic equality, supporting rival political candidates, or pushing for government reform, and it becomes a powerful tool for authoritarian repression. Its use by local police forces is particularly worrisome because it can easily reinforce stereotypes about who is likely to commit crimes. Profiling people who have been stopped in the past, but not arrested, leads to those people being stopped more often in the future in a never-ending vicious cycle. Not to mention the irresistible urge by some in law enforcement to turn it on spouses, lovers, neighbors, government officials, and anyone else in which the officer (or analyst) has an interest.

Another thing that makes Palantir's software so dangerous is that Palantir apparently felt no qualms about stealing much of its design from a competitor. In 2011, Palantir paid approximately $10 million to settle a lawsuit brought by Virginia-based i12 Group alleging that Palantir fraudulently obtained copies of i12 products and incorporated features of those programs into its own. In its defense, Palantir claimed that the "greater good" of enhancing the government's ability to analyze data possibly related to terrorism justified the theft of i12's copyrighted material.

***Determining for itself that it has the right to steal "for the greater good."*** (Not to mention, greater profits.)

At about the same time, Palantir had to apologize when word leaked out that it had conspired with the Bank of America to attack Wikileaks, and then later conducted a similar campaign against progressive organizations including Think Progress. This is why it is not surprising that a moonlighting Palantir employee, using Palantir's software, performed the Cambridge Analytica data mining operation for the Trump campaign (to which Thiel had donated $1.25 million). In fact, nothing nefarious or unnerving about Palantir should come as a surprise, in light of Thiel's rather extreme libertarian ideas about society. As Wikipedia notes:

> in *Cato Unbound,* the organ of the Cato Institute, a libertarian think-tank, Thiel wrote, "...I no longer believe that freedom and democracy are compatible ... The 1920s were the last decade in American history during which one could be genuinely optimistic about politics. Since 1920, the vast increase in welfare beneficiaries and the extension of the franchise to women -- two constituencies that are notoriously tough for libertarians -- have rendered the notion of "capitalist democracy" into an oxymoron."

It seems clear that Thiel does not propose to reconcile the contradiction between capitalism and democracy in favor of the latter. And I can only imagine how women reading this book must feel at the moment. So, if you're inclined to believe that an operation like Palantir, in the hands of Thiel and others who share his philosophy, in bed with the National Security State, is a scary proposition, *you are not alone*.

There is an old saying in the internet world: If you're not paying for a product, you *are* the product. Unfortunately, as Daniel Kahn Gillmor explained on the ACLU's Privacy and Technology blog, Facebook tracks you and compiles data on you even if you don't have, *and have never had*, a Facebook account. Every time you're mentioned or tagged in a post by a Facebook user, that info goes into your file. Facebook also captures information from other internet sites. Gillmor explains: [Emphasis added.]

Nearly every website that you visit that has a "Like" button is actually encouraging your browser to tell Facebook about your browsing habits. Even if you don't click on the "Like" button, displaying it requires your browser to send a request to Facebook's servers for the "Like" button itself. That request includes information mentioning the name of the page you are visiting and any Facebook-specific cookies your browser might have collected ... This is called a "third-party request."

This makes it possible for Facebook to create a detailed picture of your browsing history -- **even if you've never even visited Facebook directly**, let alone signed up for a Facebook account.

The same is true with Google. Turns out that in addition to all the other information it sweeps up from Google searches, Gmail, etc., Google quietly slipped into their 2017 Terms of Service agreement a provision allowing its Chrome Cleanup Tool anti-virus browser extension to scan and collect data from Windows files on users' computers.

This mass collection and sale of user data has led critics to argue that if the big data mining companies are allowed to continue doing so, at least the people whose information they share should be compensated. As Ben Tarnoff noted in The Guardian, just days before the Cambridge Analytica story broke, if you're the product, then you ought to share in the revenues. That idea has some merit, but again, when they track your info, they inevitably sweep up info from your friends and associates. There's a much better answer:

**The 39th Amendment -- The Right to Privacy**

**Section 1: The right to privacy being critical to the citizens of a free and democratic republic, no individual, organization, business entity, or department of government at any level shall**

maintain files, dossiers, or other records pertaining to any citizen except:

a) As such records shall result from the issuance of a properly noticed search warrant or subpoena applicable to that individual, or from a civil or criminal court action;

b) As such records serve legitimate civilian purpose bearing on the establishment of credit;

c) As are necessary for the granting of licenses and permits or for the effective regulation of business enterprises including charities and non-profit entities;

d) By affirmative consent by the person to the collector of such information, without such permission being imposed by the collector as a requirement of use, access, or service, or in lieu of payment for same, and with the collector restrained from selling, bartering, or otherwise communicating such information to any third party.

e) Violation of any provision of this Amendment shall be a felony resulting in the incarceration of all offending parties in a maximum security penal institution for a period, not subject to pardon, parole, commutation, suspension, or other reduction of sentence, of twenty years.

Section 2: Immediately upon ratification of this Amendment, all files, dossiers, or records in violation hereof, whether held in public or private hands, within the physical confines of the republic or abroad, shall be permanently and completely destroyed. Failure to do so by

**any person authorized or obligated to perform such destruction shall be a felony subject to incarceration in a maximum security penal institution for a period, not subject to pardon, parole, commutation, suspension, or other reduction of sentence, of twenty years.**

As Richard Stallman notes in the New York Magazine interview mentioned earlier:

> What is data privacy? The term implies that if a company collects data about you, it should somehow protect that data. But I don't think that's the issue. I think the problem is that it collects data about you period. We shouldn't let them do that.

He's right. No one should have their private information collected, disseminated, and sold for huge profits. No one should have to agree to surrender data as a condition for purchase or use of a product or service. This is *inverted transparency*:

> The government, aided by its alliances with Big Tech, gets to know everything about us but, thanks to excessive classification of information and legal concepts like "state secrets," we don't get to know almost anything of actual importance about the government.

# Chapter 15

# SOVEREIGN UNITY AND SECURITY

The battle over illegal immigration in America involves the deceitful, the delusional, and the divided. Both political parties are well-represented in all three groups.

Democratic party leaders pretend the issue is about racism and fairness, when it is really about expanding the Hispanic voting bloc that traditionally leans heavily Democratic. These Democrats are doubly deceitful, because illegal immigrants take many blue-collar jobs away from working class members of labor unions who were once the cornerstone of Democratic support. In some cases, unions have been forced to recruit and accept illegal immigrants just to remain viable. The flip side is that those same unions then often have to accept lower wages from employers than they would if there was not such a huge, non-union, competitive labor pool available. Of course, this does not bother the white-collar, liberal Democratic elements, whose jobs are not threatened, and who are happy to employ illegal immigrant nannies and gardeners at low wages paid in cash. In 1993, both of Bill Clinton's first two choices for Attorney General, Zoe Baird and Kimba Wood, withdrew after revelations that they had failed to pay income and Social Security taxes for their nannies.

The GOP also has its deceitful arguments, framing the issue as one of laws and border security to hide the racist undertones of many of its rank-and file members (not to mention, the ceaseless quest of its business sector for a limitless pool of cheap, exploitable labor). Of course, hypocrisy being totally bipartisan, two George W. Bush nominees, Linda Chavez for Secretary of Labor, and Bernie Kerik for Secretary of Homeland Security, were torpedoed by Nanny-gate revelations. The Chavez nomination, of a Latino woman guilty of exploiting a Latino nanny, and then being considered for Secretary of *Labor,* ranks exceptionally high on the irony scale.

The delusional faction, largely on the Democratic side, comprises those who contend that we can continue to absorb and provide for everyone who wants to come here. Deathly afraid that opposing illegal immigration will get them branded as racist, they fall back on the hoary canard that, "America was founded by/built by immigrants." This argument fails to differentiate between settlers and immigrants. The former came to an unfinished land with no restrictions on immigration. The latter seek to illegally enter an established country, with clearly defined borders and firmly established procedures for immigrating legally. The argument that welcoming immigrants is an American tradition also conveniently omits reference to the fact that America once had other traditions we no longer embrace, most notably slavery, segregation, and denying women the right to vote.

Wikipedia defines cognitive dissonance as, "The mental stress or discomfort experienced by an individual who holds two or more contradictory beliefs, ideas, or values at the same time, or is confronted by new information that conflicts with existing beliefs, ideas, or values." Those in the pro-illegal immigration bloc display cognitive dissonance on an epic scale. They support efforts by illegal immigrants to obtain legal status, work, send their children to public schools, or avail themselves of emergency medical care and other social services, on the basis that these people have just come to America to build a better life, that they have fled horrible economic and political conditions in their home countries. Yet these same defenders of illegal immigration often proclaim themselves environmentalists, and rail against how much of the planet's resources our society consumes. They argue that we must reduce pollution, convert to a sustainable economy, and decrease our carbon footprint by reducing our dependence on cheap fossil fuel energy. Unable to see, or unwilling to admit, the inherent contradiction between *more* people needing *more* jobs and consuming *more* material goods versus stabilizing economic output and reducing reliance on pollution-causing energy sources, they simply deny that any contradiction exists.

There is also a perverse racism buried in this coming-here-from-horrible-circumstances-to-build-a-better-life-and-follow-the-American Dream argument. Inherent in this philosophy is the notion that the countries which these illegal immigrants come from *can't be fixed.* Which is another way of saying that Mexicans, Hondurans, Salvadorans, and citizens of other countries, from the tip of South America to the former Soviet satellite republics to Ireland, are incapable of improving their government. In other words, these people are inferior to Americans, because only America can build a country with a dream for its people. Why can't there be a Mexican Dream, a Honduran Dream, a Lithuanian or Nigerian Dream? For the record, I know that the U.S. has numerous natural advantages, resources, etc. And I recognize, as pointed out in Chapter 2, that global climate change will hit these countries hard. Nevertheless, conditions in those countries are much worse than they could be, should be, and would be, if they were not in the merciless grip of a few wealthy elite. Nor is this to deny that the USA contributes to the horrid conditions in these countries by our meddling, corruption of their governments, and military misadventures. Our actions and policies help ensure that these countries remain awful places in which to live. We can, and should, help these people fix their countries while we fix ours. But ultimately, the only people who can fix another country are the citizens of that country who remain and fight for reform, which is a long, difficult, and often deadly undertaking. It's so much easier just to go to America illegally. Unfortunately, because the problems in those home countries are never solved, the flow of people trying to enter the U.S. illegally also never stops.

Illegal immigration divides both parties. Traditional, pro-business GOP leaders see illegal immigrants as a sure way to weaken unions, depress wages, and fuel the corporate lust for profits. However, many rank-and-file party supporters see the issue in terms of: a) a question of law enforcement; and b) economic warfare being waged against themselves. Hence, while Republican leadership pretends to oppose amnesty for illegal aliens, behind the scenes those same leaders would love to see such a program implemented, just as long as the Democrats carry the ball and allow the Republicans to dodge voter backlash at the polls.

Across the aisle, even though the influence of unions has waned, in many races Dem candidates still depend on unions and their members for contributions and manpower to canvas door-to-door, man phone-banks, and staff *Get Out The Vote* campaigns. However, these same Democrats have become dependent on big money donations from the same companies that have been a major traditional Republican funding source -- and traditionally eager to exploit illegal labor. Thus, in public, leaders and candidates from both parties tell the voters what they want to hear. In private, however, both vote for the interests of their campaign contributors.

President Trump has been pilloried as being a racist for his efforts to build a border wall, and for on-going raids by ICE bent on finding and deporting illegal aliens. But in typically hypocritical fashion, whenever Democrats sensed a political nerve to be tapped, they have also railed against the evils of illegal immigration. Here's Bill Clinton in his 1995 State of the Union speech:

All Americans ... are rightly disturbed by the number of illegal aliens entering our country ... That's why our administration has moved aggressively to secure our borders more, by hiring a record number of new border guards, by deporting twice as many criminal aliens as ever before, by cracking down on illegal hiring, by barring welfare benefits to illegal aliens. In the budget I will present we will try to do more, to speed the deportation of illegal aliens who are arrested for crimes, to better identify illegal aliens in the workplace...

Clinton was no outlier among Democrats. Go to YouTube and watch Dianne Feinstein's 1994 campaign ad in which she argues that, "illegal aliens compete for housing, classroom space, leech Medicaid and commit felonies." She also advocated for -- guess what?! -- *a wall* along the southern border. As one wit asked, "Should that fence be electrified?" Obama continued the Democratic charade. Here's from his floor speech on immigration reform on April 3, 2006, while he was still a senator:

But those who enter our country illegally, and those who employ them, disrespect the rule of law. And because we live in an age where terrorists are challenging our borders, we simply cannot allow people to pour into the United States undetected, undocumented, and unchecked. Americans are right to demand better border security and better enforcement of the immigration laws.

Once in office, Obama followed through. By 2014, The Economist reported that the United States, "is expelling illegal immigrants at nine times the rate of 20 years ago; nearly 2m so far under Barack Obama, easily outpacing any previous president." So, while the Democrats give lip service to illegal immigrant populations, behind the scenes they employ the same tactics for which they vilify the GOP.

In determining what defines a country an easy place to start, for those who believe in common sense, is by looking at a map of the world. All those countries are in different colors because they have *borders*. Certain countries may disagree over exactly where the border should be, or which offshore islands belong to which country, but they agree that there must be a border. Wars have traditionally started when one country's army crossed another country's border. Any country that cannot control its borders is in immediate danger of no longer functioning as a country.

Some people argue that securing our southern border by building a wall would be too difficult, even impossible. Complete bullshit. I say again: C-O-M-P-L-E-T-E bullshit. Go online, search for the world's longest bridges. You'll find ones for both high speed rail and vehicular traffic that span more than 20 miles, including over open water, such as connecting islands in the ocean. One high speed rail bridge in China is over 100 miles long. The newest vehicular bridge, which runs for 34 miles, connects Hong Kong, Macau, and mainland China. It has six lanes and required the building of four artificial islands for the support towers.

Want examples closer to home? The 1,700 mile Alcan Highway from Seattle to Alaska was completed in *eight months* (March through October 1942), through pure wilderness, which had never even been surveyed before, using equipment that would be considered rudimentary by today's standards. Something like three dozen bridges had to be constructed. Thawing permafrost turned sections of the route into muck so deep that the roadway bed had to be 12 feet deep. Professor J. David Rogers, Chairman of Geological Engineering at the Missouri University of Science & Technology, described it in an article as: "One of the Top 10 Construction Achievements of the 20th Century."

Flash forward sixty years and you have the newest way to get across historic Chesapeake Bay, using the Chesapeake Bay *Bridge* which then transitions to the Chesapeake Bay *Tunnel* under the bay so as not to impede ship traffic. There is another bridge-tunnel combination, Oresund, which connects Sweden and Denmark.

We built the Alcan highway in the middle of a world war, there are hybrid bridges and tunnels that span open ocean waterways, but somehow building a wall on solid ground is too difficult? *Get outta here*.

The real reason that people do not want to see the wall built is because *they know it will work*. President Reagan taunted Gorbachev to, "tear down this [Berlin] wall" precisely because it was so effective in keeping East Germans from escaping to the West. Prisons have walls for the same reason. Whether it's keeping people in or keeping people out, well-designed, properly constructed walls work. It is also important to keep in mind that if the sea level rise predictions come to fruition, we will need to protect all of our coastal borders from flooding, wave action, etc. So, in addition to building walls to keep out those fleeing the devastation of global upheaval, we will also be building dikes, seawalls, breakwaters, and perhaps massive surge control gates like the Dutch already employ.

Some people argue that even with an effective wall along our southern border, we could only achieve true border security by militarizing the border, both south and north. This would be wrong, why? We have by far the world's biggest military. We regularly spend as much as the next ten countries put together. In some years we spend more on our military than all other nations of the world combined. We have between 700 and 1,000 foreign military installations of one sort or another, from massive bases like Ramstein in Germany, and Aviano in Italy, to "lily pad" Special Ops camps in countries most Americans have never heard of, and couldn't find on a map. Instead of running around the world, meddling in the internal affairs of other countries, how about we bring some of those troops home to secure our own borders and enforce our own immigration laws?

Just how bad is our illegal immigration problem? The Department of Homeland Security, using Census Bureau calculations, put the number of illegal immigrants currently in the country at around 11.5 million, down from a high of 12.7 million in 2007, before the Great Recession. Other experts put the number much higher, at around 20 million. A few, like James H. Walsh, who have analyzed the data and methodology from multiple sources, say the real total is a whopping 38 million. Why such a wide disparity?

One reason is that the official DHS estimate relies on the residual method, in which the Census Bureau takes the total number of people who identify themselves on census forms as foreign-born, then subtracts out the number of aliens who are known to reside here legally. Since illegal aliens are notoriously reluctant to respond to government inquiries, and given that there is no real penalty for not replying to census inquiries, a lot of people simply don't admit to being here.

Even the Census Bureau itself recognizes this flaw in the system and adjusts the population of foreign-born residents upward, but evidently, not enough. For example, the 2000 Census first put the total U.S. population as 275 million people. However, because population determines everything from the number of representatives a state gets in Congress to the amount of federal funding that flows to states and municipalities, states and local governments challenged that number. It was subsequently revised upward by just over 6 million, including an increase in the Hispanic population of 2.5 million. Since all aliens legally living in the country are known from government records, presumably almost all of those 2.5 million subsequently added to the census estimate had to be here illegally. If the government estimated the illegal population at 11.5 million prior to the census revision, then the revised estimate should be 14 million, correct? Or, if the correct population estimate of illegal immigrants after the adjustment is 11.5 million, then before the adjustment it had to be only 9 million, meaning the initial estimate was off by over 20%.

The government has a vested interest in keeping the estimated number of illegal aliens artificially low to create an illusion of border security. But it's not just those who sneak across the border illegally who are the problem. Every year approximately 30 million people visit the U.S. on temporary visas. As Nancy Boulton pointed out in her extensive study, if just 1% of those who crossed the border legally remain after their visa expires, that would add 300,000 new illegal immigrants per year. Over a ten-year span that's another 3 million people.

Perhaps the best gauge of our government's inability, or unwillingness, to accurately estimate the number of illegal immigrants is to look at other real world examples.

- In 1986, the country was gripped by an illegal immigration "crisis" which was supposed to be solved by the Simpson-Mazzoli Immigration Reform and Control Act. A key element of that bill was amnesty, and a chance to become a citizen, for illegal immigrants who had entered the U.S. prior to a certain date and did not have a criminal record. (Other than, you know, being here *illegally*.) Leading up to passage of the bill, the government estimated that two million illegal immigrants would meet the necessary criteria. The actual figure proved to be 3.1 million, meaning that the government projections had been off by more than 50% on the low side. If the current government estimate of 11.5 million illegal immigrants is also off by that same percentage, the actual total of illegal immigrants would be 17.5 million.

- The Pew Center on Hispanic Trends estimated that in the 1980s, the U.S. population of illegal immigrants grew by about 130,000 people a year. From 1990 through 1994, that number increased to

450,000 a year, then to 750,000 through 1999. Since 2000, the rate has generally held steady at about 700-850,000 a year, although there was a dip in the overall population of illegal immigrants in 2008-2010 during the worst of the Great Recession.

- In 2005, U.S. Border Patrol Agents Union Local 2544 stated that, "There are currently 15 to 20 million illegal aliens in this country by many estimates, but the real numbers could be much higher and the numbers increase every day because our borders are not secure (no matter what the politicians tell you -- don't believe them for a second)."

Since Local 2544 released that statement, there have been significant efforts to make the southern border more secure. Illegal immigrants, and the smugglers who guide them, have been forced to take new, more difficult routes. The number of immigrants intercepted trying to cross the border has increased significantly, as have the number who die each year trying to make it across the more remote and inhospitable deserts in Arizona and Texas. Yet in 2013, Zack Taylor, Chairman of the National Association of Former Border Patrol Officers, Inc., said in an open letter that the number of illegal immigrants is still actually, "closer to 18-20 million and rising daily."

While this higher figure has been widely ignored by both elected officials and the mainstream media, lo and behold, in the early fall of 2018 a study by three professors at Yale pegged the total number of illegal immigrants at **22.1 million**. According to the authors, they used improved methodology, whereas previous, lower estimates were based on data and methods that tended, "to underestimate undocumented immigrants inflows and overstate outflows."

The 1986 Simpson-Mazzoli bill was supposed to end illegal immigration. Instead, by raising the likelihood that another amnesty would occur at some future point, it made things worse. Even the Pew Center on Hispanic Trends, which uses different methodology from the Census Bureau (but still estimates the current total number of illegal immigrants at the same 11.5 million), notes that the illegal immigrant population increased from 3.5 million in 1990 to a peak of 12.2 million in 2007. Four years after 3.1 million formerly illegal immigrants had gained either citizenship or legal status under Simpson-Mazzoli, there were still at least 3.5 million illegal immigrants living here, and the number has increased, more or less steadily, for almost a quarter-century.

The two primary camps that support illegal immigration -- businesses on the hunt for cheap labor and those looking to build political Hispanic power blocs -- are quick to argue that illegals contribute to the economy by doing jobs Americans refuse to do, because the work is too hard and/or the wages are too low. Back in the days when a majority of illegals worked in agriculture or as busboys, hotel maids, and gardeners, there might have been some truth to that argument. (As if underpaying people for performing hazardous or arduous work is somehow, in any sense, justifiable.) But over the past twenty years, in the aftermath of the Simpson-Mazzoli bill that was supposed to eliminate illegal immigration, illegal aliens have taken over many mainstream blue-collar industries that traditionally provided a middle-class living, not only to whites but also to blacks. In many parts of the country it is impossible to find any sector of the construction industry -- concrete, framing, drywall, roofing, plumbing, or electrical -- that is not dominated by illegal immigrants willing to work for lower wages than what those positions once commanded (and should still be worth).

The same is true of another, even more dangerous industry, meatpacking. It is no accident that one of the seminal works of

American literature, Upton Sinclair's 1906 novel *The Jungle*, exposed the dangerous conditions faced by workers in the slaughterhouse industry. The book, a touchstone of the populist movement for worker's rights, led to the eventual unionization of the industry. Up until the mid-1980s, it was one of the highest-paid industrial jobs in the country. All that changed in 1986 when Hormel workers in Minnesota went on strike over a reduction in wages. Hormel brought in scab workers and eventually broke the strike. Wages immediately stagnated. According to a 2007 report by the Bureau of Labor Statistics, in 1980 the average hourly wage for workers in the meatpacking industry was $8.49. Adjusted for inflation, that would have been $21.75 in 2007. Instead, the actual 2007 average hourly wage was $12.03, a 44% differential.

This decline in wages has been accompanied by an increase in injuries caused by the relentless pressure to speed up production, which has increased by more than 250% during the last two decades of the 20th century. Working at such a high rate of speed with razor sharp knives and power tools cannot help but produce an increase in injuries, especially when the danger is compounded by working in close proximity to fast-moving production line machinery, while standing on floors slippery with blood and other fluids.

The industry likes to cite statistics showing a reduction in accidents, but the Department of Labor questions the accuracy of those numbers, and has found numerous instances where accidents were not reported. In addition, accidents that befall clean-up workers on the night shift, who have to work at a break-neck pace to clean dangerous machinery with powerful chemicals, are reported under the general category of Janitorial and Maintenance, further distorting the true picture. Like a large percentage of the daytime work force, many people on those night cleaning shifts are easily exploited, and easily replaced, illegal immigrants. Even workers who are American citizens are at risk, simply because the large pool of illegal workers means that anyone can be replaced by an illegal willing to work in hazardous conditions for low pay.

In his 2002 book, *Fast Food Nation*, Eric Schlosser recounts the tragic (but hardly unique) tale of one American worker who, during his 16 years of employment, suffered a fractured vertebrae, a broken leg, and permanent lung damage from chlorine fumes, then was fired while he was in the hospital recovering from a heart attack suffered *on the job* at the age of 46. Schlosser quotes the man as saying that his employer, "used me to the point where I had no body parts left to give," then tossed him on the human scrap heap, with no health insurance and no pension. Sixteen years after *Fast Food Nation*, the Guardian reported that the American meatpacking industry averages two amputations a week among its workers. ***Two. Amputations. A. Week***.

The meatpacking and construction industries are perfect examples of how America's failure to secure its borders has enhanced the ability of employers to break unions, slash wages, and maintain dangerous working conditions. Workers may not be slaves to their employers, but they are slaves to the need to make some kind of a living, no matter how dangerous or how insufficient it may be.

Employers who hire illegals are also breaking the law and should be prosecuted, but rarely are. With many small businesses, it would be easy to do so. One problem that occurs with large corporations, such as the meatpacking companies, is that those who bear the major responsibility are insulated from the actual act of hiring. Top management never orders their facility managers to hire illegals. Instead, they set production targets and wage levels that can only be met if local managers hire illegals, who are likely the only people willing to take the extreme risks and punishing pace at the wages offered. Then, in the rare instances in which someone does get prosecuted, it's the plant managers. Those in the corporate hierarchy get off by feigning shock that illegals were part of their workforce. Fortunately, there is a solution put forth later in this chapter.

Merely securing the border is not enough. Although 79 percent of all illegals come from Mexico and other Latin America countries, as of 2012 there were still at least 1.3 million Asians, 300,000 Europeans, and another 200,000 from other countries. Since these projections are based on an estimated total of 11.5 million illegal immigrants, if the true overall number is around 20 million (or even higher), then it stands to reason that these estimates of non-Hispanic illegals also represents an undercount. At any rate, there are still at least 1.8 million illegal aliens, most of whom probably entered the country in some official fashion and then overstayed their visas. From David Seminara, at the Center for Immigration Studies:

> Nearly half of the 12 million-plus illegal aliens in America arrived legally with temporary, non-immigrant visas. The Department of Homeland Security (DHS) estimates that a 'substantial' percentage of America's illegal population is made up of visa overstays -- their estimates range from 27 to 57 percent.

According to ImmigrationPolicy.org, in 2012, Immigration and Customs Enforcement made over 278,000 arrests, most of which were inland, rather than along the border. While open border pro-illegal immigration proponents decry the idea of deploying U.S. military forces along the border, the truth is, in most countries with an illegal immigrant or refugee problem, legal points of entry are manned by Customs officials, but the borders themselves are patrolled by that country's armed forces. If we did the same thing, not only could we achieve maximum border security, but many Border Patrol agents could be redeployed to search out illegal aliens already residing inside the country. Other BP agents could be retrained to bolster the number of agents assigned to the backlog of legal immigration applications.

Illegal immigrants do more than just drive down wages and allow employers to get away with unsafe working conditions. Illegal aliens represent a huge cost to government, and put an enormous burden on social services, from law enforcement to education to health care. Here are some examples from R. Cort Kirkwood from his article, "Illegal Aliens a Drain on U.S. Taxpayers, Report Says" posted on TheNewAmerican.com in August 2012. He quotes figures from the Center for Immigration Studies:

> Given that illegals tend to earn less money and live in poverty, they are also prone to use welfare. In Texas, for instance, 58 percent of illegal households collect some form of welfare, CIS reported, with 49 percent using food assistance and 41 percent using Medicaid. In California and Illinois, 55 percent use welfare. The list of states goes down from there.
>
> Nationally, 47 percent of illegals use welfare; 39 percent use food assistance and 35 percent use Medicaid.
>
> As one would imagine, a population of more than 10 million illegals is a crushing burden on public schools. Illegals are 1.3 million of the school-age population and about 2.4 percent of 5- to 17-year-olds, CIS reported. Taxpayers provide some $40 billion to educate illegals and their offspring.
>
> School-age illegal aliens plus the U.S.-born children of illegal aliens comprise about 7.2 percent (3.9 million) of the total school-age population, CIS reported.
>
> In states like Nevada, Arizona, Texas, California, Washington, Illinois, and New Jersey illegal immigrants comprise a much larger share of the school-age population than they do nationally.
>
> Since per-student expenditures in the United States are roughly $10,000 a year, it is likely that some $13 billion annually goes to educate illegal aliens in public schools. The total cost for educating illegal aliens and

their U.S.-born children likely comes to over $39 billion a year.

As Kirkwood points out, again using CIS figures:

> "High rates of Medicaid and food assistance use by illegal immigrant households is not caused by an unwillingness to work on the part of illegals." Almost all illegal households have at least one member working, a higher rate than American households, CIS noted. But because half of all illegals didn't finish high school, "their average income in the modern economy will be very low."

Some other CIS estimates cited by Kirkwood:

> Combined total income of illegal immigrants is about $162 billion, but they would have to pay approximately 24 percent of their total family income in state and local taxes just to cover the cost of educating their children.

> Approximately 62% of illegal immigrants -- roughly 6.5 million people -- do not have health insurance. In Texas the number is 72 percent. In North Carolina, 69 percent; Colorado, 66 percent. Adding in the number of their children and the total number of uninsured illegal aliens jumps to 7.3 million. In Arizona, California, Nevada, and Texas, roughly one-fourth of all uninsured are illegal immigrants and their children. In New Jersey, Washington, and North Carolina roughly one-fifth of the uninsured are illegal immigrants.

These figures are based on an estimated 11.5-12 million illegals in the country. If the true number is around the higher estimate of 20-22 million, it's logical to assume that the number of uninsured increases proportionally. These estimates are also prior to the Obamacare expansion of Medicaid. Given its government funding, any Medicaid expansion that reduces the number of illegals without health insurance also increases the unreimbursed cost of government healthcare consumed by illegals.

Here are some costs for various states, estimated by the Federation for American Immigration Reform (FAIR). Numbers include costs for education, unreimbursed health care, criminal justice activities, welfare, and state/local general operating costs such as street maintenance, trash disposal and sewage treatment, water delivery, etc.

| State | Annual Cost to State & Local Government | Average Annual Household Cost |
|---|---|---|
| California | $25.3 billion | $2,370 |
| Texas | $12.1 billion | $1,197 |
| New York | $9.5 billion | $1,607 |
| Illinois | $4.6 billion | $1,051 |
| New Jersey | $3.48 billion | $1,327 |
| Arizona | $2.57 billion | $1,359 |
| Georgia | $2.4 billion | $743 |
| Massachusetts | $1.86 billion | $775 |
| Nevada | $1.19 billion | $1,696 |
| Michigan | $929 million | $241 |
| Minnesota | $744 million | $374 |
| Iowa | $350 million | $299 |

Notice the great disparity in per-household costs. In Iowa and Michigan, households headed by legal immigrants, naturalized citizens, and native-born citizens pay less than $300 a year to subsidize the cost of services to illegal aliens. In California, it's nearly $2,400, more than it costs to lease some cars.

Lynn, Massachusetts provides a typical example of how the failure to control immigration imposes massive costs and social disruption on local communities, even when they are far from the front lines along the border.

In 2012, large numbers of illegal immigrant children from Guatemala, Honduras, and El Salvador, who were not accompanied by a parent or other adult family member, started being caught by the Border Patrol, especially in Texas. Eventually ICE came under media criticism over the conditions in which these Un-Accompanied Juveniles (UAJs) were being held. Rather than deport these children, ICE shipped the problem off to local communities all over the country, including Lynn. But as we'll see, many of those designated as UAJs are not, you know, actually *juveniles*. (Hey, if you're dumping a federal problem off on various cities and states, why bother with details, like making sure these "children" aren't really adults?)

In the 2011 school year, Lynn had 2 UAJs (theoretically ages 14-17) from Guatemala enrolled in its schools. By 2014, that number had jumped to 101. In that same period, total out-of-country admissions to the Lynn school system leapt from 54 to 538. The impact to the city and its school district was devastating. A new middle school, intended to alleviate over-crowding, was itself already designated as over-crowded under state standards when it opened for the 2016 school year. All students in Lynn public schools have to be vaccinated. In 2011, the city health department gave out 11 free vaccinations. In July 2014, that number was up to 159 and the clinic, formerly open only on a limited basis, had to add more nurses and extend its hours of operation. In addition, on their ICE documents many of these allegedly juvenile immigrants have the exact same birth date: January 1, 1998. In a press conference hosted by the Center for Immigration Studies, Lynn Mayor Judith Flanagan Kennedy noted that:

> There were people with graying temples, hair around the temples. There were people with more wrinkles than I have around their eyes. And we were told through a directive from the Department of Justice that we were not to question or verify -- attempt to verify these ages.

***A directive not to attempt to verify ages***. And even though one illiterate "student" accidentally presented a Guatemalan *arrest warrant* with his other papers, ICE does not provide local authorities with any information on an immigrant's possible past criminal history. I wonder what the parents in the Lynn school system think of their teenage daughters going to class with adult men, some old enough to have graying temples, and who are undoubtedly criminals?

To finance the additional costs to the school system and health department, Lynn has had to cut all other department budgets. Mayor Kennedy explained the negative impact:

> I had a great program in Lynn, a community policing program, where the six sectors of the city of Lynn ... each had their own bike cop. And the bike cops were there to take care of quality of life issues, to look into problems before they got to be big problems, to keep an eye on gang recruitment -- and over the last few years, the city of Lynn has managed to bring down its number of known gang members and affiliates from about 1,300 down to 350. And I attribute that decline in large part to the community policing program that we have had in place. That program can no longer be continued because that money has had to be diverted to the school department.

The problems in Lynn are not unique. All over the country, communities are suffering under the same negative impacts of illegal immigration. Because most of these Un-Accompanied Juveniles are illiterate in Spanish as well as English, they require specialized instruction, which raises their cost of education to approximately $11,000 -- $12,000 or more, per year, *per student*. In 2014, 90,000 UAJs cost state and local governments a billion dollars ***just in education costs***. And that doesn't include the costs of UAJs already here.

Proponents of unlimited illegal immigration like to claim that illegal workers contribute to the economy and pay more in taxes than they receive back in benefits. Foremost among these arguments is that illegals who use phony Social Security numbers are helping finance Social Security, but will never receive SS retirement benefits. This argument fails, first of all, on the assumption that if the illegals were not performing this work, the work would not be done by citizens and legal residents. This is ludicrous. It assumes that contractors, and the owners of meat packing companies or manufacturing plants, would go out of business rather than hire citizens at adequate wages. In fact, the lure of hiring illegals is the ability to pay them less than the employer would have -- or **has been** -- paying citizens and green card workers.

In addition, when someone pays SS taxes, but their name and DOB don't match up with that of the person registered to that number, the taxes go into the SS Earnings Suspense File (ESF) while the administration attempts to reconcile the discrepancy by sending out a "no match" letter to the employer. Even though it is a felony under federal law to use a phony SS number, the possibility of prosecution is so remote that many employers either ignore the no-match letters or allow their illegal employees to simply supply a new, equally fraudulent number, which starts the whole notification process over again. In other cases, illegal aliens obtain Individual Taxpayer Identification Numbers (TINs) from the IRS, then submit both the TIN and a fraudulent SS number. The IRS simply credits earnings under the phony SS number to the TIN account.

However, if immigration reform included amnesty for illegal aliens currently working here, those amnestied persons would then be eligible to claim retirement credit for monies in the ESF that they earned under a false SS number. To some people, this might seem fair: *they worked for it, they should get it*. Unfortunately, this just brings us to the second problem arising out of the use of fraudulent SS numbers by illegal workers: since over half of all possible SS numbers have already been issued, there is a better than 50-50 chance that any made-up number will match one already assigned to another person.

The Federation for American Immigration Reform notes that in 2004, when the population of illegal aliens had not yet peaked, the IRS received nearly **eight million** W-2 forms where the SS number did not match the name and DOB of the person legally assigned that number. Over half of those mismatched numbers came from states like California, Texas, Florida, and Illinois that are home to massive numbers of illegals. (Ironically, one fraudulently used number belonged to an IRS agent, which is another felony for impersonating a federal employee.)

The proliferation of phony SS numbers among illegal aliens facilitates identity theft and fraud, sometimes on a massive scale. FAIR reports on one case in Colorado where 1,300 illegals used phony SS numbers to obtain over $2.6 million in fraudulent tax refunds. In other cases, the numbers have been assigned to infants who suddenly (and unbeknownst to their parents) have an earnings history, tax liabilities, and in some cases, even a criminal record tied to that SS number. FAIR describes some of the damage that results for victims of this form of identity theft:

> A person who was in a motorcycle accident and was denied disability payments from the Social Security Administration because the records showed him continuing to work hundreds of miles from his actual residence.

> [Or the] police training officer in Los Angeles County who was pursued by the IRS for $60,000 in taxes owed by individuals using his stolen SSN, and who was unable to buy a home because his credit rating had been destroyed.

> [snip]

> If an illegal alien using another person's SSN doesn't pay taxes on the income earned under that number,

the IRS demands that the true owner of the number pay the outstanding taxes. In addition, if an illegal alien has already filed a return using an American citizen's SSN, the IRS will require the citizen to clear the matter up before accepting and processing the citizen's return.

There is also another problem: Each year the Social Security Administration accidentally categorizes about 10,000 people as deceased even when they're still alive and kicking. Usually this occurs when someone transposes a number from the death certificate to the SSA files. By law, the IRS must convey notice of death to other federal agencies, so that various benefits can be halted. So now, just through accidental bureaucratic foul-ups, 10,000 people temporarily go without much needed benefits while they straighten out the mistake. Just imagine how much worse the problem is if someone using the stolen SS number of a real person dies and that information is conveyed to the SSA. There's a word for this, and it begins with *cluster*.

When they can't argue effectively using facts, proponents of illegal immigration resort to the time-honored tactic of branding their opponents as racists. This is interesting in several respects, not the least of which is that one leading opponent of illegal immigration was an icon of the Civil Rights movement, the late Congresswoman Barbara Jordan. The first African-American elected to the Texas State Senate since Reconstruction, she was also the first black woman from the south elected to the U.S. House of Representatives, and the first black woman to deliver the Democratic National Convention's Keynote speech. Wikipedia notes that she was awarded the Presidential Medal of Freedom, and upon her untimely death at age 59 from leukemia, she was the first African-American woman to be buried in the official Texas State Cemetery.

From 1994-1996, Jordan chaired the U.S. Commission on Immigration Reform, where her goal was to close loopholes in the

1986 Immigration Reform and Control Act that allowed employers to hire illegal immigrants. The introduction to the Commission's 1994 report, appropriately titled, *U.S. Immigration Policy: Restoring Credibility*, stated:

> The Commission decries hostility and discrimination against immigrants as antithetical to the traditions and interests of the country. At the same time, we disagree with those who would label efforts to control immigration as being inherently anti-immigrant. Rather, it is both a right and a responsibility of a democratic society to manage immigration so that it serves the national interest ... The credibility of immigration policy can be measured by a simple yardstick: people who should get in do get in; people who should not get in are kept out; and people who are judged deportable are required to leave.

If one prominent black leader's opposition to illegal immigration isn't enough to cast doubt on the racism argument, consider this, which appeared in the Huffington Post in 2010, from Clarence B. Jones, the Scholar in Residence at Stanford University's Martin Luther King, Jr. Institute:

> In the discussion about the new law passed in Arizona directed at addressing that state's problems associated with illegal immigrants from Mexico, the protests concerning the legislation are directed at the wrong parties, in the wrong direction. The pro-immigration community, some church groups and many Civil Rights leaders are all calling for a boycott of the State of Arizona based on their belief that the new Arizona law is focused on "racial profiling" as the method for identifying possible illegal Mexican immigrants.
>
> As an African-American who lived through and before the Civil Rights Movement, I'm no fan of assessing people based on their skin color. But holding a struggling State's feet to the fire on tactics is missing the point. Why are protests not being directed to our national government and the government of Mexico?

Why aren't these groups demanding that our porous border with Mexico be closed, once and for all? It's not impossible. We have the most sophisticated surveillance and monitoring technology in history, the most formidable military in the world, yet we are unable to stop the daily intrusion of illegal immigrants from Mexico into the United States? This is a failure of policy, not one of capability.

[snip]

Congress has been unwilling to pass an immigration bill, the first priority of which is closing the border. Why does "immigration reform" now demand a higher national priority than the crippling unemployment that is devastating the economic base and precipitating wide spread home foreclosures in our communities? ... [C]ities like Phoenix and many cities in the State of California and elsewhere are drowning in red ink with an ever-growing population demanding ever-more city services.

[snip]

The pro-illegal immigration amnesty movement shuns the classification "illegal" immigrant; preferring instead the term "undocumented immigrant." This is, of course, framing the debate. The "undocumented" immigrants entered into the United States illegally. When apprehended, deportation back to their country of origin is the customary legal procedure. Now, however, an intermediary process is advocated in lieu of deportation: an undocumented immigrant who, after following certain prescribed procedures, including the payment of taxes, will be permitted to remain in the United States. This constitutes de facto amnesty for the "undocumented immigrant." As such, it relieves the government of Mexico from any financial responsibility for the economic consequences associated with the cost of medical care, public education, public housing, welfare, police, and social services provided by the cities, counties and states in which such initially illegal immigrants choose to reside.

[snip]

The truth is that Mexico is exporting, or at the very least facilitating the export, of its poverty in the form of illegal immigrants to the United States.

[snip]

The annual cost of maintaining and providing services to illegal or "undocumented" citizens should be tabulated, assumed and paid by the Government of Mexico or credited against the annual cost of oil we import from them.

By now I think an irrefutable argument has been made that we need to enact:

### The 40th Amendment -- Sovereign Security

**Section 1: The security of a nation resting inevitably on the security of its borders, Congress shall fully fund all walls, barriers and other infrastructure necessary to secure the nation's borders and prevent any unauthorized entry.**

**Section 2: Congress shall provide all funds and enact all laws, which the Executive Branch shall fully enforce, necessary to prevent any person who has entered the country illegally from remaining therein.**

**Section 3: Until such time as the nation's southern and northern land borders have been fully and effectively sealed to prevent any unauthorized entry, Congress shall give no grant of amnesty, or exemption from the provisions of this Amendment, except to a**

**specific person by name upon demonstration of unique and meritorious circumstance.**

**Section 4: Employing, causing to employ, or facilitating the employment of a person within the territorial limits of the United States, who is not legally eligible to be so employed, shall be a felony punishable by incarceration in a maximum security facility for a period, not subject to pardon, parole, commutation, suspension, or other reduction of sentence, of not less than five years.**

Note that Section 2 and 3 work together to permit Congress to grant amnesty and a possible path to citizenship for those already here illegally, but only *after* our land borders have been sealed to prevent another surge of illegal immigration from creating yet another population of illegals intent on eventually benefiting from yet another amnesty.

No discussion of real immigration reform is honest or complete without also addressing the issue of automatically granting U.S. citizenship to anyone born on U.S. soil. This is known as birthright citizenship *jus soli* (as opposed to *jus sanguinis*, which is granted based on the nationality of one or both parents). *Jus soli* birthright citizenship motivates pregnant women to come to the U.S. illegally so that the child becomes an anchor with which to leverage legal resident status for the parent. Once the mother is legally established, she can bring in the rest of the family through the process known as family reunification. Soon, one anchor baby provides the citizenship mooring not just for the child's parents but also for numerous brothers, sisters, aunts, uncles, cousins, and grandparents. This is why opponents of illegal immigration favor a different term: *chain migration*. Wikipedia notes that birthright citizenship is more predominant in the Americas:

> Among advanced economies (as defined by the
> International Monetary Fund), the U.S. and Canada
> are the only ones that observe unconditional birthright
> citizenship ... (since) 2004 no European country
> grants citizenship based on unconditional jus soli.

[snip]

> A 2010 study found that only 30 of the world's 194
> countries grant citizenship at birth to the children of
> undocumented foreign residents.

The United States grants citizenship or permanent legal resident status to one million people a year. Only half of those people went through the traditional legal process, which can take up to ten years, and requires complying with many regulations. The other 500,000 people came here illegally and managed to obtain legal status, many under the anchor baby/family reunification policy. Ironically, while anchor babies automatically receive U.S. citizenship, children born abroad to U.S. citizens have not always been so lucky. For example: if both parents are U.S. citizens, their children born abroad gain birthright citizenship only if at least one parent has previously resided in the U.S. In cases where one parent is a U.S. citizen, his or her child gets automatic citizenship only if their American parent has lived in the U.S. continuously for one year prior to the child's birth. There are other conditions involving residency requirements and formal applications for citizenship that apply if the child is born in a foreign country to a non-American mother. (Typical example: children born in Korea or Vietnam during those respective wars.)

Another interesting aspect of the birthright citizenship issue applies to the requirement that candidates for President and vice-President must be native-born citizens. Forget the wacky birther conspiracy theories about Barack Obama being born in Africa; there was actual debate as to whether or not the late John McCain, by virtue of being born in the Panama Canal Zone while his father was stationed there, was eligible to run for President. Think about that: An anchor baby born to illegal immigrant parents could have a more clear-cut claim to meeting the native-born requirement to run for president than John McCain, whose parents were both U.S. citizens, and whose father was on active duty, on his way to becoming an admiral, at the time John was born. Whatever your opinion of John McCain, for this to even have been the subject of conjecture is absurd. If children, born to parents who come here illegally, can end up having clearer citizenship rights than the children of parents who were already citizens when their kids were born isn't ass-backward, what is?

As former Democratic Senator Harry Reid said in 1993:

> If making it easy to be an illegal alien isn't enough, how about offering a reward for being an illegal immigrant? No sane country would do that, right? Guess again. If you break our laws by entering this country without permission and give birth to a child, we reward that child with U.S. citizenship and guarantee a full access to all public and social services this society provides. And that's a lot of services.
>
> Is it any wonder that two-thirds of the babies born at taxpayer expense at county-run hospitals in Los Angeles are born to illegal alien mothers?
>
> No sane country would do that, right?

This, of course, would be the same Democratic Senate Majority Leader Harry Reid who later advocated for illegal immigrant rights and benefits once his party realized that a growing Hispanic population would produce additional Democratic voters.

As with other arguments involving illegal immigration, its proponents are quick to claim that America has always done things this way. Actually, it hasn't. It wasn't until the post-Civil War Fourteenth Amendment was enacted in 1868 that birthright citizenship *jus soli* was formally recognized in the Constitution. At various times since then -- 1924, 1940, 1952, 1960, 1978, 1994,

2001, and 2011 -- Congress has seen fit (or been forced) to adjust the criteria for American citizenship. An example was the retroactive granting of native-born jus soli citizenship status to people born in Alaska and Hawaii prior to the time that those territories became states. So, no, the U.S. has no blanket tradition of *jus soli* birthright citizenship. Ending *jus soli* citizenship is absolutely necessary to stem the tide of illegals who threaten both the physical and economic security of the country and its legal population. Thus:

**Section 5: Immediately upon ratification of this Amendment, the right of automatic citizenship will no longer confer to children when either parent is in the country illegally.**

It is interesting to note that Hispanic leaders bray about the *right* of Mexican immigrants to be here because it is rightfully *their* land. It makes a great sound bite, but those leaders never advocate for returning those lands to Mexico. You never hear demands for Texas, New Mexico, Arizona, and California to become Mexican states, with Mexican laws, Mexican political parties, the Mexican economy, and most of all, the Mexican peso. *Thank you very much, but no, we'll stick with the U.S. economy, laws, schools, public services, and the good old Yankee dollar.*

Ensuring that our borders are secure, and that the suffrage franchise remains sacrosanct through the 36th Amendment, will not be sufficient to protect American sovereignty. At the time I began this book the United States under the Obama administration was in secret negotiations on two nefarious and deceptively titled international Free Trade agreements: The Trans-Pacific Partnership (TPP) and its evil twin, the Transatlantic Trade and Investment Partnership (TTIP). Free Trade is the term applied to agreements that reduce tariffs and eliminate barriers to products from one country being imported into another. The theory is that each country benefits by exchanging an approximately equal amount of its exports for imports. Thus,

America might export sophisticated medical diagnostic equipment to country "X" and import apparel or tropical fruit from there. This theory conveniently ignores the fact that the reason tariffs and import quotas are enacted in the first place is to protect domestic industries, from farmers to automakers. When tariffs come down, the first people hurt are the workers and small business owners in those markets.

As Yves Smith noted at her widely respected and influential blog NakedCapitalism.com:

> [The TTP and the TTIP] are not about "free trade". They are, in the case of the TTP, to advance US geopolitical aims by isolating China, and in the case of both proposed pacts, to weaken national sovereignty to make the world safer for multinationals. The revolving door payoffs for the members of the US Trade Representative's office must be really juicy for them to be so eager to engage in treason.

A September 2010 NBC News-Wall Street Journal poll revealed that, "the impact of trade and outsourcing is one of the only issues on which Americans of different classes, occupations and political persuasions agree," with 86% saying that outsourcing jobs by U.S. companies to poor countries was, "a top cause of our economic woes," and 69% thinking that, "free trade agreements between the United States and other countries cost the U.S. jobs." Only 17% of Americans in 2010 felt that "free trade agreements" benefit the U.S., compared to 28% in 2007.

If the TPP and TTIP were truly about free trade, things would be bad enough. But they were not. Instead, these agreements were intended as the latest step in creating a worldwide supranational government of, by, and for mega-corporations. That's why they were being negotiated in secret. Congress didn't get to see the draft proposals, nor did the press. The only people who knew what was in these deals were the 600 private attorneys doing the actual drafting and negotiations. Despite this unprecedented secrecy, details about a couple of sections of the TPP were leaked through places like Wikileaks. After analysis of these documents, here's what Andrew Gavin Marshall wrote for Occupy.com:

> Dubbed by many as "NAFTA on steroids" and a "corporate coup," only two of the TPP's 26 chapters actually have anything to do with trade. Most of it grants far-reaching new rights and privileges to corporations, specifically related to intellectual property rights (copyright and patent laws), as well as constraints on government regulations.
>
> [snip]
>
> The agreement stipulates that foreign corporations operating in the United States would no longer be subject to domestic U.S. laws regarding protections for the environment, finance or labor rights, and could appeal to an "international tribunal" which would be given the power to overrule American law and impose sanctions on the U.S. for violating the new "rights" of corporations.
>
> The "international tribunal" that would dictate the laws of the countries would be staffed by corporate lawyers acting as "judges," thus ensuring that cases taken before them have a "fair and balanced" hearing -- fairly balanced in favor of corporate rights above anything else.
>
> [snip]
>
> The international corporate tribunal would allow corporations to overturn national laws and regulations or demand enormous sums in compensation, with the tribunal "empowered to order payment" of unlimited government Treasury funds to foreign investors over TPP claims.

This last item, suing for compensation, is particularly pernicious. It not only provides that corporations can sue to overturn state, national, and local environmental and safety regulations, but the plaintiff is also entitled to payment of *projected* lost profits caused by these regulations. Take a hypothetical example: Say that BP, the company responsible for the disastrous Deepwater Horizon oil rig disaster in the Gulf of Mexico, wants to drill for oil in the Bering Sea off Alaska, but its plans are put on hold because its drilling rig and its emergency response plans fail to meet government safety requirements. (This actually happened with a proposed Shell Oil drilling project in the Bering Sea.) With the powers granted to corporations by the TPP, BP would be able to get those regulations declared void *plus* it would be entitled to be reimbursed by the U.S. government for the profits BP *expected to make* during the period when the regulations prevented the company from drilling. Economist Dean Baker has noted that the TPP would limit the ability of state and local governments to regulate or prohibit oil fracking that permanently contaminates vast amounts of water, and has been linked to an increase in earthquakes near fracking operations.

The dangers of the TPP, and similar phony trade bills, extend into the areas of medicine, finance, and intellectual property. Sections of the proposed TPP agreement would have extended drug patents, kept less expensive generic versions of drugs off the market, and even allowed for the patenting of medical procedures. So, someone invents a new, less dangerous way to install a cardiac stent? Your doctor can only use the procedure if he, or the hospital, is willing to pay a licensing fee to the corporation that owns the right to that procedure. Under the TPP, some prescription drug prices could have gone up by 2,000 percent. (Not that they haven't already been jacked out of sight even without the TPP.)

Many of the TPP's most dangerous provisions involving the financial sector were drawn from the never-completed World Trade Organization General Agreement on Trade in Services (GATS). Yves Smith again: (Subject heading bold is original.)

**No new regulation**: The United States agreed to a "standstill provision" which requires that we not create new regulations (or reverse liberalization) for the list of financial services bound to comply with WTO rules. Translated out of GATSese, this means that the United States has bound itself not to do what Congress, regulators and scholars deem necessary -- create new financial service regulations.

**Certain forms of regulation banned outright**: The United States agreed that it would not set limits on the size of financial firms, the types of financial service one entity may provide or the types of legal entities through which a financial service may be provided in the broad array of financial services signed up to the WTO. These WTO rules conflict with countries' efforts to put size limitations on banks (so that they do not become "too big to fail") and to "firewall" different financial services (a policy tool used to limit the spread of risk across sectors).

[snip]

**No bans on new financial service "products"**: The United States is also required to allow all foreign financial firms operating here "to offer in its territory any new financial service," a conflict with proposals to limit various risky investment instruments, such as types of derivatives.

With respect to the TPP's radical changes in the area of intellectual property, here's more from Andrew Gavin Marshall at Truthout.org:

**Internet freedom is also a major target.**

The Council of Canadians, and OpenMedia, major campaigners for Internet freedom, have warned that the TPP would "criminalize some everyday uses of the Internet," including music downloads as well as the combining of different media works. OpenMedia warned that the TPP would "force service providers to collect and hand over your private data without privacy safeguards, and give media conglomerates more power to send you fines in the mail, remove online content -- including entire websites -- and even terminate your access to the Internet."

If these proposed limits on government power, and the right to sue for lost profits, seem too extreme to ever be enacted, guess again. They're already in place as part of the North American Free Trade Agreement (NAFTA). The website Public Citizen reports on six lawsuits arising from NAFTA's Investor's Rights provisions. Canada was sued four times for daring to restrict a toxic fuel additive, temporarily ban the export of cancer-causing PCBs, and limit logging. The damage amounts sought ranged from $20 million to $507 million. Mexico was sued for $90 million, for preventing a US company from re-opening a toxic waste dump *on top of an aquifer supplying drinking water to local communities*. But the biggest suit, for $725 million, was filed by a Canadian funeral home business, against the state of Mississippi, over a jury verdict awarding $25 million in punitive damages for the company's fraudulent and deceptive practices. Public Citizen reports that so far, "Damages sought from taxpayers in NAFTA cases already exceed $1.8 billion." That doesn't count the newest case, in which Quebec is being sued for $250 million because the province decided not to allow oil and gas drilling under the St. Lawrence River.

Unfortunately, NAFTA has served as a template for other multi-nation trade deals, which has led to even more lawsuits -- according to the Sierra Club, more than 500 -- for lost profits and denial of investor rights filed against governments across the globe. Both Columbia and Romania have been sued after they refused to let companies use cyanide in gold-mining operations that would threaten local drinking water. A U.S. mining company is suing Canada for $300 million in lost profits because Nova Scotia refused to allow a mining operation in an environmentally sensitive area. Other cases cited by the Sierra Club involve suits by

Dow Chemical and ExxonMobil. The arbitration tribunals hear these cases in secret, with three judges selected from a pool of lawyers who, when they're not hearing cases, are *filing* cases on behalf of other clients. A mere 15 lawyers have heard 55% of the cases brought so far. Their verdict is final and there is no appeal.

This perverse system has helped make ISDS suits so potentially lucrative that Wall Street hedge funds are investing in the costs of the suits, in return for hefty percentages (in some cases 35%) of any settlement award. One hedge fund set up a $700 million litigation fund. Compare that with the situation in countries like Costa Rica and Bolivia, where the entire justice department budget is under $20 million a year. Furthermore, because only companies can bring ISDS suits, only companies can win financially. Governments cannot bring suit against companies, and must pay their own legal expenses, even if they win.

Another treasonous free trade deal that followed NAFTA was KORUS, the Korean-United States Free Trade Agreement, ratified in 2011. According to the Economic Policy Institute, in its first year, KORUS increased the U.S. trade deficit by $5.8 billion, and caused the loss of over 40,000 well-paying U.S. jobs, mostly in the manufacturing sector. EPI projects that overall, KORUS will cost 159,000 U.S. jobs. Still, KORUS is a weak sister compared to NAFTA. EPI reported that, in the sixteen years between when it was signed into law in 1994 and the end of 2010, NAFTA increased the U.S. trade deficit with Mexico by $97.2 billion, and eliminated 683,000 jobs. The loss of manufacturing jobs has been so acute that the Obama administration attempted to hide the true extent of the disaster by changing the definition of manufacturing. Here's Lee Shepperd from Tax Analysts in the July 8, 2014 edition of Forbes, which is hardly a bastion of pro-worker sentiment: [Emphasis in the final paragraph added.]

> The Economic Classification Policy Committee, a group of federal agencies, proposes to change the North American Industry Classification system, a

classification system for data analysis by NAFTA governments, to amend the definition of manufacturing for many purposes, including labor statistics and economic indicators.

The object of this exercise is to reclassify companies that have outsourced production from the United States as US manufacturers. Some federal classification systems, including standard industrial classification, already do treat offshored manufacturing as US manufacturing. Public Citizen argues that the proposal would artificially reduce the manufacturing trade deficit while artificially raising the number of jobs classified as manufacturing jobs.

The tax law has been indulgently defining US-contracted offshore manufacturing in ways that benefit US companies for many years. The tax code contains a number of special benefits for manufacturing. Hardly anyone would qualify if manufacturing were strictly defined as metal bashing in the United States. So the IRS has been liberal in its interpretations, helping companies qualify for these breaks.

Indeed, a desperate Congress told the IRS to interpret qualification for the domestic production deduction generously. Enacted a decade ago, the deduction allows companies to deduct nine percent of their income from domestic production, provided the deduction does not exceed taxable income or 50 of associated US wages (section 199).

[snip]

The policy committee proposes to redefine manufacturing to include US-designed products that are manufactured in China. The US design activity would be redefined as "factoryless goods" production.

US executives would be redefined as factoryless goods producers, increasing reported manufacturing wages. The fabrication activity in China would be redefined as a service. And the imported Chinese goods would be redefined as imported services. The policy committee hopes to get the EU to accept the products as US-manufactured exports.

The policy committee's argument is that the person putting all the factors of production together should still be considered a manufacturer. Requiring transformation in the United States was regarded as too restrictive, **because it would prevent companies from offshoring to chase lower wages.** Yes, the policy committee really did say that.

It's disheartening that government agencies no longer even pretend that their mission is to protect American jobs. Fortunately, opposition to the TPP became a cornerstone of Trump's 2016 presidential campaign. Although it may not have killed the TPP forever -- these bogus trade agreements are like zombies, you have to kill them with fire -- Trump's election killed the momentum of the project and temporarily removed it from active debate. Trump also promised to either renegotiate NAFTA or pull the U.S. out of the agreement, and his administration has -- apparently successfully -- renegotiated the deal with Canada and Mexico.

Corporations, banksters, and politicians seek to justify the job losses sustained by these trade agreement scams by waving the banner of globalization, which they claim is inevitable, an act of nature rather than a deliberate plan concocted by the multinational elite. The argument even has its own acronym, TINA, which stands for There Is No Alternative. In a September 2013 speech, Richard Fisher, President of the Federal Reserve Bank of Dallas, said that manufacturing is, "not going to come home to the degree it used to be." Here's how two NakedCapitalism.com readers responded: (Capitalization is original.)

By screen name Petridish:

This is the weak, puny fait accompli mantra inevitably invoked in discussions such as these. Manufacturing was never going to "come" home. It was always going to need to be FORCED home through tariffs and severe tax penalties for those who would destroy what it has taken over 200 years to build. In truth, it never should have been allowed to leave at all ... As to the accusations of "protectionism" that would follow, they should be EMBRACED. The productive economy of the US deserves and demands protection and the US government, with all available FORCE, should provide it.

No country can long endure economically without producing the bulk of what it consumes. And no economy can "grow" without growing, mining or manufacturing things as its primary activities. All other activity should serve those ends.

By screen name Montanamaven:

If a country does not make as much as it can of what it needs and instead imports finished goods, it is called a colony. The Germans never gave up the making of the machines that make the machines. They did not outsource their tool and die makers ... So it is they, not us, who are selling these advanced machines to the Chinese.

There you have it: two regular citizens demonstrating a clearer grasp of economic realities than 99% of the journalists, pundits, politicians, think-tank fellows, and ivory tower academics who pollute the national narrative on a daily basis.

The acronym we need to start using is RITA. Reform Is The Alternative. RITA starts with enacting policies that defend American workers, American manufacturers, and America's ability to provide for itself:

**Section 6: Neither Congress nor the President shall bind the United States to any treaty, trade**

**agreement, or other covenant that surrenders any sovereign legal rights or judicial or military powers of the federal government, or any state or lesser jurisdiction, to any foreign entity. Immediately upon ratification of this Amendment, all such treaties and agreements previously in force are null and void.**

Last, but certainly not least, in order to assure that the U.S. becomes, and remains, the melting pot that we've historically claimed it to be, it is necessary to establish English as the unifying official language.

**Section 7: A common language being necessary to a stable economy and a unified citizenry, English shall be the official language of the nation. All business of Federal, state, and local government, and all official documents thereof including ballots and election materials, shall be in English, and only English. Recognizing the value of other languages in a global community, Congress and the States shall implement foreign language proficiency requirements as a condition of secondary school graduation.**

A common language not only unites a country emotionally, it is a crucial factor in the efficient functioning of both the economy and society in general. Iran is different from Saudi Arabia, not just because they follow different Muslim sects, but because Iranians speak Farsi, while Saudis speak Arabic. Brazil is different from Venezuela, or Argentina, because Brazilians speak Portuguese rather than Spanish. And closer to home, if ever a country presented a clear example of the divisive problem of entrenched language differences among people inhabiting the same geographic territory, it's our neighbor to the north, Canada.

Quebec, conquered by the French in bits and pieces starting in 1534, quite naturally gave rise to a population that was (and still is) heavily Catholic and French-speaking. The other areas of Canada, conquered by the British or, in the case of the western provinces, obtained from Spain, is predominately Protestant and speaks English. Combine that with the resentment of the French-speaking population to being defeated by the British in 1763, and you have a cultural problem which festers to this day.

Since adoption of the Official Languages Act in 1969, Canada has officially been bi-lingual, with both French and English theoretically sharing equal status. Wikipedia summarizes:

> Official bilingualism is generally understood to include any law or other measure that:
>
> - Mandates that the federal government conduct its business in both official languages and provide government services in both languages;
>
> - Encourages or mandates lower tiers of government (most notably the provinces and territories, but also some municipalities) to conduct themselves in both official languages and to provide services in both English and French rather than in just one or the other;
>
> - Places obligations on private actors in Canadian society to provide access to goods or services in both official languages (such as the requirement that food products be labeled in both English and French);
>
> - Provides support to non-government actors to encourage or promote the use or the status of one or the other of the two official languages. This includes grants and contributions to groups representing the English-speaking minority in Quebec and the French-speaking minorities in the other provinces to assist with the establishment of an infrastructure of cultural supports and services.

So, Canadians have the right to receive services from departments of the federal government in both official languages, and to be heard in court in either official language they choose. Easy, right? Not so fast. Again, from Wikipedia:

> At the provincial level, New Brunswick officially recognizes the equal status of French and English. While French has equal legal status in Manitoba restored due to court ruling that struck down seventy-year-old English-only laws in 1985, in practice, French language services are only provided in some regions of the province. Quebec has declared itself officially unilingual (French only). Alberta and Saskatchewan are also considered unilingual (English only). In practice, all provinces, including Quebec, offer some services in both English and French and some publicly funded education in both official languages up to the high school level (English language postsecondary education institutions are also present in Quebec, as are French language postsecondary institutions in other provinces, in particular in Ontario and New Brunswick). English and French are official languages in all three territories. In addition, Inukitut is also an official language in Nunavut, and nine aboriginal languages have official status in the Northwest Territories...

Let's total that up: Quebec rejects English. Alberta and Saskatchewan more or less ignore French. And with ten officially recognized native languages, Canada does business in twelve languages. Got it.

Despite a 1988 revision to the law, as well as the ensuing publication of regulations designed to clarify and implement the act, language issues persist. First, there is the continuing problem of defining exactly what areas have, "sufficient demand for services in both languages." Then, there are the conflicts between the national law and Quebec's Charter of the French Language. Again, Wikipedia explains:

In the 1970s the (Quebec) provincial legislature adopted two laws, the *Official Language Act* (also known as "Bill 22") and the Charter of the French Language (also known as "Bill 101"), reducing the access of Quebecers to English-language services, preventing immigrants and Francophones from enrolling their children in English schools, requiring that French be made the language of the workplace, and restricting the use of English on commercial signs.

The insistence by Quebec that French language regulations be enforced led to the creation of the infamous Board of the French Language, aka the language police, which made an international fool of itself in 2013 by fining an Italian restaurant for not using the French words for pasta, calamari, etc., in its descriptions of menu items.

All this would be funny if it didn't mask a serious issue:

**Many residents of Quebec don't really consider themselves Canadians, but rather Quebecois.**

The American Historical Association published a pamphlet titled *EM 47: Canada: Our Oldest Good Neighbor* which contained an article, *Is There A Deep Split Between French and English Canada?* that described the role language plays as follows: [Emphasis added.]

> Canada is like a double-yolked egg. French Canada and English Canada each form, as it were, *a nation within a nation*. The Dominion is *a country with a dual nationality*. Double nationality is very foreign to American ways of thinking, but it has to be recognized before one can begin to understand Canada. There are few countries in the world -- and not another in this hemisphere -- where such complete duality prevails. It dominates Canadian politics, for almost every public question must be viewed with a French eye and an English eye, or it will be seen out of focus.

Canada's dual nationality is published on every postage stamp and on the paper currency issued by the Dominion government, for they are printed in both French and English. It is echoed in the Supreme Court of Canada and in the houses of Parliament, where, according to the constitution, French stands on a par with English as an official language. Every motion in Parliament has to be put in both French and English, members may deliver their speeches in either tongue, and all federal publications -- the Dominion laws, the debates in Parliament, and government reports -- appear in two editions, one French and the other English.

Arguments over language sparked a simmering separatist movement. From the 1960s through the mid-1990s, there was a considerable effort to have Quebec break away and become its own country. Two Quebec referendums on the issue, in 1980 and 1994, failed, but by narrow margins. One analysis is that common sense prevailed. Becoming its own country sounded romantic, right up until people started adding up everything their new country would have to provide and pay for on its own, including creating a currency, enforcing its own borders and customs inspections, negotiating its own trade agreements, etc. But none of that changes the fundamental fact that French-speaking Canadians, especially those in Quebec, consider themselves distinctly separate from the rest of Canada.

We have a parallel situation here in the U.S. with the Latino community. There is a strong belief among many Latinos, especially illegal immigrants, that the U.S. stole the southwest from Mexico. They see demanding services in Spanish, and the continued use of that language, as both a right and a protest. That's why it is common to see lots of Mexican flags at Latino protests over U.S. immigration policies. Not surprisingly, this creates resentment among non-Hispanic Americans who feel that the Latino illegal immigrant community wants the benefits of living and working in the U.S., while at the same time vilifying it.

Just to be clear, we did steal parts of America from the people who were here before us, but they were Native American Indian tribes. Mexico invited Americans to settle Texas to help fight the marauding Comanches that Mexico couldn't deal with by itself. People from Mexico, who think the rest of the country should learn their language, never seem to consider that they're not asking Americans to use *Aztec*; they want us to speak *Spanish*, the language of a country halfway around the world that conquered Mexico -- and the rest of Latin America -- centuries before Texas and California became independent republics. Mexico and the U.S. fought a war over Arizona and New Mexico; we won, they lost. End of story. It is now history. Perhaps not yet ancient history, but still history.

Many who support English as an official language like to claim that, unlike today's immigrants, previous immigrants (primarily from European countries) were quick to learn and embrace English. Let's put that baloney to rest from the get-go. Many learned just enough English to get by at work. By necessity, their kids became fluent in English through school. But around home, the conversational language was that of the mother country. Germantown or Chinatown, Little Italy or Little Odessa, the distinguishing characteristic -- besides ethnic cuisine -- was (and is) the predominance of the ancestral language. Fidelity to that reality is one reason some scenes from *The Godfather* that take place here in America (like Michael and Sollozzo in the restaurant), are in Italian with English subtitles. And ethnic communities from Africa, Asia, and the Middle East still hold on to their mother tongues. (Where do you think the CIA, FBI, and the State Department look when they're recruiting translators?)

Language differences exacerbate ethnic, racial, and cultural differences. Lack of a common language encourages division into *us* and *them*. The solution is to enforce English as the official language, while at the same time mandating that kids learn a second language, starting in grade school. Every American child should become competent in multiple languages. Given the global nature of the world we live in, exposure to other cultures and competency in other languages is both sociologically and professionally valuable. But the glue of the nation still has to be proficiency in English. Which is why, unless you are over 50 and have lived legally in the U.S. for at least twenty consecutive years, to become a naturalized citizen, you have to pass a three-part test which covers reading, writing, and speaking *English*. This makes a lot of people wonder why, if citizens must be competent in English, ballots and election materials have to be provided in multiple other languages?

# Chapter 16

# PROTECTING STATE
# AND LOCAL POWER

There's an old saying: "All politics are local." That's because the impact of decisions made far away in D.C., or the state capital, are eventually felt in individual homes. Congress authorizes the Invasion of Iraq; your National Guard unit gets called up and soon you're halfway around the world dealing with ambushes and IEDs, while back home your spouse tries to keep the family afloat financially. The state reduces education funding; your daughter's Advanced Placement class at school gets the axe. Environmental regulations get weakened or enforcement funding gets cut; later your city is trucking in water because the local supply is no longer safe to drink.

Just as they have learned to manipulate states and cities for subsidies, tax waivers, and other sweetheart deals, entire industries have learned to evade what they consider burdensome regulations. (*Burdensome* being defined as "interferes with excessive profits.") If local ordinances and regulations are too strict, companies lobby legislatures to preempt local authority with weaker statewide regulations. If state regulations are too tough, they get Congress to step in. Classic examples of this involve fracking, Genetically Modified foods, zoning regulations, and the prohibitions against municipal internet services described in Chapter 14.

Hydraulic fracturing, commonly known as fracking, is the process of injecting extremely high-pressure fluids into deep underlying rock formations, causing them to fracture, which allows natural gas and oil to migrate to the well. The process is sometimes "enhanced" through the use of explosives.

Leaving aside any discussion of the effects of continued dependence on fossil fuels on global climate change, the chemicals used in fracking are a threat to public health and safety. The effects include surface land contamination, the migration of methane gas and fracking chemicals into the air, earthquakes, and even the release of radioactive elements buried deep in rock formations. In the summer of 2018, the area of Colorado known as the Front Range, which includes Denver and its surrounding communities, recorded smog levels exceeding federal health standards. The cause wasn't cars; it was airborne pollution from fracking operations in the state. But the most important threat from fracking is the ***permanent*** loss of water. Once contaminated with fracking chemicals, water's molecular structure is forever altered, and the water ***cannot*** be reclaimed. Since fracking contaminates ground water, wherever that contaminated water flows it can combine, and contaminate, more water. Would you like some hydrocarbons with your coffee?

Of 28 chemicals that researchers and scientists know are used in fracking, every single one is proven to adversely affect the skin, eyes, sensory organs, or respiratory function. Some of the more noxious fracking chemicals are:

- **Diammonium peroxodisulfate**, used in making bleach and laboratory cleaning agents.

- **Sodium tetraborate decahydrate** and **sodium borate**, both used in cleaning products and insecticides.

- **Ethoxylated branched rich alcohols**, used in industrial cleaning supplies.

- **Heavy aromatic naphtha**, used in the production of gasoline and paint thinner.

- **Poly(oxy-1,2-ethanediyl)** and **tetrakis (hydroxymethyl) phosphonium sulfate**, used in pesticides.

One or more of the seven listed above are known to affect the immune system, brain and nervous system, kidney and liver function, and the digestive tract. Several also impact the reproductive system, or adversely affect physical and mental development in children. Sodium tetraborate decahydrate, sodium borate, and tetrakis (hydroxymethyl) phosphonium sulfate are known disruptors of endocrine function. Many other harmful chemicals may be in use in fracking but are not publicly known, because the corrupt stooges in Congress *have exempted companies that engage in fracking from the Clean Water Act*, meaning they don't have to reveal the dangerous substances they use. This had led to absurd situations where fracking companies claim that there is no pollution of the ground water, yet homeowners have posted videos of setting their tap water on fire in the kitchen sink.

Concern over the disastrous environmental effects and health issues associated with fracking has driven states and local communities, all over the country, to use zoning laws, moratoriums, and outright bans to limit or prevent fracking. New York State's Southern Tier, and the Catskills, are prime targets for fracking. But by 2014, nearly 80 municipalities had banned fracking altogether, another 99 had enacted moratoria and, in 87 other jurisdictions, organized opposition to fracking was pushing for additional regulations. New Mexico's Mora County was the first county to ban fracking, and Vermont the first state to do so. New Jersey and North Carolina followed suit, while Maryland enacted a statewide moratorium until more data is available. Meanwhile, cities, counties, and other entities with jurisdiction over lands, rivers, and parks, have enacted their own bans. The list includes big cities (Dallas, Pittsburgh, and Los Angeles), wealthy enclaves (Beverly Hills), and small communities such as Wellsburg, Ohio and Lewisburg, West Virginia.

Pennsylvania, home to the oil and natural gas reserves of the Marcellus Shale, has been ground zero in the fracking war. Forced to buy out farmers and homeowners whose lands have been irretrievably polluted by fracking, the companies have insisted on gag orders that prevent even the children in these families from ever talking about the settlements.

In 2012, thanks to Republican domination of the state legislature and Republican Governor Tom Corbett's willingness to sell out to the big energy companies, Pennsylvania passed Act 13, an amendment to the Pennsylvania Consolidated Statutes which, among other things:

- Allowed fracking anywhere in the state, regardless of local zoning regulations, moratoriums, or bans.

- Exempted fracking drillers from having to reveal how chemicals used in fracking impact existing compounds and organisms in the ground around drilling operations.

- Exempted drillers from having to reveal the chemicals they use to physicians.

- If voluntarily notified by drillers of chemicals used in fracking, physicians were prohibited from disclosing that information to the patient, the public, or other physicians, including specialists.

Fortunately, in 2013, the portion of Act 13 prohibiting local jurisdictions from enacting and enforcing zoning laws and other environmental safeguards was overturned by the Pennsylvania Supreme Court as a violation of the state constitution's Environmental Rights Amendment. The court also instructed the state appeals court to reconsider the prohibition against doctors sharing information with patients, other physicians, and the public.

In Alaska, Shell Oil filed a preemptive lawsuit against a number of prominent environmental groups, seeking to prevent them from filing future lawsuits against Shell's plans to drill in the Arctic Ocean. Shell filed this lawsuit before it even submitted its Arctic drilling plan. Yes, you read that right: Shell either hadn't decided what it was going to do, or had decided and wouldn't reveal it yet, but either way, it wanted the court to prevent anyone from **ever** suing over whatever it decides to do.

Of course, when the fracking project is in your own backyard, that's a whole 'nother thing. Rex Tillerson, Trump's first Secretary of State, was quick to join a lawsuit against the construction of a water tower near his $5 mil Texas home. That the tower would supply water for fracking was both ironic and hypocritical given that Tillerson, in his role as CEO of ExxonMobil, was a fierce proponent of fracking and railed against local regulations designed to stop it. ThinkProgress.org reported:

> "This type of dysfunctional regulation is holding back the American economic recovery, growth, and global competitiveness," he (Tillerson) said in 2012. Natural gas production "is an old technology just being applied, integrated with some new technologies," he said in another interview, "So the risks are very manageable."

In shale regions, less wealthy residents have protested fracking development for impacts more consequential than noise, including water contamination and cancer risk. Exxon's oil and gas operations and the resulting spills not only sink property values, but the spills have leveled homes and destroyed regions.

Fracking is currently banned completely by France, Germany, Ireland, and Bulgaria. (That's right, we're behind *Bulgaria* when it comes to environmental protection of our water supplies.) The actions of the fracking industry, in communities all across the country, are proof that we need constitutional safeguards that enable states and local governments to protect our families and communities. If *Not In My Back Yard* is good enough for the wealthy and connected, it should be good enough for the average citizen.

In addition to using the preemption powers of the federal government to threaten your well-being through their activities in the ground, the corporate elites are also perfectly willing to do it through the air. Congress is currently considering Senate Bill S 3157, which would preempt local communities from prohibiting the placement of 5G wireless transmitter towers. It would even mandate that such towers could be erected on public buildings, including schools. The bill is opposed by the National League of Cities, and with good reason. Not only are communities required to allow positioning of these towers at absurdly low rental rates, the proven adverse health effects of radiation of this magnitude include an elevated risk of cancer, learning and memory disorders, and sleep deprivation. The idea of placing these towers on school facilities is particularly worrying because children are among the most vulnerable from exposure to excess radiation.

GMO crops are another huge problem. Most are engineered to be Round-Up Ready, which means that they can be sprayed with the herbicide Round-Up and only the weeds will die, not the crop itself. GMO corn and cotton, on the other hand, are engineered so that they **self-produce pesticides in their own tissue**. As labelgmos.org notes, "GMO Corn is regulated by the Environmental Protection Agency as an Insecticide, but is sold unlabeled." So, what you're really serving at the next holiday barbecue is *insecticide-on-the-cob*.

Even worse, the vast majority of corn and other GMO grains are fed to livestock. Thus, even people who eat organic vegetables and produce may unknowingly ingest GMO residue from the meats and poultry they consume. In addition, GMO seeds cannot effectively be contained. They get spread by wind, storms, and irrigation runoff. This is why organic farmers and others who avoid GMO seeds have found GMO contamination in their crops.

The argument against GMO food is pretty basic: Current research and real-world experience has already linked GMO foods to allergies, organ failure, impaired reproductive and immune systems, and cancer. Tinkering with the food supply could have disastrous, perhaps irreversible, consequences for the survival of the entire food chain. The primary goal of the anti-GMO movement is a ban on the use and sale of GMO products, and those that contain GMO residue. If that is a bridge too far, the fallback goal is to at least require all GMO foods and beverages to be clearly labeled, so that consumers can make an informed choice. In polls and public opinion surveys, 90% of all consumers want labeling of all food containing GMOs or GMO by-products. Again, according to labelgmos.org, by 2013:

> 61 countries with over 40% of the world's population already label genetically engineered foods, including the entire European Union. China labels genetically engineered foods...

> In 50 countries there are significant restrictions or outright bans on GMOs.

Beside the EU, other countries that either ban GMOs or require strict labeling are Australia, Japan, South Korea, Brazil, Saudi

Arabia, Russia, and Mexico. You read that right: *Russia* and *Mexico* do a better job of informing the populace and protecting their food supply than the U.S.

The movement to ban or label GMO's started in the 1990s. The EU enacted its regulations in 2004. Even though a 2012 California ballot measure, Prop 37, narrowly failed (due to a massive propaganda effort by GMO producers), by 2013 the movement to label GMOs had spread to 34 states. That's when the biotech industry got nervous. As organicconsumers.org reported:

> State GMO labeling, and other food safety and food labeling laws, are guaranteed under the Constitution. Federal law, upheld for decades by federal court legal decisions, allows states to pass laws relating food safety or food labels when the U.S. Food & Drug Administration (FDA) has no prior regulations or prohibitions in place. There is currently no federal law or FDA regulation on GMO labeling, except for a guidance statement on voluntary labeling, nor is there any federal prohibition on state GMO or other food safety labeling laws.

> But with so many states, including Washington, Connecticut, Vermont, Maine, and others, threatening to actually pass GMO labeling laws, the biotech industry is fighting back. Realizing that they can't fight GMO labeling laws in every state, they're coming after states' rights.

> [snip]

> Last year, when Vermont legislators signaled they might pass a GMO labeling law, Monsanto threatened to sue the state, causing the Governor to back down.

With Vermont's legislature hard at work on a GMO labeling law, Senator Bernie Sanders introduced Senate Amendment 965, which would have definitively established the rights of states to enact GMO labeling laws. The measure failed, 22-71. Who voted against the right of people to know what they are eating? There were 43 Republicans on the wrong side, but given their traditional deference to the interests of big business, that's to be expected. The crushing blow came from the 28 *faux*gressive Democrats, who claim to have the public's interest at heart but really do the bidding of the donors who own them. Among the traitors: Progressive darlings Elizabeth Warren (MA), Sherrod Brown (OH), Tammy Baldwin (WI), Al Franken (MN), and Michigan's Debbie Stabenow. Sometimes referred to by critics as Debbie Stab*me*now, in 2012, she scored almost $740,000 in campaign contributions from major agribusiness firms.

When Bernie Sanders can't get a bill passed to ensure states the power to exercise rights that are seemingly already guaranteed by the Constitution, then we have to set those rights in stone:

### The 41st Amendment --
### Protection of State and Local Power

**Section 1: Given the inevitable conflict between the interests of commerce and the well-being of the people, to protect its environment, economy, and natural resources a state, or lesser jurisdiction thereof, may enact and enforce laws or regulations involving environmental protections or business operating conditions that are more stringent than those of superior jurisdictions, including the federal government.**

Returning once again to Hamilton's idea that laws must be attended by penalties, for protection of our physical, business, and financial environment we must ensure that failure to follow the law lands offenders in jail. Fines are not enough; often the amount is a pittance compared to the illegally-obtained profits. It simply becomes a cost of doing business and, to make matters worse, it's generally deductible on the violator's tax return. A law against dumping toxic waste in a river is a perfect example. A company or corporation does not violate this law, a person or persons violates this law. *Somebody* ordered the dumping. *Somebody* opened the valve, or pushed the lever, or turned off the filtering device that was supposed to remove toxic elements. Those people should go to jail. Therefore:

> **Section 2: All violations of environmental protection laws involving damage in excess of $10,000 shall be a felony punishable by incarceration in a maximum security facility for a period, not subject to pardon, parole, commutation, suspension, or other reduction of sentence, of not less than five years.**

Some will argue that the only people convicted under this provision will be low-level workers tasked with carrying out the orders, while those that give the commands and make the decisions will escape punishment. This argument does not pass muster. For one thing, lower-level workers will have an incentive to provide evidence against their bosses in order to avoid being prosecuted themselves. Most importantly, we must end the notion that no one should get punished unless everybody gets punished, because too often that path leads to no punishment for anyone, and no deterrence against future repetition. At some point, if only low-level workers are prosecuted, other workers will decline to follow illegal orders.

Another argument against giving this kind of veto power to local communities is that it would stymie projects that have to be built, that a small community could obstruct the greater good. Three responses: First, when you see contentious projects, especially ones with potentially negative environmental impacts, being suggested for Beverly Hills, New York City's Upper East Side, or the Kalorama neighborhood of Washington, D.C. you might have a valid argument. Remember, the NYC landfill is on *Staten* Island, not Manhattan. Second, if a particular project is not suited for better neighborhoods, maybe it's not suited for any neighborhood?

Maybe the project shouldn't happen? Third, if a project is absolutely essential and there is no other place to put it, government will find a way, even if it means acquiring an entire community by eminent domain. (In several extreme pollution cases, whole communities have been acquired this way.)

There is nothing more important to quality-of-life issues than local zoning regulations. Every community needs a certain critical mass of population and tax base to support necessary basic public services. After a community reaches that minimum critical mass it can still accommodate and benefit from additional growth. However, despite what developers and their crony politicians claim, that growth cannot go on forever without adverse impacts. Eventually, there comes a point where population growth becomes a negative in terms of traffic, air quality, water supplies, school district capacity, and other quality-of-life issues. The local zoning process allows communities to control both density and the mix of property uses. Zoning regulations keep chemical plants from being located next to hospitals, and strip clubs away from schools.

Developers and real estate interests love to make end runs around local regulations. Real estate developers in California, wanting to bypass local zoning initiatives that limit how many units they can cram into a given area, got the state to pass legislation superseding local density limits and mandating more development. Companies that don't like a state's strict regulations on emissions, or toxic waste controls, get their puppets in Congress to hand superseding jurisdiction to federal agencies staffed by the industry's own former employees. (Employees who will come back to work in that industry when their "public service" ends.)

The great irony is that many times more growth is proposed as the solution to problems caused by previous growth and the over-development of a specific community or area. But, that doesn't prevent those who stand to profit by new development from ignoring the reality that, *if growth was the solution, these*

***communities would have grown their way to nirvana long ago***. Local zoning regulations, especially where citizens have the power of the ballot initiative and referendum, allow communities to prevent unrestrained and counter-productive growth. Local zoning power also enables small communities to protect themselves from being exploited by wealthier and more politically powerful communities.

This issue is important because there is now a movement underfoot laying the groundwork to take zoning and planning control power away, not only from local communities, ***but from states as well***. In July 2014, the Washington Post's Wonkblog headlined:

### How big cities that restrict new housing harm the economy

The gist of the article was that cities must accept unlimited, never-ending increases in housing density to benefit the greater good. (*Greater good* meaning the wealth of those at the top of the economic pyramid.) A month after the Wonkblog article, the website NakedCapitalism.com re-posted a summary of articles dealing with *The Economics of Big Cities* from Bruegel.com: (All bold is original.)

> Richard Florida writes that in the years since the economic crisis, powerhouse metros like San Francisco, New York, and Washington, D.C., have continued to grow in importance. **In 2012, the top ten largest metropolitan economies produced more than a third of the country's total economic output.**
>
> Josh Lehner writes that **the largest metros (the 51 largest have a population of 1 million or more) have seen the strongest gains in recovery** ... It is also interesting to note that only the largest cities have seen growth rates return to pre-recession levels, while the others lag. This is at least partly due to the nature

of the Great Recession in which housing and government have been large weights on the recovery. These jobs also play a disproportionately large role in many medium, smaller and rural economies than in big cities.

Chang-Tai Hsieh and Enrico Moretti write that one possible way to minimize this negative externality would be for **the federal government to constrain U.S. municipalities' ability to set land use regulations**. Currently, municipalities set land use regulations in almost complete autonomy, since the effect of such regulations have long been perceived as predominately localized. But if such policies have meaningful nationwide effects, then the adoption of federal standard intended to limit negative externalities may be in the aggregate interest.

Enrico Moretti [also] writes that, historically, **there have always been prosperous communities and struggling communities**. But the difference was small until the 1980s ... The mounting economic divide between American communities -- arguably one of the most important developments in the history of the United States of the past half a century -- is not an accident, but reflects a structural change in the American economy. Sixty years ago, the best predictor of a community's economic success was physical capital. With the shift from traditional manufacturing to innovation and knowledge, the best predictor of a community's economic success is human capital.

Kristian Behrens and Frêdêrick Robert-Nicoud write that **inequality is especially strong in large cities**. Large cities are more unequal than the nations that host them. For example, income inequality in the New York Metro Area (MSA) is considerably higher than the US average and similar to that of Rwanda or Costa Rica. Large cities are also more unequal than smaller towns. While larger cities increase the income of everyone, the top 5% benefit substantially more than the bottom quintile.

Let's unpack these articles:

- Local zoning laws inhibit the creation of gigantic mega-cities.

- Giant mega-cities would be in the best interest of the economy. (In other words, *profits*.)

- Thanks to the de-industrialization of the economy, human capital is now more important than physical capital. (Land, plants and equipment, transportation infrastructure, etc.)

- The best way to **exploit** that human capital is to concentrate it in mega-cities **that have the greatest income inequality**.

So, the more inequality we create, the better it is for the economy? Whose economy?

*The plutonomy, dummy!* Because, as Citibank explained, *nobody else counts.*

Although the Moretti and Hsieh article points out that trying to make local land use policy a federal prerogative is probably unrealistic, this is exactly how such movements get started. Academic studies are used to float ideas. There is initial pushback, but the drumbeat continues. Over time, resistance is worn down. Compromises are made. The concept creeps incrementally closer to reality, until finally it is an almost unstoppable force.

With respect to the distortion of the U.S. economy over the past forty years, a commenter at NakedCapitalism.com who uses the screen name Glen posted: "Kill off manufacturing leaving only rent seeking industries and then marvel at the importance of cities. Wow!" It is also interesting that in his thesis, Moretti examined the impact of housing limitations in the San Francisco area, where lower-income renters are being forced out by tech industry yuppies willing to pay inflated rents. One of those recent battles involved the city of San Francisco doling out a waiver of the city's income tax to employees of Twitter if the company agreed to stay in San Francisco, rather than move south to Silicon Valley. According to the city, the value of that tax break is $22 million. However, in analyzing it as part of Twitter's Initial Public Offering, the SEC valued it at $56 million. Other companies locating around the new Twitter headquarters will also qualify. Perhaps this example of corporate welfare and race-to-the-bottom economics shouldn't be surprising in a city where Google's private buses are allowed to use the city's public bus stops, free of charge.

Speaking of race-to-the bottom economics, this is also a good time to reiterate that economics is often referred to as the dismal science, but in fact, is not a science at all. Economics is the analysis of economic events that happened in the past, and *theories* about what will happen in the future under various conditions and government policies. The science of physics has laws, like the *Law of Gravity*. The science of chemistry has laws; combine copper and tin in the correct proportions and you'll get bronze. Every time. It's been that way since mixing the two metals was first discovered about fifty-five hundred years ago. However, with economic theories there is no such thing as surety of outcome. Some theories have been shown to work in the past, while others failed. Or, *are failing*. However, even when they fail, economic theories like austerity remain in use because they favor the banksters and other ruling elite.

On the local, national, and international level we are told that growth is essential, that the economy must grow. Completely ignoring the reality that the Earth has finite resources, growth is prescribed as the cure for every problem. Back in the years leading up to the Great Recession, those of us in California were told that the state's population would go up by some 20 million people by 2040 and we had to plan for that increase. The solution would be "smart growth," with high-density housing and "live-work" centers clustered along major high-speed mass transit systems. At a regional planning meeting to devise various visions of how this scheme could be implemented, I asked: "Say we come up with a great plan, a plan so perfect that it is adopted by all the government agencies involved. What happens then? In 2040, does growth stop? Do people suddenly stop wanting to move to California? Or will we have another meeting like this one, in 2025 or 2030, to plan for even more growth? Because it seems to me that there can only be two possible outcomes: either growth continues forever, or at some point it must stop. And if it's the latter, why not stop now before we ruin whatever quality of life is left for us who are here now?" I was escorted from the meeting and told not to come back.

The whole farce and fiasco of transit-oriented development did not go away simply because of the Great Financial Crisis/Great Recession. Like those creatures who burrow deep under dry lake beds, and wait dormant for years until there is another rainfall, these developer scams simply hunkered down to re-emerge once economic conditions improved. Take, for example, California Senate Bill 827, introduced in 2018 by three San Francisco Bay area legislators. Here's how curbed.com described the bill:

> [The bill] would spare new housing developments from certain restrictions if they qualify as "transit-rich housing." The initial version of the bill defines such housing as "parcels [...] within a half mile radius of a major transit stop or a quarter mile radius of a high-quality transit corridor."

The actual text of the bill stated that it:

> ...would exempt a project [from] maximum controls on residential density or floor area ratio, minimum automobile parking requirements, design standards that restrict the applicant's ability to construct the maximum number of units consistent with any

applicable building code, and maximum height limitations.

So, tiny little places crammed into very tall buildings. With minimal or even no parking. There is a name for these buildings: tenements. And the fact that they would tower over single-family homes, increase school enrollment beyond current capacity, add to demands on law enforcement and paramedics, and increase already dense traffic? *Tough shit*. Don't like the idea of people in tall buildings being able to look down into your backyard, or your bedroom window? *Tough shit*. The developers who profit will continue to live in their gated communities, send their kids to private schools, and get lots of work done on their way to work in their chauffeur-driven limo. Tough shit? More like *fuck you*.

Those who oppose this kind of intrusive over-development are often accused of NIMBY-ism, NIMBY standing for *Not In My Back Yard*. A very savvy and articulate local guy, Eugene Soloman, who serves on my city's Budget & Finance Committee, came up with a perfect alternate acronym: SIMBY: *Stupid In My Back Yard*.

Nobody wants stupid in their back yards. If having state legislatures, often situated hundreds of miles away from where development will take place, over-rule zoning and land-use planning at the local level where the impacts will be felt the most seems crazy, that's because **it is crazy**. And if Moretti's lunatic idea of giving Washington power over what can be built in your community sounds even scarier, that's because **it is**. Hubris married to stupidity on a biblical scale.

Growth is not the answer, nor is concentrating more and more economic activity in fewer and fewer mega-cities that widen the gap between the haves and the have-nots. A key step in converting from a growth-oriented economy to a sustainable economy is preserving the ability of local jurisdictions to protect themselves and their residents from economic exploitation and environmental degradation by private industry. Critics say that this is discrimination, that it unduly favors those who are already in a particular area or community. And this is bad, why?

At some point, we have to accept the twin tenets that: a) not everybody can live where they want; and b) being first has to count for something. Imagine your family is out to dinner. The restaurant is popular and crowded, not an empty table to be had. Another family of total strangers shows up and demands that you move over, squeeze in, and make room for them at your table. You would be outraged, insulted, and refuse to comply. But somehow in the identical situation applied to housing, one of the most precious components in determining quality of life, you're supposed to move over, pack in, and accept it with a smile, because it's inevitable? Developer puppets in the California legislature have enacted, and are hoping to expand, laws that mandate local communities build more and more residential housing, year after year, regardless of local conditions, or the desire of local residents. Similar measures and policies are a fact of life in other states, especially where citizens are denied the right of initiative and referendum. Again, it's all in the service of unlimited and unending growth. To reiterate:

*If growth was the solution, many areas would have grown themselves to nirvana long ago*.

As previously noted, this doesn't mean that communities should be able to stymie bona-fide public projects like highways, schools, and so forth. Where necessary for public use, eminent domain can still be employed to obtain the required land and overcome local resistance.

Zoning and land use aren't the only issues where state and local power must be protected. By now almost everyone knows that the primary cause of the GFC was massive systemic fraud in the FIRE (Finance-Insurance-Real Estate) sector of the economy. But for those who aren't conversant with the specifics, a quick recap: Big banks and mortgage firms found a lucrative market for securities backed by packages of mortgages. By offloading existing loans, these banks and other lenders received cash with which to make new loans. However, because of the commissions and bonuses that these RMBS (Residential Mortgage Backed Securities) generated, the demand for more mortgages to package soon outgrew the ability of the industry to find qualified buyers, especially for traditional fixed-rate loans that required a substantial down payment. This led to the rise of "innovative" new types of mortgages with Adjustable Rates, low or no down payment, and even loans with payments that only covered the interest. Collectively known as subprime mortgages, these instruments were innovative all right. They innovated new opportunities for fraud. Buyers were lured into loans that had low initial payments, which later reset to much higher interest rates and monthly payments. Usually they were told that they could refinance later, with another low teaser-rate loan.

Other people were deceived into thinking they were getting a fixed rate loan, only to learn later that language converting it into an ARM was buried in the fine print. In many cases, mortgage company staff simply forged the borrower's signature and replaced key pages in the original loan documents. There was also a big increase in "Stated Income Loans," in which borrowers did not have to provide income documentation. Not surprisingly, these became known as "Liar's Loans." Last but not least, homeowners were encouraged to strip equity out of their homes with new loans and HELOCS. (Home Equity Lines of Credit.)

The big Wall Street banks assembled huge bundles of these loans into packages and sold them to investors. Many institutional buyers, like pension funds, are legally required to buy only AAA-rated securities. The need to meet this threshold fostered corruption throughout the process. Real estate appraisers found they had to inflate appraisals or lenders would find appraisers who did. Instead of actually examining the credit-worthiness and verifying financial information supplied by borrowers, the three major bond rating agencies -- Standard & Poors, Fitch, and Moody's -- cooperated by rating just about everything that came in the door as AAA. Everybody, up and down the line, made money. Real estate agents, mortgage lenders, and securities brokers got their commissions. Executives at the big financial firms got their raises, bonuses, and cashed in stock options made ever more valuable by ever-rising profits that boosted the company's stock price. Meanwhile, back in residential neighborhoods, home prices skyrocketed. Speculators had a field day flipping properties. Some homeowners took equity out of their homes for valid reasons, such as college tuition or major medical expenses. But many blew the cash on vacation homes, RVs, boats, vacations, and so forth. It was all wonderful. It was also all a gigantic, fraud-inflated bubble.

When that bubble burst, the economy crashed. Sales of cars, appliances, electronics, clothes, furniture, and other staples of everyday life crashed. Stores, even well-known chains, went out of business almost overnight. (Remember Circuit City, CompUSA, Linens & Things, Lord & Taylor, K-B Toys, Mervyn's, and Levitz?) Other chains closed a huge number of stores. All the folks laid off by these closings joined the ranks of those who had over-bought, or been duped by nefarious mortgage schemes. The result was a sea of foreclosures and a major economic crash.

A mortgage consists of two elements: the documents for the loan itself (note), and the title to the property. When a note is transferred, the title is supposed to travel with it. For RMBS security sales to qualify for certain preferential tax treatment, the title has to be transferred to the securitization package within ninety days after the sale of the security. However, recording changes of titles at the local or state registrar's office is an expensive, labor-intensive process. Unwilling to let following the law slow down the sales of RMBS, the big banks formed MERS, the Mortgage Electronic Recording System, and used it to file notices of change of title. This allowed the banks to save hundreds of millions in filing fees that otherwise would have gone to state and county governments. And it was all done without a single state or federal statute being passed to authorize the creation of MERS.

If the banks and mortgage brokers had actually used MERS as intended, the biggest problem would have been the lost registration revenue to states and counties. However, MERS did not function that way. With no oversight, millions of title transfers were never recorded when the accompanying notes were packed and sold. In addition, millions of notes were never endorsed (signed over) to their supposed new owners. This contributed to the fraudulent resale of the same mortgage loan two, or even three times, to different parties. In some cases, this was accidental; in other cases, the lack of proper endorsement was intentional, to facilitate the fraudulent resale to multiple parties. In both cases, the failure to properly endorse and transfer notes and Deeds of Title blew a gigantic hole in a system of land chain-of-ownership that had served the nation for centuries. That's when differences in state laws and foreclosure procedures became important.

Twenty states only allow judicial foreclosure, where a foreclosure application has to be approved in court. Before long, some homeowners became aware that the original title was not attached to the loan documents presented to the court. In other cases, the entity claiming the power to foreclose could not produce a properly endorsed note. In the beginning, courts viewed these cases as isolated events and tended to give foreclosure filers the benefit of the doubt. Knowing that they could not depend on this type of judicial forbearance to go on forever, the companies that processed foreclosure applications began a massive new fraud, called robo-signing, in which people were hired off the street to sign affidavits attesting that new replacement documents were valid. But these documents were not valid, and in many cases the robo-signers were executing so many documents per hour that they could not have actually reviewed the files as required by law before signing the affidavits. (Anyone who has slogged through the mountain of paperwork required to close escrow on a house knows that no one, short of the Lord himself, could review an entire file, especially one that had been transferred numerous times, in *forty-five seconds*, as many robo-signers were claimed to have done.)

Eventually, the bad guys foreclosed on the wrong person, Florida attorney Lynn Syzmoniak. After discovering that the documents in her file were forgeries, Syzmoniak dug deeper. The robo-signing scandal she discovered ended up on *60 Minutes*. It was revealed during the segment that one woman, named "Linda Green," had executed thousands of affidavits for her employer, a company named DOCX, on behalf of several different banks. Her handwriting and signature, however, varied wildly from document to document. In a case brought by the Missouri Attorney General, DOCX and its founder, Lorraine Brown, were indicted on 136 counts of forgery. At least 79 documents bearing Linda Green's name had been signed by someone else. Eventually Brown pleaded guilty to fraud charges and was packed off to a Florida prison for five years, followed by another forty months in prison after pleading guilty to racketeering charges in Michigan. Syzmoniak sued everyone involved and was awarded $18 mil in damages. She used the money to start a foundation to help other victims of mortgage fraud.

Once the issue of falsified and missing documents came to light, state courts started to have a big impact. Maine's Supreme Court ruled that a MERS assignment was not legally sufficient to prove authority to foreclose, essentially ending MERS ability to do business in the state. New York's Unified Court System instituted a new affidavit that every attorney for a foreclosure applicant had to sign, under penalty of perjury. With attorneys facing fines, jail time, and disbarment for violating the new affidavit requirements, foreclosure filings immediately plunged from hundreds a day to only a few per month.

California adopted a new Homeowner's Bill of Rights that not only bans several nefarious foreclosure and mortgage transfer practices, but allows for defendants in foreclosure proceedings to have their attorney's fees paid by the bank if the foreclosure documents are not authentic, or procedures aren't properly followed. In one case, a bank and its law firm paid over $100,000 in fees for improperly trying to foreclose on a house with an appraised value of about $275,000. In some cases, when nobody could prove that they held both the note and the Deed of Title, homeowners were given title to their property, free and clear. Technically, they owed *somebody* the balance of the mortgage, but nobody could prove that they were that party. Therefore:

> **Section 3: A state may enact and enforce on financial institutions and insurance companies doing business within its borders, or with its residents, laws and regulations more stringent than those imposed by the federal government and its agencies or chartered entities. All violations involving financial fraud in excess of $10,000 shall be felonies punishable by incarceration in a maximum security facility for a period, not subject to pardon, parole, commutation, suspension, or other reduction of sentence, of not less than ten years.**

A lot of the problems that are addressed by the 41st Amendment stem from the vagueness of Article IX of the Constitution, the Commerce Clause, and how it interacts with, or is limited by, Article X, which assigns to the states all powers not specifically granted to the federal government. Over the past two hundred years, the Supreme Court went from having a very narrow view of the Article IX powers granted to the federal government to having a more expansive interpretation, which allowed for more wide-ranging federal regulation, and intervention into commercial activities. Under Justice Rehnquist it swung back toward a more limited view that still prevails. Given the history of the court to interpret the vagueness of Article IX (and the limits on federal power in Article X) more by political philosophies than by clear-cut and consistent legal principles, it is important not just to specifically reinforce the existing protections given states by Article X of the original Bill of Rights, but to extend that protection to subordinate jurisdictions. Whether it's fracking or foreclosure fraud, GMO food labeling or zoning regulations, or some entirely new issue, if companies don't like a particular state's or municipality's regulations there's a simple solution: *Don't do business there*. Of course, somebody else will, and they'll be the ones making the profits.

# Chapter 17

# UNIVERSAL COMPULSORY
# MILITARY SERVICE

Our Founding Fathers were notoriously averse to the concept of standing armies.

James Madison, at the 1787 Constitutional Convention:

> A standing military force, with an overgrown Executive will not long be safe companions to liberty. The means of defence [*sic*] against foreign danger, have been always the instruments of tyranny at home. Among the Romans it was a standing maxim to excite a war, whenever a revolt was apprehended. Throughout all Europe, the armies kept up under the pretext of defending, have enslaved the people.

Thomas Jefferson, in 1789:

> There are instruments so dangerous to the rights of the nation and which place them so totally at the mercy of their governors that those governors, whether legislative or executive, should be restrained from keeping such instruments on foot but in well-defined cases. Such an instrument is a standing army.

Followed by this, in 1814:

> The Greeks and Romans had no standing armies, yet they defended themselves ... Their system was to make every man a soldier, and oblige him to repair to the standard of his country whenever that was reared. This made them invincible; and the same remedy will make us so.

Jefferson also famously expressed the idea that the only thing more dangerous to democratic government than a standing army are banks. This was not intended to diminish the danger from armies, but rather to emphasize the threat from banks. Jefferson also opposed any kind of compulsory military service. Believing that the true mission of military force was to defend the country from foreign attack, Jefferson felt that people would be sufficiently motivated to defend their country to rally to military service, as they had during the Revolutionary War.

So, why quote Madison and Jefferson arguing against standing armies and compulsory service in support of a constitutional amendment that makes national military service mandatory? Because the world has changed. Everything that was true then has now been reversed. An enemy can now attack us in minutes instead of weeks, using weapons never imagined in that era. Given events of the past hundred years, although we can and should reduce our military footprint considerably, there is no possibility that we can abandon having one entirely. But most importantly, the very nature and purpose of our modern military has been inverted, turned upside down.

For the first century of its existence, the Army was a small force designed as a first response against attacks on our soil. The Navy's job was to protect our coastlines and discourage pirates (like those in Tripoli) from raiding American flag vessels on the high seas. As the 20th century dawned, all that changed. First came the Spanish-American War of 1898, in which a country, founded on freedom from colonial imperialism, officially acquired its first ~~colonies~~, I mean, *territories*: Cuba, Guam, Puerto Rico, and the

Philippines. In 1903, President Theodore Roosevelt sent U.S. Navy warships to ensure that Panamanian rebels succeeded in breaking away from Nicaragua, which had refused to allow the U.S. to build the Panama Canal. A year later, the newly independent Panamanians sold the U.S. rights to the Canal Zone for ten million dollars.

During the first three decades of the 20th century, U.S. military interventions in Latin America, on behalf of American corporate interests (oil, agriculture, and mining), became so numerous that they acquired a title, *The Banana Wars*. American military power and clandestine subversive activities toppled governments in Honduras, Columbia, Haiti, Mexico, and the Dominican Republic. These actions were based on the 1904 Roosevelt Corollary to the Monroe Doctrine, which proclaimed the right of the United States to intervene in the internal affairs of Latin American countries. As Wikipedia notes: [Emphasis added.]

> In its altered state, the Monroe Doctrine would now consider Latin America as an agency for expanding U.S. **commercial interests** in the region, along with its original stated purpose of keeping European hegemony from the hemisphere. In addition, the corollary proclaimed the explicit right of the United States to intervene in Latin American conflicts **exercising an international police power**.

From these humble beginnings grew America's self-appointed right to interfere in the internal affairs of countries around the world, nominally on behalf of democracy, but in reality, to benefit American companies and the global economic elite. Aside from occasional legitimate military actions, such as WWII and Korea, the predominant role of the U.S. military, and our spy agencies, in the last hundred years has been to ensure that American companies gain access, on favored or exclusive terms, to exploit the natural resources and markets of foreign countries.

The CIA's very first operation -- in 1947, before it was even the CIA and was still the Office of Strategic Services -- was intervention in the Greek Civil War. This was followed by the overthrow of the legitimate governments of Iran in 1953, and Guatemala in 1954. But we didn't stop there. As noted earlier, the list of Western Hemisphere countries where the U.S. either assisted in overthrowing democratically-elected governments, or helped repressive but corporate-friendly dictators stay in power, includes Chile, Bolivia, Brazil, Uruguay, Panama, Peru, Nicaragua, Guatemala, El Salvador, and Grenada. Similar actions took place in other parts of the world. The turning point, at least in military terms, came in Vietnam, where using American lives to back corrupt dictators on the pretense of deterring communism reached its zenith.

The military learned many lessons from Vietnam, not the least of which was that it is virtually impossible to sustain a war -- using an army primarily composed of unwilling conscripts -- against a far-off enemy who poses no direct threat to the American public. Although the Vietnam-era draft sent disproportionate numbers of minorities to the killing fields, its impact was also deeply felt in many white middle-class households. This is why the face of the anti-war movement was largely white, middle-class, and educated.

The Vietnam anti-war movement gave birth to the all-volunteer army, the personification of what Jefferson and Madison feared most: a standing army composed entirely of professional soldiers. Today, the U.S. military consists of a career officer corps, generally dedicated to the concept of American superiority and imperialism, leading enlisted ranks made up mostly of people with no other viable job options, many of whom join to get technical training that holds out the prospect of future employment in the private sector. In other words, an aristocracy of career officers commanding a manpower base produced by a de facto economic draft.

Although they feared and opposed standing armies, the concept of universal military service was not foreign to our Founding Fathers. Madison, in fact, supported the underlying concept: "A well-regulated militia, composed of the body of the people, trained in arms, is the best most natural defense of a free country." Not a select few, but *the body of the people*. Or, as another Founding Father, George Mason, put it: "What is the militia? It is the whole people except for a few public officials."

Since we can't get rid of our military forces, our only choice is to make them as representative of the country as possible. We must offset authoritarian career militarists with a vastly larger number of citizen soldiers, Mason's "whole people."

The first and foremost benefit of compulsory universal military service is to apply a natural check on the tendency to instigate or prolong military actions primarily to enrich the Military-Congressional-Industrial-Surveillance Complex. As George Orwell famously noted, in modern times, "The war is not meant to be won; it is meant to be continuous." As in, continuously *profitable*. Every time the U.S. engages in military action in some far-off country, defense contractors rake in the dough. Aside from our nuclear-powered aircraft carriers and submarines, virtually every piece of equipment the U.S. military operates requires fuel in massive amounts, both to get to the theater of operations and to fulfill its mission once there. Every bullet fired, bomb dropped, and missile launched comes with a price tag, and the inventory must be replenished. In April 2018, President Trump fired 118 missiles of various types, including 58 Raytheon Tomahawks, at a supposed Syrian chemical weapons installation. The cost? $165 million. Here's The Real News Network host Sharmin Peries talking about the correlation between war-making and defense contractor profits:

> ...last year, Fortune magazine calculated that defense contractors and companies, their share prices rose by

as much as $5 billion after Trump launched his attack on the Syrian air base.

Reliably, the day after Trump's second missile attack, defense company stocks, including Raytheon and Lockheed Martin (which makes Hellfire missiles) again rose.

President Reagan's former Director of the Office of Management and Budget, David Stockman, has excoriated what he calls the abandonment of the "America First" defense policy. Here's what he wrote on davidstockmanscontracorner.com just after that Syrian missile strike: [Emphasis is original.]

> When the Cold War officially ended in 1991, Washington could have pivoted back to the pre-1914 status quo ante. That is, to a national security policy of ***America First*** because there was literally no significant military threat left on the planet.
>
> Post-Soviet Russia was an economic basket case that couldn't even meet its military payroll and was melting down and selling the Red Army's tanks and artillery for scrap. China was just emerging from the Great Helmsman's economic, political and cultural depredations and had embraced Deng Xiaoping proclamation that "to get rich is glorious".
>
> The implications of the Red Army's fiscal demise and China's electing the path of export mercantilism and Red Capitalism were profound.
>
> Russia couldn't invade the American homeland in a million years and China chose the route of flooding America with shoes, sheets, shirts, toys and electronics. So doing, it made the rule of the communist elites in Beijing dependent upon keeping the custom of 4,000 Wal-Marts in America, not bombing them out of existence.
>
> ***In a word, god's original gift to America -- the great moats of the Atlantic and Pacific oceans***

*-- had again become the essence of its national security.*

After 1991, therefore, there was no nation on the planet that had the remotest capability to mount a conventional military assault on the U.S. homeland; or that would not have bankrupted itself attempting to create the requisite air and sea-based power projection capabilities...

Indeed, in the post-cold war world the only thing the US needed was a modest conventional capacity to defend the shorelines and airspace against any possible rogue assault and a reliable nuclear deterrent against any state foolish enough to attempt nuclear blackmail.

But the America First doctrine Stockman describes and advocates for would not have resulted in record profits for the defense contractors who employ so many retired military personnel. And thus was born the Global War on Terror whose main product, aside from defense contractor welfare, has been the creation of more jihadists. The original target was Al Qaeda and its partner-in-crime, the Taliban. Then it was Iraq and Saddam Hussein's fictitious weapons of mass destruction. Later it was weapons and air support for Libyan "freedom fighters." Then came funneling weapons from Benghazi in Libya to "moderate" Islamic rebels fighting Assad in Syria. Lo and behold, a lot of those weapons and so-called moderate rebels morphed into the new bogeyman, ISIS, whom former CIA Director Leon Pannetta claims will require a thirty-year war. ***Thirty. Fucking. Years***. Of profits from killing people halfway around the world, who have darker skin and speak languages other than English.

In November 2018, Newsweek published a story by Tom O'Connor titled:

**U.S. Has Spent Six Trillion Dollars on Wars That Killed Half a Million People Since 9/11**

Citing a report by the Brown University Watson Institute for International and Public Affairs, the article asserted that, "[the] high costs in war and war-related spending pose a national security concern because they are unsustainable." It also noted that the casualty figure of 500,000 did not include another 500,000 deaths from the civil war in Syria, which the U.S. helped initiate and fund in an effort to topple the Russian-friendly government of Bashir Assad.

So, *one million dead* from a *War on Terror* that started out as a hunt for Osama bin Laden and probably less than one thousand total members of Al-Qaeda. But even these numbers are small compared to what James A. Lucas found when he did a deep-dive for Global Research into the total number of dead from U.S. military actions in what he described as 37 "Victim Nations" since WWII. The number: 20 million. ***Twenty million people***. (The article is meticulously researched and includes a detailed list of sources from which the numbers were compiled.)

News flash folks: People in other countries don't hate us for our freedoms. They hate us for the bombs we drop on their families, and our bases on their land, and our interference in their internal affairs just so Exxon-Mobil, Goldman Sachs, Halliburton, and other American companies can get rich. It would be much harder to continue this policy if every American family faced the prospect that their son or daughter could be sent in harm's way. In 2013, Christopher Yates, a former British Army officer, gave a clear example of this in an article for the UK Guardian describing his experience as an observer during a Greek Army training mission. A Greek officer explained that since Greece has compulsory military service, the Greeks could never agree to send troops to join a coalition in Iraq, or other parts of the Middle East, because, "every mother in the country would need to know why."

***Every mother would need to know why.***

Yep. And every father, too.

Yates also argues that universal military service should be thought of as a progressive political issue, because it doesn't allow certain elements of society to be insulated from the impact and consequences of national decisions. He's absolutely right; universal military service doesn't allow us to go on our merry way, oblivious to the costs attendant to our lifestyle.

Compulsory universal military service, with a post-basic training civilian component for those not currently needed for military operations, is the exact opposite of militarism and tyranny, and would allow the country to reap multiple benefits beyond merely applying the brakes to American military adventures in the service of global elites. For starters, we could return to the traditional military system where soldiers performed the menial chores necessary for everyday living. The peeling of potatoes and mopping of restrooms would once again be done by military personnel, at a fraction of the cost which now goes to private contractors. A little manual labor never hurt anyone, especially the young, and often serves as a catalyst for a better appreciation of how others live.

After six months of basic military training, a portion of the conscripts would be randomly selected (with severe criminal penalties for interference in the process) to finish out their service in the military, subject to deployment anywhere in the world, including border security. Everyone else would be assigned, based on their talents and aptitude, to a variety of tasks:

- As aides in child care facilities for working parents, especially single mothers.

- Demolition of abandoned buildings, debris removal, and salvage of recyclable materials in blighted neighborhoods.

- Debris removal from our nation's waterways.

- Additional staffing for national parks, thus allowing longer hours of operation.

- Habitat restoration and mitigation of environmental degradation resulting from natural resource extraction or simple neglect. (Ex: mountain-top removal mining.)

- Emergency response and rebuilding efforts after natural disasters, such as floods, earthquakes, and hurricanes.

- As staffing aides in hospitals and clinics.

- Digital transfer and duplication of historical and reference materials which have not yet been processed due to lack of funds and/or manpower.

- Aides in animal shelters and wildlife sanctuaries.

- Apprentice job training on infrastructure projects.

- Humanitarian response to natural disasters in foreign countries.

- Educational tutoring for fellow conscripts with deficient skills in math, reading comprehension, English composition, etc.

- Assignment to states and municipalities to bolster manpower available for public services. (Imagine going to the DMV and finding enough clerks that the wait was only a few minutes, rather than several hours.)

- Assignment to state and local offices responsible for administering elections to ensure that all elections function smoothly across all precincts.

- Assist in the physical inventorying necessary to produce a comprehensive true audit of the Department of Defense. (This alone is estimated to require at least ten years.)

Mandatory universal military service would also help break up the de facto caste system that has developed in America. Let's force upper crust kids to rub elbows with commoners. Let the cloistered liberals from coastal enclaves mix with equally cloistered kids from the heartland and rural areas. This might produce some understanding and acceptance of those from different circumstances and cultures.

Support for a universal draft, and some sort of mandatory national service, spans the political spectrum. Here's retired Army Colonel Andrew Bacevich, a West Point grad who served in Vietnam, writing eloquently for The American Conservative:

> With the ongoing "war" approaching the 10-year mark, the U.S. economy shed a total of 7.9 million jobs in just three years. For only the second time since World War II, the official unemployment rate topped 10 percent.
>
> [snip]
>
> The political response to this economic calamity paid less attention to forecasting long-term implications than to fixing culpability. On the right, an angry Tea Party movement blamed Big Government. On the left, equally angry members of the Occupy movement blamed Big Business, especially Wall Street. What these two movements had in common was that each cast the American people as victims. Nefarious forces had gorged themselves at the expense of ordinary folk. By implication, the people were themselves absolved of responsibility for the catastrophe that had befallen them and their country.
>
> Yet consider a third possibility. Perhaps the people were not victims but accessories. On the subject of

war, Americans can no more claim innocence than they can regarding the effects of smoking or excessive drinking. As much as or more than Big Government or Big Business, popular attitudes toward war, combining detachment, neglect, and inattention, helped create the crisis in which the United States is mired.

A "country made by war," to cite the title of a popular account of U.S. military history, the United States in our own day is fast becoming a country undone by war. Citizen armies had waged the wars that made the nation powerful (if not virtuous) and Americans rich (if not righteous). The character of those armies -- preeminently the ones that preserved the Union and helped defeat Nazi Germany and Imperial Japan -- testified to an implicit covenant between citizens and the state ... war was the people's business and could not be otherwise. For the state to embark upon armed conflict of any magnitude required informed popular consent. Actual prosecution of any military campaign larger than a police action depended on the willingness of citizens in large numbers to become soldiers. Seeing war through to a conclusion hinged on the state's ability to sustain active popular support in the face of adversity.

In their disgust over Vietnam, Americans withdrew from this arrangement. They disengaged from war, with few observers giving serious consideration to the implications of doing so. Events since, especially since 9/11, have made those implications manifest. In the United States, war no longer qualifies in any meaningful sense as the people's business. In military matters, Americans have largely forfeited their say.

As a result, in formulating basic military policy and in deciding when and how to employ force, the state no longer requires the consent, direct participation, or ongoing support of citizens. As an immediate consequence, Washington's penchant for war has appreciably increased, without, however, any corresponding improvement in the ability of political and military leaders to conclude its wars promptly or successfully. A further result, less appreciated but with even larger implications, has been to accelerate the erosion of the traditional concept of democratic citizenship.

In other words, the afflictions besetting the American way of life derive in some measure from shortcomings in the contemporary American way of war. The latter have either begotten or exacerbated the former.

[snip]

Apathy toward war is symptomatic of advancing civic decay, finding expression in apathy toward the blight of child poverty, homelessness, illegitimacy, and eating disorders also plaguing the country. Shrugging off wars makes it that much easier for Americans -- overweight, overmedicated, and deeply in hock -- to shrug off the persistence of widespread hunger, the patent failures of their criminal justice system, and any number of other problems. The thread that binds together this pattern of collective anomie is plain to see: unless the problem you're talking about affects me personally, why should I care?

[snip]

The crux of the problem lay with two symmetrical 1 percents: the 1 percent whose members get sent to fight seemingly endless wars and that other 1 percent whose members demonstrate such a knack for enriching themselves in "wartime." Needless to say, the two 1 percents neither intersect nor overlap. Few of the very rich send their sons or daughters to fight. Few of those leaving the military's ranks find their way into the ranks of the plutocracy.

[snip]

Yet a people who permit war to be waged in their name while offloading onto a tiny minority responsibility for its actual conduct have no cause to complain about an equally small minority milking the system for all it's worth. Crudely put, if the very rich are engaged in ruthlessly exploiting the 99 percent who are not, their actions are analogous to that of American society as a whole in its treatment of soldiers: the 99 percent who do not serve in uniform just as ruthlessly exploit the 1 percent who do.

[snip]

As a remedy for all the ailments afflicting the body politic, war -- at least as Americans have chosen to wage it -- turns out to be a fundamentally inappropriate prescription. Rather than restoring the patient to health, war (as currently practiced...) constitutes a form of prolonged ritual suicide. Rather than building muscle, it corrupts and putrefies.

The choice Americans face today ends up being as straightforward as it is stark. If they believe war essential to preserving their freedom, it's incumbent upon them to prosecute war with the same seriousness their forebears demonstrated in the 1940s.

[snip]

...the dilemma just described may be more theoretical than real. Without the players fully understanding the stakes, the die has already been cast. Having forfeited responsibility for war's design and conduct, the American people may find that Washington considers that grant of authority irrevocable. The state now owns war, with the country consigned to observer status.

Bacevich has a Ph.D. from Princeton and is currently a professor at Boston University. This certainly places him among our upper-middle class intellectual elite. Yet he and his family practice what he preaches, and know full well the cost of doing so. In 2007, his son, 1st Lt. Andrew John Bacevich, was killed in Iraq by an IED.

On the other end of the political spectrum, long-time liberal African-American Congressman Charles Rangel regularly introduced legislation to reinstitute the draft for all Americans, including women. Rangel is highly critical of the fact that so many members of the military come from minority urban and white rural communities, which share a common denominator: limited employment options. Having put himself through college on the G.I. Bill, Rangel notes that many enlistees see military service as their only possible path to education and a viable economic future.

Rangel is hardly the only prominent person on the left to advocate for a universal draft. Thom Hartmann and David Sirota, both well-known progressive authors and radio personalities, have come out on multiple occasions in favor of universal compulsory military service. As Hartmann notes, a universal draft is, "one of the best ways to prevent a military from becoming its own insular and dangerous subculture." Draftees are more likely to become whistleblowers simply because, in addition to not being naturally authoritarian or militaristic, they don't have to worry about damaging their opportunities for career advancement.

Sirota also makes a great point about the responsiveness of the government to public pressure when he says, "The federal government only reacts to popular will when the upper-middle professional class starts making noise. Everyone else's voice falls on deaf ears." Sirota rightly notes that it is only when their kids might be in the line of fire that the middle and upper classes hit the streets, jam congressional phone lines, and bury their representatives in hostile emails.

The most important point that Hartmann, Sirota, Rangel, and others make is that with universal military service, the public will only support military action on foreign soil that is unavoidable, and in pursuit of a clear objective considered worth the cost to the vast majority. WWII was; war with Iran is not. Nor is kicking the Russian bear in the name of worldwide American hegemony.

Both Hartmann and Sirota support the provision for alternative forms of service. However, one point must be clear: all alternative assignments must come *after* compulsory basic training, with ensuing military and combat assignments based primarily on random selection. We accomplish nothing if we acquiesce to a system in which those who don't want to serve in the military -- those affluent middle and upper-class kids of our social circle -- have a chance to perform nice, safe alternative jobs. Anyone whose sense of patriotism, or desire to pursue a military career, prompts them to volunteer for extended duty should be able to do so. (With commensurate increased compensation and options in terms of training and specialization.) However, under no circumstances should volunteers be allowed to replace anyone randomly selected for a combat or forward base assignment. This is necessary to counter a key argument against universal service: that it would not be administered fairly; that should military action be necessary, those with money or influence would buy their kids out of harm's way. Random selection, with a heavy mandatory prison term for attempting to influence assignments, is the only way to prevent this from happening.

With respect to the idea of a random lottery selection for combat assignments, some will argue that the military must not be constrained from selecting the troops that are best for each mission. This argument fails on two counts. First, it presupposes that there should be a mission. The defining purpose of universal military service is to ensure that military action on foreign soil is only undertaken in the most compelling circumstances. Second, using specially-trained elite forces for a commando-style operation like killing Bin Laden is appropriate, but when we invaded Iraq and Afghanistan it was the regular troops, the men and women who entered the military in search of a job, that bore the real burden. It was the reservists from your local big box store, car dealership, and real estate office who had their lives uprooted. It was career enlistees and reservists who had to serve three, four, five, even six tours. With universal military service, it's likely that we would never again have to call up reservists. In fact, we might do away with reservists entirely.

Like other contentious issues that would fundamentally change how the country operates, the idea of universal military service has its opponents. Some see it as government interference in the lives and liberties of the people. However, as Sirota has noted, anyone who believes in the necessity of the military but doesn't want any part of actually serving, or having members of their family serve, is offering an immoral argument based on selfish hypocrisy.

The argument has also been made that the existence of our previous post-WWII draft did not prevent America from becoming embroiled in Korea and Vietnam. That argument fails to consider that the Korean War started with a ground invasion of the South by North Korean troops. With memories of WWII still fresh in everyone's mind, many leaders and citizens alike felt that aggression had to be stifled right away, not appeased, as the British and French had tried to do with Hitler. And although it is commonly referred to as the Korean *War*, it was actually a *police action* conducted under the auspices of the United Nations, and it included troops from a number of nations. If the UN was to have any hope of preventing widespread future wars, it had to demonstrate success in stopping Communist aggression on the Korean peninsula.

Korea represented a direct attempt at imposing a communist dictatorship on an unwilling neighbor. Comparing the prosperity and living standard of democratic South Korea with the horrendous conditions in the North leaves little doubt that the Korean Police Action, which re-established the pre-war border, was worth the cost. Vietnam, on the other hand, was a legitimate war of national reunification, falsely sold to the American public as crucial to preventing all of Southeast Asia from going commie. (It's interesting that soon after the Viet Cong achieved victory, they got into a nasty border war with their northern neighbor, China, over grievances going back centuries. So much for Chinese -- or Russian -- domination of a reunited Vietnam.) We also now know that the *casus belli*, the so-called Gulf of Tonkin Incident, where North Vietnamese gunboats supposedly attacked U.S. naval vessels, never happened.

What is most interesting about the idea that we got into Korea and Vietnam in spite of a draft is that this argument fails to acknowledge the role the draft played in getting us out of both of those conflicts. By 1952, Americans were tired of the costs in lives, money, and domestic stability. This was particularly true of WWII vets, who had just begun to rebuild their civilian lives, only to be called up again. Many wives, parents, and siblings, having seen a son, husband, brother, or fiancé survive WWII, were not anxious for them to perish in Korea. Dwight Eisenhower won the 1952 election, in part, because of his pledge to bring an end to the fighting. Who knows how long the war may have lasted had all our troops been volunteers, victims of a de-facto economic draft.

Vietnam is the same story. The Pentagon Papers revealed that President Johnson and Secretary of Defense Robert McNamara knew the war was unwinnable from the start, yet they continued to send American boys to kill, die, and be maimed in the name of political expediency and some distorted, perverse sense of national honor. It was only after the draft lottery was introduced, and children of the upper-middle class began to face a realistic threat of combat, that public pressure brought an end to our participation. So, in point of fact, the threat of *universal* and *unavoidable* military service does have a direct impact on where, when, and how long America chooses to engage in military action.

The central challenge is simple: our Military-Industrial-Congressional-Complex seeks to create a *never-ending* series of enemies, requiring a *never-ending* series of wars, to provide a *never-ending* flow of profits, and ensure that the American military can forever be used as the point of the spear for corporate interests. It's perpetual war as a business model. Going into Afghanistan was supposedly about getting Bin Laden, but we conveniently allowed him to slip out of Tora Bora. (U.S. commanders wanted many more U.S. troops but were overruled in favor of hiring local warlords, who have centuries of history as double-crossers. Guess what? They took our money, then let Bin Laden slip away. Who could have predicted?!)

Not getting Bin Laden early-on was a great excuse to stay in Afghanistan for what is now approaching two decades. Why do that? Lithium. It's in almost every electronic gadget from cordless power tool batteries to cell phones. Afghanistan is loaded with it, and has enormous reserves of other rare-earth metals critical for modern technology applications. (Not to mention Union Oil's desire to build a pipeline across Afghanistan from the oil fields in the Caucuses.)

The only way we are ever going to rein-in our corporate/imperial military is to put every family at risk. Therefore:

### The 42nd Amendment --
### Universal Military Service

**Section 1: The responsibilities of the people being no less important to the well-being of the republic than the responsibilities of government, Congress shall pass, and the President shall sign, legislation to establish universal compulsory National Military Service. Such service shall be for a minimum period of twenty-four months, with at least six months of basic military training followed by either continued military service or in such civilian projects as Congress may designate.**

**Section 2: Service shall begin no later than sixty days after reaching the age of eighteen, or graduation from high school, whichever**

occurs last. **Exemption from service shall be granted only to those having such permanent and severe physical or mental infirmities that they can fulfill no useful role or function in civilian life. Persons afflicted with lesser, but still significant permanent physical or mental infirmities such that they cannot reasonably participate in military action, shall be assigned appropriate other duties.**

**Section 3: Persons incarcerated at the time of normal induction into service shall serve the full term of their service upon release from incarceration. For the safety of the public, those inducted after incarceration shall be excused from weapons and tactical training.**

**Section 4: With the exception of specialized units, composed of career personnel serving a minimum initial enlistment of at least eight years, all combat assignments shall be made by random lottery. It shall be a felony punishable by incarceration in a maximum security facility for a period, not subject to pardon, parole, commutation, suspension, or other reduction of sentence, of not less than ten years, for influencing, or attempting to influence, the assignment of any person to or away from any theater of combat operations.**

How, exactly, could we finance universal military/national service? First, start with the savings achieved by not having to bribe people to enlist. This includes getting rid of post-service college tuition assistance as a military benefit and moving it into whatever national, universal tuition-assistance or free college program the people see fit to have Congress to enact. Second, we would not have to pay draftees the salaries we now bestow on our volunteers. All draftees really need is enough spending money for recreation. Third, we can eliminate the wasteful cost of outsourcing support operations. Many functions that have been out-sourced to private, for-profit contractors can be handled as they used to be, by draftees. We can certainly save enormous amounts by cutting back on the extravagantly over-priced new weapons systems that keep so many former colonels and generals employed by defense contractors.

What if even these savings aren't enough to offset the greater cost of universal service? The best answer will come in the next series of amendments dealing with economic security. But, for the time being, let's just say that we can always tax the wealthy and corporations. They get a disproportionate share of the benefits that come from America being the world's only remaining superpower. It's only fitting that they should carry a little more of the cost.

# PART III

---

# THE ECONOMIC
# BILL OF RIGHTS

# Chapter 18

# ECONOMIC SECURITY -- PART ONE

*"Let me issue and control a nation's money and I care not who writes the laws."*
--Mayer Ameschel Rothschild,
founder of the House of Rothschild banking empire

The real source of power in the United States is the banking system. Banks and other financial institutions have been allowed to become Too Big To Fail, which means their key executives are Too Big To Jail. To rectify this situation, we must first abolish the Federal Reserve Bank, which despite its name, is not a government agency. The U.S. Supreme Court in 1928:

> Instrumentalities like the national banks or **the federal reserve banks, in which there are private interests, are not departments of the government. They are private corporations in which the government has an interest.**

The long-time Chairman of the House Banking and Currency Committee, Louis Thomas McFadden, in 1932: [Emphasis added.]

> Some people think the Federal Reserve Banks are US government institutions. They are not. ... They are **private credit monopolies** which prey upon the people of the US for the benefit of themselves and

their foreign customers and domestic speculators and swindlers, and rich and predatory money lenders. The sack of the United States by the Federal Reserve Board and the Federal Reserve Banks ... is the greatest crime in history. Every effort has been made by the Fed to conceal its powers, but the truth is the Fed has usurped the government ... It controls everything here and it controls all our foreign relations. It makes and breaks governments at will.

The Fed likes to play a semantic game of whack-a-mole. It will admit that the Federal Reserve Board is a federal agency, and thus subject to Freedom of Information Laws. But, it has contended in a number of suits, including ones filed by Bloomberg and by Joe Weisenthal at Business Insider, that the various regional Federal Reserve Banks are separate institutions. During a 2011 Bloomberg FOIA request hearing, San Francisco Federal Reserve research analyst David Lang testified that, "the Federal Reserve Banks are 'independent corporations', which are 'not agencies', are 'privately held', and have 'private boards of directors'." The Fed contended that this meant that the regional Federal Reserve banks were thus *not subject to federal regulations governing record keeping and disclosure.* Therefore, since the bank bailout during the crash of 2007-2008 was conducted by the New York Fed, it didn't have to turn over the records of which banks got bailout money and how much. Lower courts ruled that this assertion was basically bullshit. The Fed appealed all the way to the Supreme Court, but got a cold shoulder. Five days later the NY Fed had to turn over the requested data, which was both revelatory and embarrassing.

That the Fed would try to conceal its inner workings is not surprising, considering that the Fed was born in secrecy during a clandestine retreat at the Jekyll Island Hunt Club, off the Georgia coast, in November of 1910. The island was owned by a group of multi-millionaires led by J.P. Morgan. Members of the club not invited to the meeting were told not to visit the island. Wikipedia quotes Bertie Charles Forbes, financier and founder of Forbes Magazine, describing the incident:

> Picture a party of the nation's greatest bankers stealing out of New York on a private railroad car under cover of darkness, stealthily riding hundreds of miles South, embarking on a mysterious launch, sneaking onto an island deserted by all but a few servants, living there a full week under such rigid secrecy that the names of not one of them was once mentioned, lest the servants learn the identity and disclose to the world this strangest, most secret expedition in the history of American finance. I am not romancing; I am giving to the world, for the first time, the real story of how the famous Aldrich currency report, the foundation of our new currency system, was written ... The utmost secrecy was enjoined upon all. The public must not glean a hint of what was to be done.

### *The public must not glean a hint of what was to be done*.

All this secrecy was necessary because the nation was enraged over the economic devastation caused by the Panic of 1907, a precursor of the Great Depression. Public pressure forced Teddy Roosevelt to appoint a National Monetary Commission to devise reforms to the banking system. Given the public's raging distrust of the big money east coast banks that controlled the existing system, and which were (correctly) believed by the public to be responsible for the 1907 Panic, if those banks were going to control how reform was structured, they had to do so in secret. Leading the group was the chairman of the National Monetary Commission, Senator Nelson Aldrich of Rhode Island. According to Wikipedia, also on board the Jekyll Island Express were:

> A.P. Andrews (Assistant Secretary of the United States Treasury Department), Paul Warburg (a naturalized German representing Kuhn, Loeb & Co.), Frank A. Vanderlip (president of the National City Bank of New York), Henry P. Davison (senior partner of J. P. Morgan Company), Charles D. Norton (president of

the Morgan-dominated First National Bank of New York), and Benjamin Strong (representing J. P. Morgan), together representing about one fourth the world's wealth at the time...

Of these men, Paul Warburg was the most important. A German immigrant with experience in European banking, Warburg was married to Nina Loeb, daughter of Solomon Loeb, founder of Kuhn, Loeb & Co. His wife's brother-in-law, Jacob Schiff, was a senior partner at the firm. In his book about the Warburg family, Ron Chernow describes Paul Warburg as, "the only man who understood how a central bank works," and credits Warburg with drafting the final plan for the Federal Reserve System which emerged from the Jekyll Island meeting.

Although the original Aldrich Plan failed to be enacted, the subsequent Federal Reserve Act was virtually identical. As an example of the propaganda campaign that accompanied the bill, instead of creating a central *bank,* the founders titled their creation the Federal Reserve *System*, which functioned exactly like the existing European central banks. The bill itself was passed late on December 23, 1913, after some members of Congress had departed for the Christmas recess. Once President Wilson signed the bill, Paul Warburg became one of the directors of the New York Fed.

How exactly does the Fed get its power? Article I, Section 8 of the United States Constitution gives Congress the responsibility and the authority to, "coin Money, regulate the Value thereof, and of foreign Coin, and fix the Standard of Weights and Measures." However, the Federal Reserve Act transferred that power to the Fed. At one time, our currency bore the title *U.S. Treasury Note.* Now the title is *Federal Reserve Note.* By having the power to increase or decrease the supply of money in circulation, the Fed can control inflation, or induce deflation, which is a fancy way of saying that it can inflate, and then pop, economic bubbles at will. The dot.com bubble of the early 90s, and the subprime mortgage bubble that triggered the Great Recession, are classic examples of how the Fed's control of money operates for the benefit of the mega-banks that run it.

Perhaps the best way to understand the pernicious nature of the Fed is through some telling quotes. The first, from Mayer Ameschel Rothschild again, speaking about a central bank system:

> The few who understand the system will either be so interested in its profits or be so dependent upon its favors that there will be no opposition from that class, while on the other hand, the great body of people, mentally incapable of comprehending the tremendous advantage that capital derives from the system, will bear its burdens without complaint, and perhaps without even suspecting that the system is inimical to their interests.

*Inimical to their interests*. You got that right.

From Montagu Norman, Governor of the Bank of England, addressing the United States Bankers' Association in New York, in 1924:

> Capital must protect itself in every possible way, both by combination and legislation. Debts must be collected, mortgages foreclosed as rapidly as possible. When, through process of law, the common people lose their homes, they will become more docile and more easily governed through the strong arm of the government applied by a central power of wealth under leading financiers.
>
> These truths are well known among our principal men, who are now engaged in forming an imperialism to govern the world. By dividing the voter through the political party system, we can get them to expend their energies in fighting for questions of no importance. It is thus, by discrete action, we can secure for ourselves that which has been so well planned and so successfully accomplished.

From Charles Binderup on the floor of the House of Representatives in March 1937:

> It was Henry Ford who said, in substance, this: "It is perhaps well enough that the people of the nation do not know or understand our banking and monetary system, for if they did I believe there would be a revolution before tomorrow morning."

And more from Congressman McFadden of Pennsylvania, to Congress in 1934:

> "We have, in this country, one of the most corrupt institutions the world has ever known. I refer to the Federal Reserve Board. This evil institution has impoverished the people of the United States and has practically bankrupted our government. It has done this through the corrupt practices of the moneyed vultures who control it."

Two things make this last quote particularly powerful. First, before joining Congress, McFadden had been a banker, and knew how the system worked from the inside. Second, after making the famous speech from which this quote is taken, there were *three* attempts on his life. He was shot at in front of a D.C. hotel, then unsuccessfully poisoned at a banquet, where a doctor saved his life. The third try proved to be a charm and McFadden died from "a sudden attack of influenza" at another banquet.

Then there is Woodrow Wilson himself, who later regretted signing the Federal Reserve Act:

> However it has come about, it is more important still that the control of credit also has become dangerously centralized. It is the mere truth to say that the financial resources of the country are not at the command of those who do not submit to the direction and domination of small groups of capitalists who wish to keep the economic development of the country under their own eye and guidance. The great

monopoly in this country is the monopoly of big credits. So long as that exists, our old variety and freedom and individual energy of development are out of the question. A great industrial nation is controlled by its system of credit. Our system of credit is privately concentrated. The growth of the nation, therefore, and all our activities are in the hands of a few men who, even if their action be honest and intended for the public interest, are necessarily concentrated upon the great undertakings in which their own money is involved and who necessarily, by very reason of their own limitations, chill and check and destroy genuine economic freedom.

When it comes to fears about central banks like the Federal Reserve, Wilson has plenty of company among former Presidents:

Theodore Roosevelt:

> Issue of currency should be lodged with the government and be protected from domination by Wall Street. We are opposed to...provisions [which] would place our currency and credit system in private hands.

James Madison:

> History records that the moneychangers have used every form of abuse, intrigue, deceit, and violent means possible to maintain their control over governments by controlling money and its issuance.

Thomas Jefferson:

> The eyes of our citizens are not sufficiently open to the true cause of our distress. They ascribe them to everything but their true cause, the banking system ... I sincerely believe that banking establishments are more dangerous than standing armies.

James Garfield:

> Whoever controls the volume of money in our country is absolute master of all its industry and commerce ... and when you realize that the entire system is very easily controlled, one way or another, by a few powerful men at the top, you will not have to be told how periods of inflation and depression originate.

So, exactly which banks own or control the Federal Reserve? Nobody knows, because the Fed, a privately held corporation, doesn't have to reveal who its shareholders are. In 1983 and 1992, two books (by Eustace Mullins and Gary Kah, respectively) made the case that the Fed is partly owned and controlled by foreign banks. Unfortunately, both of these sources are suspect. Eustace Mullins was a racist of the first order who once authored the book titled, *Adolph Hitler: An Appreciation.* A fervent anti-Semite, bankers were an easy target for Mullins because, traditionally, many of them are Jewish.

Gary Kah is a former Europe & Middle East Trade Specialist for the Indiana state government who traveled abroad in the course of his job. He is also a born-again Christian who likes to intertwine religion and world domination theories. However, that does not mean that, on this point, he and Mullins are necessarily wrong. Twenty years ago, it was commonplace to dismiss anyone who warned about the Trilateral Commission or the Bilderburg group as a conspiracy nut. Now, when the secret meetings of the Davos clique are widely reported on, theories about international economic conspiracies are not so easily dismissed.

Kah claims direct foreign ownership of a controlling number of shares in the New York Fed by eight banks, four of them foreign:

- Rothschild Banks of London and Berlin
- Lazard Brothers Banks of Paris
- Israel Moses Seif Banks of Italy

- Warburg Bank of Hamburg and Amsterdam

Mullins argued that control was exercised more covertly through foreign bank ownership of key domestic banks in the twelve Fed districts. The claims of both Kah and Mullins have been attacked as based on supposedly "secret sources" whose anonymity made them suspect. So, let's dismiss Mullins and Kah as unreliable. Instead consider what actually happened during the Great Financial Crisis of 2007-2008 (and beyond to present day).

During the period from December 1, 2007 through July 21, 2010, the Fed handed out **$16.1 trillion** in secret loans. How do we know this? Normally the actions of the New York Fed's Open Market Committee (FOMC), which makes Fed policy, are secret. Thanks to outrage over the bank bailout, Congressman Ron Paul of Texas and Senator Bernie Sanders of Vermont forced a bill through Congress to audit the Fed. Although the bill was watered down before passage, the results of even this limited audit were still astounding. And while the top beneficiaries (offenders?) were U.S. banks, trillions went to foreign banks:

- Barclays PLC (Britain) -- $868 billion
- Royal Bank of Scotland -- $541 billion
- Deutsche Bank (Germany) -- $354 billion
- UBS (Switzerland) -- $287 billion
- Credit Suisse (Switzerland) -- $262 billion
- Bank of Scotland -- $181 billion
- BNP Paribas (France) -- $175 billion
- Dexia (Belgium) -- $159 billion
- Dresdner Bank (Germany) -- $135 billion
- Societe Generale (France) -- $124 billion

So, even if the Fed is not secretly controlled by foreign banks (as Mullins and Kah allege), it certainly doesn't have any compunction about giving gigantic stacks of American dollars to foreign financial institutions.

Imagine, if even a fraction of this money had gone instead to regular people, in the form of mortgage refinancing, aid to state governments, or infrastructure projects. In fact, it would have cost far less to give every citizen $1 million each. Consider, also, that one recent estimate puts the true cost of the *on-going* bank bailout at **$27 trillion**.

Defenders of the Fed argue that abolishing it would cause worldwide financial panic and the end of life as we know it. Bullshit. Only three things would change:

- First, the printing of money would return to the Department of the Treasury as required by the Constitution.

- Second, the government would not have to borrow money. As a sovereign nation that prints its own currency, the United States government doesn't have to borrow, all it has to do is print however much money it needs. The only limitation on that power is that it cannot print so much money that other countries cease to give it sufficient value. It could still print more than it takes in through taxes, but the process wouldn't enrich the banks as it does now.

- Third, the management of the money supply, which is to say the management of the economy, would be yanked from the secret hands of the worldwide financial elite and returned to the government. Some argue that the last thing we want is control of the money supply in the hands of politicians, who could not resist the temptations to manipulate the currency, to ensure favorable political outcomes.

You mean, like ensuring a better life for the vast majority of citizens? What a novel idea! I mean, *how much worse could it be than what we have today*? And assuming the other Restoration Amendments were enacted, these politicians will have been elected with public financing, and hence responsive to the people.

The Fed is economic royalty, and here is what FDR said on that subject in his 1936 speech to the Democratic National Convention upon accepting the nomination for another term:

Out of this modern civilization, economic royalists carved new dynasties. New kingdoms were built upon the concentration of control over material things. Through new uses of corporations, banks, and securities, new machinery of industry and agriculture, of labor and capital -- all undreamed by the fathers -- the whole structure of modern life was impressed into this royal service.

There was no place among this royalty for our many thousands of small businessmen and merchants who sought to make worthy use of the American system of initiative and profit. They were no more free than the worker or the farmer. Even the honest and progressive-minded men of wealth, aware of their obligation to their generation, could never know just where they fitted into this dynastic scheme of things.

It was natural and perhaps human that the privileged princes of these new economic dynasties, thirsting for power, reached out for the control of the Government itself. They created a new despotism and wrapped it in the robes of legal sanction. In its service, new mercenaries sought to regiment the people, their labor, and their property. And as a result, the average man once more confronts the problem faced by the Minute Man...

Against economic tyranny such as this, the American citizen could appeal only to the organized power of the Government...

The royalists of the economic order have conceded that political freedom was the business of the Government, but they have maintained that economic slavery was nobody's business. They granted that the Government could protect the citizen in his right to vote, but they denied that the Government could do anything to protect the citizen in his right to work and his right to live...

The economic royalists complain that we seek to overthrow the institutions of America. What they really complain about is that we seek to take away their power. Our allegiance to American institutions requires the overthrow of this kind of power.

*Our allegiance to American institutions requires the overthrow of this kind of power*.

You're damned right it does.

### The 43rd Amendment -- Economic Security

**Section 1: The Federal Reserve system is hereby dissolved and Congress shall establish, under the Department of the Treasury, a central bank, operated solely by the government, and vested with all powers necessary to protect the value of the national currency, properly regulate the amount of money in circulation, and ensure the lasting strength of the domestic economy.**

If you worry that this proposal goes too far, that it is impractical, or poorly thought-out, I have one final argument, which I believe you will find persuasive. Martin Goodfriend, a 2018 nominee to the Federal Reserve Board of Governors, wrote two papers in 2016 advocating ***abolishing cash***. Supposedly, this would allow the

Fed to stimulate the economy in times of recession by adopting negative interest rates, meaning that instead of the bank or other financial institution paying you interest, **you pay them a fee** to keep *your* money in *your* accounts. Savings, checking, retirement, money market, etc. You get hit with a fee every day for the money that just sits there, and additional fees every time you make a purchase, pay a bill, or even make a deposit.

The theory is that during tough times, instead of people sitting on their money in a Tupperware can in the backyard, they would be encouraged to spend it and stimulate the economy. This is also supposed to create a true free market, except free markets never actually exist in real life. Of course, the bankers will get those fees, 24/7/365, even when times are good.

There are, however, two big upsides for government and the Fed to abolishing cash: in addition to already knowing all the stuff in those Big Data dossiers, these satanic bankers will also know every transaction you make because everything will have a record attached to it. And if you get out of line, start agitating for something they don't like, they can just freeze your accounts. Isn't that wonderful?! Like I said, two big upsides for the most evil men and women on the planet.

### Fuck the Fed. And the horse it rode in on.

Unfortunately, to put an effective choke-chain on the voracious wolves of Wall Street, we have to do more than just end the Fed. We must also break up the dominant mega-banks into smaller, more manageable units. We must limit the size and reach of each bank, both geographically and in terms of financial power, so that no single institution, or interconnected cluster of institutions, is a threat to the country's, or even the world's, financial structure.

In October 2018, Bernie Sanders introduced a bill in the Senate to break up certain huge financial institutions. According to the press release announcing the bill, which is co-sponsored in the House by Rep. Brad Sherman of California: [Emphasis added.]

> Today the six largest banks in America control assets equivalent to more than half the country's GDP and the four largest banks are on average about 80 percent larger today than they were before the bailout. The legislation introduced Wednesday would cap the size of the largest financial institutions so that a company's total exposure is no more than 3 percent of GDP, about $584 billion today.

> By applying a cap on the size of financial institutions, the bill would break up the six largest banks in the country: JP Morgan Chase, Bank of America, Citigroup, Wells Fargo, Goldman Sachs and Morgan Stanley. The bill would also address large non-bank financial service companies such ase [*sic*] Prudential, MetLife and AIG.

> "Too big to fail should be too big to exist," said Sherman ... "Today they can claim: 'if we go down, the economy is going down with us.' By breaking up these institutions long before they face a crisis, we ensure a healthy financial system where medium-sized institutions can compete in the free market."

> In the 10 years since Wall Street caused the financial crisis and was bailed out by taxpayers, the five largest banks have raked in more than $583 billion in profits. The six biggest banks have a combined total exposure of over **$13 trillion** which exceeds **68 percent of our nation's GDP**.

As Sanders' asked in a GIF posted on Facebook:

> If these banks were too big to fail 10 years ago, what would happen if any of them were to fail today?

The answer, of course, is that we, and the world economy, would be -- and ***will be*** -- screwed.

The Sanders-Sherman bill has no chance of being passed. Even if the Democrats regain control of Congress, they are too beholden to (and in love with) Wall Street to ever pass such legislation. Even if it were to pass, Trump would veto it, and over-riding his veto would arguably be impossible. The only way a bill of this type is ever going to get passed is *after* another monumental financial meltdown. In other words, after the damage is done.

This does not mean that introducing the bill is merely political theater. It puts Sanders on the record -- before the next inevitable crisis hits -- about the dangers posed by these gargantuan institutions It also means that when the financial institutions again crash and burn, as they surely will, his bill could become a handy, off-the-shelf, ready-to-go response.

The problems, in my opinion, with Sanders' solution involve the details. Determining percentage of GDP is one. GDP fluctuates, as does a bank's size. Lawyers and accountants are adept at fudging figures. Deals can be carried off-the-books, on what are known as external balance sheets, as was done by Enron. A simpler solution is to confine banks and insurance companies both with monetary limits and geographically. This would not affect consumers or businesses in any meaningful way. ATMs would still be accessible via systems like Star. Money could still be transferred using PayPal or some alternative. (Rest assured, the financial institutions would fall all over themselves making sure that their customers have convenient transactional access, which would be a prominent feature of their ad campaigns.) Therefore:

**Section 2: To protect the public interest, and prevent concentrations of economic influence detrimental to the security and well-being of the people, no bank or other purveyor of financial instruments or insurance shall hold or control more than ten percent of public or private deposits, insure more than ten percent of the population, or operate in more than ten**

**states. No bank or other financial institution shall also own or control any insurance entity.**

If this sounds simple, that's because it is. Often the best solutions are simple. The thing is, they're just not painless, especially to those who benefit from the status quo. *Cry me a river.*

# Chapter 19

# ECONOMIC SECURITY -- PART TWO

**The 43rd Amendment (continued)**

> **Section 3: Within 180 days after ratification of this Amendment, Congress shall enact National Industrial Policy legislation to create, protect, and ensure a robust, diverse, and self-sufficient domestic economy producing, within the borders of the 50 states, all goods required for the security of the nation and the comfort, prosperity, and well-being of its people. The National Industrial Policy, regularly amended as time and need require, shall include such tariffs, import duties, and other regulations necessary to protect American workers and industries from unfair foreign competition.**

Wresting control of the currency and the economy back into the proper hands will not be enough to cure our economic ills or address the economic challenges we face. J.P. Morgan exerted tremendous power in the Gilded Age, but it was still the industrial and business robber baron tycoons like Rockefeller, Carnegie, and the mine owners, who really held the working class by the throat. Thanks to the rise of unions and social movements, things got better for a few golden decades between the 1930s and the 1970s. Most of those gains have since been eroded, or vanished altogether, and wealth inequality is greater now than it was in the Gilded Age.

The use of *industrial* policy instead of *economic* policy is important. Nations that have real power and real wealth *make things*, for both domestic consumption and export. That's why Germany has a strong economy, and why many worry about the seeming inevitability that China will rule the 21st century. A National *Economic* Policy is about who gets rich; a National *Industrial* Policy is about how the economy is organized and prioritized, how a country decides which domestic industries to protect, which economic activities are to be encouraged (or discouraged), how its natural resources are managed, and so forth. Every developed nation has one.

The U.S. national economic policy is not formally enunciated, because formally admitting the government's economic intentions would foment revolution in the street. Instead, our policy is hidden in the tax code and various pieces of special-interest legislation, dots that only the oligarchs and rapacious corporations know how to connect. For example, we have no stated national policy to export jobs and throw workers at home out on the street. But under the U.S. tax code, a company that does so *qualifies for a tax break*. No wonder that in the decade from 1999--2009, U.S. companies terminated 2.9 million domestic jobs while adding 2.4 million jobs in low-wage foreign countries. In the period between 2001 (when China was allowed to join the World Trade Organization) and 2013, trade with China alone cost America approximately 2.8 million jobs. In 2011 alone, another 2,273,392 U.S. jobs were lost to outsourcing. Manufacturing led the way with a 53% loss of jobs. EconomyInCrisis.org summed up the situation: [Emphasis is original.]

> It's obvious that while we are gaining short-term profit and a few jobs, we are forfeiting our manufacturing and industrial base. Eventually, we'll be left with few to no American-owned factories, leaving the nation

completely dependent on other countries for work, resources and a fair standard of living.

**These are the economic characteristics of a third-world country. These are the chains that our forefathers fought to shake off more than 200 years ago. That is a vision of the U.S. that no American is comfortable imagining.**

The killing of American jobs isn't just a corporate campaign, it's government policy. Remember the bailout of General Motors, heralded as saving the cornerstone of the American auto industry? What really happened is that GM agreed to immediately close sixteen manufacturing facilities, including four domestic assembly plants, putting 21,000 hourly wage employees out of work. GM also agreed to close three more plants by 2014. But that wasn't the worst of it. According to UAW Legislative Director Alan Reuther in a letter to Congress:

> Between 2010-2014 GM's restructuring plan also calls for a 98% increase in the number of vehicles it will be importing into the United States from Mexico, Korea, Japan and China, with the number of imports from these countries increasing from 371,547 to 736,743.

Our tax money effectively subsidized, and is continuing to subsidize, increased imports by GM into the U.S. from Mexico, China, and Korea. William Greider, writing at The Nation, asked, "How is this in our national interest?"

The answer: *It isn't.*

Who would negotiate such a deal? His name is Steve Rattner. What kind of guy is Stevie-boy? Described by Rolling Stone writer Matt Taibbi as "the Rat," he's the kind who pays $16.2 million in fines for bribing state officials in order to get $150 million in investment business from the New York State public employee pension fund. Eight other conspirators pleaded guilty to criminal charges but Rattner, a major fundraiser for Obama and other

Democratic candidates, got off with only a civil charge, and he did not have to admit wrongdoing. Worth hundreds of millions, Rattner's lifestyle was not impacted by a $16 million fine. Most importantly, instead of a lifetime ban from working on Wall Street, he skated with a measly two-year suspension.

Despite the GM example, it is incorrect and foolish to think of the outsourcing crisis just in the strict traditional terms of industrial and manufacturing jobs. For anyone who has had to deal with tech support, it will come as no surprise that according to that same Akron study, 43% of the jobs outsourced between '99 and '09 were in IT Services. What is truly scary is that another 38% of the jobs lost were in the field of Research and Development. As a result, the Akron study concludes, "We are not innovating, jeopardizing our competitiveness with countries who continue to support Research and Development."

The measures described in the previous chapter to end illegal immigration will not be sufficient to ensure that American jobs go to qualified Americans. We must also curtail the ability of employers to abuse legal work-visa programs such as the category known as H-1B. Enacted in 1990, the H-1B program allows up to 65,000 people a year to enter the U.S. to work when they provide "highly specialized knowledge" in fields Wikipedia described as:

> ...including but not limited to biotechnology, chemistry, architecture, engineering, mathematics, physical sciences, social sciences, medicine and health, education, law, accounting, business specialties, theology, and the arts, and requiring the attainment of a bachelor's degree or its equivalent as a minimum (with the exception of fashion models, who must be "of distinguished merit and ability").

Fashion models? Yep. Before she was Mrs. Tom Brady, this was how supermodel Giselle Bündchen lived and worked in the U.S., even though her contract required her to be paid in *euros* because of "worries" about the fluctuating value of the U.S. dollar.

The limit of 65,000 new H-1B workers a year makes the problem sound far less serious than it really is. Aside from the fact that most of these jobs (gorgeous babes excepted), are in fields that require high skill-sets, and should be favorably compensated, there are other problems. First, these visas are for three years, but can be extended to six, and even in some cases, for up to ten years. Second, the 65,000 person-per year limit isn't actually, you know, a *limit*. There are exceptions for people who have advanced degrees, as well as for those who work at universities, research facilities, the Department of Defense, or security agencies. This last category includes people who work for contractors. Amazon, for instance, provides cloud computing and storage services to the CIA. Theoretically, Amazon (or Google, or any of the other Police State-assisting) tech companies, can get approval for an unlimited number of H-1B visa immigrants to perform these assignments. Whether they do (or not) isn't known, but merely the possibility that foreign nationals are being given priority over American citizens, for work involving national security, should be cause enough for worry. What we do know is, in 2012, the U.S. Customs and Immigration Service approved 136,890 new H-1B visa applications, more than double the so-called limit of 65,000. There is no word on how many fashion models were included in that figure, but USCIS also approved another 125,679 renewal applications.

There is no disputing the fact that H-1B immigrants reduce wages for jobs that Americans would otherwise gladly perform. In 2017, Harvard economist George J. Boras, an Hispanic immigrant who grew up in a single-parent home after his father died young, decided to find out what kind of impact immigrants had on wages and employment rates for similarly-skilled citizens. Besides an enormous, mind-boggling drop-off in wages for native workers without a high school diploma, Boras also found a significant decline in wages and employment for highly-skilled employees such as mathematicians.

This decline in wages for highly-skilled employees occurs because H-1B immigrants are totally dependent on employment for their legal status. If you rock the boat, complain about pay or working conditions, make noise about trying to form a union, you can be fired and sent home immediately. Although ICE sometimes gives terminated H-1B workers between ten days and a month to settle their affairs, this is merely a courtesy. The law provides for no grace period, and fired workers can be deported the same day they are terminated. Business Week reported, as far back as 2008, that there were approximately 500,000 H-1B workers who are "usually beholden to employers that can transfer them home at will."

So, half a million foreign workers worry about instant deportation if they complain about wages and working conditions. Maybe that explains why so many American tech workers are unemployed, underemployed, or underpaid. According to Josh Harkinson, writing for Mother Jones in February 2013: [Emphasis added.]

> According to the Economic Policy Institute (EPI) ... from 2001 to 2011, the mean hourly wage for computer programmers didn't even increase enough to beat inflation.
>
> [snip]
>
> More than 80 percent of H-1B visa holders are approved to be hired at wages **below those paid to American-born workers for comparable positions**, according to EPI ... older, more expensive workers are particularly vulnerable to being undercut by their foreign counterparts. "You can be an exact match and never even get a phone call because you are too expensive," says Norman Matloff, a computer science professor at the University of California-Davis. "The minute that they see you've got 10 or 15 years of experience, they don't want you."

America has no shortage of qualified college graduates in the STEM (Science, Technology, Engineering, Mathematics) field to fill entry-level jobs. But, because they don't want to pay competitive wages, employers go to great lengths to avoid hiring them. As Joe's Union Review explained:

> The brighter of our countrymen, the Techie geeks, are under attack. Not just from the threat of offshoring, but by the threat of misuse of H-1B Visa's by unscrupulous employers on our own shores. It is called the PERM process and the following video made by Immigration attorneys from Cohen & Grigsby explains just how to disqualify qualified US Workers in favor of foreign workers, who by the way must keep their job at all costs or be deported...

> Immigration attorneys from Cohen & Grigsby explain how they assist employers in running classified ads with the goal of NOT finding any qualified applicants, and the steps they go through to disqualify even the most qualified Americans in order to secure green cards for H-1b workers. ... Microsoft, Oracle, Hewlett-Packard, and thousands of other companies are running fake ads in Sunday newspapers across the country each week.

The difficulty getting employment in STEM occupations is believed to have induced a number of students, especially those who intend to get a master's degree, to pursue other fields. Professor Matloff again, in a Josh Harkinson piece for Mother Jones: "In terms of the number of people with graduate degrees in STEM, H-1B is the problem, not the solution."

The flip side of this involves cases where H-1B workers qualify under what is known as dual intent, meaning that while they are here on temporary H-1B work visas they can apply for permanent worker green card status, and eventually even citizenship. Once someone acquires green card status, they are no longer included in the annual tally of H-1B visas. Likewise, H-1B applicants can also bring their families along, and if they then have a child born on U.S. soil, that baby becomes the anchor for the whole family to gain permanent resident status. Thus, figures like the ones cited above for 2012, do not accurately reflect the ongoing long-term impact of H-1B immigrants on skilled labor job opportunities for Americans. But even this isn't the most insidious aspect of the H-1B program. That has to do with how the rotation of H-1B workers back to their home country facilitates off-shoring *of the job itself*.

Take Pfizer, for example. In 2008, it announced plans to shift much of its IT work to Indian outsourcing giants Infosys and Satyam Computer Services. But first, it required the American employees, *who were about to be laid off*, to train between 800 and 1,000 Indians brought over on H-1B visas **to learn the jobs being outsourced back to India**. You can't make this up, yet it's common practice. As Ron Hira, an assistant professor of public policy at Rochester Institute of Technology and co-author of "Outsourcing America," noted in a 2008 article for e-week.com:

> It's not surprising to have a company bring in [workers on] H-1B or L-1 visas to transition that work to companies like Infosys and Satyam ... (but) you shouldn't have to dig your own grave by bringing in someone on an H-1B and training them to do your job.

Not content with just using the H-1B visa program to train foreigners for IT jobs being shipped overseas, Pfizer also off-shored more than 11,000 jobs in manufacturing and supply operations.

Using H-1B workers to learn jobs that can then be outsourced back to the immigrant's home country is understandable, considering that in most cases it is not the U.S. company that actually hires the H-1B immigrant. That job is contracted out to foreign-based employment agencies and recruiting companies. Here's Josh Harkinson for Mother Jones in February 2013:

> *ComputerWorld* revealed last week that the top 10 users of H-1B visas last year were all offshore outsourcing firms such as Tata and Infosys. Together

these firms hired nearly half of all H-1B workers, and less than 3 percent of them applied to become permanent residents. "The H-1B worker learns the job and then rotates back to the home country and takes the work with him," explains Ron Hira, an immigration expert who teaches at the Rochester Institute of Technology. None other than India's former commerce secretary once dubbed the H-1B the "outsourcing visa."

Of course, the big tech companies claim H-1B workers are their last resort, and that they can't find qualified Americans to fill jobs. Pressing to raise the visa cap last year, Microsoft pointed to 6,000 job openings at the company.

Hmmm, 6,000 unfilled job openings. Could any of them be like the programmer position advertised by one company for which *all* **25,000** applicants were deemed unqualified by a software program? We'll never know for sure, but in 2014, IBM paid a paltry $44,400 fine for discriminating against American workers in favor of H-1B immigrants. *Wow, $44,400 will certainly stop IBM from ever doing this again!*

There is little wonder that these foreign employment agencies and their U.S. clients have tried repeatedly to get the yearly cap of 65,000 new H-1B visas doubled, or even tripled to 195,000. Customs and Immigrations opens the H-1B application process for the following year on April 1st. In 2014, the entire allotment of 2015 H-1B visa petition applications was reached by April 5th. Unable to get all the H-1B allotments they covet, some firms have taken to bringing in workers on traditional B-1 visas, intended for short-term business travelers here to visit facilities or conclude deals. One India-based giant, Infosys, paid $34 million to settle a federal lawsuit over this type of "systematic visa fraud."

Undercutting American workers and defrauding the American government isn't enough; these companies defraud and exploit the immigrant workers as well. Business Week ran a story about an

Indian worker, promised a starting salary of $44,000, who ended up getting paid only $23,310. Even with multiple roommates, try living anywhere near Silicon Valley on $23K a year. In January 2014, reporter James Tapper revealed that Indian outsourcing giant Tata Consultancy had paid a $30 million fine for forcing employees it placed with American tech companies to sign over their individual U.S. tax refund checks.

The worst part of our current suicidal economic policy is the tax benefits bestowed on companies who engage in outsourcing and off-shoring. This is an example of Gresham's Dynamic, the theory that, "bad behavior drives out good behavior." In a market where government or regulatory forces do not restrain or punish bad behavior by some parties, others will be driven to engage in that same bad behavior simply in order to remain competitive. Therefore:

> **Section 4: Ensuring American citizens priority to American jobs being of the utmost importance, the importation of foreign workers under any temporary grant of work status shall be strictly limited to 20,000 persons per year, who shall be selected strictly on the basis of their extraordinary knowledge and skills, and thus compensated at a rate at least twice that paid to American citizens performing the same or similar work for any employer in the same or similar field.**

The lack of a true, sound, official National Industrial Policy is also reflected in how corporate special interests are able to manipulate the tax code with respect to paying -- or more precisely, *not* paying -- taxes on their profits. They do so in two ways. The first is to revise the company's Articles of Incorporation so that the entity is now (ostensibly) headquartered in a foreign tax haven with a low corporate income tax. The technical term is "inversion."

Sometimes inversion is part of a merger where the new entity opts to designate its new headquarters in a foreign tax haven.

The thing is, the headquarters doesn't really have to move, only its nominal address. Ugland House, a modest five-story building on Grand Isle in the Cayman Islands, is the registered headquarters for 18,857 companies. More accurately, it's headquarters to nearly 20,000 private mailboxes. According to the Center for Tax Justice, "About half of these companies have their billing address in the U.S., even while they are officially registered in the Caymans." Any mail that does arrive at these tiny "headquarters" boxes is dutifully forwarded to the company's real headquarters in the U.S.

The second method employed by companies to defraud taxpayers by not paying their fair share in taxes involves setting up foreign subsidiaries in low tax/no tax countries. This allows the company to use accounting charades to move profits from where they are actually earned to a subsidiary in a tax haven. Once again, *the money doesn't have to actually be offshore*. It can stay right here, safely in the hands of mega-banks like Citigroup, Chase, and Bank of America.

According to reports about the abuses of inversion and offshore tax avoidance produced by Tax Justice Network, as of 2011, 290 of the Fortune 500 companies sheltered nearly *$1.6 trillion* from U.S. taxes by stashing the profits abroad in tax haven countries. Just these Top Twenty offenders accounted for nearly half that total. (Figure in billions.)

| | |
|---|---|
| General Electric | 102,000 |
| Pfizer | 63,000 |
| Microsoft | 60,800 |
| Apple | 54,300 |
| Exxon Mobil | 47,000 |
| Merck | 44,300 |
| Johnson & Johnson | 41,600 |

| | |
|---|---|
| Procter & Gamble | 39,000 |
| IBM | 37,900 |
| Cisco Systems | 36,700 |
| Citigroup | 35,900 |
| PepsiCo | 43,100 |
| Abbott Labs | 31,900 |
| Hewlett-Packard | 29,100 |
| Google | 24,800 |
| Chevron | 24,376 |
| Coca-Cola | 23,500 |
| J.P. Morgan Chase | 21,800 |
| Oracle | 20,900 |
| Goldman Sachs | 20,630 |
| | |
| Total | 793,606 |
| Other Fortune 500 Corps | 794,307 |
| Grand Total | 1,587,913 |

Tax Justice Network estimates that in 2012, between $21 and $32 **trillion** in profits was sheltered in unreported tax havens worldwide.

Companies manage to evade taxes through strategies with exotic names like "the Dutch Sandwich," or the "Double Irish." While complex in terms of paperwork, they are relatively simple in design. Companies set up a number of entities in countries with very low corporate tax rates. (In the case of a country like Bermuda, *no* corporate tax at all.) They then create paperwork purporting to sell or otherwise transfer costs -- and especially revenues -- between those entities until finally whatever profit remains can be claimed in the jurisdiction with the lowest rate. In some cases, the companies can avoid paying taxes in both the U.S. and the various foreign shelter countries as well. In other cases, companies can reduce the nominal U.S. corporate tax rate of 35% down to a real, effective rate of, in the case of Google, 2.4%.

Meanwhile, both the U.S. and the E.U. face budget and tax revenue gaps in the trillions.

Who makes up this shortfall in government revenue? Either the average taxpayer and small business owner, or the government simply uses the revenue falloff as a handy, but entirely phony, excuse to cut programs like unemployment benefits, Medicare reimbursements, food stamps, and the rebuilding of roads and bridges.

Technically, these off-shored profits are taxed when the money is repatriated back to the parent company. However, that rarely happens. Instead, the company simply borrows the money it wants, using the off-shored profits as collateral. Since the bank making the loan is often the same bank where the money is already on deposit, the company is borrowing its own money, and the bank has no risk of non-payment. Nominally, the corporate tax rate is 35% but, thanks to all the gimmicks, loopholes, and licenses to steal built into the tax code, no company of any size really pays anything close to that. But even at a 15% rate, if the interest rate on the loan is 5%, the company still saves 10%. When the profits are in the billions, the savings from tax avoidance are also frequently in the billions. Even worse, the company **gets to deduct the interest on the loan from its taxes** when reporting profits from its domestic U.S. operations. How nice.

When loan schemes aren't enough, the companies lobby Congress for a repatriation window, a period when they can repatriate offshore profits at a special, discounted rate. The usual justification is that the companies will use this money to expand operations and create more jobs. The truth is, during the repatriation window in 2004, companies used most of the repatriated money for stock buy-backs to increase the stock price, increase stockholder dividends, and trigger bigger bonuses for executives.

In 2018, companies pushed the Republican-controlled Congress to pass (with the strategic assistance of several pathetic Democrats), President Trump's massive tax cut, which created an unofficial repatriation amnesty, taxing the money brought home from offshore books at a much lower rate than it would have been otherwise.

The public was once again promised that this tax cut would result in companies adding jobs. Instead, those companies used the money to buy back stock (raising stock prices on which executive bonuses are calculated), and increase dividends (so stock holders wouldn't feel left out), while simultaneously laying off thousands of workers. Here's a short list:

### Pfizer Pharmaceuticals
- Tax Cut Bonanza: $5 billion
- Executive Bonuses: $100 million
- Stock Buybacks: $10 billion
- Jobs Cut: 300

*Note:* After the 2004 tax amnesty on repatriated foreign profits, Pfizer bought back $17 billion in stock **and laid off 11,748 employees**.

### AT&T
- Tax Cut Bonanza: $2.4 billion
- Jobs Cut: 4,000

### Comcast
- Tax Cut Bonanza: $12 billion
- Stock Buybacks: $5 billion
- Jobs Cut: 500

## Walmart

- Tax Cut Bonanza: $2 billion
- Stock Buybacks: $4 billion
- Jobs Cut: 1,000

*Note:* Also 11,000 more jobs were cut by closing Sam's Club stores

## Tenet Health Care

- Tax Cut Bonanza: $10-$20 million
- Jobs Cut: 2,000

No new jobs, just a lot fewer old jobs. Moreover -- *surprise, surprise* -- many of the jobs eliminated here are likely to be replaced by new jobs in low-wage foreign countries. And here's a partial list of stock buybacks planned for 2018, for which these companies' tax cut windfall has not yet been published:

| | |
|---|---|
| Boeing | $18 billion |
| Home Depot | $15 billion |
| Oracle | $12 billion |
| Cisco | $25 billion |
| Alphabet (Google) | $8.6 billion |
| PepsiCo | $15 billion |
| Lowe's | $5 billion |
| Visa | $7.5 billion |
| eBay | $6 billion |
| Amgen | $10 billion |
| AbbVie | $10 billion |
| Wells Fargo | $22.6 billion |

Wells Fuckin' Fargo, quite possibly the most consistently criminal bank of the past forty years, gets to buy back $22.6 billion in stock to boost the bonuses of executives who, if there was any justice in the world, would be in jail? For those that don't know, Wells Fargo's history of evil is so extensive that both the State of

California, and the City of Chicago, have barred the bank from doing any official business with those government entities. In addition, the federal government has issued an order preventing Wells from increasing its business, meaning that it cannot acquire other financial institutions, or expand its commercial loan activities, and it can only attract enough new customers to offset losses in deposits from accounts that are closed.

Here's a partial list of the fines Wells Fargo has paid over the past twenty-five years for various violations. (Hat tip to Philip Mattera at Corporate Research Project for these numbers, which come from a story he wrote, Wells Fargo Corporate Rap Sheet, which is linked-to on the TrueReform.org website.)

1992 -- $43 million for conspiracy to fix the interest rates on millions of credit card accounts.

2002 -- $150,000 for improperly switching customers among mutual funds.

2005 -- $3 million for improper sales of mutual funds.

2011 -- $125 million for misrepresenting mortgage-related securities.

2011 -- $85 million for steering customers with good credit into subprime mortgages

2011 -- $37 million to settle a lawsuit for municipal bond bid rigging.

2011 -- $4.1 million for improper sales of securities and exchange-traded funds.

2012 -- Part of $25 billion subprime mortgage fraud settlement

2012 -- $175 million for engaging in a pattern of discrimination in mortgage lending

2012 -- $6.5 for failure to fully research the risks associated with mortgage-backed securities

2013 -- Its share of $8.5 billion to resolve claims of foreclosure abuses by ten lenders

2013 -- $42 million for neglecting maintenance of foreclosed properties

2013 -- $869 million to repurchase non-conforming homes sold to Freddie Mac

2016 -- $1.2 billion for falsely certifying Dept. of Housing and Urban Development loans

2016 -- $4 million for illegal student loan servicing practices

2016 -- $185 million for creating 3.5 million bogus new accounts not requested by customers

In 2018 it got worse. Wells FuckYou got fined another $1 billion, but that was more than offset by the $3.7 billion it got from the Trump tax cut. Not content with being $2.7 billion ahead, Wells announced that it was closing its domestic call centers and shipping those jobs overseas. By doing so, Wells not only saves millions, but it also gets those call centers out from under U.S. regulations concerning the privacy and security of customer's financial records.

When the largest state, and one of the country's biggest cities, both bar you from getting their business, and the federal government prohibits your company from expanding, but you still get to buy back over $22 billion of stock, in order to reward top executives with undeserved bonuses, something is very wrong with both our government and our economic system. Therefore:

**Section 5: Congress shall pass no law, and no court or agency shall issue any ruling or**

**regulation that has the effect of providing a reduction, waiver, or deferral of any tax for any enterprise, or its subsidiary, for producing goods in a foreign country, territory, or jurisdiction for importation into the United States, or for providing services in or from a foreign country, territory, or jurisdiction in lieu of basing those services in the United States or its territories. Nor shall profits from foreign revenues be given special tax treatment.**

Not content to savage both white-collar and skilled blue-collar employees by moving jobs offshore, or replacing them with H-1B and H-2B workers, companies have learned how to manipulate cities and states into desperate competition with each other for business. Companies that like to complain loudly about government interference in free enterprise because of workplace and environmental regulations have no compunction about extorting government for subsidies, tax waivers, and even free land and infrastructure improvements as a condition of opening a new facility or expanding an existing one. They play state-against-state, community-against-community, in a never-ending race to the bottom. The political justification is jobs, but the costs often outweigh the benefits. Worse, these kinds of special deals are a direct affront to the concept of free enterprise, which is based on the principle that rewards derive from risks taken. In the perverted reality that these deals produce, the risk is all on the government entity, and the rewards all accrue to the corporate beneficiary. ***Privatize the profits, socialize any losses.***

Remember GM, who closed all those factories and moved so much production to China as part of its taxpayer-funded bailout? Louise Story, writing in December 2012, for the New York Times, summed up the situation with her opening line, "In the end, the money that towns across America gave General Motors did not matter." Despite decades of tax breaks and other incentives, about

50 facilities were closed. Even when Ohio and Wisconsin offered over $200 million in additional incentives, they still got the cold shoulder. In Michigan, GM's tax breaks and incentives for 2009 totaled almost $800 million but GM still closed seven plants, including Ypsilanti, which over the years had provided over $200 million in subsidies and tax breaks, including hard cash and free buildings. As Story noted, all that remained in these communities which had, "spent scarce funds in exchange for thousands of jobs that no longer exist ... is a shuttered plant."

Worse yet, after the bailout and plant closings, GM's various domestic facilities still continue to receive approximately a billion dollars in state and local incentives, which come in a variety of forms: cash grants and low-or-no-interest loans; income tax credits or exemptions; property tax discounts or complete waivers; free water or trash pickup services; exemption from taxes on energy usage. Other key findings in Story's article:

- Each year cities, states, and counties give away more than $80 billion to oil and coal conglomerates, technology and entertainment companies, banks and big-box retail chains. That adds up to $9.1 million per hour.

- Many times, there is no follow-up accounting to see if the promised number of new jobs was actually created. And it is impossible to know if the jobs that were created, would have come about without the aid.

- Texas awards more incentives, over $19 billion a year, than any other state. Alaska, West Virginia and Nebraska give up the most per resident.

- Oklahoma, West Virginia, and Nebraska give up amounts equal to roughly one-third of their budgets.

- Taxes lost to state and local budgets by incentives are often reflected in cuts to vital programs. The same year that Kansas gave the theater giant AMC $36 million in incentives to move its headquarters across the border from Missouri, it cut the state education budget by $104 million.

- The amount New York State gives away each year to film and television productions equals the cost of hiring 5,000 public school teachers.

One reason automakers are among the biggest recipients of these incentives is because they helped pioneer the concept. The website ReliablePlant.com, which tracks developments in the manufacturing and industrial sector, headlined a story *Foreign-owned Auto Plants Netted $3.6B in Subsidies* and listed the beneficiaries:

- Honda, Marysville, Ohio, 1980, $27 million
- Nissan, Smyrna, Tenn., 1980, $233 million
- Toyota, Georgetown, Ky., 1985, $147 million
- Honda, Anna, Ohio, 1985, $27 million
- Subaru, Lafayette, Ind., 1986, $94 million
- Honda, East Liberty, Ohio, 1987, $27 million
- BMW, Spartanburg, S.C., 1992, $150 million
- Mercedes-Benz, Vance, Ala., 1993, $258 million
- Toyota, Princeton, Ind., 1995, $30 million
- Nissan, Decherd, Tenn., 1995, $200 million
- Toyota, Buffalo, W.Va., 1996, more than $15 million
- Honda, Lincoln, Ala., 1999, $248 million
- Nissan, Canton, Miss., 2000, $295 million
- Toyota, Huntsville, Ala., 2001, $30 million
- Hyundai, Montgomery, Ala., 2002, $252 million

- Toyota, San Antonio, Texas, 2003, $133 million
- Kia, West Point, Ga., 2006, $400 million
- Honda, Greensburg, Ind., 2006, $141 million
- Toyota, Blue Springs, Miss., 2007, $300 million
- Volkswagen, Chattanooga, Tenn., 2008, $577 million

The story notes that these figures, which span more than a quarter of a century, are taken from published news accounts (which may understate the actual value) and are not adjusted for inflation. Thus, they do not completely reflect the current value of the benefits.

Six years after forking over $577 mil in 2008, Tennessee came back, in 2014, with a $600 million package to induce Volkswagen to locate a new design center at the Chattanooga plant, and to expand the facility to produce the new VW crossover SUV. According to the Chattanooga Times Free Press, the package included:

- A $165.8 million grant from the state of Tennessee for costs associated with site development and preparation, infrastructure, production equipment acquisition and installation, and facility construction.

- $52.5 million in local government assistance to VW, split equally between the city of Chattanooga and Hamilton County, for upfront expenses for the plant addition. VW will pay back $2.5 million in an economic development fee each year, for the next 10 years, to repay about half of the loan, and VW will transfer 300 acres at Enterprise South industrial park back to the city and county.

- $12 million in state grants for training new employees

- $33 million for property tax breaks expected to be offered for the $600 million expansion over the next decade

And here you thought things like the acquisition of production equipment, building a facility, or training workers was a cost of doing business in our heralded free enterprise capitalist economy. But don't worry: property taxes will still be levied on local small businesses and homeowners.

After a 2008 strike at its main Seattle facility, Boeing went hunting for a new location where it could escape the pesky demands of the Machinists Union. Anti-union, Right-To-Work (for Less) South Carolina happily went into debt to the tune of $218 million to help, and threw in ten years of tax breaks. This was nothing new for Boeing. In 2001, the company pitted Dallas, Denver, and Chicago against each other for the right to land Boeing's new company headquarters. Chicago won, but only after the city, Cook County, and the state of Illinois put together $60 million in tax breaks. Among the benefits: 20 years of property tax abatements, an annual tax credit equal to the income taxes *its employees pay to the state*, and building a downtown heliport so that execs can commute in and out conveniently.

Determined to avoid what it saw as the drawbacks of its highly-skilled but also highly-paid Seattle workforce, when it came time to assemble the 787 Dreamliner, Boeing opted to do so in South Carolina -- but not before deciding to outsource both the manufacturing *and the design* of thirty percent of the components to subcontractors, including ones in South Korea, Italy, Sweden, and even China. The goal was to save money. Instead, the Dreamliner turned into Boeing's nightmare. Parts from different suppliers did not fit. Other suppliers couldn't meet delivery deadlines, stalling the production line with partially finished planes. Delivery of the plane was delayed by three years, there were massive cost overruns, and Boeing even had to buy some subcontractors, such as Vought Aircraft Industries, that couldn't meet delivery schedules. But that wasn't the end of the story.

Once the planes were delivered, problems cropped up everywhere. One website that tracks commercial aircraft accidents and equipment failure incidents chronicled 109 instances of everything from fuselage cracks to lithium battery fires, which forced a global grounding of the planes while an investigation took place. A January 2013 article in the UK Guardian described the Dreamliner as, "a nightmare waiting to happen." It would have been cheaper, faster, and safer to do the work in-house, which is exactly what one of the company's own senior tech analysts warned, way back in 2001.

Having learned from the Dreamliner fiasco, Boeing decided to keep the design and building of the fuselage, wings, interiors and many other major components for its next-generation 777X in-house. However, still relentlessly focused on weakening its supremely talented and experienced union workforce, Boeing initially announced that it would also assemble the 777X in South Carolina. Boeing's Seattle unions fought the move tooth-and-nail, and finally the company relented, but only after the union agreed to end its members defined-benefit pension package in favor of a 401(k) plan and the state of Washington agreed to $8.7 billion in incentives, the largest state tax subsidy in U.S. history. What did Washington get in return? Boeing promptly shipped 4,300 jobs to Florida, Missouri, Alabama, and California. This shouldn't have come as a surprise. As the Seattle Times noted, Ray Goforth, Executive Director of the Society for Professional Engineering Employees in Aerospace (SPEEA), warned Washington Gov. Jay Inslee, before the bill was passed, that, "the legislation was crafted with loopholes that would allow Boeing to take the $9 billion and outsource jobs anyway."

Alas, all of Boeing's efforts may be for naught. In May 2018, a group of flight line mechanics at the South Carolina facility voted to join the Machinists Union. Boeing is intent on not giving up without a fight, and has promised to try to get the election nullified in court. But if it stands, this could be the first chink in Boeing's anti-union armor. If unions can ever successfully organize in a place like South Carolina, the whole south may no longer remain a sanctuary for companies that make billions but pay peanuts.

As the Boeing and GM examples prove, incentives don't guarantee that jobs will remain in the city or state which forks over the cash. Hell, they may not even remain in the country. More importantly, incentives don't create jobs; they simply redistribute employment. Foreign automakers began making vehicles in the U.S. in the 1980s for two reasons: First, to counteract protectionist arguments for higher tariffs on imported vehicles. Second, cars are bulky and heavy. A cargo ship that can carry 1,000 vehicles can carry tens of thousands of flat screen TVs or millions of smart phones. When labor costs can be pushed down to a certain point, it becomes economically advantageous to build some models in the U.S. rather than ship them from overseas. Therefore, if Volkswagen doesn't build its new SUV plant in Tennessee, it will build it in South Carolina, or Alabama, or some other state.

When Boeing moved its headquarters to Chicago, the same jobs moved to the new location. Every time a company relocates, some existing employees move, while others (especially those able to retire) elect to stay where they are. Then, somebody else gets hired to do their old job in the new location. In some instances, by consolidating operations from various other states, a company actually reduces the size of its workforce, resulting in a net loss of jobs.

Note: GM management deserves a good deal of the blame for the situation the company found itself in when car sales plummeted in 2007-08. Nevertheless, the fact remains that $1,500 of every car GM sold went to pay retiree pensions and health benefits that foreign manufacturers do not have to shoulder. So, Toyota could build the equivalent vehicle and sell it for $1,500 less, or it can put more features into a car and sell it for the same price as the equivalent GM model. (Although their situations varied somewhat, Ford and Chrysler were at a similar disadvantage.) It's also important to note that, when discussing quality issues that used to plague American-made cars, the men and women on the shop floor only assembled the cars, they didn't design them.

When companies move to more "business-friendly" states with lower wages, lower corporate taxes, and other incentives, the result is increased income inequality. Even though labor can be as low as 10-15% of total product cost, lower labor costs for business are really lower wages for employees. A 2014 study, by economists David Neumark and Jennifer Muz of the University of California, showed that lowering business costs to stimulate economic growth widened the gap between the richest segment of the population and those on the lower rungs of the economic ladder. "The same tax and cost related indexes that are associated with higher economic growth are also associated with increases in inequality." This should come as no surprise. When a company can lower its labor costs and tax burden, it can sell its product for the same price but make more profit. And who benefits from these higher profits? Executives and stockholders.

This brings us to the aspiring kingpins of tax incentive deals: FoxConn's project to build a new manufacturing plant in America, and Amazon's plans for a second corporate headquarters.

FoxConn is an interesting animal (in roughly the same sense that a hungry croc is interesting). It's a Taiwanese company, but its primary manufacturing facility is a notorious mega-plant in mainland China, where "brutal working conditions" hardly describe the situation. Anytime you have to erect suicide nets around your buildings to thwart workers trying to jump off the roof, things are way past bad. In 2017, FoxConn decided to build a plant in the U.S. This set off frantic bidding by states trying to give away as much as possible in order to land the plant with its lure of jobs. Ostensibly the plant will produce LCD panels for various electronic devices, but the real reason FoxConn came to America is up for conjecture. Maybe its management foresees the day when tariffs and import duties, or rising shipping costs, will negate the cost savings offered by offshore production. Maybe having jobs in America will create new opportunities for pressure on U.S. politicians. Or maybe FoxConn simply got so many goodies from Wisconsin -- ***$4 billion*** -- it just couldn't say no. As much as $1 billion of this giveaway is for roads, utilities, and other infrastructure upgrades which FoxConn was originally supposed to pay for, but is now being let off the hook for so taxpayers will have to foot the bill.

But hey, after all, what's $4 bil when the state Legislative Fiscal Bureau estimates that the money will not be recouped until 2043 at the earliest, and when FoxConn can replace most of its employees with robots by 2032. But the pillaging and giveaways don't end there. Now that the plant deal is signed, FoxConn wants a waiver from the Great Lakes Compact, which limits new or expanded diversion of water from the Great Lakes (to places not in the Great Lakes basin itself) to 100,000 gallons a day. How much does FoxConn propose to use?

### *Seven million gallons a day*.

Worse, where the Great Lakes Compact calls for diverted water to be treated and then returned to the source, an estimated 2.7 million gallons a day will be lost through evaporation and thus not returned to the lake. Since Racine, where the new plant will be located, straddles parts of both the Great Lakes Basin and the Mississippi River basin, it is likely that this diversion will be approved, or if a waiver is denied, that the decision will be overturned in court.

As if this isn't bad enough, thanks to the appalling SCOTUS ruling in *Kelo v. New London* discussed in Chapter 13, in 2018, Wisconsin started using eminent domain to seize private property that was allegedly "economically blighted" in order to give FoxConn the land the state had promised. So, the state is not only giving away its own tax revenues, it is trying to give away its residents' property, including, in at least one case, a family's dream house that is less than a year old. Beltmag.com, which covers news of interest to the Farm Belt states, featured a scathing article about this injustice from Lawrence Tabak. Here are a few choice quotes from those faced with eviction:

> The Village is telling us our land is worthless, while at the same time you're telling Foxconn it's the best property in the world. I don't know how any of you guys can sit here and do this.

> I've lived in my home for 28 years. I'm a tax-paying citizen and I deserve better than this, to just be kicked to the curb and thrown out of my residence.

*Kelo v. New London*: Thanks, John Paul Stevens, Anthony Kennedy, David Souter, Ruth Bader Ginsberg, and Steven Breyer. *And fuck you.*

The sordid FoxConn tale took a number of twists in the fall of 2018. First, FoxConn announced that its original $10 billion investment would be scaled down to a much smaller $2.5 billion, and the plant would make much smaller screens than the mammoth ones promised earlier. This meant that the original promise of 13,000 jobs would likely turn out to be much less, and the mix tilted heavily toward managerial and administrative positions, so-called "knowledge workers." Most of the assembly work would be done by -- you guessed it -- robots. Then came the announcement that, due to an alleged shortage of qualified local workers, FoxConn was considering bringing in **Chinese** workers. Finally, the legislative analyst's best-case projection of the subsidy being paid back by 2043 was contradicted by a sobering assessment published in Forbes by an economic professor at the University of Georgia, Jeffrey Dorfman, who said, "At $230,000 [or more] per job, there is no hope of recapturing the state funds spent."

With the $4.1 billion subsidy penciling out to an astronomical $315,000 per job, Wisconsin Governor Scott Walker, the moving force/prime patsy behind this boondoggle, attempted to distance himself from the project. But alas, it was too late. The Gods of Karma struck and he lost his reelection bid.

As for Amazon, for two years the mega-company engaged in a nationwide hunt for a location for its Second Headquarters, known by the acronym HQ2. Originally, 238 cities made bids. In 2017, Amazon narrowed the list down to 20 finalists. Finally, in November 2018, Amazon announced that it was splitting the project in two, with one part to be built in the Long Island City portion of Queens, New York, and the other in the Crystal City area of Virginia, just across the Potomac from DC. New York agreed to pony up at least $1.52 billion, and Virginia is dispensing a total of at least $596 million in state and local funds. Some observers think that by the time the dust clears, the total tab will come in at $3 billion.

The astounding part is, Amazon could have gotten much more. New Jersey agreed to fork over a total of $7 billion, and Maryland offered $8.5 billion. Why take the lower deals? One possible answer is that the whole HQ2 search was a charade from the beginning, a shakedown exercise to ensure that Amazon got the best possible deal for what it was always going to do: locate its new facilities in the two traditional American power centers of NY and DC. Being in Arlington, Virginia puts it close to both the various regulatory agencies that it needs to deal with (FAA, FCC, FTC, etc.), and the nation's premier lobbying firms. NY is the financial center of the economy and locating there also guarantees that state and city officials will be happy to help Amazon get whatever it might want.

Thankfully, not everyone was happy about the announcement. Incoming Congresswoman from Queens Alexandra Ocasio-Cortez immediately took to Twitter, reporting that her office was being flooded by calls expressing outrage. She condemned the idea of giving away a huge subsidy and tax breaks to a billion-dollar company when the city is struggling with a subway system on the verge of collapse. She also questioned whether Amazon will hire from the existing local workforce or merely bring in new workers who will drive up housing costs and displace current residents.

New York State Assemblyman Ron Kim announced that he was introducing legislation to void the deal and instead use the money, which he estimated at a total of $3 billion, to pay off the student debt hanging over the heads of one million state residents. Kim also dismissed the notion that this was some kind of second headquarters for Amazon. He claimed that it is really just a planned expansion of the company, and that the supposed 50,000 jobs that will be created across the two new locations were already, "in the pipeline."

How these deals will ultimately play out remains to be seen, but there is always the straw that breaks the camel's back. Maybe this will be the one for corporate welfare. Of course, it doesn't hurt that critics of the deal have pointed out that Amazon head Jeff Bezos, as the world's richest man, makes $191,000 a minute. *One-hundred-ninety-one-thousand-dollars a minute*. For running a company that pays no federal taxes. The best way to permanently stop these kinds of race-to-the-bottom corporate welfare rip-offs is to make them unconstitutional:

> **Section 6: No official or employee of a state or lesser jurisdiction of government shall offer or provide any subsidy or any reduction, deferment, or waiver of taxes, fees,**

**assessments, or cost of public services as an inducement to establish, conduct or expand any business. No official or employee of a state or lesser jurisdiction shall act in concert with another to evade the intent or effect hereof. Violation of such shall be a felony punishable by incarceration in a maximum security facility for a period, not subject to pardon, parole, commutation, suspension, or other reduction of sentence, of not less than ten years. Conviction or plea of guilty shall result in the forfeiture of all pension benefits accrued while in public office or employment.**

Enacting a National Industrial Policy that corrects all of the evil policies and activities described so far (and initially in Chapter 2: Larger Issues) will not be sufficient to cure our unemployment problems. Just getting all those jobs back from overseas will also not be enough. Neither will job re-training programs, or sending people back to college for more education. Millions of people with plenty of job skills, and high levels of education, are currently out of work, or working at jobs far below their qualifications, simply because *there are not enough jobs*.

Even worse, the relentless march of technology means that, in the future, there will be even fewer jobs. Forget about the reduction in store clerks brought about by self-checkout at markets and big box stores. Forget about robots in factories and warehouses. Amazon is pushing to allow drones to deliver packages. Sure, there are drawbacks to the idea. What about liability if a drone drops a package on someone? What about residential resistance to the constant whirring and whizzing over neighborhoods? But suppose Amazon is successful? It will surely be joined by other companies. Taking tens of thousands of delivery trucks off the road would ease traffic, and reduce carbon emissions, but what happens to all those UPS, DHL, and FedEx drivers? Same with Google, Tesla, GM, etc., and their plans for self-driving cars and trucks. Bye-bye truckers and taxi drivers.

What happens when we arrive at a point where the legal work force permanently outnumbers all available jobs by any significant margin? There are several options:

## Draconian Population Reduction

We could just let the least fortunate (or some would say, the laziest) die from starvation, suicide, and disease born of malnutrition and intolerable living conditions. I'm not joking. There are plenty of psychopaths at the top of the current food chain who view poor people, and those of a lower socioeconomic strata, as expendable. Their attitude is, "If these people are not productive, if they aren't smart enough to do well, what good are they?" No less a plutocrat than war criminal Henry Kissinger once referred to this great mass of people as "useless eaters." Of course, these psychopaths are often children of privilege who, as the saying goes, "Were born on third base and think they hit a triple." The problem with this approach is that expendable people tend not to go quietly. At some point, they recognize that there is no alternative but to fight back. On a small scale this results in increased crime. At a higher level, it produces riots, and even topples governments. At its apex, it devolves into civil war and the kind of dystopian landscape which has become a staple of novels and movies.

## Job Sharing

One partial solution could be public and private sector job-sharing, where two people both do the same job, probably at the same desk or work station, but only part-time. For example, one person works Monday, Tuesday, and a half-day Wednesday. The other person comes in on Wednesday and finishes the week. For jobs where the business is open every day, people work three days one week and four the next, or alternate months of three-day and four-day weeks.

The problem with job sharing is that both workers will probably have to earn enough to support themselves, or at least contribute their necessary share of their required family income. This means wages would have to increase significantly. In effect, people would be getting full-time pay for doing a part-time job. Although experts like Yves Smith at Naked Capitalism have cited studies that put labor at only 10-15% of the overall cost of manufacturing operations, staffing costs are often considerably higher in more service-oriented employment. This increase in wages would trigger a vicious perpetual inflationary circle where wages rise, then rising prices outstrip the buying power of those higher wages, which requires another increase in wages and so on.

## Workfare

Another partial solution is workfare, welfare tied to a weekly work obligation, where you are required to put in a set number of hours at some task in return for a monthly stipend. Australia has such a program, albeit with its share of shortcomings. Because it is a compulsory transitional program designed to tide recipients over and give them some work experience until they can get a regular job, many potential employers look askance at the participants, whom employers suspect may not actually be much inclined to work, or to do a good job if hired.

Here in the U.S., we have had a number of job training and re-training programs, but most are often nothing more than a token fig leaf for jobs lost thanks to phony trade bills like NAFTA. These programs tend to produce people trained for jobs that either don't exist, or not in sufficient numbers to employ the number of people in the program. The only people who benefit are politically-connected grifters who deliver the training while sucking at the government teat.

## Jobs Guarantee

With a Jobs Guarantee the federal government funds, and sometimes administers, programs that provide a guaranteed job at a living wage for everyone who is able to work. These jobs can span the entire spectrum, from infrastructure projects and environmental mitigation to artistic and cultural endeavors. The idea of using government funds to finance art or cultural efforts elicits howls of protest from those who fear that art, with a political or religious message with which they disagree, will be subsidized by their tax dollars. This is a valid concern, but should be directed toward setting parameters for the commissioning of works rather than a blanket prohibition. It's hard to see how objections could be raised to art depicting the great natural wonders of the country. Much of our modern urban and suburban landscape is so sterile, that works of art (statuary, monuments, historical replicas) could add a more appealing look, while also serving an educational function.

The classic example of a jobs program was FDR's Works Project Administration, which helped lift us out of the Depression. There are countless public buildings, bridges, dams, canals, and works of art that are still in use, or still being admired. And while the idea of guaranteeing someone a job would have been scoffed at by the majority of people just a few years ago, it is now making remarkable in-roads in terms of both public awareness and official consideration. In 2018, Bernie Sanders introduced a bill to establish such a program. It is not as comprehensive as what is proposed here, which will be decried by lots of opponents as just another cockamamie socialist scheme to destroy the rugged individualism that marks America's greatness. Nor will Bernie's bill ever be enacted by a Republican-controlled Congress, or signed by a president like Trump. But history has shown that control of Congress and the White House changes, and with Congress, sometimes rather quickly. Make no mistake: no action ever occurs without discussion first, and Sanders has put the concept on the national discussion agenda.

## Universal Basic Income or
## Supplemental Income Guarantee

A Universal Basic Income (UBI), is a minimum payment made to all citizens (or residents) by the government, without regard to their other sources of income. Naturally, the thought of giving government money to people who are already well-off elicits howls of rage, and justifiably so. By comparison, a Supplemental Income Guarantee (SIG), is a means-tested distribution of funds in which people with a certain level of income receive no money at all, and those below that level get pro-rated amounts offset against whatever other income they may have. For example, a sole head of household may get a higher stipend than someone whose spouse, parent, etc., has a regular job. The idea is to get everyone up to a minimum acceptable standard of living.

As a stand-alone proposition, UBI is not a panacea. In fact, it's a downright sinister plan to undermine wages. In 2018, Chris Hedges, a former divinity student who became a Pulitzer Prize-winning war correspondent and is now a leading civil liberties activist and author, wrote a scathing takedown of proposals for a UBI put forth by various oligarch billionaires, such as Mark Zuckerberg and Elon Musk. Hedges nailed their proposals for what they are: an attempt to ensure that "future consumers, plagued by job insecurity, substandard wages, automation and crippling debt peonage" will still have enough money to buy what the rich will be trying to sell. These oligarchs are desperately seeking some way to prop up consumer spending, without actually improving the lives of those consumers, and especially without seeding any of the economic control with which the rich now hold the country hostage. The rich want, as Hedges puts it, "a deindustrialized wasteland," where wages remain artificially low, and desperate citizens can be pitted against each other for economic scraps, left over from the banquet tables of the elite.

Unfortunately, all of these concepts -- a Jobs Guarantee, UBI, and a Supplemental Income Guarantee -- share two enormous problems. First, they run counter to America's work-hard-and-get-ahead, Land-of-Opportunity, tradition. Because this attitude is so engrained, squaring this circle will be an enormous task. Outraged cries of socialism and worse yet, communism, will reverberate across the land. Second, those who do not understand how the economy and government finance really work, will proclaim that we cannot afford the enormous cost of a program like this. Let's put that idea to rest right off the bat:

### *As a sovereign government that prints its own currency, the United States can never go broke.*

This is the basis of the economic doctrine known as Modern Monetary Theory. MMT is based on how actual, real-world fiscal policy has worked since governments went off the precious metals standards. (U.S. currency used to be redeemable in gold or silver, but Nixon did away with that. Likewise, the British pound used to be redeemable in sterling silver.) Now, we have what is known as *fiat currency*, which means that it is money because the government says it is. Another way to explain fiat currency is that it's money because the government will accept it as payment for taxes.

If you find MMT hard to accept, consider the following: If we're constrained by some artificial spending limit, why is it critical *only* when the subject is healthcare, education, social services, etc.? How come we can waste trillions on wars at the drop of a hat, without any concern for the effects on the budget deficit? How come any time the banks need bailing out, or the elite want another rapacious tax cut, somehow Congress is able to pull it off?

The answer is:

> **Worries about the federal deficit are all bullshit, economic fakery designed to serve the elite and screw the rest of us**.

And don't fall for the argument that, "government has to be run like a household, or a business." Households can't print money, and neither can businesses, so the next time a politician or expert tells you that the federal government must be run like a household budget, tell them that they're both a liar *and* a moron.)

Don't take my word for it. No less a conservative icon than former vice-president Dick Cheney said, "Reagan proved that deficits don't matter." Cheney and his puppet, George W., racked up deficits that made Reagan look like piker. Now, the Trump tax cut has created monster future deficits in the many trillions. Watch as the GOP bastards in Congress use this as an excuse to attempt cutting Social Security, Medicare, and other progressive safety net programs. Deficits are always a handy excuse for why, as the derisive adage goes, "we can't have nice things."

So, if the federal government doesn't need tax revenues to finance government operations and programs, what's the purpose of federal taxes? Good question, and there are several answers. One is that taxes serve to remind everyone that we should pay a price, variable according to income, for the benefits we receive as citizens and legal residents who work here. A second is to help control the supply of money in circulation, as a way to control inflation. A third is to destroy wealth, to keep the rich from becoming too disconnected from everyone else. If destroying wealth sounds like some kind of nefarious and evil Marxist plot, well, it probably is. But that doesn't mean it doesn't serve a useful function. Most people are not against others getting rich, they just don't want them to freeload off the rest of society, and not get an inordinate return for the benefits they receive. That seems fair. To me, anyway.

It must also be made clear that MMT *only* applies at the federal level. States and municipalities cannot print their own currency, so at those levels of government, tax and fee revenues limit what government can afford. This is why something like SIG or a Jobs Guarantee needs to be funded at the federal level, but can be administered by states and local government entities. And even if the relationship of spending to taxes was a legitimate issue at the national level, we could always solve that problem simply by raising taxes on the obscenely wealthy, right?

Damn right.

While it will take a long, determined effort to make most people realize the truth about MMT, it will take even more work to demonstrate that, even after we re-shore all those lost jobs, the labor pool will exceed workforce needs. When the new economic reality sinks in, a solution awaits: a combination of a Jobs Guarantee with a Job Sharing/Supplemental Income Guarantee program.

> **Section 7: Within one year of ratification of this Amendment, Congress shall create a federally-funded Jobs Guarantee, paying a living wage to all citizens unable to find other employment. Where state, municipal, or district administration of programs is deemed most effective, funds shall be distributed accordingly. Jobs created under this program shall encompass all endeavors which add to the safety, defense, environmental protection, economy, education, or cultural enrichment of the nation. For those who, by disability or other legitimate reason, are unable to work, or whose part-time employment is insufficient to provide the adequate necessities of life, Congress shall institute a Supplemental Income Guarantee.**

Most people want to work; they derive satisfaction from doing a job and being a productive member of society. In fact, many people who slide into substance abuse, or commit suicide, do so because they have lost any hope of having a job that provides a measure of self-respect. A main driver of the women's rights movement was the desire of women to get out of the house, to show that they could contribute. (As they had so undeniably demonstrated during WWII.) These women craved the interaction with other people, the challenge of the job, the feeling of independence and self-worth that having a job produces. It was a lack of employment opportunities that drove so many housewives to seek solace in alcohol against lives of quiet desperation.

With a Supplemental Income Guarantee, the government can fill the income gap for those who have to share a job (in either the public or private sector) with someone else, thus allowing wages and prices to grow at a controlled rate. A Supplemental Income Guarantee would also cover those who are too physically or mentally infirm to participate in the normal Jobs Guarantee program. This includes people whose ability to work is compromised by an obligation to care for aging parents, severely disabled children, etc. (Whether these people would come under the SIG, or their caregiver job simply becomes part of the larger Jobs Guarantee program, is a semantic exercise of little consequence.)

With a federally-funded Jobs Guarantee, governments at all levels can address the needs of society in a fast, comprehensive manner. Much like the Universal Military Service program described in Chapter 17, think of how great it would be if every time you went to the Post Office, the DMV, your local city hall or library, there was ample staff and wait times were minimal. Imagine the benefits of having multiple teachers' aides in classrooms, or having free, quality childcare for parents. Think of all the environmental clean-up programs that could combine young people, during their military service period, with older workers who would otherwise be excluded from the work force.

Yes, indeed, think how great it would be.

# Chapter 20

# EMPLOYMENT & RETIREMENT PROTECTIONS

Unions, both in the public and private sector, have fallen into disfavor with much of the public. Partly this is the result of a long, sustained, brilliantly crafted propaganda campaign orchestrated by big business. A key part of this campaign has been convincing white-collar workers that they are superior, that they're not really part of the *labor* class, are better able to care for themselves, and thus not in need of union representation. It's a classic example of class warfare. Those who buy into this delusional argument should remember one truism:

*If someone else signs your paycheck, you're a worker, a part of labor.*

The reduction in union power is also due to decades of decapitating unions by moving jobs to foreign countries or Right-to-Work (For-Less) states. It's also partly the result of adverse rulings by courts, and the National Labor Relations Board, which have enabled companies to mount intense and highly sophisticated campaigns against union organizing efforts. Tactics include high-pressure campaigns against union organizing votes, intimidation, discrimination in work assignments, threats of physical violence, and termination. Currently, there are no criminal penalties for these actions, which makes trying to start a union at a person's place of employment a risky endeavor.

Union workers have been blamed for poor quality products, especially in the auto industry. While, in some instances, slipshod workmanship took place, it should be remembered that a lot of the blame belonged to those white-collar types in the design, engineering, procurement, and risk management areas. Workers on the assembly line did not design the cars, did not decide to cut corners on materials, and did not decide to sell unsafe cars just because the cost of settling lawsuits was less than the cost of fixing the problem.

Another factor in the decline of unions is the fact that younger generations lack knowledge of what things were before unions. Just like today's youth cannot imagine a world without smart phones or the Internet, they also take for granted days off, vacations, and safe work environments, as if they were the natural order of things rather than benefits for which earlier generations fought, and sometimes died.

Unions themselves bear much of the blame. Too many times, they have insisted on policies and procedures that protect the lazy employee as much as the industrious one, the slipshod as much as the diligent. That's because unions do not exist to protect workers; they exist to protect workers *who belong to that union.* This leads to situations where the ability to do the job is secondary to the ability to also get into the relevant union. Some unions have apprentice programs that offer a pathway to union membership. Other unions have a system whereby, if you get the job, you qualify for union membership, and then can work your way up the ladder at your employer. But many unions operate as closed clubs, which naturally generates animosity from those who are excluded, especially since entry into union membership is often affected by nepotism or favoritism, or even racial bias. The Writers Guild -- which insists that it is not a union despite the fact that it collects dues, negotiates wages and working conditions, and occasionally conducts strikes -- does absolutely nothing to assist outsiders in breaking into a writing career, but is only too happy to pounce once you've sold a script or convinced a company to hire you. The first call you get is from the Membership Office, but don't expect to hear congratulations on starting your career. The only thing that call will be about is reminding you to get your membership initiation fee and initial dues payment in right away. Far too many other unions and guilds have a similar attitude. It's all very insular.

Union leadership at the national level has also become a weak, sniveling, captured appendage of the Democratic party. Fat-cat union leaders, pulling down salaries of up to $400K a year, have less and less in common with rank-and-file members. These so-called leaders talk a good game, but they always fold and support Dem presidents or Dem congresses when they stab workers (union and non-union alike) in the back. By failing to deliver real, tangible benefits, unions have diminished their only true selling point. However, one fact remains:

**No union ever drove a company out of business with demands for better wages and working conditions *unless that company faced non-union competition*.**

If all the companies in the same field have equal labor rates, economic winners will be determined by which has the best product, or provides the best service. Instead of employees who actually do the work suffering in a price war, it will be the profits of the owners, and the bonuses of the executive ranks. The best way to improve the internal operation of unions is to put more people in them. Unions like to preach "solidarity" with other unions, and with workers in general. When the number of people enrolled in unions reaches a certain critical mass, real solidarity will likely help foster a climate of transparency and accountability. Therefore:

## The 44th Amendment --
## Employment & Retirement Protections

**Section 1: All citizens and legal residents shall have the absolute unrestrained right to form or join unions, to participate in union activities, and to have said unions engage in collective bargaining, including strikes and boycotts, on their behalf. It shall be a felony punishable by incarceration in a maximum security facility for a period, not subject to pardon, parole, commutation, suspension, or other reduction of sentence, of not less than ten years, to interfere with, or retaliate for, the free exercise of these rights.**

Just before this book went to press, the Supreme Court issued its eventually-to-be-infamous *Janus* decision, in which it ruled that public employees cannot be compelled to pay *any* portion of union dues, including that which supports core union activities -- the negotiation of wages and working conditions, pension benefits, grievance procedures, and protections against arbitrary or wrongful termination -- if the employee disagrees with any policy or political position the union takes. The contrived First Amendment basis behind this ruling is that people should not have to support a union *in any way* if they disagree with *any* aspect of union activity, especially union support of political candidates and parties whose policy positions conflict with those of the employee.

The Court, anxious to further eviscerate the already shrinking power of unions, conveniently neglected to address the elephant in the room, namely the other laws and judicial precedents that require unions to provide services and benefits to *all* employees in any workplace covered by union jurisdiction. Thus, those who refuse to pay union dues still get all the benefits of union representation. These *free riders* get the same salaries as their union co-workers, the same vacation and sick leave benefits, the same workplace safety and termination protections. The goal of *Janus* is to slash the money public employee unions get from dues, thus restricting the ability of the union to advocate for and protect workers, while at the same time weakening the unions' ability to be effective in the political arena.

Historically, except for the brief period from 1953 through 1969 under Chief Justice Earl Warren, the Supreme Court has always been a conservative, reactionary body preoccupied with the rights of businesses, investors, and land owners, the hostility of the current court toward unions should come as no surprise. That the Court would stretch the scope of the First Amendment to justify *Janus* is also just another example of how the justices on the Court create or infer some rights when it suits them, and ignore obvious others -- *Can you say, the right to good government?* -- when it does not.

Given that Trump, after his victory in the Kavanaugh nomination battle, may eventually get the opportunity to appoint additional arch-conservative justices, any hopes that the Court will reverse itself on *Janus* in the coming decades seems fanciful at best. Likewise, proposing a constitutional amendment to reverse *Janus* would be fraught with danger. Given ingrained resistance to the concept of unions among many voters, trying to include such an amendment could well sink the entire Restoration Amendments movement. It just isn't worth the risk.

Nevertheless, two factors can vastly reduce the impact of *Janus*. Section 2 of the 33rd Amendment, The Public Financing of Elections, will prevent unions and employers alike, whether in the public or private sector, from participating in the electoral process. This eliminates some of the First Amendment justification for *Janus*.

However, even if unions and employers cannot back candidates and parties, individual union members, government officials, and business people will still retain their personal right to endorse candidates and ballot measures, and to volunteer in campaigns during non-work hours. Inevitably, this will produce situations where some potential union members have a moral, philosophical, or religious objection to a position taken by others in the union. There will also be some rugged individualists who cling to the idea that they can fend better for themselves by negotiating personally on the subject of compensation, terms of employment, and so forth. The obvious solution is to let them.

By the same token, those who eschew the power of union representation should also relinquish any attendant benefits. Shocked to discover that the salary you negotiated is less than that of your union co-workers? *Tough shit*. Cheated out of overtime on your paycheck? *Get a lawyer*. Wrongfully terminated? *Keep paying that lawyer*. But don't suddenly try to avail yourself of union grievance procedures, or union attorneys with expertise in labor law, and so forth. You want to be on your own? ***Be on your own***. Therefore:

> **Section 2: No union shall provide, or be required to provide, any benefit or service, including but not limited to: negotiation of wages, job classifications, promotion criteria, working conditions, grievance procedures, or seniority rights; protection from termination; or inclusion in any pension plan, to any person who elects not to join said union when eligible to do so.**

Some will argue that this could boomerang, by encouraging government agencies to pay higher salaries to those who decline union membership, because the government body will save on the back-end in terms of pension funding. This is a possibility, but not one to which I give much credence. The reason involves my next subject, pensions.

Providing for workers during their productive life is not enough. Some people love their jobs, and work happily right up to death's door. But most people cannot, and do not wish, to work forever. This is particularly true when the work involves strenuous physical exertion, takes place outdoors in the elements, or imposes long-term health consequences. That's why a critical part of a person's working life is the ability to provide for retirement. Other than those who are fortunate enough to have significant investment income, this is best accomplished through a combination of Social Security and a pension.

Many people fundamentally misunderstand the concept of pensions. Pensions are not simply payments made to retired workers. Pensions and Social Security are not older retired workers freeloading off younger generations who are still working. ***Pensions are payment of deferred compensation***. Pensions result from an agreement between workers and their employer to put aside a certain amount of money, each month, so that it accumulates, and is then available to be paid out at a prescribed rate after the worker retires. Even interest that pension funds earn from investments is still earned by the workers, because it's *their* money that is invested.

Some critics ask, "What about retirees who end up being paid more than the amount they paid in?" That's the wrong question. The correct one is, "What about employees who paid into the plan but don't live long enough to get their contribution back?"

With the exception of some small local businesses, employers, in general, *hate* employees, and therefore they hate pensions. Big corporations are interested in their employees, considered a necessary evil, only to the extent that they provide current value in excess of their compensation. Pensions represent money, which must be set aside now, so that it can be paid in the future to past employees *who will then no longer be producing for the company*. Pensions represent money that management can't give to itself, or to stockholders, in the form of salaries, bonuses, dividends, stock buy-backs, or spend on market expansion. At a more visceral level, pensions are also an uncomfortable reminder to the titans of industry that no matter how brilliant their app is, or how many robots they employ, their success depends, at some level, on the effort and ability of those regular people whom they shun as inferiors.

In tying companies to pensions (and thus to workers), pensions also tie workers to the company. Pensions give workers and retirees a stake in the continued viability of the company. Ever see ads or signs that say, "Established 1953" or, "In business for 75 years" or, "Family-owned for three generations?" Phrases like those are designed to convey to new customers a feeling that the company makes and stands behind a good product, or provides service in a dependable, timely manner. This is why brand names are so important. Whether it's Chevy or Toyota for cars, Frigidaire or Samsung for appliances, Levi's or Versace for apparel, a brand's importance results from having a long history of supplying products, **made by the people now collecting pensions,** that the buyer believes have value equal to, or exceeding, their cost.

Pensions allow society to have a self-sustaining circle of life: When their productive life is over, parents with pensions are able to retire and live decently, without being a burden on either the children they worked to raise and educate, or to government and society at large. Absent adequate pensions, people who are no longer able to work are either forced into a depraved existence without dignity, or must be supported by their children, who then find it difficult, sometimes impossible, to provide adequately for their own children. Money that must go to aging parents cannot go to growing children. Retirees with adequate pensions are not a burden on their offspring, and are often able to help with things like a down payment on a first house, or college costs for grandchildren. The decades-long attack on defined benefit pensions is a lynchpin in the War on the Middle Class.

In all honesty, *the ideal natural order for business is slave labor*. Fortunately, true slavery is no longer socially acceptable. So, the economic elite opt for the next best thing: de facto, or virtual slavery.

Virtual slavery starts by off-shoring, which creates downward pressure on wages for jobs that remain and can't be outsourced. (If you run a restaurant in Dallas, your staff pretty much has to be *in Dallas*, not New Delhi.) Outsourcing also eliminates the power of those pesky unions, with their demands for safe working conditions, vacations, humane work schedules and, of course, fair pay.

Wages can stagnate over long periods, as they have since the 1970s, but prices rarely do. This sets the stage for the second step in creating virtual slavery: consumer debt, especially credit card debt and, in the run-up to the Great Recession, using home equity as an ATM. Excessive debt fuels a delusional economy, where people spend money they don't really have, on everything from school supplies and college tuition to flat screen TV's and boats. It may be fun while it lasts, but it never lasts forever. Miniscule monthly payments are designed to encourage over-spending, but inevitably result in a massive buildup of overhanging debt. When things go south, as they did in 2007-2008, the bottom falls out. People no longer have money to spend. Companies fail due to the inability of people to afford their products and services. This puts more people out of work and that further reduces consumer spending. Large numbers of people end up broke, whatever assets they had having been swallowed up by creditors in bankruptcy. If they're over fifty, chances of finding another job, especially one that pays decently, are slim. People who tried to maintain their middle-class lifestyle, despite the ever-decreasing buying power of stagnant wages, found themselves moving in with parents, grandparents, or adult children.

Compounding all this is the skyrocketing cost of college tuition. If retiring parents have adequate pensions to supplement their monthly Social Security checks, their children may have a fighting chance to eventually dig their way out. But, if recent grads must also contribute to parental support, there is just no way. Their entire life becomes one long story of debt for student loans, credit cards, mortgages, end-of-life care for their parents, and then finally, themselves. There is no light at the end of the tunnel. Because it's not a tunnel, it's just a very dark cave.

Note: One solution to the problem of college costs is free public university for all who desire it, and meet appropriate entrance criteria. But that requires federal funding, because individual states could not afford it. It also begs questions about the supply of facilities, teachers, and so forth. A well-crafted law would address these issues, but a constitutional amendment is probably not the correct approach. And forgiveness of existing student loans, which would give a massive boost to the economy, is also only possible at the federal level.

The solution for the issue of secure pensions is to require all but the very smallest employers to provide safe, secure, adequately funded and insured pensions *that are portable from job to job*. Most small companies would probably end up joining a multi-employer pension system geared specifically to their needs. And even when the employer is so small that they are not required to be in a pension fund, their individual employees must have the option to have a portion of their salary -- and a matching contribution from their employer -- diverted to a pension plan. Granted, many small business employees would likely elect not to make pension contributions. Some will be young enough that they do not yet see the wisdom of planning for retirement. Others will have such pressing current expenses that they just cannot go without that extra money in their weekly paycheck. But the system proposed here at least puts the decision in their hands.

> **Section 3: All business entities with five or more employees shall enroll in a pension plan having fair and reasonable conditions for vesting and enrollment, which ensures the payment of a defined-benefit pension to employees who meet fair and reasonable retirement criteria, and which is transferable by the employee from employer to employer. Such pensions shall be approved, regulated, enforced, and guaranteed in full by the Federal Pension Benefit Guaranty Agency.**

> **Section 4: Individual employees of firms with fewer than five workers may elect to enroll in a pension plan of their choice, have a portion of their salary contributed thereto, and have that contribution matched by their employer.**

Interestingly enough, while some employees of very small businesses might opt out of pension plan enrollment, a lot of their employers may elect to join such pension plans, rather than take the risks associated with private retirement accounts like 401K plans. (More on the fatal defects of 401K plans later in this chapter.) Therefore, pensions, as a key to a secure and dignified retirement, must be sacrosanct:

> **Section 5: In business bankruptcy proceedings, pension claims, including contributions for pensions already vested but not yet exercised, shall be supreme above all other claims, including for taxes. No court or government entity shall in any way void, reduce, or delay payment of any pension, or post-employment benefit, negotiated between employer and employee. To assist in funding pension**

**obligations, courts may confiscate, from those charged with responsibility for operation of the enterprise, any previous compensation which the court considers excessive.**

For those executives who like to reward themselves with golden parachutes, while the businesses they ran plummet to Earth:

**Section 6: In business bankruptcy proceedings, unpaid wages and severance benefits shall have second priority, after pension obligations, before taxes and other creditors. No bonus or severance benefit shall be paid to any executive of a bankrupt entity unless all pension contributions, unpaid wages, and severance benefits have been paid to non-executive employees.**

People want to run a company, and make decisions that impact thousands of workers? Great. That's the true heart of free enterprise. But, they don't get to privatize the profits and then socialize the losses. Make great decisions and get rich? Wonderful. Screw the pooch and kill the company? You suffer at least as bad a fate as those who depended on you for their livelihood.

Public employee pensions are a horse of a different color because, in addition to the employer and the employees, two other parties are involved: taxpayers and politicians. Unfortunately, when it comes to public employee bargaining agreements, the taxpayers are betrayed by both Democrats (who don't care about anything except using the negotiations to gain or repay union campaign support), and Republicans (who are dead set against taxes on businesses and the wealthy to help fund these benefits). This toxic stew has led to a system of overly lavish, and yet wildly underfunded, public employee pension systems.

How lavish?

In 2012, over 12,000 former California state employees received pensions in excess of $100,000 a year from CalPERS. The most egregious at that time was Michael D. Johnson, a former administrator of the County of Solano, at $371,042, which is $30,920 *a month*. There were another 6,600 retired teachers/school administrators who got over $100,000 a year from CalSTRS, the teachers and school administrators fund. Leading that list was the former head of the Modesto City Elementary School District, James C. Enochs, at $302,064. An additional 2,200 retirees from the University of California Retirement Plan took home over $100,000 annually, led by Marvin Marcus, formerly of UCLA, at $337,346/year.

Five short years later, those numbers had skyrocketed. Thanks to Cost-of-Living adjustments, Mr. Johnson's top pension of $371K in 2012 had jumped to $390,485 in 2017. According to a story by Jeff Housemen in the Riverside Press-Enterprise, which was then picked up by dailynews.com, using figures compiled by the group Transparent California, the total number of retirees collecting six figure pensions grew by 63%, almost doubling to 23,000. According to an article in Forbes by contributor Adam Andrzejewski, those six-figure CalPERS pensions total $2.8 billion and are equivalent to the state income taxes of 1.6 million Californians. Houseman's article notes that when you add in the numbers from other California public retirement plans, like CalSTRS, LAPD, the U.C. system, and various other small plans, over 53,000 people collected six figure public pensions in California in 2017.

Illinois isn't far behind. In 2013, it had 9,900 retirees receiving $100,000 or more annually, but that was an increase of 47% in just one year. In fact, the top 200 highest Illinois state pensions are all in excess of $189,000. Leading the list is Dr. Alon P. Winnie, who makes his California counterparts look like pikers. In 2013, Dr. Winnie became the first Illinois public employee to receive an annual pension of over a half-million dollars. By 2018, it was up to $508,597.

According to TaxpayersUnitedofAmerica.org, others living high on the taxpayer hog included: [Emphasis added.]

> Tapas Das Gupta, retired from the University of Illinois at Chicago. He collected a cool **$439,672** in his last annual pension payment and will accumulate a stunning **$5.2 million** in lifetime pension payments.
>
> Beverly Lopatka retired from DuPage Government HSD 88 at the ripe old **age of 56** and has an annual pension of **$399,652**, with a staggering estimated lifetime payout of **$11,524,643**. Her contribution of the estimated lifetime payout would be only **0.8%**.
>
> The highest lifetime payout estimate goes to Larry K. Fleming, from ... school district Lincolnshire-Prairie View 103 ... at the **age of 55** with a cushy annual pension of **$258,163**, he will accumulate a breathtaking **$11,868,155** in pension payments over a normal lifetime.

Taxpayers United calculated the lifetime pension benefit according to the retiree's age at retirement, their initial benefit compounded by 3% annual cost-of-living adjustments, and a life expectancy of 85 years. Three years earlier, in 2010, the website ForeclosureBlues.com used a similar formula to project that the Top 100 Highest Paid retirees from the Illinois State Teacher's Retirement System will collect nearly ***$888 million*** over their combined lifetimes.

New Jersey saw the number of its retirees earning pensions in excess of $100,000 jump by 75% just between 2010 and 2013. Still, residents of New Jersey might consider themselves lucky. The state only has a little over 1,700 members in the Six Figure Pension Club, and the highest annual benefit is a mere $195,000 a year.

Across the river in New York, the number of six-figure pensions continues to rise, but things still might be considered good compared to California and Illinois. According to the New York Observer, in 2018, the New York State and Local Retirement System had only 3,817 retirees in the Six Figure Pension Club. However, this fund does not cover retirees from New York City. Nor is it clear whether this total includes those in the NYFD retirement fund which, in the past, has refused to supply data, even though it's required by state public information laws. The highest paid retiree (that we know about) was Dr. Shashikant Lele, formerly of the Roswell Park Cancer Institute, at $436,356.

Typical of the pension abuse that takes place in many states is the case of Long Island, New York's James H. Hunderfund. In 2006, he started collecting a pension of $316,245, slightly more than three-quarters of his $400,310 a year final salary from the ironically named Commack Union Free Schools district. The next year, 2007, Hunderfund began serving as the "interim" superintendent of the Malverne School District. In 2014-2015, his MSD salary was $235,238. Let's see: $316,245 + $235,238 = $515,483. How ever does Mr. Hunderfund make ends meet?

Defenders of public employee pensions counter by arguing that the average retiree pension is far less than the exorbitant examples cited above. For 2017, CalPERS put the average retiree pension at about $2,700 a month or $32,400 per year, after an average length of employment of just over 20 years. However, that figure is deceptive in that it fails to consider how the average is pulled down by older retirees, who had far lower salaries (and thus lower pensions), and by people who retired with as few as five years, the minimum required to vest in the plan. By comparison, seven years ago in 2011, Steve Malanga published this in The City Journal:

> State treasurer Bill Lockyer, a Democrat who has received union backing in his political campaigns, claimed that the average retired state worker in California was getting just $2,500 a month in benefits.

When *Contra Costa Times* columnist Daniel Borenstein investigated, he found that Lockyer's average included people who had worked for the state for as little as five years and were collecting partial benefits, as well as those who had retired years before the state significantly enhanced pension benefits in 1999.

But if you limit the average to currently retiring workers who have spent more time working for California and thus can retire with full benefits, a different picture emerges, Borenstein found. The average state worker retiring in 2009 with full benefits received a pension of nearly $67,000 a year. Local government workers in California did even better. Looking at his own town, Contra Costa, Borenstein found an average pension for new retirees of $85,500 annually. There's more: though government workers don't automatically qualify for Social Security, about 65 percent of the retired government employees who are members of CalPERS, the state's government-employee pension system, do get Social Security benefits because the state has made contributions for them for years. The average benefit comes to $19,000 a year. So sweet are California's pension deals that a report by the state's Little Hoover Commission, a government watchdog agency, estimated that the average government worker retiring with full benefits and Social Security will get 109 percent of his final working salary as a pension.

Still, union advocates have found that citing misleading pension figures makes for effective sound bites. During a rally against New Jersey governor Chris Christie's pension reforms last year, an official of the Communications Workers of America claimed that the average pension in New Jersey was a mere $20,000 a year for state workers and $13,000 for local workers. But the *Newark Star-Ledger* reported strikingly different numbers: an average of nearly $40,000 a year for state workers who retired with 25 years of service; $46,486 for teachers; and $73,571 for police and firefighters.

Similar statistics in New York are just as deceptive. Union reps argue that state workers receive just $19,000 a year, on average, but the actual median pension for those recently retired with full benefits is more than $50,000 a year, according to state pension-fund documents. For New York teachers, the median pension is often reported as slightly more than $48,000; for those retiring now with full benefits, though, it's about $71,000.

The difference in these numbers is significant, especially because in most state systems, current workers are earning benefits at the same high levels as recent retirees, not at the levels of those who retired years ago or retired with partial benefits. That's why the annual contributions that many governments must make to pension systems for current workers are exploding. Take the case of a New York teacher retiring at 60 with a $71,000 pension. To finance that pension over the retiree's expected remaining lifetime would require a guaranteed lifetime annuity of $1.2 million, according to a pension calculator constructed by the Manhattan Institute's Empire Center for New York State Policy.

Let's be honest here. The purpose of pensions was, and should still be, to ensure that workers can retire at a reasonable age and live out their years in reasonable comfort and security, without being a burden to either their family or society. That's why, in high-cost states like California and New York, pensions of $60,000 to $80,000 are probably not excessive. But pensions were never intended to ensure that travel agencies, cruise ship operators, and motor home manufacturers remain profitable. The biggest problem rests with the obscenely lavish, uncapped pensions at the top. This is compounded by the deliberate underfunding of many state plans. In general, Republican politicians hate imposing taxes, and have contempt for public employees. Democrats, who want to curry favor with the public employee unions that support their campaigns, are also loathe to provoke voter anger by arguing for more taxes to pay for those pension bennies. So, they employ three tricks:

- Trick One is to kick the can down the road, which is what happened in the 1990s. By the time the bill came due, the politicians who approved or supported increasing pension benefits were either in higher office, or out of office entirely, and collecting their own cushy pensions from the same public employee pension fund.

- Trick Two is to invest the money in stocks, bonds, and real estate ventures, and then game the projections of the returns the funds will make on those investments, to make it seem like there is plenty of money in the fund, when actually there are huge underfunded deficits. Most underfunded state employee pension plans use an annual projected Return On Investment figure of around 7%. The problem is, for decades, no pension fund has come close to consistently earning returns anywhere near that rate. Over the past 20 years, the true annual return has hovered around 3%. And since these are compounded projections, every year in which the real ROI is significantly lower than predicted, the deficit which must be made up grows, meaning that even if a state fund hits the magic 7% figure the following year, it has still fallen behind in terms of the money needed to provide for pensions coming due in the future.

- Trick Three is for the state and local governments to simply not make the legally-required annual contributions necessary to meet actuarial projections. This is often rationalized and defended as a "one time only" emergency measure to balance

the state's budget. The legislature and governor
promise to make it all up next year, when things are
better. Except things don't get better, and even if
they do, spending for current projects that were
also postponed takes precedence over back-filling
pension obligations.

How big and how dangerous are these underfunded public
pension liabilities? That depends on how you define the problem.
By sheer underfunded dollar volume, California leads the way at
somewhere between $213 billion and $500 billion, with a worst
case scenario of as much as $1 *trillion*. The low figure is based on
the optimistic 7.5% ROI projections of CalPERS and CalSTRS (the
teacher's retirement system which is $70 billion underfunded),
plus $63 billion in unfunded retiree health benefits. The $500
billion figure comes from using more realistic ROI projections,
and adding in the liabilities of the University of California
Retirement Fund. Because the deficit will continue to compound,
the CalSTRS' current $70 billion estimate -- which CalSTRS itself
admits is "unsustainable" under current funding formulas -- could
balloon to as much as $600 billion by 2043. This is one reason the
top end estimate of $1 trillion might not be unreasonable.

Judged on the basis of how much each taxpayer owes (per capita)
and how close the state fund is to going broke, Illinois is number
one. In New Jersey, the situation is also dire. Back in 1994, one of
Governor Christine Todd Whitman's first acts was to engineer a
30% cut in the state income tax and balance the budget by
eliminating a $3 billion payment to the state retirement fund.
Twenty years later, Gov. Chris Christie got a judge's okay to cut
$900 million from the state's required 2014 pension fund
contribution. When the total robbed from the pension fund hit
$2.4 billion, the unions sued, but eventually lost in state court. On
his way out the door when his term was over, Christie tried to put
some lipstick on the pig by cutting the ROI that the pension fund
used to calculate earnings from 7.65% to 7%. But within months

after taking office in 2018, new Governor Phil Murphy rescinded that change on the grounds that having to make up the $400 million difference would put undue stress on local governments. One can only wonder what kind of undue stress the entire state is going to be in when it finally comes time to pay the piper.

It's not only blue states that are in trouble. In 2011, the Wall Street Journal profiled ten states with dangerously underfunded pension liabilities, including Colorado, Kansas, Oklahoma, New Hampshire, and Kentucky. Two years later, an article by California Political News compared California with other states using new, more strict accounting rules for calculating true pension debt. Besides those already named, that report identified Mississippi, Connecticut, and Alaska as states with big pension problems looming on the horizon.

Eventually, politicians run out of road, and are no longer able to kick the can any farther. Their only choices: raise taxes, cut money for current public services to back-fill pension obligations, or declare municipal bankruptcy in an attempt to renegotiate or slash previous pension deals. San Bernardino County and the city of Stockton were among the first to try the bankruptcy route. The latest was Detroit. Public employees and their union leaders have long put their faith in state constitutional provisions that prohibit pension reductions for public employees. However, in the Detroit case, the Federal Bankruptcy Court judge ruled that federal bankruptcy law trumped the state constitution. Rather than risk having that ruling affirmed by the decidedly anti-employee Supreme Court, retirees in Detroit's pension system voted to accept drastic cuts of up to 50% in pension and health care benefits.

Despite the current problems with public employee pensions, public employees must enjoy the same basic right to union representation as private sector workers. Therefore:

**Section 7: Employees of government and public entities shall have the absolute, unrestrained, and unimpeded right to form or join unions, to participate in union activities without retaliation, and to have said unions engage in collective bargaining, including strikes and boycotts, on their behalf. The right to strike shall not apply to police officers, firefighters, or those responding to a current or imminent emergency. It shall be a felony, punishable by incarceration in a maximum security facility for a period, not subject to pardon, parole, commutation, suspension, or other reduction of sentence, of not less than ten years, to interfere, or attempt to interfere in any way, in the free exercise of these rights.**

**Section 8: Once agreed to, pension obligations to public employees shall not be reduced, deferred, or otherwise negated in value.**

**Section 9: Pensions to employees of state and local government entities shall be insured by the Federal Pension Benefit Guaranty Agency, which shall have all powers and authority necessary to see that each pension entity is adequately and properly funded.**

Bringing public employee pensions into the Federal Pension Benefit Guaranty program (FPBGA) will add another layer of protection against excessive pensions. The FPBGA will have explicit constitutional authority to ensure that states and local government pensions are linked to viable and realistic funding. Want to provide reasonable pensions for public employees? Great. All you have to do is fund them adequately. Want to let some high-level retirees live like aristocrats? *Not. A. Chance.*

Reality-based economists have an axiom, which is the basis of bankruptcy: "Debts that cannot be repaid will not be repaid." Once one or more major state pension funds gets to the point where bankruptcy is the only way forward, there will be a court decision allowing public pensions to be retroactively reduced. At that point, the 33rd Amendment, Public Campaign Financing, will demonstrate its merit. When unions are no longer able to impact campaigns, elected officials will be able to represent their constituents, and negotiate without the inherent conflict-of-interest that now attends every election from dogcatcher to president. They will be able to go forward with reasonable public pensions that serve their legitimate original purpose and are no longer golden perks for higher echelon personnel.

The harsh realities of skyrocketing public employee pensions, combined with rising public awareness and outrage, have led some states to enact reforms. These usually involve some combination of changes in how pensions are calculated, caps on benefits, prevention of double-dipping, or even requiring new hires to accept 401(k) type defined-contribution plans. Still, many ask, "Why should we pay taxes so that public employees can get pensions when we, in the private sector, don't?" Their outrage is both warranted and understandable, but the real question is:

***Why shouldn't private sector employees also enjoy adequate, properly funded and safely insured defined-benefit pensions?***

The answer: They should.

The solution, therefore, is to bring public employee pensions under control while also ensuring that private sector workers have plans which are comparable and equally secure.

This brings us to the subject mentioned earlier, of government entities trying to induce workers to renounce union membership in return for a higher up-front salary. The problems with this hypothetical are twofold: First, with a Jobs Guarantee there will be fewer people desperate for a job that pays a decent wage. Second, with virtually all private sector employees enrolled in the defined-benefit pension plans instituted by the 44th Amendment, why would anyone in their right mind take a public sector job where an equally secure pension is offered, and then turn down that benefit just for a little more current cash? The guy at the local hardware store will have a pension plan. The clerks at the supermarket will have a pension plan. But you're going to go to work for a government entity, and turn down the opportunity to have a secure, guaranteed pension, just because you dislike the idea of a union? Few people are likely to be that stupid. Those who are deserve to pay the price.

The bottom line is that public and private sector employees, who perform comparable work, should enjoy approximately the same wages, and both should have comparable, fair, and secure pensions that will actually be there throughout their retirement. And that doesn't mean 401(k) plans, which are one of the biggest frauds ever perpetrated on the public. Who profits from 401(k) plans? a) The companies, who get out from having to fund future benefits; and b) everybody in the financial community from stockbrokers to financial advisers, who skim a fee off the top for managing those invested funds. And who loses? Workers. For a number of reasons.

First, since only the contribution is guaranteed and not the benefit, if the stock market drops, your 401(k) goes in the crapper. Second, even if the overall market remains relatively stable, 401(k) plans depend on having a roughly equal number of buyers and sellers in whatever sector of the economy your plan has most of its shares. Third, and most important, a 401(k) only works *if you know how long you're going to live*. Need $30,000 a year for retirement expenses and have $300,000 in your 401(k)? Great! You're set for ten years. (Forgetting, for a moment, the fact that even at only a 4% annual rise in the cost of living, the price of something doubles every 18 years. Thus, by the tenth year of your planned retirement, that $30K a year needs to be about $46,000.) And what if you live longer than ten years?

*Too bad, so sad.*

To compound the injustice of 401(k) plans, they are often shoved down employees' throats because, "the company is experiencing difficult times and everyone must sacrifice." Everybody except the stockholders and the execs in upper management, that is. Defined Benefit pensions are current wages deferred for payment in the future, after retirement. If a Defined Benefit pension program is ended or frozen, do the workers receive that additional income, that was formerly deferred, in the form of a raise they can invest on their own? *Of course not.* The company gets to save later on employee benefits, but spend now on management and investor compensation. On numerous occasions, employees have been forced to convert from defined benefit to defined contribution/401(k) type plans at the same time that upper management gave themselves raises and bonuses, or cashed in on lucrative stock options.

There is a war going on, between the ownership/stockholder/ investor rentier class on one side, and the people who do the real work on the other. Employers who can offshore jobs, dodge unions, and cut sweetheart race-to-the-bottom tax and subsidy deals in Right-to-Work-for-Less states will never willingly alter their business model to do right by their retired workers. What we have to do is give everyone the ability to form or join a union, to enroll in a pension plan if they so desire, and then make the unions serve their membership, instead of their leadership. Both employers and unions must be compelled by the constitution to be fair to the men and women who actually produce goods and services. The employer side currently has money and political muscle, but it's a small group. *We the people* have a vast numerical superiority. But to win, we must force enactment of the employment and retirement protections in the 44th Amendment.

# Chapter 21

# UNIVERSAL HEALTHCARE

### The 45th Amendment --
### The Right to Healthcare

**Within one year after ratification of this Amendment Congress shall establish a federally funded national healthcare system, delivered by such combination of public and private entities as may be most practical and effective, covering the full and true cost of treatment for all illnesses and injuries, for all citizens and all legal resident aliens. No citizen, legal resident alien, organization, or business entity shall be required to purchase or provide private healthcare insurance.**

Americans grow up being taught that *We're Number One*, that America is exceptional. In some ways we are. Take health care, for instance, where we're definitely Number One -- in cost. We spend far more on healthcare, both on a per-capita basis and as a Percentage of Gross Domestic Product, than any other country. And the quality of our healthcare is exceptional, all right. *Exceptionally bad.*

- **2000 World Health Organization** study: **38th,** behind not only most of Europe but also countries like Costa Rica, Columbia, Cyprus, and Morocco. However, we did place one spot ahead of ... Slovenia.

- **2013 World Bank/International Monetary Fund/World Health Organization** study: **46th**. Among those countries now ranked ahead of the U.S.: Iran, the Dominican Republic, Bulgaria, Libya, and Mexico.

- **2010 Commonwealth Fund** study: **Dead Last** among the seven most-developed countries.

- **2014 Commonwealth Fund** study: Upped the number of nations included in the study to eleven but, yet again, the U.S. came in **Dead Last**. This prompted NBC News to headline their story, *We're Last! Again!* The L.A. Times went with, *U.S. Healthcare system: Worst in the developed world.* The Atlantic magazine summed it up with, *Most Expensive and Worst Performing.*

These studies were conducted by organizations with the staff and funding to aggregate massive amounts of data and perform accurate, in-depth analysis. They all used multiple criteria, including such things as infant mortality rates, average life expectancy, cancer survival rates, patient safety, access (physical and geographic proximity to providers), and equity (access relative to economic status). And things have only gotten worse since 2014.

Fifty-nine countries currently provide universal health care, but not all use a single-payer system. Many have a system of private health insurance. So why not use this system in the United States? Because in those countries with a hybrid system, the insurance companies are all non-profit and tightly regulated. We, however, have a history of regulators being captured by the industries they are supposed to regulate. In addition, in the United States, non-profit status is an IRS designation, the standards for which are easily manipulated. For example, the National Football League was, believe it or not, for the first seventy or so years of its existence, a non-profit organization, and as such got a property tax break on its New York headquarters. Under intense public pressure, it finally relinquished its non-profit status in 2015.

Goodwill -- which is actually Goodwill *Industries* -- is another example where being non-profit doesn't mean what people think it means. In 2013, Goodwill paid seventeen top executives more than $1 million each. Others, like Oregon Goodwill CEO Michael Miller (at $856,043), weren't far behind. In 2016, Goodwill CEO James Gibbons made $1,114,375. The San Diego Union Tribune reported that in 2013, seventy CEOs of non-profit organizations were paid in excess of $200K each, *just in San Diego County*. Merely because an entity is non-profit doesn't mean that the people who run it aren't profiting. But these companies are all pikers. In 2013, while it was still non-profit, the NFL paid Commissioner Roger Goodell $44 million.

*Forty-Four. Million. Dollars*.

If the thought of government-paid health care conjures up visions of care being provided by the medical equivalent of the Post Office, or the DMV, stop worrying. Single-payer does **not** mean single provider. In marketplace-delivered single-payer systems, care is delivered by doctors, clinics, and hospitals operating either as private or public entities. Bellevue in New York City is a public hospital; Lenox Hill and New York Presbyterian are privately owned and operated.

Obama falsely promised that under Obamacare, "If you like your doctor, you can keep him." Under a single-payer system, you really can keep your favorite (or most conveniently located) doctors, clinics, pharmacy, and hospital. That's because under single-payer, except for purely discretionary cosmetic procedures, **all** providers and **all** services are covered. (Most cosmetic surgery, other than reconstructive surgery after accidents or breast cancer surgery, is not covered by current medical policies, so there would be no change there.)

Ever made a trip to the doctor? With it comes a mountain of paperwork. (Especially if your condition involves more than one trip.) Notices from your insurance company itemizing each visit, each provider, and each procedure, along with what the company paid, what may have been waived because the provider was in-network, what you have to fork over in terms of co-pays and deductibles, and the additional money you're liable for because some charges exceeded Regular and Customary rates for your area. These notices must be reconciled with individual bills from your doctor, clinic, anesthesiologist, physical therapist, etc. Some bills arrive before payments from your insurance company have been received and applied, so you wait to get a later bill that matches up with your insurance company's Statement of Benefits. If the insurance company makes a mistake, such as incorrectly billing an in-network doctor as out-of-network, you have to go through an appeals process, usually in writing. If you have Medicare Advantage and the provider's billing department erroneously bills Medicare directly, you have to fill out more forms and wait months to get that cleared up.

There is none of this nonsense with single-payer. If you qualify by virtue of being a citizen or legal resident alien, you go to the doctor or hospital, get treated, and go home. The bill goes to the government payment office. The only time a patient or their family gets bothered with paperwork is if they're randomly selected for a spot check fraud audit, to verify that they really did get the treatment the government is being billed for by the provider.

How can we afford to cover everybody? We can start by using the savings from eliminating health insurance company profits and administrative bureaucracy at every level of health care delivery. According to a 2014 study published by Physicians for a National Health Program, over 25% of hospital budgets are consumed by administrative overhead:

> "We're squandering $150 billion each year on hospital bureaucracy," said lead author Dr. David Himmelstein, a professor at the CUNY/Hunter College School of Public Health and lecturer at Harvard Medical School. "And $300 billion more is wasted each year on insurance companies' overhead and the paperwork they inflict on doctors."

Similarly, according to a 2013 article by Dr. David Dvorak published at CommonDreams.org:

> The nonpartisan U.S. General Accounting Office concluded that single-payer health care would save the United States nearly $400 billion per year, enough to cover all of the uninsured.

In 2012, economist Gerald Friedman, Ph.D., a professor at the University of Massachusetts Amherst, analyzed the benefits from the single-payer health care plan offered by Congressman John Conyers in HR 676: [Emphasis added.]

> While it would raise some costs by providing access to care for those currently uninsured or under-insured, it would save much larger sums by eliminating insurance middlemen and radically simplifying payment to doctors and hospitals. While **providing superior health care**, a single-payer system would save as much as **$570 billion** now wasted on administrative overhead and monopoly profits.

A year later, Friedman revised his projections based on newer data:

> Under the single-payer system created by HR 676, the U.S. could save an estimated $592 billion annually by

slashing the administrative waste associated with the private insurance industry ($476 billion) and reducing pharmaceutical prices to European levels ($116 billion). In 2014, the savings would be enough to cover all 44 million uninsured and upgrade benefits for everyone else.

Specifically, the savings from a single-payer plan would be more than enough to fund $343 billion in improvements to the health system such as expanded coverage, improved benefits, enhanced reimbursement of providers serving indigent patients, and the elimination of co-payments and deductibles in 2014.

[snip]

HR 676 would also establish a system for future cost control using proven-effective methods such as negotiated fees, global budgets, and capital planning. Over time, reduced health cost inflation over the next decade ("bending the cost curve") would save $1.8 trillion, making comprehensive health benefits sustainable for future generations.

Favorable cost savings estimates for single-payer health care plans are not new. As far back as 1991, the General Accounting Office concluded:

If the US were to shift to a system of universal coverage and a single payer, as in Canada, the savings in administrative costs [10 percent of health spending] would be more than enough to offset the expense of universal coverage.

Later that same year, the Congressional Budget Office reported:

All US residents might be covered by health insurance for roughly the current level of spending or even somewhat less, because of savings in administrative costs and lower payment rates for services used by the privately insured.

Remember, under MMT, the government can simply print the money it needs for universal healthcare. Or it could reduce some of the obscene, bloated Defense Department budget. Note: In 2018, faced with its first ever serious audit attempt, the Pentagon admitted that it could not account for $21 **trillion**. Some believe this admission is the Defense Department trying to get out in front of a story that is already bad and only going to get worse.

For the sake of argument, let's say that you don't believe in MMT, or that at some level it won't work, and we will have to use federal tax revenues to pay for healthcare. Fine. Studies have shown that under single-payer, individuals and families would not pay anywhere near as much in taxes as they now pay in monthly premiums, deductibles, co-pays, etc. But what if those studies are wrong? Let's take a worst case scenario: What if the health insurance premiums currently paid by those who can afford a policy went, instead, to the government as taxes? A hypothetical family of four that pays $6,000 a year in insurance premiums would continue to be out $6K, but would still be way ahead because they would have *no other out-of-pocket medical expenses.* No co-pays or deductibles. No out-of-network charges. No uncovered costs for medications. And they could see any doctor, visit any clinic, or go to any hospital -- without the mountains of paperwork.

No discussion of health care reform is complete without an examination of Obamacare. At the time this book is being written, the status of Obamacare remains unclear. The Republican Congress failed to repeal the law outright, but it did succeed in cutting some funding and other elements (such as the individual mandate to purchase insurance), as part of the 2018 Budget Act. Some state Medicaid programs are likely to end, or be drastically reduced, which is sad because this is probably the one beneficial feature of Obamacare. In other areas, subsidies to buy Obamacare's over-priced policies will end, or be cut back. But all this depends on a number of factors, including litigation from some states, plus the possibility that backlash from constituents might force some in Congress to push for revisions in future bills.

While we cannot know for sure how Obamacare will fare in the short and medium term, by examining the bill as passed, we can still learn a lot about what *not* to do. Although it was billed as health *care* reform, Obamacare was, in fact, health *insurance* reform. Or more correctly, a corporate welfare program for the medical insurance industry.

Officially titled the Affordable Care Act, Obamacare provides very little care and is generally not very affordable. The low-premium basic Bronze plans feature high co-pays, extremely high deductibles (as much as $10K), narrow provider networks, and tight drug formularies that exclude many common drugs. Originally advertised during the Obama campaign as offering health care to those who were currently uninsured, the ACA fell far short. At best, Obamacare enrolled about nine million people, leaving thirty million more without coverage or care. A substantial number of those who did enroll, did so through expanded state Medicaid programs. This presents its own set of problems, the first of which is that Medicaid is limited to those far down the poverty ladder, and provides no relief to the middle class.

Second, whenever Medicaid provides care to anyone between 55 years of age up to the Medicare qualifying age of 65, the cost of that care is a lien against the person's assets and estate. Say that you have a modest home that you purchased many years ago and finally own, free and clear. But your employer shipped your job to China or Mexico, or you were downsized and job prospects for someone in their late fifties are virtually non-existent. So now, you're surviving on food stamps and help from your children. You have a heart attack, come down with cancer, develop diabetes, or some other serious medical condition. Sure, Medicaid will provide the minimum basic care. But that house you planned to leave to your kids, to give them a little jumpstart in life, or maybe as an asset for retirement? It's gone. Eventually it will be seized and sold to reimburse Medicaid for the cost of your care. What makes this so perverse and pernicious is that people with higher incomes who qualify for subsidies to purchase regular Obamacare plans don't have to repay anything. So, the poorer you are, the more you have to give up, even after you're dead. *Is this a great country or what?*

Third, both Medicaid eligibility and the qualifying thresholds for Obamacare subsidies are income-related. If you qualify at the beginning of the year, but end up earning too much income, at the end of the year you have to reimburse the government. *"Hi, congratulations on that promotion that finally got you out of poverty! Now give back that Obamacare subsidy or we'll garnish your paycheck. Have a nice day."*

Fourth, Medicaid (and Medicare) is in the process of slowly being privatized. Here's blogger David Dayen, who has followed the healthcare issue since the beginning of the Obamacare debate, explaining the situation in Florida and Arkansas for NakedCapitalism.com in 2013:

> Over the past week, both houses of the Florida legislature have rejected the Medicaid expansion program endorsed by Governor Rick Scott. You may recall the huzzahs from the progressive world when Scott, a self-possessed anti-Obamacare warrior, decided to accept the Medicaid expansion. What didn't get reported as much is that Scott's announcement coincided with the go-ahead from the Administration for Florida to fully privatize their Medicaid system.
>
> [snip]
>
> So what was up with the Legislature's rejection? Tea Party politics? Some unlikely show of principle against crony capitalism and corporate welfare?
>
> No. They just want a different kind of privatization.

Arkansas privatization, in particular -- which would just completely liquidate the public Medicaid program and have the state, in the immediate term, pay for premiums for everyone up to 138% of the poverty line to purchase private health insurance. There would be no more public disposition of Medicaid for the poor. It folds Medicaid into the as-yet-untested insurance exchanges.

[snip]

This actually jacks up costs over time, perhaps as much as 50%, as Medicaid is cheaper to administer, and always will be, considering that it involves the direct provision of services rather than running them through a middleman ... It makes the system more fragmented and unsustainable. It may not even be legal; it's based on a fairly dubious reading of a 25 year-old clause in the Social Security Act.

So how did that Arkansas Medicaid privatization program work out? Predictably, not well. As the National Review and other media reported, according to a federal government report, the program enrolled 61,000 more people in its first year than originally estimated. By mid-2016 over 40% of the entire state was covered by expanded Medicaid. The problem was, this privatized version, ensnared in the gorilla grasp of predacious health insurance companies, was far more expensive than predicted.

### *$778 million more expensive in just the first three years*.

The enrollment numbers are clear proof of how many poor and low-income people needed health care. The skyrocketing costs prove that, due to the necessity of making a profit, privately-funded healthcare is more expensive than single-payer.

One group that did benefit enormously from the Obamacare expansion of Medicaid is hospitals, especially the for-profit chains. Here's a Business Week headline in September 2014:

## Medicaid Expansion Is a Windfall for Hospitals

The article went on to explain how the Obamacare expansion of Medicaid resulted in more people becoming paying customers, rather than waiting until they had to seek emergency room care, which is generally an unreimbursed expense for hospitals. Not surprisingly, this resulted in better financial results for over 500 for-profit hospitals. The article closed by noting that, "The shift has been good for for-profit hospitals' stock prices."

*Yeah, no shit.* In the first nine months of 2014, stock prices for the three major hospital chains were between 130% and 145% higher than the S&P 500 average.

One reason that Obamacare has been profitable for the Medical Industrial Complex, but not much help to sick people, is that insurance companies are pros at gaming the system. Besides offsetting low premiums with high co-pays and deductibles, insurers have squeezed their networks of participating doctors and hospitals. Seattle Children's Hospital filed suit against the Washington State Insurance Commissioner's Office because five of the seven Obamacare insurance plans offered in Seattle's King's County don't include Children's Hospital in their network of providers. A Seattle Times article quoted hospital spokesperson Sandy Melzer as saying, "The notion that a major insurance plan is going to exclude us from their network is truly precedent-setting and represents a new level of degradation in children's access to care."

Medicare for All is often thrown out as code for single-payer healthcare, but that is inaccurate. While certainly a boon to senior citizens, Medicare has its own disadvantages, starting with the fact that it only covers 80% of costs. Back in 1965 when Medicare was instituted, that wasn't seen as a big problem. The cost of health care in relation to average incomes was not nearly as extreme as it is today. In addition, lots of workers, especially in unionized sectors of the economy, got to keep their company health care in retirement. Between Medicare and the company plan, all care was covered. However, over time, the cost of health care ballooned far ahead of both the rate of inflation and any growth in worker income. As more and more jobs were outsourced, or moved to anti-union states in the south, fewer and fewer retired workers had supplemental coverage from their former employer.

Never wanting to miss an opportunity to exploit our flawed health-care system, private insurance plans convinced Congress to approve Medicare Advantage, a system of private supplemental health insurance. Medicare is financed by a $138 per month deduction from each Social Security recipient's retirement check. The way Medicare Advantage works is that the government gives the retiree's Medicare money to whatever private health insurance company the retiree selects. In turn, that company manages all of the retiree's health care needs and services, including billing. The rationale is that the companies will negotiate better deals with doctors, hospitals, drug companies, and so forth. The money saved can then be used to reduce most of the 20% that traditional Medicare doesn't pay, leaving the retiree with lower overall health care costs. Sadly, it was all a scam.

The health insurance companies desperately wanted to insert themselves into Medicare, in order not only to profit, but to further entrench themselves into the system, to make their position as middlemen seem indispensable. Once entrenched, they gradually set out to squeeze everyone involved: patients, doctors, hospitals, clinics, labs, physical therapists, right on down the line.

Medicare Advantage in Southern California is a perfect example. Blue ~~Crucifix~~ Cross Medicare Advantage Preferred Standard used to be offered in L.A. County as a PPO option. Starting in 2013, BC/BS instituted an additional $38 per month premium on top of the $138 a month Social Security already kicked in. In 2014, Social Security recipients got a 1.6% per month Cost of Living Adjustment (COLA). However, BC/BS upped its premium surcharge for these *preferred* policy holders to $80 per month, meaning that everyone who selected that plan and wasn't at the very top end of the SS payment scale actually got a smaller monthly SS check than the previous year. This again demonstrated how insurance-driven inflation in the medical field has consistently outpaced inflation at large. (I can't help but notice that when you abbreviate Blue Cross Blue Shield, it comes out BC BS.)

Coincidental with BC's 2013 institution of the premium surcharge, it also doubled the co-pay on many medications. In 2014, the company went a step further, eliminating certain popular medications from its formulary of covered drugs. One of those was Hydrocodone, one of the least expensive, most effective, and most prescribed generic painkillers. So, Blue Crucifix Advantage Preferred Standard policyholders who endured long-term pain while recovering from major injuries or surgery paid a lot more than they would have before. *Ain't it wonderful to be preferred?*

Eventually, even that expensive BC Preferred Standard policy ended. There are still about 25 Medicare Advantage plans currently offered in the Southern California region. Not one of them is a PPO program. So, if the ability to choose the physician you want, freedom from needing a referral to see a specialist, or office/clinic/hospital location is important, you're dead meat. Which is fine with the insurance companies; they'd rather you die than cost them money. Literally. Really.

The topper? BC Medicare Advantage Preferred Standard was, like most Medicare Advantage policies, offered only as a regional policy. Some policies cover an entire state, but many cover only a particular county. Imagine living in one county, working in another, and not having in-network health coverage if you have a heart attack at work. When signing up for regional policies, people have to balance the advantages of the policy against the possibility of becoming ill or injured while out of their region. If you need medical attention in another region, even though there may be an identical plan available, your care can be -- and probably will be -- billed as out-of-network.

Speaking of costs and billing, ever wondered why your COAL (Cost Of Actual Living) outpaces the government's official Consumer Price Index? For one thing, the government claims that because the quality of care is hard to measure, health care insurance and non-hospital costs are **not** included in the formula the government uses to measure inflation. Isn't that convenient? (It's also why, in a deliberate attempt to make official figures look better than things really are, the government does **not** measure monthly increases in food or fuel costs when calculating inflation and the CPI.) According to author Michael Snyder at The Economic Collapse website, if the Cost-of-Living inflation rate was still calculated using the formula in place in 1990, it would be 6%. If calculated using the 1980 formula, it would be 10%. But 10%, even 6%, would mean massive increases in Social Security payments, as well as downward revisions to GDP figures.

With a system so corrupted by greed, and so at odds with the concept of actual care, it's no surprise that overwhelming medical costs are the leading cause of bankruptcy. And because Obamacare plans either have really high premiums, or really high deductibles and co-pays, it doesn't improve the situation, which comes as no surprise to those who follow the healthcare issue closely. Here's former health finance expert at Nerdwallet Health, Christina LaMontagne, way back in 2013:

> I don't think Obamacare is going to get rid of the situation. The data suggests that already-insured Americans are struggling. With the expansion of insurance, it doesn't seem like that problem will go away entirely. It's not a panacea.

No, it sure wasn't. Obamacare has been in operation for four years now, and 30 million Americans are still without both health care and health insurance. Indicative of the problem of depending on health *insurance* to pay for health *care* is the fact that 8% of all medical-related bankruptcies are filed by people 65 or older. In other words, *people on Medicare.* That's not surprising when you consider that, according to Rosemary Gibson, author of several books on problems in our healthcare system, seniors spend 23% of their Social Security checks on Medicare Part B and Part D premiums, deductibles, co-pays and uncovered procedures or out-of-network charges. (Part B is Medicare Advantage, while Part D is the infamous prescription drug program, in which Medicare is forbidden, *by law*, to negotiate lower drug prices with the pharmaceutical companies.)

Seniors aren't the only ones who face financial difficulty paying for medical care. Even after the implementation of Obamacare, and its accompanying expansion of Medicaid, medical expenses still exceed all other causes of bankruptcy.

There's also the problem of paying health care providers. Congress struggles constantly with what has become known as the "Doc-Fix." As Sarah Kliff of the Washington Post explained, "Ever since Medicare was created in 1965, the federal government has struggled to decide how much to pay Medicare doctors for their services."

Congress has good reason to worry that a cut in Medicare reimbursement rates would cause doctors to flee the system. Without these periodic emergency funding increases, Medicare providers would have seen their reimbursements fall by as much as 27% in a given year. Even with one Doc Fix after another, in many communities, a number of doctors already refuse to accept straight Medicare, and treat only patients who have either a Medicare Advantage or MediGap policy. (Medicaid has similar problems, and Medicaid providers are often found only in low-income areas. In rural areas, Medicaid providers can be few and far between.)

In 2013, there was much discussion in Congress about finding a permanent solution to this recurring crisis. But with Congress unwilling, or incapable, of actually governing, nothing happened. As the Washington Post headlined:

**For 17th time in 11 years, Congress delays Medicare reimbursement cuts as Senate passes 'doc fix'**

*Seventeen times in eleven years.* Really inspires faith in both government and our health care system, doesn't it?

The root problem involves both contradictory philosophies toward government and outright refusal to face facts. The Republicans hate the very idea of public-provided healthcare, and the Democrats are afraid of being branded fiscally irresponsible socialists. So, every year, Congress underestimates what Medicare will cost, then acts surprised when there is a funding crisis. And both sides refuse to accept the principle of MMT, because they would lose a valuable talking point when trying to prevent some government program on the basis that, "we can't afford it."

Given the problems already infecting Medicare, expanding it to everyone will not solve the problems of how we deliver health care, or how we pay for it. When it comes to dissecting the problems of our health care system, Lambert Strether, who writes for both Corrente.com and NakedCapitalism.com, sums up the situation:

> The key point to remember in all discussions of ObamaCare is that neither it, nor indeed the entire private health insurance "industry," should exist. They are rent-seeking parasites, economic tapeworms. One does not improve a tapeworm; one removes it.

Exactly right. But if we remove the private health insurance tapeworm that has attached itself to our entire healthcare system, including Medicare and Medicaid, what happens to all those jobs, to the people currently employed managing the paperwork maze of our present system? This is a valid concern, and, during the Congressional debate over Obamacare, some companies in the Medical-Industrial-Complex gave employees paid time off to demonstrate and carry picket signs. Naturally, if your family is one of those affected by the switch to single-payer, you are going to be concerned. But the problem extends beyond that. People who lose their jobs stop spending, and this results in a ripple effect of more job losses throughout the rest of the economy. However: *We cannot continue to protect jobs that bankrupt the rest of society*.

We cannot prioritize jobs in an industry that is predatory, perverse, and parasitic. Some of the people who lose private sector jobs at health insurance companies, hospitals, and doctor's offices will get hired to help manage the single-payer system. The estimates of cost savings by switching to single-payer include calculations on how much it will cost to deliver health care to all those who presently lack access to care. Obviously, the government cannot process payments for 30 million more patients without hiring some additional staff. Likewise, health care providers will need more admissions personnel, more nurses and lab techs, etc. Many of the people who will be displaced by the end of private health insurance have office and managerial skills that can be employed in new industries, or in the re-institution of the traditional manufacturing jobs that we have shipped abroad. If you can process paperwork for an insurance company, you can learn to process paperwork for a company that makes solar heating systems or electric cars.

Other people who now work in the private health insurance system can find employment through the Jobs Guarantee program, outlined in chapter 19. But the first step remains removing the health insurance tapeworm operated by the medical mafia. Everything else proceeds from that.

# Chapter 22

# BENEFITS FOR MILITARY SERVICE

### The 46th Amendment --
### Veteran's Rights and Benefits

**Once a benefit for service in the Armed Forces is offered, Congress shall make no law, and no court shall order or enforce any action, which results in the delay or reduction of said benefit. Benefits heretofore promised members of the military, but later rescinded or reduced, are retroactively restored in full.**

There is no greater myth than the one about how the United States honors and cares for the men and women who serve in its Armed Forces. Parades, flyovers at sporting events, and speeches on Veteran's Day, Memorial Day, and the 4th of July notwithstanding, the history of the U.S. military is one of sending troops into combat without the best equipment, and then reneging on post-service benefits. Sadly, with the exception of the WWII G.I. Bill, it's always been that way.

Perhaps a hundred thousand Union soldiers died needlessly in the Civil War because the War Department refused to outfit troops with the new, lever-action 15-shot Henry Rifle which had been patented in 1860. (The Henry, with some modifications, later became the famed Winchester "that won the West.") The Army's stated justification for not adopting the Henry? Soldiers would *waste too much ammunition.* The real reason: the political connections of companies with contracts to supply conventional muzzle-loaders.

In WWI, American doughboys died in droves after being forced to use the worst combat firearm ever made, the French Chauchat light machine gun, which jammed more often than it fired. The U.S. could have had the vastly superior Vickers, but didn't want to pay its British patent holder a licensing fee.

The semi-automatic M-1 Garand was introduced in 1936 as the new, standard infantry combat weapon. But six years later, the Marines on Guadalcanal still carried the vastly inferior pre-WWI bolt-action 1903 Springfield. It took the Marines seven bloody months to capture Guadalcanal, longer than it took to capture Tinian, Saipan, Iwo Jima, and Okinawa *combined.* Eisenhower proclaimed the Garand the weapon that made the difference in defeating Nazi Germany. No telling how many Marines might have lived if they'd had the Garand on Guadalcanal.

During the Battle of the Bulge, GI's had to fight frostbite and pneumonia, as well as the Germans, because they didn't have proper winter clothing. Did the Pentagon learn from this experience? Of course not. In Korea, the same lack of winter clothing caused many soldiers to freeze to death at the battle for the Chosun Reservoir.

In the early days of the Vietnam war, GI's went into combat with the wildly inaccurate M-14 instead of the new M-16. Why? Because those in charge of small arms procurement at the Pentagon didn't like the idea that the M-16 was independently developed by a private company. It was NIH -- *Not Invented Here.* When Defense Secretary Robert McNamara finally forced the brass to issue the new weapons, military procurement officers changed the type of powder in the cartridges and failed to accommodate for that change by chrome-plating the receiver. Until the problem was corrected, hundreds of GI's died when their M-16s jammed in combat. It was so bad that, in some cases, the standard defensive fighting alignment was three men to a foxhole: two firing and one constantly clearing jammed weapons. Try that sometime in the dark with hot casings raining down on you.

Iraq and Afghanistan were no different. A decade after *Blackhawk Down* demonstrated the vulnerability of unarmored Humvees, our soldiers were still dying in them. It got so bad that resourceful GI's scavenged steel from destroyed Iraqi vehicles to fabricate their own "hillbilly armor." Other soldiers died due to defective flak vests, while back home bureaucrats played semantic games with test results, and lobbyists pushed profits over safety and performance.

The problems service men and woman have to deal with, while in uniform, is often matched by what happens when they leave active service. WWI vets were promised bonuses, but they weren't payable until 1945. In 1932, during the depths of the Great Depression, 17,000 of them set up camp in D.C. as the Bonus Army and demonstrated for immediate payment. President Hoover sent in troops and tanks under Gen. Douglas MacArthur to burn them out. *And thanks for your service.* Finally, in 1936, with the country still mired in the Depression and the winds of a new war appearing on the horizon, Congress agreed to pay the bonuses early. *Because soon we're gonna need those guys to go fight and die again.*

When WWII finally did roll around, the still-fresh memories of the Bonus Army problem forced Congress to create the GI Bill. It paid the tuition and living expenses for over two million vets to attend college, something average people rarely had an opportunity to do in those days. It also provided low interest rate/no down payment home mortgage financing, and low-interest loans to start businesses, both of which contributed greatly to the post-war boom and growth of the middle class. Similar bills were passed for Korean War and Vietnam War vets. Eventually, the program was expanded to cover service members who served in peacetime. But what Congress giveth, Congress can taketh away, so each subsequent bill contained fewer and lower benefits. Unemployment payments, to ease the transition from military service to the civilian workforce, were cut, and subsidies for college soon fell far below the actual cost.

The real turning point came in the aftermath of the invasion of Iraq and Afghanistan. As the cost for Veteran's Administration health-care grew by leaps and bounds, Congress had three choices. First, it could embrace the concept of MMT. But nobody ever wants to do that, because admitting that the government can print all the money it needs, means that the cost of a program can no longer be used as an excuse not to fund it. The second option was to tax the wealthy and big, tax-dodging corporations. (No need to explain why that idea failed to find a big following.) Third, they could underfund the VA, then profess shock and surprise when horrible conditions and huge backlogs of untreated patients came to light. By 2013, the backlog of unprocessed VA disability claims reached 400,000. VA facilities across the country were discovered falsifying records to hide the fact that wait times for appointments with doctors stretched up to seven months. Not surprisingly, an average of 22 vets with PTSD were committing suicide *every day*. *And still are.* In fact, here's a sobering and disturbing fact: in the period from 1999 through September 2018, deaths of active-duty U.S. military personnel stands at 5,273. The total for veteran's suicides in the same period? 128,480.

### *One hundred twenty-eight thousand four hundred-eighty.*

VA health care isn't the only veterans benefit that has suffered. In 2013, Congress voted a 20% reduction in retirement benefits that had previously been promised to service members. Remember those recruiting ads, which promised to pay a soldier's college tuition when they finished their military service? In 2014, Congress yanked the rug out from under vets by reneging on that promise. But once again, *thank you for your service*. The group The Other 98% posted a GIF on Facebook in 2018, listing all the proposed programs that the GOP-controlled Congress failed to enact:

- Clay-Hunt Suicide Prevention Act
- Health Benefits & Retirement Pay Restoration Act
- Wounded Veterans Job Security Act
- Veterans Retraining Act
- Homeless Veteran Reintegration Act
- Disabled Veterans Home Accessibility Act
- Job Corps Act
- Torture Veterans & Victims Relief Act
- Veterans Business Center Act

This cannot be tolerated. Promises made to those who go in harm's way simply must be kept. And when veterans need special help as a result of their service, it must be provided.

Some people may wonder why, if we are going to have both universal military service and universal single-payer healthcare, we need to have a separate amendment ensuring the benefits of military service?

- First, we have a national moral obligation to restore benefits that were promised to service men and women in the past and then subsequently rescinded.

- Second, we need to ensure that promises made to those who join the military as a career are kept, and those career personnel do not find that benefits once promised are later yanked out from under them whenever it suits Congress.

- Third, those who serve in combat under their mandatory two-year service period may suffer wounds and physical or psychological injuries that require special assistance. Having universal healthcare may eventually result in no longer needing to have separate VA health facilities, but it is not going to help the disabled veteran get his house made wheelchair accessible. It's not going to provide him a wheelchair van. Nor will healthcare help veterans retrain for jobs for which they may be best suited, instead of having to depend on something provided by the Jobs Guarantee Program.

There are two tiers to mandatory military service: those who do two years in peacetime and get out versus those who are directly exposed to the horrors of war. We have a pragmatic duty, and a moral obligation, to see that those in the second group get the special support they have earned.

# PART IV

---

# GAME PLAN

# Chapter 23

# REDRESS OF GRIEVANCES

The First Amendment establishes the right of the people to, "assemble peaceably and petition their government for redress of grievances." That's exactly what we're going to do. Only we're going to do the petitioning first, and leave the assembling until we have achieved a critical mass and built sufficient public awareness.

Let's get clear right out of the gate what kind of petition we're talking about: We are going to follow the general format and procedures in place in states where citizens have the right to put forth initiative and referendum ballot measures. This involves printing petition books with the complete text of the proposed amendments, along with signature blocks where registered voters print and sign their name along with their address. Most petition books that I've worked with in local campaigns have around 100 signature blocks, but a book does not have to be full to be valid.

Naturally, we will also have websites where people can download, sign, and mail back a single petition for their state. However, this will only be an auxiliary tool, and not a primary focus. Why? First, because this will not be a one- or two-page petition; to include all the information required it will be a number of pages long. This alone will discourage a few people from going the print-it-yourself route. But more importantly, paper petitions that you access online involve people taking individual action, rather than organized, collective action.

***Nothing replaces the visibility and commitment of people in the streets***.

As more and more circulators carry petition books, more and more people will take notice of what is happening. Feeling that, *you are not alone*, and that, *yes, something can be done by regular people like me*, is an empowering experience, one that the elites hope we never feel to any large degree.

In states which allow citizen initiatives, we will go through the formal application process, in which proponents submit the measure to the appropriate official. For state-wide measures this is usually the Secretary of State or the Attorney General. That official writes up an ostensibly unbiased Title and Summary of the measure. These summaries usually run 200 to 500 words and sometimes include reference to the fiscal costs of the measure if enacted, as well as what, if any, existing laws it will replace, delete, or amend. If proponents feel that the summary is not fair or accurate, they can go to court where judges often direct the drafting official to make certain changes. In some cases, judges will even write the new summary themselves.

Then a Notice of Intent to Circulate an Initiative Petition, including the Title and Summary, plus the signatures of the measure's proponents, is posted in various public places, and published in one or more newspapers. Once proof of publishing has been presented to the appropriate election official, the process of collecting signatures may begin. Typically, initiatives proponents have around 120-180 days to gain the signatures of enough registered voters to meet a certain threshold. Sometimes it's a percentage, usually 10%, of the registered voters in the area (state, county, city, district) impacted by the measure. Other times, the threshold is a percentage of the votes cast in the last general election.

Once the proponents collect enough signatures to exceed the threshold, the petition books go to the proper election official to be compared to the voter rolls. If the total number of valid signatures meets the required minimum, the measure then goes to the voters. In many states the governing body of the jurisdiction impacted by the measure (legislature, city council, school board, etc.) has the option to simply adopt the initiative, word for word, just as if it had been approved by the voters. Measures adopted in this fashion can only be repealed by a vote of the public. (Governing bodies generally take this approach when the volume of signatures, plus their analysis of the temperament of the citizenry, indicates that the measure will pass anyway, and fighting it will only provoke unnecessary hostility, which might cost some officials their seats.)

Will this approach work? No. Most states have laws limiting ballot measures to a single issue. It is highly unlikely that elected officials, entrenched and enriched by the very system which we propose to change, are going to rule that reform is a single issue. Another problem is that the petition will call for each state legislature to demand Congress enact these amendments, or call for a constitutional convention to do so. Most states have laws preventing an initiative from mandating legislative action. So, in those states where citizens can propose initiatives we will go through the process, knowing that we will be denied. This way, we can say we tried all official channels.

Once we are turned down, we will simply circulate the petition for signatures anyway. We will write our own Title and Summary, and also publish and post as normally required. There is a silver lining to being denied official status: if we do not qualify for official sanction, we are also not bound by any limitations, such as a specific time period to collect the necessary signatures. Instead of

180 days we can take a year if necessary. There are two reasons for pushing ahead even with an unofficial initiative petition:

- First, it gets the idea of expansive, effective constitutional control in front of the public in the best possible way: one-on-one, person-to-person conversation. (Naturally, we will have explanatory hand-out materials and websites with information about how to volunteer, donate, get a lawn sign, etc.)

- Second, it will gradually create a wider awareness of the issue among the public at large. Eventually, small local media will start reporting on the petition drive effort. This is the first step in generating a conversation on a state, and then national scale, which is vital because ***conversion to a cause always starts with a conversation.***

Often it occurs person to person, but it also happens through the media. Whenever you see a video of Bernie Sanders giving a speech, he's having a conversation with you.

What about states that do not allow citizens to propose initiatives? We will employ the same tactics in those states, only without the charade of submitting the initiative for approval. In those states, we can point out how the 36th Amendment will expand the right of initiative, referendum, and recall to all who currently do not enjoy the benefit. We can give voters in those states a peek at how direct democracy works. Think the citizenry in places like New York, which has been in the iron grip of corrupt machine politics for 150 years, might like a chance to enact some of their own reforms (starting, perhaps, with getting a handle on their obscene property taxes, or enacting binding term limits)? *You betcha, Red Ryder.*

The beauty of this strategy is that all we will be doing is peacefully petitioning for redress of grievances. No need to divert time, money, and resources into organizing protests and demonstrations, and no need for the massive police presence those activities require. All our initial efforts will be one or two people engaging in conversation with their neighbors. What could be more quintessentially American and patriotic?

The effort required to pull this off will be enormous, possibly bigger than any previous domestic reform movement, including the battle for women's suffrage, the civil rights movement, and the anti-war protests in the 60s and 70s. While all of those were huge undertakings, what we're after is peaceful reform, but on a scale that amounts to a genuine Second American Revolution.

If the overall scale of the project seems daunting, once broken down into its individual parts, it's not so bad. Looking at the D-Day Invasion of Europe from Eisenhower's perspective at headquarters, or looking back at it through the lens of history, it was almost overwhelming. But at ground level it was much simpler: Get this ship, or this boat, or this plane, to this point at a set time. Once ashore, each man was simply trying to reach his objective and maintain contact with the rest of his unit. Our task will be the same.

The campaign will require a massive number of dedicated, motivated warm bodies. Many can and will be volunteers. Many operations can be run out of private homes, across the dining room table, but will still involve the cost of printing the petition books and campaign materials, running local ads, etc. Other operations will require a bona fide campaign HQ. In small or sparsely populated states, a single office will suffice. Larger states, with multiple population centers, will require local offices, probably on the county level, but perhaps even at the city level. Someplace like NYC may require an office in every borough. These offices will need some paid staff, office equipment and so forth.

Hopefully, a lot of this stuff will be donated or available cheap off Craig's List and eBay. But there are still going to be hard dollar costs.

Most staff will be local, but some people will have to travel to conduct training sessions, make public appearances, perhaps even execute documents. Traveling staff may bunk in someone's guest room or even on the couch. This happened a lot in the days of the civil rights movement. More than a few earnest volunteers slept on living room floors. But we can't count on that, so there will be hotel costs on top of plane fares, meals, and gas reimbursements. No matter how you slice it, the campaign is going to need money, including for legal representation. This money may come from donations, merchandise and apparel sales, fund-raising concerts, etc., but it will still have to come from somewhere. Assuming that this book sells well enough and provides the necessary genesis momentum to the movement, I plan to donate a portion of the proceeds to TrueReform.org. We can also take heart in the way Bernie Sanders was able to parlay millions of small contributions into enough money to wage a significant campaign.

Since initiative and referendum laws vary from state to state, even though we will not get official approval, we'll need an election law attorney in each state to make sure that our forms and applications, as well as our method of collecting signatures, conform to state statutes. We want to give the maximum appearance of conforming to all the legal requirements for an official petition. Plus, if even one state grants our initiative legal status, that would be a tremendous credibility boost and, while unlikely, might even be legal leverage to get other states to follow suit.

Conforming to ballot measure regulations in states with citizen-initiative provisions won't be the full extent of our need for legal representation. In states where there is no provision for citizen initiatives, local and state governments will be confronted by a new phenomenon, and on a scale for which they are not prepared. There will be issues of where, when, and how circulators may solicit signatures. The *where* will include both purely public spaces like parks, sidewalks, library and civic center grounds, etc., and semi-public/semi-private sites, such as shopping centers and malls. State laws vary with respect to what is protected permissible First Amendment activity and what is not, or what requires certain permits, limits hours of operation, mandates identification or registration of solicitors, etc. Rest assured that those who oppose reform will leave no legal stone unturned, nor will they let one dirty trick go unused, to stop us. They will likely resort to legal action, which they know will not withstand judicial scrutiny, but will still tie up our time and resources.

A question that is bound to come up is, "Will True Reform run or endorse candidates for office?" The answer is no. We will remain laser-focused on enacting the Restoration Amendments. We will not allow attention or resources to be diverted from principles to personalities. First off, candidates and politicians change their minds, or say one thing and then do another. Second, candidates or current officeholders who proclaim support for the Restoration Amendments may hold other views that are deemed unsatisfactory by some of our supporters. Abortion is a prime example. Support for Israel is another, as is gun control. We can sidestep all those potholes and prevent fracturing of the movement by following this simple credo:

> *Candidates and office holders can endorse the Restoration Amendments, but TrueReform.org will not endorse or campaign for them.*

# Chapter 24

# INFLECTION POINT

Let's be honest. Victory will not be easy. As I noted at the beginning of this book, the current system is rigged, and the people who rigged it like it that way. But as Mahatma Ghandi reportedly said, "First they ignore you; then they ridicule you; then they fight you; then you win." The establishment will fight us. They will not take their feet off our throats voluntarily.

Since collecting petition signatures is the opening salvo in a struggle for the restoration of the republic, it is likely that at some point the opposition will make stopping circulation of the petitions a priority. They will try to nip the prospect of genuine reform in the bud, before it can grow and spread. Pushing back against our efforts will validate the notion that the elites fear the movement.

This initial counteroffensive will likely employ multiple tactics. The enemy's first move could be attempting to get courts to enjoin circulation of the petitions. We will respond, and should prevail, but victory in all jurisdictions cannot be assured. With or without a ruling in our favor, there will be attempts to prevent us from soliciting signatures in public or quasi-public locations. There are legal precedents holding that malls and shopping centers constitute today's equivalent of the old town square, traditionally accepted as a venue for discussion of issues. (Circulating petitions has traditionally been included under a wide First Amendment interpretation of free speech.) But since there are other court decisions that place conditions on the gathering of petition signatures at such locations, we cannot be sure how things will turn out on the legal front in every situation.

Experience has shown that circulating petitions at locations with lots of foot traffic will not be sufficient to gather enough signatures. Nor will supplemental returns, from people going online to print and mail their own petition, be enough to cover the shortfall. Inevitably, large numbers of people will need to go door-to-door collecting signatures. While this would seem to be a constitutionally protected right, it is not without limitation. Cities and states have the authority to limit hours of solicitation. Normally these regulations apply to people selling items door-to-door, but even in some states where citizen initiatives are permitted, the hours when door-to-door signature collecting may take place are specified by law. In states where petition rights do not yet exist, vagueness in the language defining or prohibiting solicitation for commercial purposes may lead opponents to argue in court that it applies to our efforts as well. In addition, some gated communities and senior citizen or public housing complexes may have additional regulations restricting or prohibiting door-to-door contact. Initially, each of these cases will have to be fought on an individual basis. However, if we can secure a series of favorable court decisions, legal precedent should turn in our favor, thus making each new challenge easier to overcome. On the other hand, things could go against us. And, in some fairly isolated instances, we may have to simply defy the law and accept the consequences, which range from being ticketed to being arrested, and even assaulted, either by law enforcement or private security.

Other than being arrested in a deliberate test case against unfair restrictions on signature gathering, volunteers who circulate petitions should have little to fear. Same for those who support the movement or sign the petitions. However, it will probably be best for supporters to be careful mentioning the True Reform movement at work. If you work for a Fortune 500 company, defense subcontractor, public agency, health insurance company, etc., your co-workers may share your desire for reform, but it is unlikely that management will. Better to keep your head down as long as possible.

One tactic that will definitely be employed at some phase of the movement is cutting off our ability to communicate, not only across social media sites like Facebook and Twitter, but on the internet itself. Do not be surprised if our website goes down. Blocking of our phone connections, both cellular and landline, is also likely. In March 2018, the Defense Department's Special Operations Command held a symposium titled, "Sovereignty in the Information Age." Seven months later a summary of this conference for the Atlantic Council surfaced. This document is not only revelatory, it is incendiary. For one thing, sovereignty is defined as *the ability of the state to impose its will on the populace.* (So much for the idea that government derives its power from a grant by the people.)

The need for the state to impose its will is justified on the grounds that the internet has provided a mechanism by which alternative political ideas have caused a drop in the public's willingness to trust government. The report goes on to explain that the wide dissemination of alternative viewpoints via the internet has nullified the ability of traditional "professional gatekeepers" (i.e. the captive mainstream media) to control information flow and the desired official narrative. This has created a situation where, "facts themselves are not sufficient to combat disinformation." And why is this, pray tell? Because, "the truth is too complex." The result of all this free exchange of ideas is, "conflict and disruption," and the only solution is censorship of political speech. And the best mechanism for achieving this desired level of censorship and, "*promoting pro-government narratives*"? Private sector, "technology giants, including Facebook, Google, YouTube, and

Twitter," because they can, "determine what people see and do not see."

Fear not; many successful revolutions in world history occurred without benefit of the telephone or internet. In fact, some succeeded precisely because their leaders avoided using methods of communication that could be easily monitored. There are still ways we will be able to communicate.

Eventually, despite attempts to stop us, the movement will reach critical mass. Millions and millions of signatures will be collected, and then delivered, with a great public show, to every statehouse. Only then will we start to demonstrate demanding enactment of the Restoration Amendments. And that is when things will get ugly. This is when the gloves will come off.

Not everyone who participates will become a target, although tactics aimed at leaders sometimes inflict collateral damage on others. Those in leadership positions, however, will definitely have to steel themselves against several types of retaliation. The first, arrest, has already been mentioned in connection with signature gathering.

Being arrested -- either deliberately, or as a by-product of simply exercising your (alleged, nominal) constitutional right to free speech -- has been a tactic of social justice activists for more than a hundred years. It was used by women agitating for the right to vote, union organizers, civil rights activists, and anti-war protestors. On various occasions, and for various causes, protestors have deliberately chained themselves to the fence around the White House. People protesting construction of the Keystone XL pipeline chained themselves to everything from earth-moving equipment on the job site to trees in the pipeline's path. More recently, getting arrested without meaning to, as a byproduct of nonviolent protest, has been a common occurrence. It happened to members of Occupy, and to people protesting against the DAPL pipeline across Native American lands in North Dakota. (I know of one woman who proudly boasts of being arrested more than 80 times going back to the 60s. Someone like Medea Benjamin of Code Pink probably has a rap sheet longer than the New York phone directory.) Unfortunately, the nature of these types of arrests has recently begun to change dramatically.

For many years, there was a ritualized process. Protestors refused orders to disperse, were arrested, carted off to jail, and then released soon after, sometimes by being bailed out, other times by signing an affidavit to appear in court when summoned. Even where charges were not dropped or reduced, the ultimate penalty (aside from the inconvenience of being arrested) was usually a modest fine. Now, the tactics are much harsher and more draconian. Now, the authorities like to instigate and choreograph opportunities to arrest protestors. One favorite technique is *kettling*, in which protestors are herded into an area, sometimes cordoned off by plastic fencing, and then arrested for not dispersing when ordered to do so. Trapped in a place where they can't escape, then arrested for not leaving. The NYPD employed this with Occupy. Another trick employed by the NYPD, in connection with Occupy, involved a protest march over the Brooklyn bridge. Officers at the start of the march told protestors that there were too many of them for safe transit on the sidewalks, and directed them to use the adjacent traffic lane. When protestors got to the other side of the bridge they were arrested for impeding traffic.

The widespread use of flex-cuffs, oversize zip ties designed to function as handcuffs, has created another opportunity for the authoritarian minions of the powerful to inflict pain on citizens exercising their constitutional right to protest. Some officers and departments have taken to pulling the ties so tight they cut off circulation. A few victims have suffered permanent nerve damage as a result of either regular handcuffs, or flex cuffs, being applied too tightly and/or for too long. Another tactic of law enforcement is to pack arrested demonstrators into a paddy wagon like sardines, close the doors, and leave them (preferably in the hot sun) for as long as possible before transporting them to the station for booking. The police don't care if this leads to fainting spells, heat prostration, or even heart attacks. For them it's not about exercising constitutional rights, it's about *compliance with their authority*.

At the police station, more indignities may await. Sometimes cells are packed to overflowing, leaving little or no room for older protestors to sit down. Air conditioning is turned off, or the heat turned on. Booking paperwork is deliberately slow-walked. Water can mysteriously get shut off, leading to both a lack of drinking water and overflowing toilets. These are all tactics, not just of a police state, but a *frightened* police state, desperate to punish citizens for attempting to practice democracy.

With the advent of the Trump administration, conditions have gotten worse. Now, it's not just a few nights in jail that demonstrators have to worry about. Various levels of law enforcement have tried putting long prison sentences on the menu. (To be fair, not all of these changes can be blamed on Trump. Many of the anti-democratic actions against protestors began under the Obama administration, and have their roots in the protests which helped scuttle the Trans Pacific Partnership trade agreement, as well as the prolonged protests against the Keystone XL pipeline and the Dakota Access Pipeline.)

Aghast at Trump's election, thousands showed up at his inauguration for various "Not My President" demonstrations. The organizers of the demonstrations -- dubbed J20 for the January 20th inauguration date -- and most of the participants, were intent on peaceful protest. Sadly, these days nearly every major demonstration is infiltrated by elements of the notorious anarchist movement, whose favorite tactic is the destruction of private property, especially store-fronts and cars. In typical police state fashion, instead of selective, targeted arrest of these anarchists, large numbers of protestors were swept up -- "kettled" -- and arrested en masse. Then, unlike the usual ritual of arrest, booking, and release, 234 protestors were charged with various felony rioting charges, carrying potential sentences of up to sixty years in prison, for property damage that the prosecution estimated at more than $100,000. Twenty-one defendants pleaded guilty. (Whether each of them was, in fact, guilty, or simply took a plea deal to avoid the expense and uncertain outcome of a trial is unclear.)

Eventually, charges were dropped against all but 59 protestors, six of whom volunteered to have their cases heard first. Among them was a nurse from Pittsburgh attending the event as a volunteer medic. Another was one of the nine journalists arrested. The prosecution's ludicrous allegations included:

- That the membership of some of the defendants in the Industrial Workers of the World union constituted proof of a conspiracy.

- That the normal kind of organizing that goes into setting up a protest constitutes a "criminal conspiracy."

- That anyone wearing black was showing their allegiance to the anarchist elements. (This, of course, denies that black could be symbolic of Trump's inauguration being a dark day for the country. Or that black was simply the color of the protestor's warmest jacket.)

The real purpose of these prosecutions was to intimidate and deter future protest organizers and participants. Fortunately for the republic, things did not go well for the prosecution. The six initial defendants were acquitted on all charges. From Sam Adler-Bell's account in The Intercept:

"This is a demonstration that the jury didn't buy the prosecution's absurd theory of the case," said Sam Menefee-Libey, of the Dead City Legal Posse, which is providing legal support to defendants ... "This is a big win for these six defendants and a big relief to everyone else who's still fighting."

[snip]

...a juror who only gave his name as Steve [said] it was not ultimately a close call. "The prosecution admitted the morning of day one that they would present no evidence that any of the defendants committed any acts of violence or vandalism ... From that point, before the defense ever uttered a sound, it was clear to me that ultimately we would find everyone not guilty."

After the trial, the judge ruled that the lead prosecutor had unlawfully withheld exculpatory evidence which would have aided the defense. (That the defendants were acquitted anyway is just further proof of how pathetic, baseless, and vile this entire prosecution really was.) A second trial of other defendants resulted in either acquittals or hung juries. Finally, in a classic Friday afternoon news dump -- compounded by it being on the Fourth of July weekend -- prosecutors dismissed the charges against the remaining 39 defendants. Although the good guys won in the end, they did so at significant cost. One defendant correctly noted the distorted and abusive power prosecutors have, "to overcharge people, disrupt their lives, and then drop cases before having to face any consequences in court." That charges like these eventually get dropped does not offset the time, money, and aggravation involved in mounting a defense. And the punch line?

The prosecutor who had withheld exculpatory evidence, Jennifer Kerkhoff, *was **promoted** to Chief of the Felony Major Trials Section.*

This prosecution is not the only case where officials have sought to advance the War on Dissent. By February 2018, almost sixty anti-protest bills had been introduced in 31 states. Here's Traci Yoder, Director of Research and Education for the National Lawyers Guild:

The first round of anti-protest legislation introduced in 2016 and 2017 produced mixed results. Many of the bills were so poorly written or so blatantly unconstitutional that they were defeated within a short period of time. Bills calling for the removal of driver liability for killing protesters, using racketeering laws to punish protesters, trying to drastically redefine the meaning of "riot," or challenging the right to picket mostly failed right out of the gate. However, conservative lawmakers have learned from their early mistakes, and are now re-introducing some of these bills in stronger revised form...

[snip]

In January 2018, ALEC formalized a new model policy that had been introduced at its annual meeting last December -- The Critical Infrastructure Protection Act ... that criminally penalize and fine anyone trespassing on "critical infrastructure," and prescribe criminal penalties and financial liability for any "conspiring organizations" that assist protesters. Drafted by ALEC's Energy, Environment and Agriculture task force, this policy is a thinly-veiled attempt to stop protesters from interfering with fossil fuel extraction infrastructure, including oil pipelines, petroleum refineries, liquid natural gas terminals, and railroads used to transport oil and gas. A week after the finalization of this model policy, legislators in Ohio and Iowa introduced "critical infrastructure" bills. Both of these states are currently home to major pipeline projects owned by Energy Transfer Partners (ETP), who assisted in the drafting of legislation. These kinds of bills are clearly an attempt to address the successes of environmental and Indigenous activists who have pushed back against projects like the Dakota Access Pipeline.

New bills concerning "critical infrastructure" are cause for alarm for several reasons. First, a key component of these bills is the attempt to redefine and expand the meaning of terms like "terrorism," "sabotage" and "trespass" to allow prosecutors to punish more people for a broader range of activities. ... Furthermore, these bills aim to penalize organizations that support protesters by holding them "vicariously liable" for damage undertaken by individuals. Based on the myth of the "paid protester," these bills seek to punish supportive organizations with fines of up to 10 times the amount paid by an alleged trespasser.

While some of these new anti-protest laws are aimed at deterring and punishing protest against fossil fuel industries, the overarching goal of anti-protest legislation is to discourage people from protesting against any aspect of our patently unfair current system. To succeed, it is not necessary for authorities to get convictions. Arrest and trial imposes significant costs for legal defense, puts the defendants under severe psychological stress for an extended period, can lead to them losing jobs, and may put them in danger of damaging other relationships. Another purpose of some of these laws is to remove liability for "independent actors" who employ physical violence against protestors. Many times, corporations and law enforcement don't need to act; they can simply foment a situation where frustrated individuals who disagree with the protestors (for whatever reason) feel free to act violently on their own. Witness the tragic death of Heather Heyer, run down by a racist while protesting against the *Unite The Right* white nationalist march in Charlottesville, Virginia, in 2017.

Another concern, also already mentioned, is employment retaliation. Sooner or later, if you work for a big company or a public agency, and if you are publicly linked to the movement, someone in management who fears these reforms may fire you, or pressure those who can fire you to do so. This is why I predict that many protest leaders will come from occupations where employment retaliation is difficult, if not impossible, to enforce.

And thanks to the gutting of the economy by the elite, there are millions of unemployed workers who are both quite skilled, and *highly* motivated, to join the movement, especially when our fundraising reaches the point where they can be adequately compensated. If you're in your fifties, and your job got sent to China or Mexico, which would you rather do? Sit in your living room watching daytime television, or go out and try to stick it to the bastards who screwed you?

Naturally, if you lose your job as a result of your involvement with the True Reform movement, we will try to assist you in filing an unfair termination claim and/or a civil suit for damages. But, given vagaries in state laws, as well as each person's individual circumstance and employment field, there is no guarantee that we can do so in all cases, or that we will prevail. And even when we do win, the reward may not be sufficient to make you whole again. Financial ruin will be a valid concern for some, which is why some supporters will have to take great care before deciding to become too actively involved.

There are also three other dirty tactics with which volunteers may have to contend. The first is civil litigation. Several activists in my area, who took on a coalition of developers and their city government cronies, were sued for allegedly violating various election statutes. It was all bullshit, and eventually the judge ruled for the activists on all counts, calling the suit itself "a sham" and the plaintiffs "shills" for the developer secretly bankrolling it. Nevertheless, each activist had to hire counsel, submit to depositions, depose the other side, etc. Although it appears inevitable that the defendants will be awarded their legal fees and court costs, none of them knew for sure that would be the outcome. So even with fellow supporters kicking in at fundraisers, the costs and risks were still enough to cause a few sleepless nights. As mentioned earlier, at some point True Reform will have funding to deploy legal eagles, but there is no guarantee that we can adequately assist everyone who might end up in the litigation crosshairs.

The second dirty tactic will be reputational destruction. The enemy will look for anything in your background that you'd rather friends, relatives, employers, and neighbors not know. If they can't embarrass you directly, they'll try to do it through your family. At this point, it's good to remember that the surveillance community may already have most of the information they need, stored in those cavernous data centers and the bowels of Big Tech. What they don't have they can find, the old-fashioned way, through background investigations.

If they can't find what they need, they'll try to entice you into something. If that fails, or isn't practical, they will just invent something scurrilous. Planting drugs will be one preferred tactic. Planting illegal firearms or bomb-making materials will be another, especially in states with strict gun control and gun registration policies. However, planting child porn is perhaps the most likely option.

In 2013, intellihub.com picked up a story by Amber Harrison on American Live Wire titled, *The Government Is Planting Child Porn On Your Computer,* which outlined how a computer virus called Win32/MoliVampire is spread across P2P networks. According to the story, Operation Flicker, a program started by ICE to snare child sex traffickers, has the unfortunate collateral effect of attaching child porn images to other files from P2P sites such as LimeWire.

If the government can do this accidentally, they can do it on purpose, especially when an agency like the NSA or the CIA is involved. And remember, it doesn't have to be child porn. It could be schematics for making a bomb, a formula for ricin, even pictures of government buildings, installations, infrastructure, etc., where taking photos is prohibited. Moreover:

***The government can do it and hide all trace of where it came from. Or even attribute it to a fake source.*** (For example, from one member of the movement to another, indicating a conspiracy.)

In 2017, Wikileaks released Vault 7, a collection of 800 files showing that the CIA used a program, code-named Marble, to hack into computer networks but leave behind telltale code traces that made the hack appear to originate from Russia, China, North Korea, or Iran. According to Wikileaks, the Vault 7 files also demonstrated that the CIA can hack into smart phone applications and bypass the encryption features of WhatsApp, Signal, Telegram, Weibo, Confide, and Cloakman. Given the close cooperation and collaboration between high-tech private security companies and government intelligence agencies, the dirty work could be done by the private contractors without official government involvement.

Even if whatever is planted on a person's phone or computer is eventually proven false, the damage may be irreparable. The accusation will lurk on the internet forever. Whatever it is will find its way into employment records, credit reports, and security clearance background files, and the target will have to expend tremendous time, energy, and money fighting to clear their name. So, while supporters and most volunteers will likely not be targets, everyone in a leadership position within the movement must operate on the assumption that we will be smeared with either embarrassing truth or scandalizing fiction, and whatever it is will be portrayed in the most slanted, distorted, sensationalistic way.

The last threat we face is assassination.

In 2014, Pulitzer Prize-winner Chris Hedges, quoted previously in Chapter 19 concerning the diabolical perils of stand-alone Universal Basic Income, outlined his *Rules of Revolt* for

TruthDig.com. He left the most important, and the most chilling one, for last. Rule 12 states: [Emphasis added.]

**The generation that begins a revolt often does not live to see its conclusion.**

Hedges uses *generation*, but in our case, I think the more appropriate term would be *leaders*. For one thing, we don't have the luxury of taking a generation. Second, the seeds of reform have already been simmering for fifteen years, starting with the foolish and fraudulent invasion of Iraq, then expanding in the aftermath of the bank bailout during the Great Financial Crisis.

Hedges' premise is that non-violence only works *after* violence, instigated and imposed by the regime against early protestors, proves insufficient to deter further demonstrations. Sadly, this initial violent response, while failing to extinguish the revolt, may still result in martyrdom for a few movement leaders. Paradoxically, sometimes the death of one or more early protestors ignites even larger, and ultimately successful, additional demonstrations. In this respect, we will be not unlike the union organizers, civil rights advocates, and anti-war protestors of the past century.

Many people don't realize how widespread the use of murderous official military power has been in the history of American citizens fighting for basic human rights and fair economic treatment. During the battle to establish unions in the West Virginia coal fields, a five-day pitched battle was fought in 1921 at Blair Mountain, where a private army of over 2,000 men organized by the mine owners, **and reinforced by the West Virginia National Guard**, used machine guns and even bombed the miners from aircraft. In the end, *over a million rounds were fired*, around 100 people were killed, and 985 miners eventually stood trial for murder and other charges, including **treason against the state of West Virginia**.

The Ludlow Massacre is another event not known by nearly enough Americans. Here is how Wikipedia describes the event: [Emphasis added.]

> The Ludlow Massacre was an attack by the **Colorado National Guard** and Colorado Fuel & Iron Company camp guards on a tent colony of 1,200 striking coal miners and their families at Ludlow, Colorado on April 20, 1914 ... The massacre, the seminal event in the Colorado Coalfield War, resulted in the violent deaths of between 19 and 26 people; reported death tolls vary but include two women and eleven children, asphyxiated and burned to death under a single tent.

Anyone tempted to dismiss Blair Mountain and Ludlow because they took place a hundred years ago, or even Kent State because it was fifty years ago, should consider this: A Freedom of Information Request (FOIA), filed by the Partnership for Civil Justice Fund, led to the release of an official FBI document showing that the FBI knew of a plan by some organization to use snipers to assassinate Occupy leaders in Houston. In the end, the FBI was able to convince a federal judge that revealing any more information about the plot would disclose the identities of "members of organized violent groups" who were confidential informants, and was thus exempt from FOIA requirements.

It is abundantly clear that the FBI was more concerned about protecting the identity of these violent, potentially murderous organizations than it was about protecting the civil rights and saving the lives of Occupy leaders. This begs the question: Did these "organized violent groups" include other law enforcement agencies? Or private corporate security forces? Because of redactions in the documents, the answer is impossible to determine. However, activist Ryan Shapiro, who submitted the FOIA request which resulted in the disclosure of this potential assassination plot, was asked by Amy Goodman on her *Democracy Now!* television show, "Why was the FBI appearing to pay far more attention to peaceful protesters in their investigation than to the actual terrorists who were plotting to kill those protesters?" I'll supply one obvious answer:

***Because it's their job to protect the establishment, not those who upset the status quo.***

It's the authoritarian careerist mindset -- order above all else -- on clear display. Compliance with authority has priority over honor, principle, morality, and most importantly, the constitutionally-protected free exercise of civil rights.

There is, perhaps, one glimmer of hope: According to the previously mentioned Atlantic Council summary of the conference for "imposing" sovereignty on the populace, the wildly misnamed Department of *Defense* has concluded that, "eliminating" -- killing or imprisoning dissidents -- can be counterproductive because it may amplify the credibility of those leaders and movements. (Thus, the emphasis on censorship to thwart growth of the movement through covert anti-democratic means.) However, the reluctance of the military to employ deadly force is not likely to be shared by those who are in, or employ, private security companies.

It is hard to predict exactly when the elites will turn savagely against us. It may vary from state to state, but given the history of what happened to Occupy, it is likely to be a simultaneous, nationwide effort, directed by the White House, coordinated by the Justice Department and Department of Homeland Security, in cooperation with our corporate and banking overlords. Naomi Klein described the crackdown on Occupy for The Guardian on December 29, 2012 as, "totally integrated corporate-state repression of dissent."

Boy, was it ever. The newly released documents contain a number of disturbing revelations. Not only did orders for the crackdown originate in the White House and involve law enforcement at all levels, *major banks shared information about the protestors, and were involved in the planning and execution* of the crackdown.

Local police and sheriffs, who are supposed to be accountable to their communities, were instructed by federal agencies not just to participate, but to use things like local zoning laws, and no camping ordinances, as justification for the evictions and arrests. Even worse, the documents prove that the Department of Homeland Security and the FBI characterized Occupy as a "terrorist threat."

For anyone who likes to use the word *fascism*, **this is fascism**: direct collaboration between business and government against the general welfare of the people.

Note: Characterizing Occupy -- which lacked a viable administrative structure, and failed to articulate a clear set of demands, much less a viable path toward achieving them -- as a terrorist threat only demonstrates how much the elites fear any reform movement which seeks to unify and motivate people on a large scale. Were those picket signs and drums lethal weapons? Of course not. Occupy's greatest achievement, planting the concept of the 99% in the public consciousness, was purely symbolic, yet the mere *idea* of widespread public discussion of inequality struck terror in the hearts of the bankers and government officials alike.

There are seriously bad people, in both government and the private sector, that we will be going up against. Studies have shown that both our current political system, and our corporate hierarchy, self-select for those with sociopathic and psychopathic tendencies that facilitate ruthless advancement. You need only watch the CEOs of health insurance companies get wealthy, beyond all reason, by killing people through the denial of care, to know that concern for others does not flow in their veins. What people need to accept is the fact that many of the rich aren't just greedy, or power-mad; they actually *hate* poor and middle-class people, and think of them as lesser beings, subhuman, Henry Kissinger's "useless eaters." And not only are you a useless eater, so is your whole family. (Unless, of course, one of them is a really attractive woman, in which case exceptions are often made.)

Because our goals are much more ambitious than Occupy, and so explicitly defined, and because our plans to achieve them are so clear, the True Reform movement will scare the elites far more than Occupy ever could, especially since the math is against them:

***There are very few of them, and a great many of us.***

In fact, if the oligarchs, sub-oligarch elites, police, and management-level enablers who benefit from the current system number two million people, with somewhere around three hundred million American citizens, the bad guys are outnumbered 150 to 1. **One-hundred-fifty to one.** If the establishment forces number only one million, they're outnumbered ***300 to 1***. This is precisely why we can expect the enemy to use every underhanded tactic in the book.

For instance, they don't need to use something crude like snipers as in the Houston plot against Occupy. Hackers have already demonstrated how to take remote control of the computers which control a modern automobile's accelerator, braking, and other systems. Some believe this is exactly what happened in the death of investigative journalist Michael Hastings. As Wikipedia notes, "Former U.S. National Coordinator for Security, Infrastructure Protection, and Counter-terrorism Richard A. Clarke said that what is known about the crash is "consistent with a car cyber attack." So, one or more of us may suddenly experience a stuck throttle and go hurtling off a bridge, or into a light pole, at which time the car's air bag will mysteriously fail to deploy.

At this point, it may seem like I've just given the establishment a game plan for fighting us. Rest assured: Nothing that I've mentioned hasn't already occurred to the mercenary leaders in government and private industry. Their Oppressive Tactics

Playbook is already written, contains measures we haven't even thought of yet, and is ready to be deployed in all its evil glory.

It may also seem like I'm trying to talk people out of getting involved with the True Reform movement. That's partly true. A number of people have urged me to tone down this section of the book. My editor naturally wants to eliminate anything that might decrease sales (read: revenue), but decreased sales would also have the effect of reducing exposure to the Restoration Amendments. Others share this fear, and think that being too direct about the scope of the challenge may well prevent the movement from catching fire. These are valid concerns. But I think those people fail to grasp how wide and deep both anger and despair run in this country. I believe that there are millions of Americans who have been searching, waiting, hoping for some fresh new approach to reform, an approach that holds out the prospect of concrete material gains for average people in a much fairer society.

Most importantly, I believe that it does us no good to pretend that this won't be a tough, perilous undertaking. Soft-pedaling the challenges would open up me, the book, and the entire movement premise to valid criticism for being naive, impractical, even detached from harsh reality.

Embarking on a campaign to force enactment of the Restoration Amendments will not be the same as donning a pink "pussy hat" and marching for a day in your local city. It will not be the same as attending a candidate rally. Nor will it be the equivalent of signing an internet petition, or calling your elected representatives about an issue.

True Reform will attempt a fundamental reordering, within the broad confines of our existing Constitution, of nearly every facet of our current political and economic structure. Our success will result in the breaking of a great many rice bowls, and the owners of those rice bowls are going to protect them fiercely. Desperately. Fanatically. But success will also mean a lot more rice, and much bigger rice bowls, for many millions of our fellow citizens.

As I've stated before, most True Reform supporters and volunteers will probably not experience the kind of nasty tactics and dangerous threats that I've outlined. But those who rise to any position of leadership or prominence, surely will. That's why the movement is likely to be driven largely by three groups:

- Young people, burdened by student debt, facing bleak job prospects, who see little alternative but substantive reform.

- Older folks, fed-up with the current trajectory of the country, well-enough established to weather the storm, and whose concern for their offspring offsets whatever fears they might harbor.

- Discarded workers, seething at having been tossed on the economic scrapheap by outsourcing, union-busting, and the gig economy.

The late progressive journalist and magazine publisher Alexander Cockburn asked young reporters interviewing for a job: "How pure is your hate?" for the elite. We must ask ourselves, "How strong is our outrage?" Because outrage is quite likely the only emotion strong enough to propel us to victory. Those people, no matter how sincere and well-meaning, who believe in traditional political maneuvering, electing "more and better Democrats," and polite discourse with the opposition as a way to fix our problems are not the target audience for this book. Nor are they likely to back many of the reforms suggested because for them the current system can be made to work. (They are also unlikely to support certain of the amendments, especially the one mandating universal compulsory military service.) In rejecting the need for the sweeping reforms proposed here, I submit that they are either willfully blind to the severity of our situation, or are tragically delusional.

The biggest questions we must ask is, "Can we win?" Again, Chris Hedges provides insight and encouragement in his *Rules of Revolt*. Among his observations is that reform movements often start out with modest demands, presented rather politely. It is only after this approach is met with indifference that reform leaders become more aggressive. Then, when non-violent protests begin to garner exposure and momentum, the elite get scared very quickly. However, what really terrifies them is the prospect of an alliance between the working class and what Hedges calls, "Déclassé intellectuals." These are the children of the middle and upper classes, and when they start showing signs of revolting against their own class, the elite sense real danger. Hedges describes, "the state's relentless demonization of the protesters, something we saw in the United States in response to actions of the Occupy movement," as a tactic aimed primarily at preventing a student/worker alliance. The state will go to great lengths to prevent this kind of alliance from forming or destroy it in its infancy.

Hedges also notes three more key aspects of non-violent reform: First, it often takes more courage to remain non-violent in the face of an attack than it does to fight back, which only plays into the hands of those wishing to portray the movement as a dangerous mob of vandals. Second, many of those employed to crush the resistance are members of the same exploited class as the protestors. Hence, it is critical to the long-term success of the movement to embrace them as people, and to use respect and compassion as tools to slowly win them over to the side of reform.

The third point that Hedges makes is profound, even if counterintuitive: Reform movements must be transparent and open. Attempts at secrecy allow the forces of the state to portray the reformers as dangerous people with something to hide. But most importantly, a movement of any size simply cannot maintain operational secrecy. Between modern technological surveillance capabilities, and good old-fashioned infiltration, the forces of fascism will inevitably know what we are planning in terms of policies, strategies, and tactics. This is why True Reform has no choice but to be exceptionally open and transparent. Our communications will be monitored. We will be infiltrated by spies. Those in power will go to great lengths to make their foot soldiers in the military, police, and private security forces believe they are in mortal danger. Traditionally, the way to do this is to send in agent provocateurs to engage in violent actions which can then be used to vilify the movement and justify a violent response. (During the Vietnam war protests, there was a saying: "Whoever suggests bombing the local draft board office is the undercover cop.")

Given these realities, it is only prudent to operate on the premise that the government and their corporate puppet-masters will know everything we're planning. This is fine, because this type of spying never stays hidden for long. The truly un-American tactics which they will employ will simply expose their corrupt, anti-democratic mindset. At some point, even Americans who didn't initially support our cause will become upset at the lack of fairness displayed by those in power.

When the movement becomes strong enough, the military will be called in. Whereupon I expect some units to fire at protestors. But I don't expect this to continue for long. In fact, I personally believe that our military is much less likely to use deadly force than civilian law enforcement agencies. I just don't see a large number of soldiers, many from disadvantaged backgrounds, turning their weapons on people that look like their families, their friends, their classmates.

Private security forces are a different matter. In the long run, we may have more to fear from them than from either traditional law enforcement or our own military. Private security personnel are much better paid than regular military troops, and most have honed their skills overseas. Many come from countries with traditionally dictatorial governments. They are mercenaries, today's version of the Hessians employed by the British during the first American Revolution.

History teaches that revolutions succeed when the enforcement arm of the ruling class changes sides and joins those demonstrating for justice. Once our uniformed military at field level refuses to follow the commands of their superiors, and turns to stand with us against the private security forces, victory will be close at hand. But what happens leading up to this point, and at the moment of victory, is crucially important.

There will come a time when the politicians and oligarchs are on the verge of losing control. It is then that they will attempt to sabotage the movement through compromise. They will propose, and perhaps even enact, weaker versions of some of the Restoration Amendments. Chances are these will be laws, not constitutional amendments, and thus subject to being repealed or modified by subsequent legislation. Even if these substitutes are enacted as constitutional amendments, you can be sure that they will contain loopholes and vague language. Meaningful punishments and effective means of enforcement will be missing. The Restoration Amendments are designed to be an interlocking set of comprehensive reforms; omitting or weakening some of them leaves an open door for the elites to do what they've been doing for decades: manipulate the system. This is why we must stand firm and remember the Iron Law of True Reform:

***The bad guys always win any compromise.***

This brings us to the climax and resolution of the movement. When the military, paramilitary, and regular law enforcement forces can no longer maintain control, when the economy suffers as people flock to protests (or simply stay home from work), when even martial law is no solution, Congress will be forced to act in one of two ways: enact the Restoration Amendments as written, or declare a Constitutional Convention. The problem with a

Constitutional Convention is that it probably cannot be legally restricted to just enacting the Restoration Amendments. This would present an opening for reactionary elements of the elite to move toward exactly the opposite of democratic reform, the formal imposition of a fascist dictatorship. Such an attempt would cause enormous pushback by True Reform supporters. In the end, if that proves not enough, the ultimate result is likely actual civil war, fighting in the streets between reformers and fascist goon squads.

The thing about civil wars is, *they tend to be bad for business.* Those who benefit to a great degree from the current system will be faced with a choice: accept a lesser, but still healthy, share of the economic pie, or perhaps risk losing everything to street warfare. As British political scientist Mark Blyth noted: "The Hamptons are not a defensible position." The same can be said for the thousands of big box stores, bank branches, office buildings, car dealerships and other physical facilities that the elite depend on for their wealth. In addition, history shows that when governments and societies fail due to civil war, while the true elite often escape to some faraway shore, their enablers usually end up in brutal prisons or at the end of a rope. Thus, there is reason to believe that the enablers may strike a deal, and switch sides in an effort to escape with their lives. In the end, enacting the Restoration Amendments may be the easiest path toward the least damage for the elite. They may end up suffering some financial pain, and a loss of power, but at least they will not be hanging from the nearest light pole.

The great mystery writer Mickey Spillane once said, "The most important part of any story is the ending. Nobody ever read a book for the middle." I believe that the ending of our story of reform goes like this:

We can win. We will win. We must win. History demands victory. Despite its shortcomings, American democracy has been the foundation of the American Dream, and an inspiration to so many people world-wide for more than two centuries. It cannot be allowed to pass into history. It cannot be allowed to become an artifact, a distant memory of some by-gone era where freedom and the quest for justice once burned brightly. The United States of America must regain its intended place as the eternal flame of government of the people, by the people, for the people.

History also predicts victory. Every time the future of the republic, or the core fabric of our society, has been threatened, the people have responded. Add it up: The War of 1812. The Civil War. Women's Suffrage. World War II. The Civil Rights Movement. Vietnam.

The strength of America is not the 1%, or their enablers among the 10%, or even the 20% for whom life is still comfortable. It is, and has always been, the 80%, the so-called average citizen, about whom almost nothing is average. Sure, there are a few frightened souls who slavishly follow one party or another, beguiled by propaganda that appeals to their own fears and insecurities. But they are on the fringes, just as deluded as our power-mad overlords. And if you think the election of Donald Trump somehow proves that many voters are idiots, you should reexamine your perspective. Many of Trump's marginal voters, the people who helped him flip states that had gone for Obama twice, were desperate people who saw their lives and livelihoods going down the drain. They turned to Trump only after realizing that the established hierarchy of the Democratic party had no intention of delivering on its lip-service promises to ordinary people.

If you need motivation to believe that the Restoration Amendments can actually be enacted, think back to the colonies. We remember and extol the leaders of the Revolution, but they were not the ones who made victory possible. It was the everyday men and women, who met in quiet corners of taverns and general stores to denounce the tyranny of the English. It was the butchers and blacksmiths, carpenters and candlestick makers, farmers and fur trappers who answered the call to arms. It was the women who sewed uniforms, tended to the wounded, and sometimes carried secret messages, all the while keeping their families fed when the men were off in battle.

Are we lesser men and women? I submit that we are not. In fact, today most women would be insulted by the suggestion that they should stay out of the forefront of the effort, and accept a passive or supporting role.

The D-Day Invasion of WWII provides another example. Almost everything that could go wrong, did go wrong. Bombs meant to destroy beach defenses fell harmlessly inland because overcast skies obscured landmarks and impeded celestial navigation. Intense anti-aircraft fire caused paratroopers to be dropped far from their intended targets. Specially modified amphibious tanks were sunk by higher than expected waves, leaving the troops on the beach with no heavy firepower. Yet the attack succeeded because American GIs put their training to work. Even when their officers went down, enlisted men cobbled together makeshift units, devised tactics on the fly, overran enemy positions, and captured vital bridges and crossroads to prevent German reinforcements from advancing.

As Americans we have a lifetime of training -- *in democracy*. We have been raised to understand how it is supposed to work. In fact, it is that knowledge and training which makes us realize how wrong our life is, how much our government has been corrupted and perverted, how far is has gone off course. This is also precisely why the forces of elitist tyranny cannot succeed against us: ***too many of the people they intend to rely on <u>will not persist</u> in fighting reform***. Sure, in the beginning many in law enforcement, even some in the military, will see demonstrations in support of the Restoration Amendments as a threat to their notion of law and order, of unquestioned compliance with authority. But this will not last. Because the majority of them have been trained to believe in, and practice, *democracy*.

At some point they will realize that they should not fight their fellow citizens. And unlike many demonstrations of recent times, which have tended to be directed against someone or something, our efforts will be *for* something, for a balanced economy, and a better life for themselves, their neighbors, their children and families.

Last but not least, the future demands victory. To let things continue as they are is to let things continue to deteriorate. Without reform, conditions will steadily worsen. Naturally, this leads many people to worry about what might be in store for their children and grandchildren, which is why it is not uncommon for politicians, and backers of one cause or another, to cry, "Think of the children," to justify some agenda or policy. Sometimes the appeal is legitimate, but often it is a smokescreen for some questionable, if not downright vile, action or proposal. But when it comes to supporting the Restoration Amendments:

*Forget.*

*The.*

*Kids.*

Worry about yourself. Without True Reform, if you're not financially very, very secure, *your* future will be an ever more dangerous, oppressive, and inhospitable world. So, let us once again heed the words of Margaret Mead:

> Never doubt that a small group of thoughtful, committed citizens can change the world; indeed, it's the only thing that ever has.

*Let the movement begin.*

Thanks for reading. Visit TrueReform.org for more information. Since we cannot yet know what the response to this book will be, at the beginning we will not be asking for financial contributions, nor will we be starting local chapters. All we want at this point is contact information and an indication as to how much support people will be willing to provide. Once we know that the movement has enough initial support to be viable, we will move on to chartering chapters, interviewing candidates for local coordinators, setting up initiative campaigns, and implementing the other steps necessary to enact:

### *The Restoration Amendments*

# Chapter 25

# THE RESTORATION AMENDMENTS™

## The 28th Amendment -- The Right to Good Government

Section 1: The right of the people to fair and honest government, which neither favors nor discriminates, is hereby established, and any citizen shall have standing at law to enforce and preserve such right, and when they prevail to be fully compensated, including the full costs of litigation plus treble damages, which shall be calculated on the cost of litigation, or the total amount of fines and settlement awards, whichever are greater. All prior laws and decisions to the contrary are hereby null and void.

Section 2: In interpreting the applicability of laws the Supreme Court shall consider the manner and degree to which said laws conform to and support the principles enunciated in the Preamble to the Constitution.

Section 3: Inescapable accountability being a cornerstone of honest government, all powers of the President, governors, judges, and official bodies to pardon, parole, commute, suspend, or otherwise reduce mandatory minimum sentences for crimes involving corruption, misuse of office, or violation of election statutes is hereby abolished.

Section 4: No legislative or regulatory body, including Congress, shall exempt itself from compliance with any statute, rule, or regulation of its own enactment. Nor shall Congress or any legislative body confer on itself by virtue of office any benefit, other than those related to compensation, which are not available to all citizens.

Section 5: Corruption is hereby defined as the self-serving use of public office for private gain, including, without limitation: bribery; public decisions to serve private financial gain made because of economic, professional, or familial relationships; public decisions to serve executive power made because of economic, professional, or familial relationships; use of public positions to become wealthy, whether by the officeholder, public official, or others seeking privately to influence same; and any failure to recuse by an officeholder, official, or public employee which thus creates the appearance of possible corruption or conflict of interest.

Section 6: All offenses involving corruption or fraud upon the public, or against the cause of good government, shall be felonies punishable as prescribed in Section 10.

Section 7: No legislation at any level of government shall contain any provision not explicitly germane to the central purpose and title of said legislation. Every element or provision of every bill shall include the name and title of the person who introduced or drafted said provision. Any element or provision that is not germane, or not identified as to author, shall be null and void, and shall impose on the bill's primary authors a prison term as prescribed in Section 10.

Section 8: Except for true matters of national security, subject to judicial review if necessary, all actions and discussions by public officials or employees of government bearing on the creation, drafting, enactment, revision, repeal, or implementation of legislation, or regulations deriving from legislation or from an order of the Executive or Judicial branch, shall be conducted only in open public proceedings, contemporaneously disseminated by mass media and subsequently archived for convenient public examination.

Section 9: No member of any legislative body shall have the power, granted by rule or courtesy, to prevent in any way the advancement of any matter before said body or committee thereof. Any matter may be advanced by a vote of twenty-five percent of the members of the relevant committee or twenty percent of the legislative body as a whole. Refusal to grant such a vote, or refusal to abide by the results of such a vote, shall result in the immediate disqualification and removal from office of the committee or chamber chair by the Chief Justice of the State Supreme Court, or in the case of Congress, by the Chief Justice of the U.S. Supreme Court.

Section 10: Violation of Section 6 shall be a felony punishable by mandatory incarceration for a period of not less than ten years. Violations of Sections 7 and 8 shall be felonies punishable by mandatory incarceration for a period of not less than five years. All sentences prescribed herein shall be served in maximum security and not subject to pardon, parole, commutation, suspension, or other reduction of sentence. Conviction or plea of guilty shall result in the forfeiture of all pension benefits accrued while in public office or employment.

## The 29th Amendment --
## The Public's Right to Information

Section 1: An informed electorate being critical to the health and survival of democratic government, no person disseminating information to the public at large shall be compelled to reveal any source of information or documentation alleging a violation of law or regulation, abuse of power or position, or act against the public good, nor shall any such person supplying or disseminating such information as described here suffer prosecution under any statute or definition of espionage.

Section 2: No person deemed a possible source of information or allegation obtained by the press, or otherwise disseminated to the public at large, alleging a violation of law or regulation, abuse of power or position, or act against the public good shall be asked, compelled, or coerced to waive confidentiality, and any attempt to do so shall be a felony punishable as prescribed in Section 9.

Section 3: Acts of retaliation taken against any person invoking these rights, or against their employer or supporters, shall be a felony punishable by maximum security incarceration for a term, not subject to pardon, parole, commutation, suspension, or other reduction of sentence, of at least ten years

Section 4: Except as pertains to true issues of national security, subject to federal judicial review and confirmation, no official or employee of government at any level, nor any vendor or consultant thereto, shall be required to sign a Non-Disclosure Agreement as a condition for hiring, transfer, or promotion, or as a condition of benefits upon retirement. This provision shall not apply to legal staff bound by attorney-client privilege, or to those involved in the negotiation of contracts during the term of the negotiation.

Section 5: No claim of secrecy invoked by government in furtherance of national security shall prevent the inspection by a court of competent jurisdiction of all materials the government wishes to deny plaintiffs or defendants for the purposes of determining the validity of the government's assertion. No claim of state secrets itself alone shall be sufficient to prevent an action for remedy at law.

Section 6: Except as may apply to proceedings involving juveniles, neither Congress nor the States shall pass any law, and no court shall issue any order, preventing the live audio and visual dissemination of any proceeding, or permanent preservation by private parties of records of said proceedings, and any attempt to do so shall constitute a felony punishable by maximum security incarceration for a term, not subject to pardon, parole, commutation, suspension, or other reduction of sentence, of at least five years.

Section 7: Concentration of media in the hands of an elite few being contrary to the public good, no person or entity shall own or control more than one entity engaged in the dissemination of news by electronic, digital, print, or other means in any geographical area comprising a market as determined by Act of Congress. Nor shall any person or entity own, or control the news or informational programming of more than ten such entities on a national basis.

Section 8: The free exchange of ideas and information being critical to the effective functioning of the republic, the internet, and such future technologies as may supplement or replace it, shall be delivered either as a service of municipal government or as a public utility, without discrimination in any way as to speed of service, cost of service, or ease of access to content.

Section 9: Violation of Sections 2 or 3 shall be a felony punishable by mandatory incarceration for a period of not less than ten years. Violation of Section 6 shall be a felony punishable by mandatory incarceration for a period of not less than five years. All sentences provided for herein shall be served in a maximum security facility and not subject to pardon, parole, commutation, suspension, or other reduction of sentence. Conviction or plea of guilty shall result in the forfeiture of all pension benefits accrued while in public office or employment.

## The 30th Amendment -- Limits on Presidential Power

Section 1: No President may pardon, parole, commute, suspend, or grant other reprieve from sentence to any person serving, or who has served, as President or Vice President, or who has advised or served in an official or unofficial capacity any administration or campaign of the President or the Vice President.

Section 2: No President, Vice President, or official of any branch of government shall be exempt from full and complete compliance with any law.

Section 3: Should the President disagree with Congress over the constitutionality or enforcement of any provision of any law, or of a regulation derived there from, the Supreme Court shall hear arguments and issue a binding ruling forthwith. Any order or directive asserting the power of the President or the Executive branch not to comply with any provision of any law, regulation, or resolution passed by Congress shall result in the automatic immediate impeachment and trial of the President. All such statements or assertions previously made by any President, and any rulings, regulations, procedures, or precedents derived as a result thereof are null and void.

## The 31st Amendment -- Accountable Government

Section 1: The Government Accountability Office is hereby established as an independent branch of government. Within sixty days after ratification of this Amendment, a GAO Office of Special Prosecutor shall be established. The Special Prosecutor shall be appointed using the same procedures as currently used to appoint the Comptroller General, and shall serve a single, non-renewable term of fifteen years.

Section 2: Should the President at any time abrogate his responsibility to appoint a Special Prosecutor, the Senate shall appoint one, subject to confirmation by two-thirds vote of the House of Representatives.

Section 3: The Comptroller General shall retain all existing current investigative and audit powers and duties, and shall continue to issue reports as necessary or as Congress or the President may request.

Section 4: The Special Prosecutor shall have the authority and duty to prosecute any and all crimes involving officials in federal, state, or lesser government office, and in furtherance thereof, without limitation or restriction, to compel the production of records for examination; compel testimony under penalty of perjury, contempt, or imprisonment; and issue grants of immunity.

Section 5: Congress shall appropriate all funds necessary for the Government Accountability Office and the Office of Special Prosecutor to faithfully and completely discharge their duties and obligations. Should Congress, in the judgment of the courts, fail to properly fund the Office of the Special Prosecutor, Congressional immunity from arrest during session shall be void and all members of the House Appropriations Committee shall be immediately confined without bail until such time as Congress appropriates sufficient funding.

Section 6: One-third of all fines and proceeds resulting from successful prosecutions shall be retained as supplemental funding for department operations; one-third shall be distributed as bonuses to all GAO employees, pro-rata according to position; and one-third shall be remitted back to the government agency exploited by the actions of the individuals or entities convicted.

Section 7: The Inspectors General or equivalent officials of all federal and state agencies, and all public or civilian oversight boards, shall provide the Government Accountability Office and the Special Prosecutor with the results of their audits, investigations, and oversight functions, together with all supporting material as may be requested.

Section 8: The Special Prosecutor may assist citizens filing suit to enforce laws under the 28th Amendment Right to Good Government.

Section 9: The annual salaries of the Special Prosecutor and the Comptroller General shall be One Million Dollars each, adjusted every five years using the cost-of-living formula set for retiree benefits by the Social Security Administration. Upon completion of term in office, Special Prosecutor and the Comptroller General shall continue to receive the same salary and benefits of office for life.

Section 10: During their term of office and upon retirement the Special Prosecutor and the Comptroller General shall not receive any other compensation except as might derive from properties and investments held prior to appointment, nor shall they accept any gifts or benefits from any organization, person, foreign government or business entity. Retired Special Prosecutors and their deputies shall not obtain other employment, lecture at any institution, or represent litigants except on a pro bono basis.

Section 11: Willful or negligent failure by the Special Prosecutor to perform the duties of office shall be a felony punishable by mandatory maximum security incarceration for a period not subject to pardon, parole, commutation, suspension, or other grant of reprieve from sentence of at least ten years.

## The 32nd Amendment -- Rotation from Power

Section 1: Senators elected subsequent to ratification of this Amendment shall serve no more than twelve years. Senators appointed to serve out unfinished terms shall serve no more than fourteen years. Senators in office upon the ratification of this Amendment shall serve no more than one additional term.

Section 2: Members of the House of Representatives elected subsequent to ratification of this Amendment shall serve no more than twelve years. Members of the House of Representatives in office upon ratification of this Amendment who have served less than twelve years may serve additional terms until reaching twelve years.

Section 3: Except for persons returning from active government service abroad, candidates for congressional, state, or local office shall have maintained a residence in that jurisdiction for at least one year prior to election, and shall have been present in said jurisdiction for at least 120 days during that year. Officeholders shall maintain a residence in their district, or for Senators, in that state, throughout their term of office, and shall be physically present thereat for at least 60 days of every year. Violation hereof will result in immediate removal from office by order of the Chief Justice of that state's Supreme Court.

Section 4: Perpetuation of a permanent political class being detrimental to the health of the republic, for a period of five years after having left elected office, appointed Cabinet or sub-cabinet position, or employment of any type in a government agency, no person shall be employed or retained in any capacity by any person or entity having previous or current business under the authority of any office, committee, or department position previously held by former official or employee. No family member shall succeed another family member in the same office until six years has elapsed.

Section 5: Except for true matters of national security, subject to judicial review if necessary, after leaving elected office, appointed Cabinet or sub-cabinet position, or employment of any type in a government agency, no person shall attempt in any way to influence policies or legislation, or to provide advice pertaining thereto, except through public testimony or written communication subject to unrestricted public review.

Section 6: Any violation or attempted violation of the provisions of this Amendment shall be a felony punishable by mandatory maximum security incarceration for a term not subject to pardon, parole, commutation, suspension, or other reduction, of at least ten years.

## The 33rd Amendment -- Campaign Financing

Section 1: All elections shall be funded exclusively by grant of sufficient public funds, distributed equitably without favor or discrimination as to candidate, party, or measure. No candidate shall contribute to their own campaign any amount in excess of a reasonable filing fee for said office. Except as provided for in Section 5 below relating to the support of political parties, no business, domestic or foreign government entity, foundation, organization, association, or person shall contribute any funds to any candidate, party, campaign-related activity or event, or to either side in a measure before the voters.

Section 2: Unions, associations, charitable or non-profit organizations, and entities created for the purpose of engaging in business or advocating on behalf thereof, shall be artificial persons not accorded or entitled to the same political rights and free speech protections as natural persons, and therefore prohibited from participating in any way in any election.

Section 3: Proponents of initiatives, referendums, and recalls that qualify for the ballot shall be reimbursed on a prompt and timely basis, by the legislative body or office or jurisdiction subject to the petition measure, for the true, documented, and, if necessary, court-approved expenses involved in securing the required number of signatures.

Section 4: For 120 days prior to any election, all electronic media falling under the jurisdiction of or licensed to operate by any branch of government shall grant, at no cost, without favor or discrimination as to candidate, party, or issue, adequate periods of time across all hours and days of the week for campaign advertising.

Section 5: Commencing one year after ratification of this Amendment, all operation and administration of national political party offices and entities shall be funded solely and exclusively by membership dues not to exceed $50 per year. Membership dues for the operation and administration of each state or territorial party office shall not exceed $50 each per year. After ten years, and each ten years thereafter, the dues limits imposed herein shall be adjusted for compound inflation according to the same formula used to calculate Social Security increases.

Section 6: No person or entity shall disseminate, attempt to disseminate, or otherwise facilitate the dissemination of the presidential voting results from any state, or any predicted outcome of a presidential election, prior to the closing of the last polling place in the last state. Violation hereof shall be a felony punishable by incarceration in a maximum security facility for a period, not subject to pardon, parole, commutation, suspension, or other reduction of sentence, of not less than five years. This applies to the press in all forms, and revises the First Amendment accordingly.

Section 7: All persons who violate, or cause others to violate, Section 1 shall be guilty of a felony punishable by mandatory maximum security incarceration for a period, not subject to pardon, parole, commutation, suspension, or other reduction of sentence, of not less than ten years.

## The 34th Amendment -- Election Integrity

Section 1: On the first Wednesday of October of the year preceding each Presidential election, Congress shall conduct a random drawing to determine the order and dates on which states may conduct a Presidential primary or caucus.

Section 2: States having twenty or more electoral votes and those having four or fewer shall be excluded from the first drawing. From the remaining states and jurisdictions, the Parliamentarian shall draw five to conduct their primaries or caucuses on the third Tuesday of February.

Section 3: All remaining states and jurisdictions not yet assigned dates shall then be drawn in groups of five. The first group drawn shall conduct primaries or caucuses on the first Tuesday of March; the next on the third Tuesday of March. All subsequent groups shall, in the order of their selection, conduct their respective primaries or caucuses on the first, second or the third Tuesdays of April, May, and June, as necessary.

Section 4: All elections, including partisan primaries, shall be conducted completely under the control of each jurisdiction's primary election officer. Any failure to ensure a fair and impartial election, with equal access, materials, equipment, and staffing across all polling sites, or any failure to properly maintain voter rolls that results in disenfranchisement of eligible voters, shall be a felony punishable as prescribed in Section 10.

Section 5: All elections shall be conducted using hand-marked paper ballots which shall be deposited in transparent ballot boxes which are under constant public observation and constant recorded electronic surveillance. All ballots shall be hand-counted in public at the location where cast, and the results shall be announced to the public and disseminated via live media before said ballots are moved to any other location. All ballots shall be maintained under security by the chief election official of that state or jurisdiction for a period of five years.

Section 6: No person not a citizen of these United States shall be eligible or allowed to vote in any election. Any legislation, regulation, practice, custom, or court ruling which is, or may be, contrary to this principle, including those attendant to the process of voter registration, is hereby null and void. Any non-citizen who votes shall be guilty of a felony punishable as prescribed in Section 10 and shall be deported upon completion of sentence.

Section 7: Any person charged with responsibility for the enforcement of election laws who fails to act diligently to prevent voting by non-citizens, or who in any way facilitates such illegal voting, shall be guilty of a felony punishable as prescribed in Section 10.

Section 8: All states and lesser jurisdictions thereof shall ensure that every person eligible to vote has free and convenient access to any documentation necessary to prove citizenship. Any person responsible for implementation of voter identification documentation who fails to discharge those duties with the greatest possible diligence shall be guilty of a felony punishable as prescribed in Section 10.

Section 9: All presidential general elections shall be a national holiday. Government agencies (other than those engaged in public safety or election management) and private companies who cannot suspend operations for the entire day shall give all employees a minimum of four hours paid time in which to vote. Public safety employees shall be given a minimum of two hours paid time and shall have priority at their appropriate polling place.

Section 10: Violation of Sections 4 or 5 shall be a felony punishable by mandatory maximum security incarceration for a period of not less than ten years. Violation of Sections 6, 7, or 8 shall be a felony punishable by mandatory maximum security incarceration for a period of not less than five years. All sentences prescribed herein shall not be subject to pardon, parole, commutation, suspension, or other reduction of sentence. Conviction or plea of guilty shall result in the forfeiture of all pension benefits accrued while in public office or employment.

## The 35th Amendment -- Fair Apportionment

Section 1: Upon completion of the first census after ratification of this Amendment, and continuing with each census or other redistricting thereafter, all federal, state, and local election districts shall be drawn by a computer or other automated program that utilizes, to the maximum degree possible with the technology available at the time, features of terrain and geography, whether natural or man-made, and the existing boundaries of parks, educational institutions, penal or military facilities, and subordinate political jurisdictions to minimize odd-shaped districts. Technologies employed to create election districts shall not consider the race, ethnic origin, or political party affiliation of any voter, and shall draw the most compact districts possible.

Section 2: An attempt to manipulate the determination of districts shall be a felony punishable by mandatory maximum security incarceration for a period, not subject to pardon, parole, commutation, suspension, or other reduction of sentence, of at least five years. Conviction or plea of guilty shall result in the forfeiture of all pension benefits accrued while in public office or employment.

## The 36th Amendment -- Participatory Democracy

Section 1: The right of voters in all states and lesser jurisdictions thereof to participate by legally binding initiative, referendum, and recall is hereby established. Any initiative or referendum petition containing valid signatures, of voters residing within the jurisdiction subject to said measure, equaling ten percent of the votes cast in that jurisdiction during the last general election shall be put before the voters within a period of not less than 90 nor more than 150 days after certification of qualification.

Section 2: For measures to recall elected officials, the percentage of registered voter signatures necessary to qualify for the ballot shall be no more than fifteen percent of the votes cast in that jurisdiction during the last general election, and said recall election shall take place no less than 60 nor more than 90 days after certification of qualification.

Section 3: Proponents of initiative or recall measures shall have 180 days to collect and present the necessary signatures. Proponents of referendums shall have 70 days after official approval of the resolution, law, or other action of government being contested.

Section 4: Certification of petition signature validity shall be performed in a timely manner by the official who is normally responsible for the conduct of elections in that jurisdiction. In the event that a petition is deemed short the required signatures, proponents shall have a reasonable right of appeal, including to court of law, to protest disqualified signatures.

Section 5: Once approved by voters, an initiative shall not be repealed or amended except by another vote of the people. If any portion of a measure is later overturned by a court of law, all other provisions shall remain in full force and effect.

Section 6: Any attempt to obstruct, impede, or delay the provisions provided for herein shall be a felony punishable by mandatory maximum security incarceration for a period, not subject to pardon, parole, commutation, suspension, or other reduction of sentence, of at least five years. Conviction or plea of guilty shall result in the forfeiture of all pension benefits accrued while in public office or employment.

## The 37th Amendment -- Equal Justice

Section 1: Supreme Court justices appointed subsequent to ratification of this Amendment shall serve for a single term of 15 years, or to age seventy-five, whichever shall occur first.

Section 2: Immediately upon ratification of this Amendment the annual salary for justices of the Supreme Court shall be One Million Dollars, adjusted every five years using the cost-of-living formula set by the Social Security Administration for retiree benefits. Upon retirement not resulting from impeachment or threat thereof, justices shall continue to receive the same salary and benefits of their office for life.

Section 3: Justices of the Supreme Court shall be bound by the U.S. Judicial Code of Ethics, and shall recuse themselves accordingly. Under no circumstances shall a sitting justice participate in cases which involve, or might reasonably be seen to involve, any financial benefit to themselves or to those with whom they have a personal, professional, or familial relationship. Failure to adhere to this obligation shall be punishable by impeachment followed by felony criminal prosecution carrying a mandatory sentence of incarceration in a maximum security facility for a period, not subject to pardon, suspension, commutation, parole, or other reduction of sentence, of not less than ten years. Conviction, or plea of guilty for violation hereof, shall result in the forfeiture of all pension benefits accrued while in public office or employment.

Section 4: During their term in office, and upon retirement, Justices of the Supreme Court shall not receive any compensation except as might derive from properties and investments held prior to appointment, nor shall they accept any gifts or benefits from any organization, person, foreign government or business entity. Nor shall retired justices represent future litigants, or lecture at any institution, except pro bono.

Section 5: No person shall be nominated to the Supreme Court after attending the same university or school of law as two or more justices currently serving.

Section 6: Fair enforcement of the law being critical to the cause of justice, all persons charged with the administration of justice who perjure, falsify evidence, or withhold that which is exculpatory, shall forfeit all immunity from civil liability and shall be guilty of a felony punishable by incarceration in a maximum security facility for a period, not subject to pardon, parole, commutation, suspension, or other reduction of sentence, of not less than ten years. Conviction, or plea of guilty for violation hereof, shall result in the forfeiture of all pension benefits accrued while in public office or employment.

Section 7: The objectives of our legal system being truth and justice, all attorneys and other officers of the court shall, at all times in matters before the court, be bound to tell the whole truth and nothing but the truth. Violation hereof shall be a felony punishable by maximum security incarceration for a period not subject to pardon, parole, commutation, suspension, or other reduction of sentence, of not less than ten years.

Section 8: The right to life being the bedrock of innocent until proven guilty, deadly force by law enforcement officers shall be employed only after actual danger to their own lives, or that of others, is clearly established, and non-lethal measures are unable to be employed with sufficient speed and effectiveness. Any violation hereof resulting in death shall be a felony punishable by maximum security incarceration for a period not subject to pardon, parole, commutation, suspension, or other reduction of sentence, of not less than twenty years.

## The 38th Amendment -- Sanctity of Private Property

Section 1: The sanctity of one's home and business being of utmost importance, no process of government, except as results from a criminal conviction, shall seize or transfer directly, or indirectly, real property belonging to any person or private entity to another person or private entity.

Section 2: Assets of individuals, organizations, and business entities may not be forfeited except upon conviction of a crime or as the result of civil judgment. Victims of illegal asset seizure shall be awarded return of the seized property, reasonable attorney's fees, and punitive damages of three times attorney's fees or the value of the seized property, whichever is greater.

Section 3: The right not to be taxed twice on the same income being fundamental to economic justice, all taxes, fees, and assessments levied by federal, state, or local governments shall be deductible from federal taxes levied on income. Home ownership being a cornerstone of a stable society, all residential mortgage interest shall also be deductible from state and federal taxes levied on income.

Section 4: The imposition of price controls on rental property constitutes a taking of value from the property owner without just compensation and is thus illegal in all forms.

## The 39th Amendment -- The Right to Privacy

Section 1: The right to privacy being critical to the citizens of a free and democratic republic, no individual, organization, business entity, or department of government at any level shall maintain files, dossiers, or other records pertaining to any citizen except:

a) As such records shall result from the issuance of a properly noticed search warrant or subpoena applicable to that individual, or from a civil or criminal court action;

b) As such records serve legitimate civilian purpose bearing on the establishment of credit;

c) As are necessary for the granting of licenses and permits or for the effective regulation of business enterprises including charities and non-profit entities;

d) By affirmative consent by the person to the collector of such information, without such permission being imposed by the collector as a requirement of use, access, or service, or in lieu of payment for same, and with the collector restrained from selling, bartering, or otherwise communicating such information to any third party.

Section 2: Immediately upon ratification of this Amendment, all files, dossiers, or records in violation hereof, whether held in public or private hands, within the physical confines of the republic or abroad, shall be permanently and completely destroyed. Failure to do so by any person authorized or obligated to perform such destruction shall be a felony punishable as prescribed in Section 3.

Section 3: Violation of any provision of this Amendment shall be a felony resulting in the incarceration of all offending parties in a maximum security penal institution for a period, not subject to pardon, parole, commutation, suspension, or other reduction of sentence, of not less than twenty years. Conviction or plea of guilty shall result in the forfeiture of all pension benefits accrued while in public office or employment.

## The 40th Amendment -- Sovereign Security

Section 1: The security of a nation resting inevitably on the security of its borders, Congress shall fully fund all walls, barriers and other infrastructure necessary to secure the nation's border and prevent any unauthorized entry.

Section 2: Congress shall provide all funds and enact all laws, which the Executive Branch shall fully enforce, necessary to prevent any person who has entered the country illegally from remaining therein.

Section 3: Until such time as the nation's southern and northern land borders have been fully and effectively sealed to prevent any unauthorized entry, Congress shall give no grant of amnesty, or exemption from the provisions of this Amendment, except to a specific person by name upon demonstration of unique and meritorious circumstance.

Section 4: Employing, causing to employ, or facilitating the employment of a person within the territorial limits of the United States who is not legally eligible to be so employed shall be a felony punishable as prescribed in Section 8.

Section 5: Immediately upon ratification of this Amendment, the right of automatic citizenship will no longer confer to children when either parent is in the country illegally.

Section 6: Neither Congress nor the President shall bind the United States to any treaty, trade agreement, or other covenant that surrenders any sovereign legal rights or judicial or military powers of the federal government or any state and lesser jurisdiction to any foreign entity. Immediately upon ratification of this Amendment, all such treaties and agreements previously in force are null and void.

Section 7: A common language being necessary to a stable economy and a unified citizenry, English shall be the official language of the nation. All business of Federal, state, and local government, and all official documents thereof including ballots and election materials, shall be in English, and only English. Recognizing the value of other languages in a global community, Congress and the States shall implement foreign language proficiency requirements as a condition of secondary school graduation.

Section 8: Violation of Section 4 shall be punishable by mandatory maximum security incarceration for a period, not subject to pardon, parole, commutation, suspension, or other reduction of sentence, of at least five years.

## The 41st Amendment -- Protection of State and Local Power

Section 1: Given the inevitable conflict between the interests of commerce and the well-being of the people, to protect its environment, economy, and natural resources a state or lesser jurisdiction thereof may enact and enforce laws or regulations involving environmental protections or business operating conditions that are more stringent than those of superior jurisdictions, including the federal government.

Section 2: All violations of environmental protection laws involving damage in excess of $10,000 shall be felonies punishable by mandatory maximum security incarceration for a period, not subject to pardon, parole, commutation, suspension, or other reduction of sentence, of not less than five years.

Section 3: A state may enact and enforce on financial institutions and insurance companies doing business within its borders, or with its residents, laws and regulations more stringent than those imposed by the federal government and its agencies or chartered entities. All violations involving financial fraud in excess of $10,000 shall be felonies punishable by maximum security incarceration for a period, not subject to pardon, parole, commutation, suspension, or other reduction of sentence of at least ten years.

## The 42nd Amendment -- Universal Military Service

Section 1: The responsibilities of the people being no less important to the well-being of the republic than the responsibilities of government, Congress shall pass, and the President shall sign, legislation to establish universal mandatory National Military Service. Such service shall be for a minimum period of twenty-four months, with at least six months of basic military training followed by either continued military service or in such civilian projects as Congress may designate.

Section 2: Service shall begin no later than sixty days after reaching the age of eighteen, or graduation from high school, whichever occurs last. Exemption from service shall be granted only to those having such permanent and severe physical or mental infirmities that they can fulfill no useful role or function in civilian life. Persons afflicted with lesser but still significant permanent physical or mental infirmities such that they cannot reasonably participate in military action shall be assigned appropriate other duties.

Section 3: Persons incarcerated at the time of normal induction into service shall serve the full term of their service upon release from incarceration. For the safety of the public, those inducted after incarceration shall be excused from weapons and tactical training.

Section 4: With the exception of career personnel serving a minimum initial enlistment period of at least eight years, all combat assignments shall be made by random lottery. Influencing, or attempting to influence, the assignment of any person to or away from any theater of combat operations shall be a felony punishable by maximum security incarceration for a period, not subject to pardon, parole, commutation, suspension, or other reduction of sentence, of at least ten years.

# TRUE REFORM

# THE ECONOMIC BILL OF RIGHTS

## The 43rd Amendment -- Economic Security

Section 1: The Federal Reserve system is hereby dissolved and Congress shall establish under the Department of the Treasury a central bank operated solely by the government and vested with all powers necessary to protect the value of the national currency, properly regulate the amount of money in circulation, and ensure the lasting strength of the domestic economy.

Section 2: To protect the public interest and prevent concentrations of economic influence detrimental to the security and well-being of the people, no bank or other purveyor of financial instruments or insurance shall hold or control more than ten percent of public or private deposits, insure more than ten percent of the population, or operate in more than ten states. No bank or other financial institution shall also own or control any insurance entity.

Section 3: Within 180 days after ratification of this Amendment, Congress shall enact National Industrial Policy legislation to create, protect, and ensure a robust, diverse, and self-sufficient domestic economy producing, within the borders of the 50 states, all goods required for the security of the nation and the comfort, prosperity, and well-being of its people. The National Industrial

Policy, regularly amended as time and need require, shall include such tariffs, import duties, and other regulations necessary to protect American workers and industries from unfair foreign competition.

Section 4: Ensuring American citizens priority to American jobs being of the utmost importance, the importation of foreign workers under any temporary grant of work status shall be strictly limited to 20,000 persons per year, who shall be selected strictly on the basis of their extraordinary knowledge and skills, and thus compensated at a rate at least twice that paid to American citizens performing the same or similar work for any employer in the same or similar field.

Section 5: Congress shall pass no law, and no court or agency shall issue any ruling or regulation that has the effect of providing a reduction, waiver, or deferral of any tax for any enterprise or its subsidiary for producing goods in a foreign country, territory, or jurisdiction for importation into the United States, or for providing services in or from a foreign country, territory, or jurisdiction in lieu of basing those services in the United States or its territories. Nor shall revenues from foreign operations be given special tax treatment.

Section 6: No official or employee of a state or lesser jurisdiction of government shall offer or provide any subsidy or any reduction, deferment, or waiver of taxes, fees, assessments, or cost of public services as an inducement to establish, conduct or expand any business. No official or employee of a state or lesser jurisdiction shall act in concert with another to evade the intent or effect hereof. Violation of such shall be a felony punishable by maximum security incarceration for a period not subject to pardon, parole, commutation, suspension, or other reduction of sentence, of not less than ten years. Conviction or plea of guilty shall result in the forfeiture of all pension benefits accrued while in public office or employment.

Section 7: Within one year of ratification of this Amendment, Congress shall create a federally-funded Jobs Guarantee, paying a living wage to all citizens unable to find other employment. Where state, municipal, or district administration of programs is deemed most effective, funds shall be distributed accordingly. Jobs created under this program shall encompass all endeavors which add to the safety, defense, environmental protection, economy, education, or cultural enrichment of the nation. For those who by disability or other legitimate reason are unable to work, or whose part-time employment is insufficient to provide the adequate necessities of life, Congress shall institute a Supplemental Income Guarantee.

## The 44th Amendment –
## Employment & Retirement Protections

Section 1: All citizens and legal residents shall have the absolute unrestrained right to form or join unions, to participate in union activities, and to have said unions engage in collective bargaining, including strikes and boycotts, on their behalf. Any attempt to interfere with or retaliate for the free exercise of these rights shall be a felony, punishable as prescribed in Section 10.

Section 2: No union shall provide any benefit or service, including but not limited to: negotiation of wages, job classifications, promotion criteria, working conditions, grievance procedures, or seniority rights; protection from termination; or inclusion in any pension plan, to or on behalf of any person who elects not to join said union when eligible to do so.

Section 3: All business entities with five or more employees shall enroll in a pension plan having fair and reasonable conditions for vesting and enrollment, which ensures the payment of a defined-benefit pension to employees who meet fair and reasonable retirement criteria, and which is transferable by the employee from employer to employer. Such pensions shall be approved, regulated, enforced, and guaranteed in full by the Federal Pension Benefit Guaranty Agency.

Section 4: Individual employees of firms with fewer than five workers may elect to enroll in a pension plan of their choice, have a portion of their salary contributed thereto, and have that contribution matched by their employer.

Section 5: In business bankruptcy proceedings, pension claims, including contributions for pensions already vested but not yet exercised, shall be supreme above all other claims, including for taxes. No court or government entity shall in any way void, reduce, or delay payment of any pension or post-employment benefit negotiated between employer and employee. To assist in funding pension obligations, courts may confiscate any excessive compensation from those charged with responsibility for operation of the enterprise.

Section 6: In business bankruptcy proceedings, unpaid wages and severance benefits shall have second priority, after pension obligations, before taxes and other creditors. No bonus or severance benefit shall be paid to any executive of a bankrupt entity unless all pension contributions, unpaid wages, and severance benefits have been paid to non-executive employees.

Section 7: Employees of government and public entities shall have the absolute right to form or join unions, to participate in union activities, and to have said unions engage in collective bargaining, including strikes and boycotts, on their behalf. The right to strike shall not apply to police officers, firefighters, or those then involved in emergency response. Any attempt to interfere with or retaliate for the free exercise of these rights shall be a felony, punishable as prescribed in Section 10.

Section 8: Once agreed to, pension obligations to public employees shall not be reduced, deferred, or otherwise negated in value.

Section 9: Pensions to employees of state and local government entities shall be insured by the Federal Pension Benefit Guaranty Agency, which shall have all powers and authority necessary to see that each pension entity is adequately and properly funded.

Section 10: Violation of Sections 1 or 7 shall be a felony punishable by mandatory maximum security incarceration for a period, not subject to pardon, parole, commutation, suspension, or other reduction of sentence, of at least five years.

## The 45th Amendment -- The Right to Healthcare

Within one year after ratification of this Amendment Congress shall establish a federally funded national healthcare system, delivered by such combination of public and private entities as may be most practical and effective, covering the full and true cost of treatment for all illnesses and injuries, for all citizens and all legal resident aliens. No citizen, legal resident alien, organization, or business entity shall be required to purchase or provide private healthcare insurance.

## The 46th Amendment -- Veteran's Rights and Benefits

Once a benefit for service in the Armed Forces is offered, Congress shall make no law, and no court shall order or enforce any action, which results in the delay or reduction of said benefit. Benefits heretofore promised members of the military but later rescinded or reduced are retroactively restored in full.

# SOURCES AND REFERENCES

For the Sources and References used in this book, as well as news, commentary, analysis, and events relevant to The Restoration Amendments, visit True Reform.org

# ABOUT THE AUTHOR

Raised in a politically active family, Jess Money majored in Political Science with a minor in Economics. He sold his first magazine article at the age of 16 and has since written everything from ad copy and political mailers to a screenplay for DreamWorks, which earned him membership in the Writers Guild of America. Along the way he had a career in professional motorsports, worked with the U.S. Women's Olympic Volleyball program, managed two of the entertainment industry's most acclaimed screenwriting programs, and worked as a bar bouncer when that's what it took to keep the wolf from the door.

Previously, he published the highly-rated political thriller, Public Enemies, which is available in e-book, hardcover, paperback, and audiobook.

No longer the handsome devil he once was, he decided against posting a picture, even though using an old one might boost sales.

www.ingramcontent.com/pod-product-compliance
Lightning Source LLC
Chambersburg PA
CBHW020600270326
41927CB00005B/104